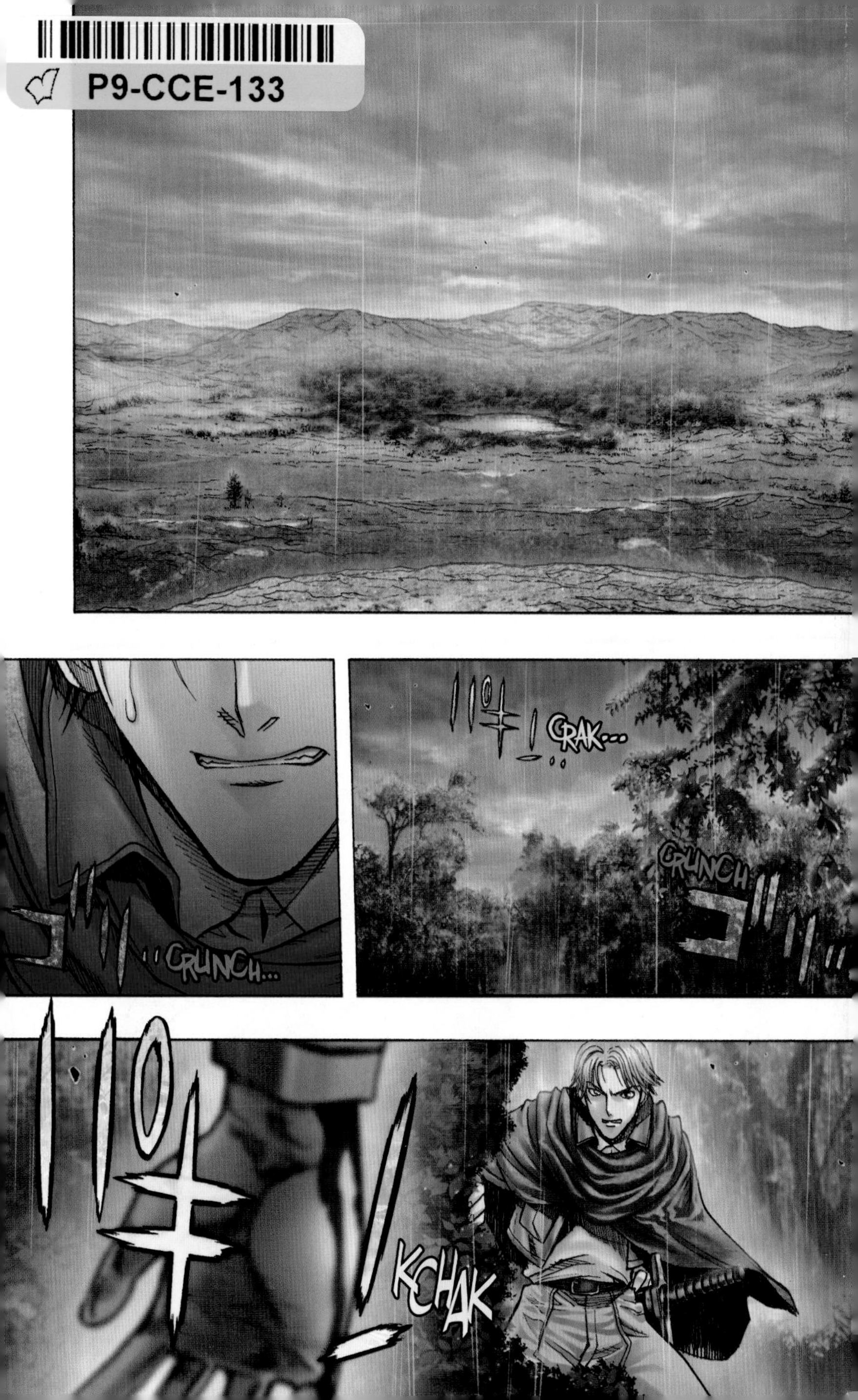
CRAK...
CRUNCH
CRUNCH...
KCHAK

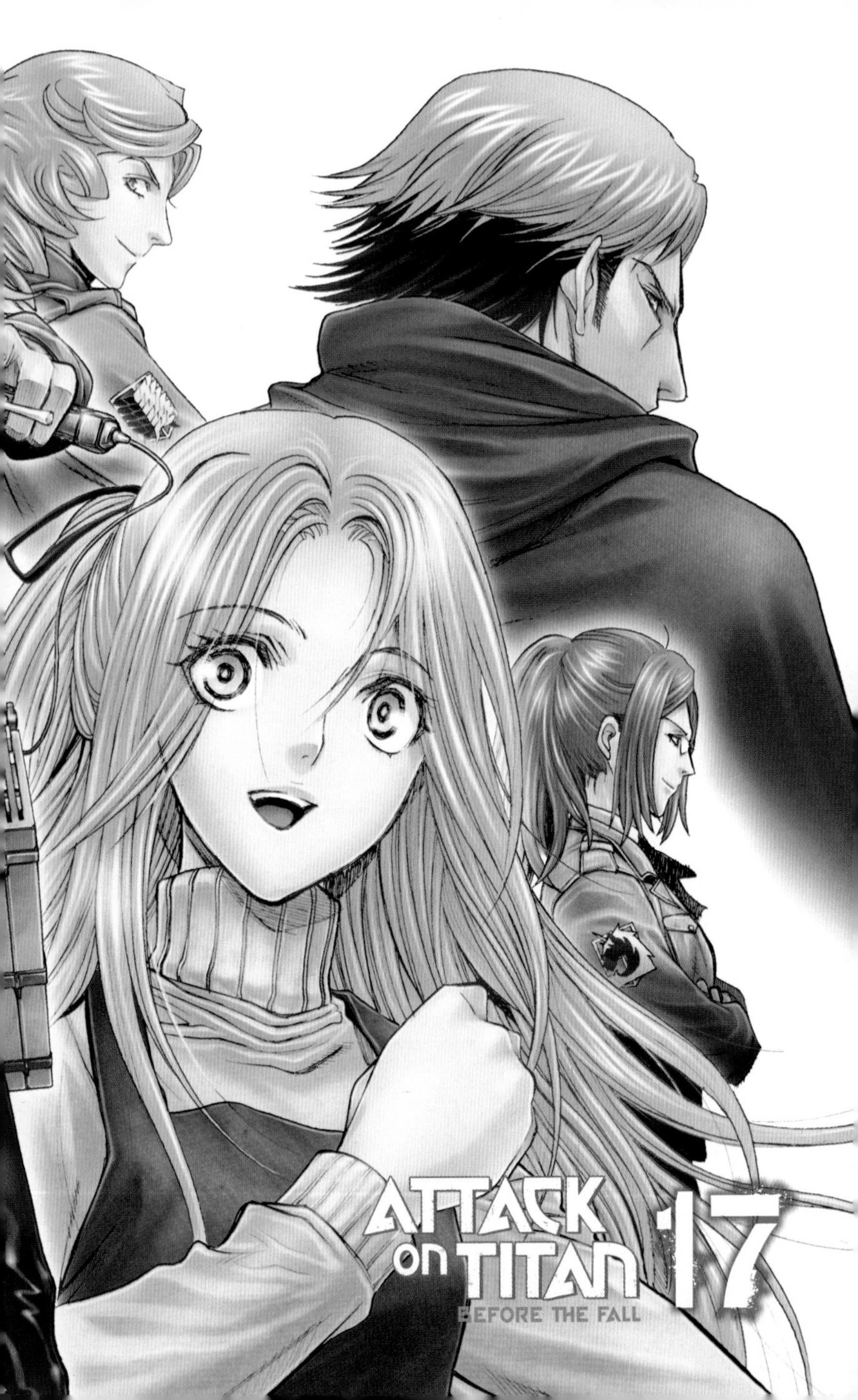
ATTACK on TITAN
BEFORE THE FALL
17

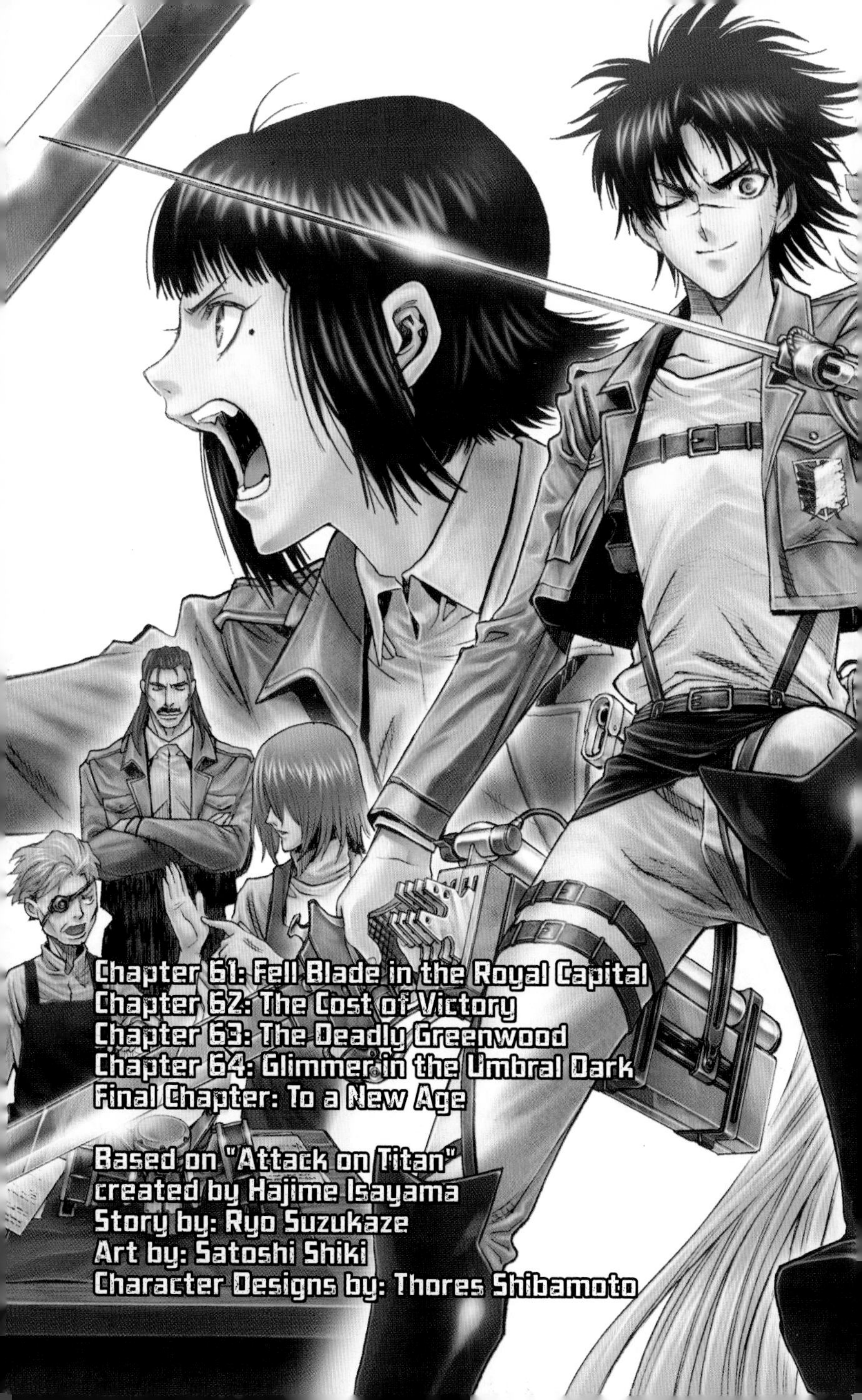

Based on "Attack on Titan"
created by Hajime Isayama
Story by: Ryo Suzukaze
Art by: Satoshi Shiki
Character Designs by: Thores Shibamoto

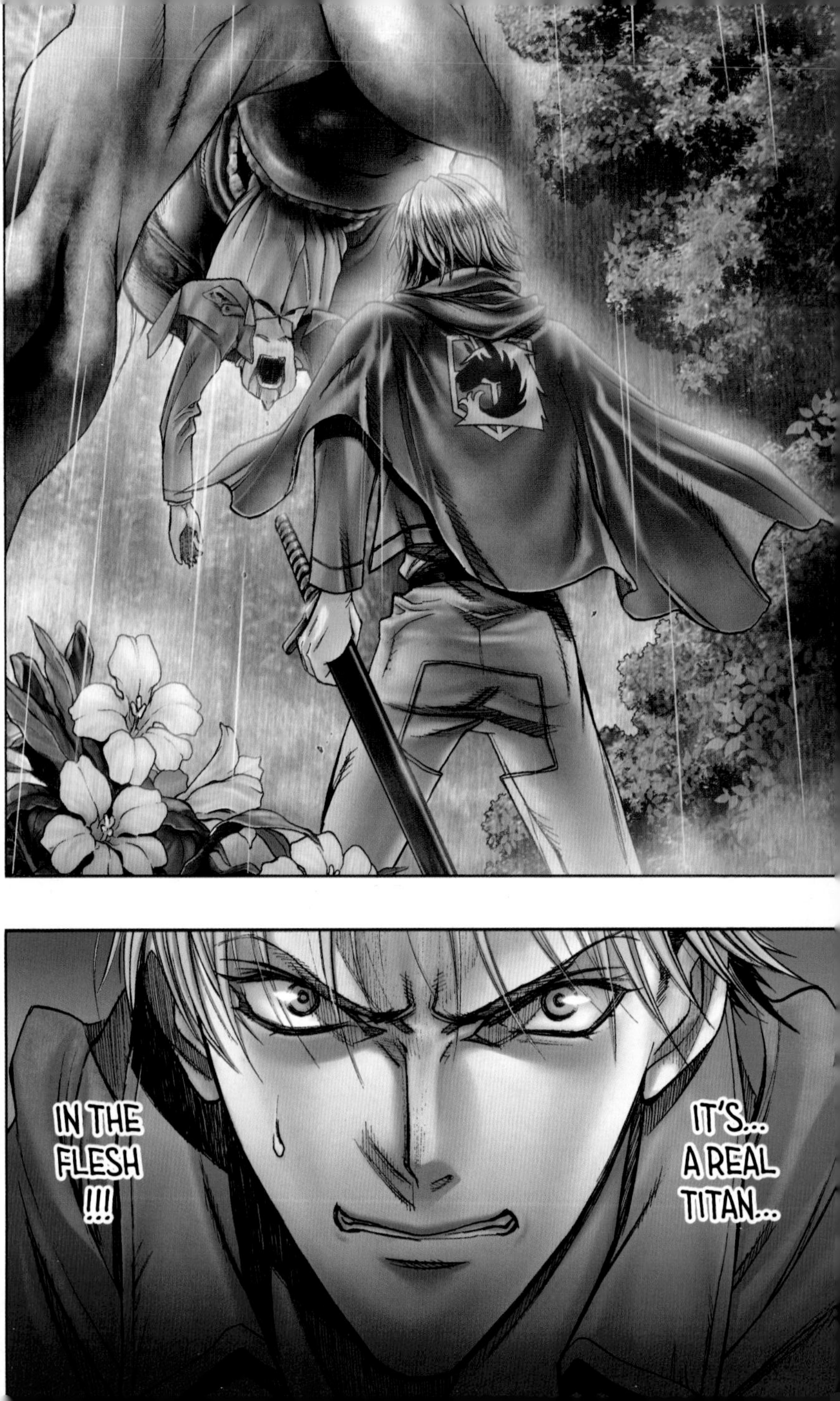
IT'S... A REAL TITAN...
IN THE FLESH !!!

Before the fall — Character Profiles

Kuklo

A 15-year-old boy born from a dead body packed into the vomit of a Titan, which earned him the moniker, "Titan's Son." He is fascinated with the Device as a means to defeat the Titans. Currently an assistant instructor with the Survey Corps, training hopeful recruits for battle. Member of Team Ten.

Sharle Inocencio

First daughter of the Inocencios, a rich merchant family within Wall Sheena. When she realized that Kuklo was a human, she taught him to speak and learn. She escaped her family home and apprenticed under Xenophon the weapons-master, bringing about solutions for developing the Vertical Maneuvering Equipment.

Cardina Baumeister

Kuklo's first friend in the outside world, and his companion in developing the Device. A member of Team Ten with Kuklo.

Carlo Pikale

Jorge's son and current captain of the Survey Corps. Since they battled Titans together, he's had great respect for Kuklo.

Jorge Pikale

Training Corps instructor. A former Survey Corps captain who was hailed as a hero for defeating a Titan. Currently on assignment with the Survey Corps.

Xavi Inocencio

Head of the Inocencio family and Sharle's brother. Working with the Survey Corps as a monitor for the Military Police.

Rosa Carlstead

The daughter of Maria and Sorum, Angel's longtime friends. Leader of Team Ten in the Survey Corps expedition force.

Angel Aaltonen

A former inventor who developed a tool to fight the Titans 15 years ago, known simply as "The Device."

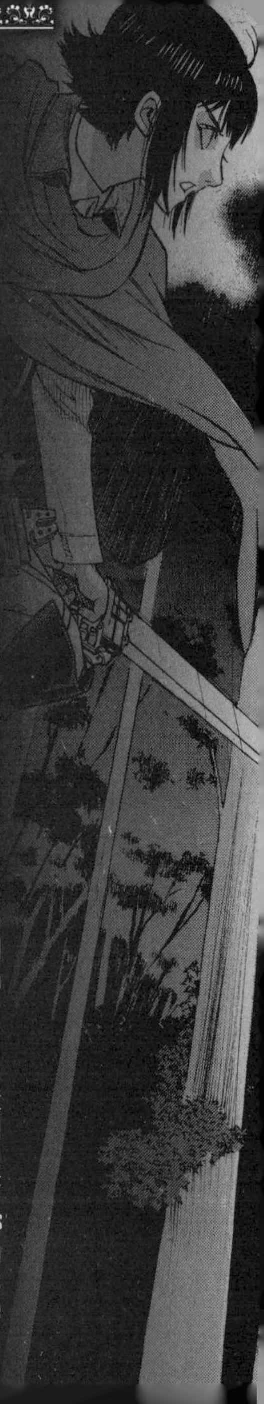

When a Titan terrorized Shiganshina District and left behind a pile of vomit, a baby boy was miraculously born of a pregnant corpse. This boy was named Kuklo, the "Son of a Titan," and treated as a sideshow freak. Eventually the wealthy merchant Dario Inocencio bought Kuklo. Dario's daughter Sharle learned that he was human and not the son of a Titan, and decided to teach him the words and knowledge of humanity. Two years later, Kuklo escaped from the mansion along with Sharle, who was being forced into a marriage she did not desire.

In Shiganshina District, the Survey Corps was preparing for its first expedition outside of the Wall in 15 years. Kuklo snuck into the expedition's cargo wagon, but the Titan they ran across was far worse of a monster than he expected. He helped the Survey Corps survive, but inside the Walls he was greeted by the Military Police, who wanted the "Titan's Son" on charges of murdering Dario. In prison, he met Cardina, a young man jailed over political squabbles. They hoped to escape to safety when exiled beyond the Wall, but found themselves surrounded by a pack of Titans. It was through the help of Jorge, former Survey Corps Captain, that the two boys escaped with their lives. The equipment that Jorge used was the very "Device" that was the key to defeating the Titan those 15 years ago. Kuklo and Cardina escaped the notice of the MPs by hiding in the Industrial City, where they found Sharle. It is there that the three youngsters learned the truth of the ill-fated Titan-capturing expedition 15 years earlier, and swore to uphold the will of Angel, the inventor of the Device.

Next, Kuklo and Cardina headed back to Shiganshina to test out a new model of the Device developed by Xenophon, Angel's friend and rival, but while they were gone, a rebellion by anti-establishment dissidents broke out in the Industrial City. Kuklo was able to slip through the chaos to rescue Sharle from the dissidents, but then Sharle's brother Xavi—now a member of the Military Police—arrived and turned his sword on Kuklo. Xavi won the battle by inflicting a grievous blow on Kuklo, who fell into the river and only survived thanks to the help of Rosa, the daughter of a man named Sorum, who lost his life on the fateful expedition 15 years earlier.

After a month and a half of recovery, Kuklo accepted Jorge's offer of an assistant instructor position with the Survey Corps. Sharle escaped Xavi's grasp and visited Angel, inventor of the Device, who unveiled his finished version, the Vertical Maneuvering Equipment. Two months later, Kuklo was among Team Ten of the Survey Corps, outfitted with Vertical Maneuvering Equipment with Rosa as his team captain, as the corps departs on an expedition beyond the Walls. Fighting poor rain visibility and muddy terrain, they headed to the oasis ten kilometers southwest of Shiganshina District, chasing after Captain Carlo and the main force of the expedition.

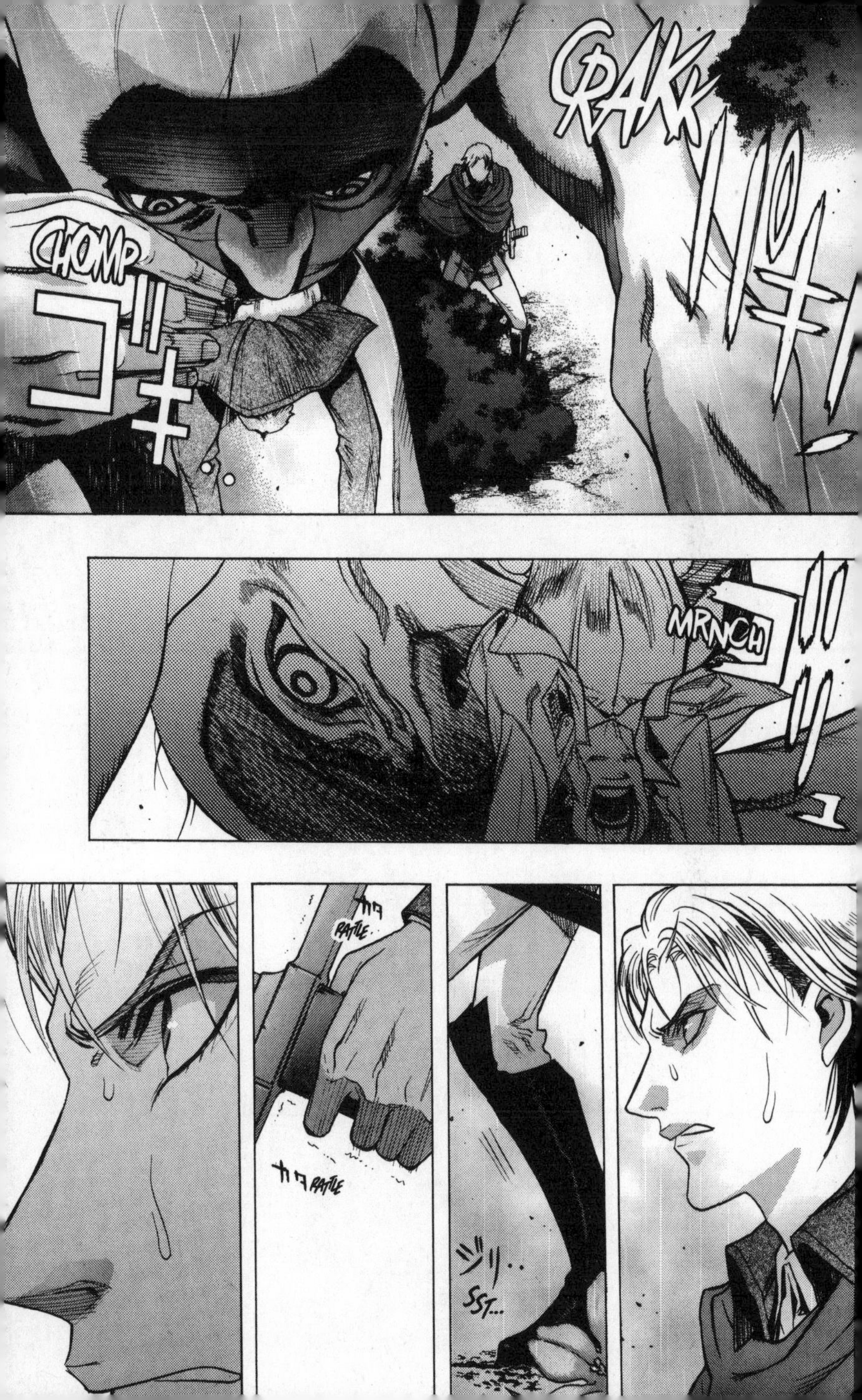
CRAKK
CHOMP
ゴキ
MRNCH
SST...
RATTLE
RATTLE

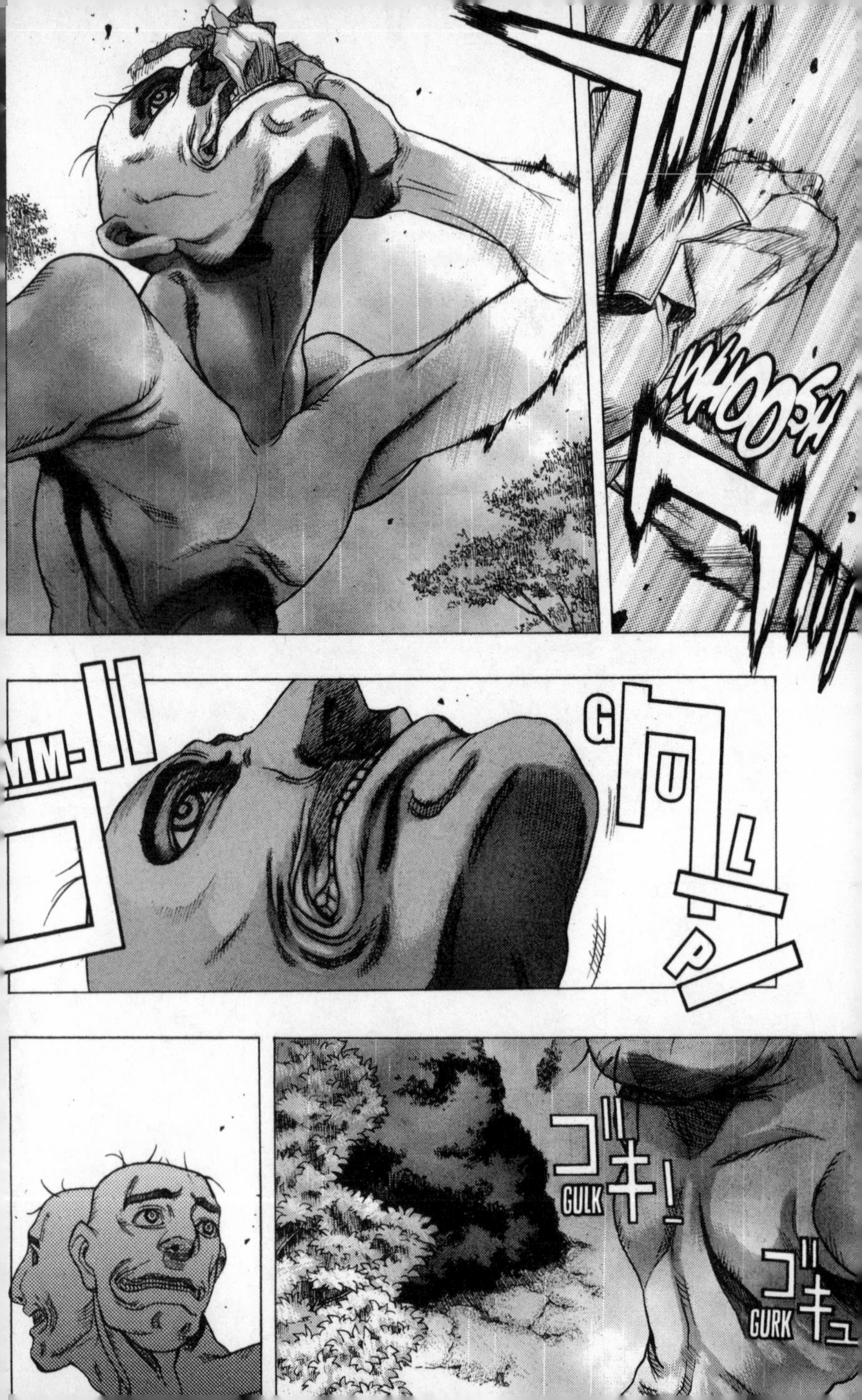
WHOOSH
GULP
MM-
ゴキ!
GULK
ゴキュ
GURK

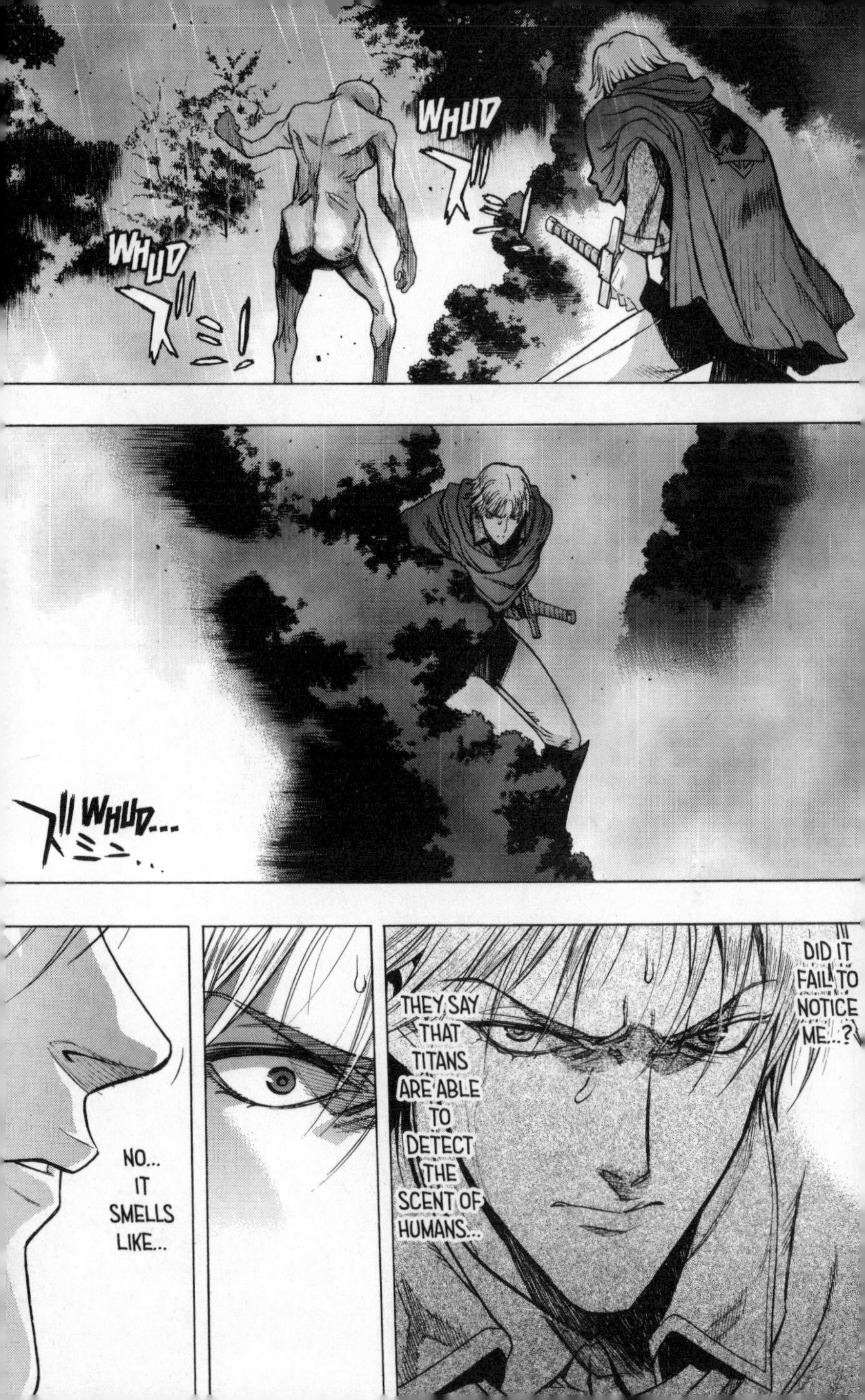
WHUD
WHUD
WHUD...
DID IT FAIL TO NOTICE ME...?
THEY SAY THAT TITANS ARE ABLE TO DETECT THE SCENT OF HUMANS...
NO... IT SMELLS LIKE...

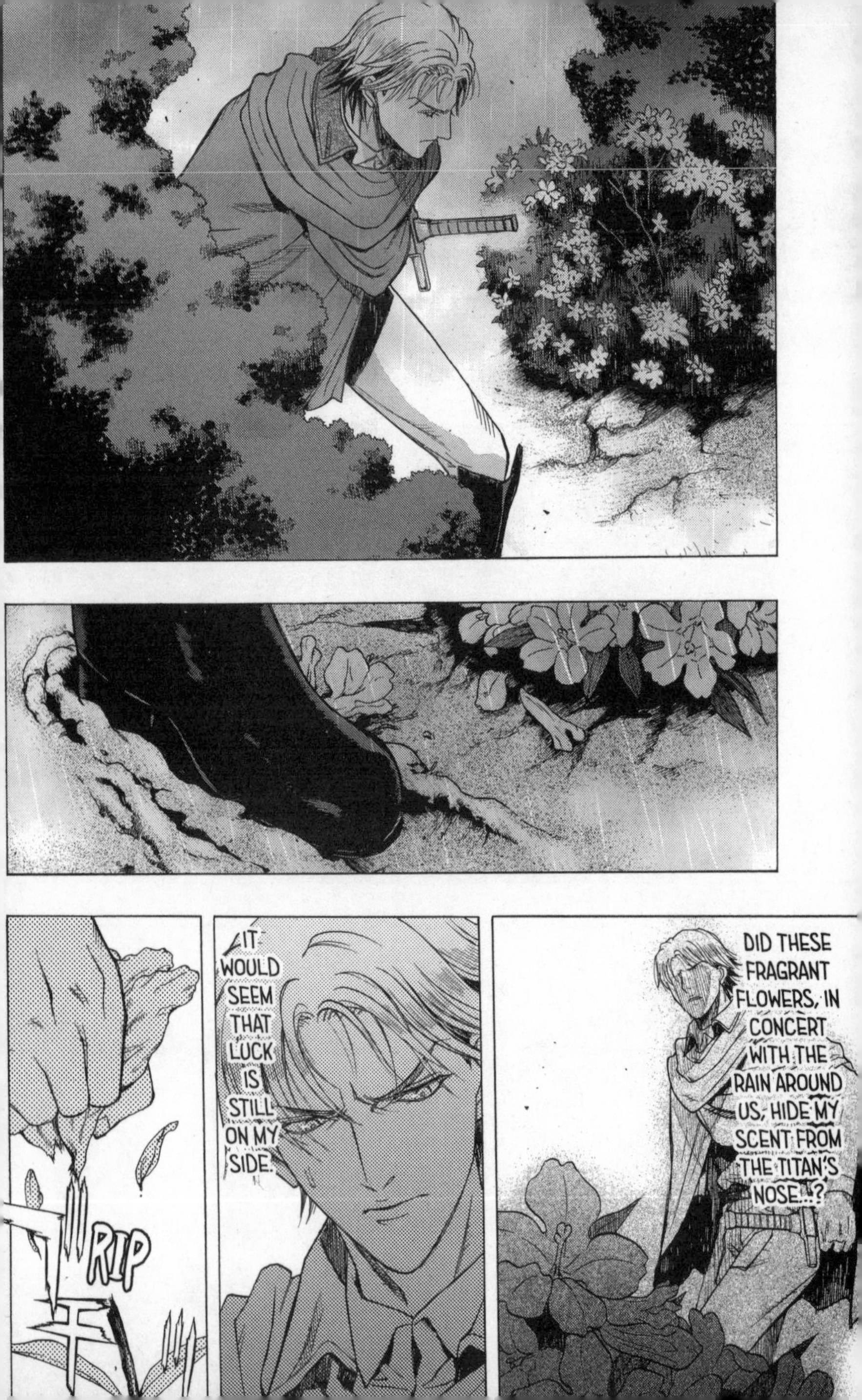
DID THESE FRAGRANT FLOWERS, IN CONCERT WITH THE RAIN AROUND US, HIDE MY SCENT FROM THE TITAN'S NOSE...?
IT WOULD SEEM THAT LUCK IS STILL ON MY SIDE.
RIP

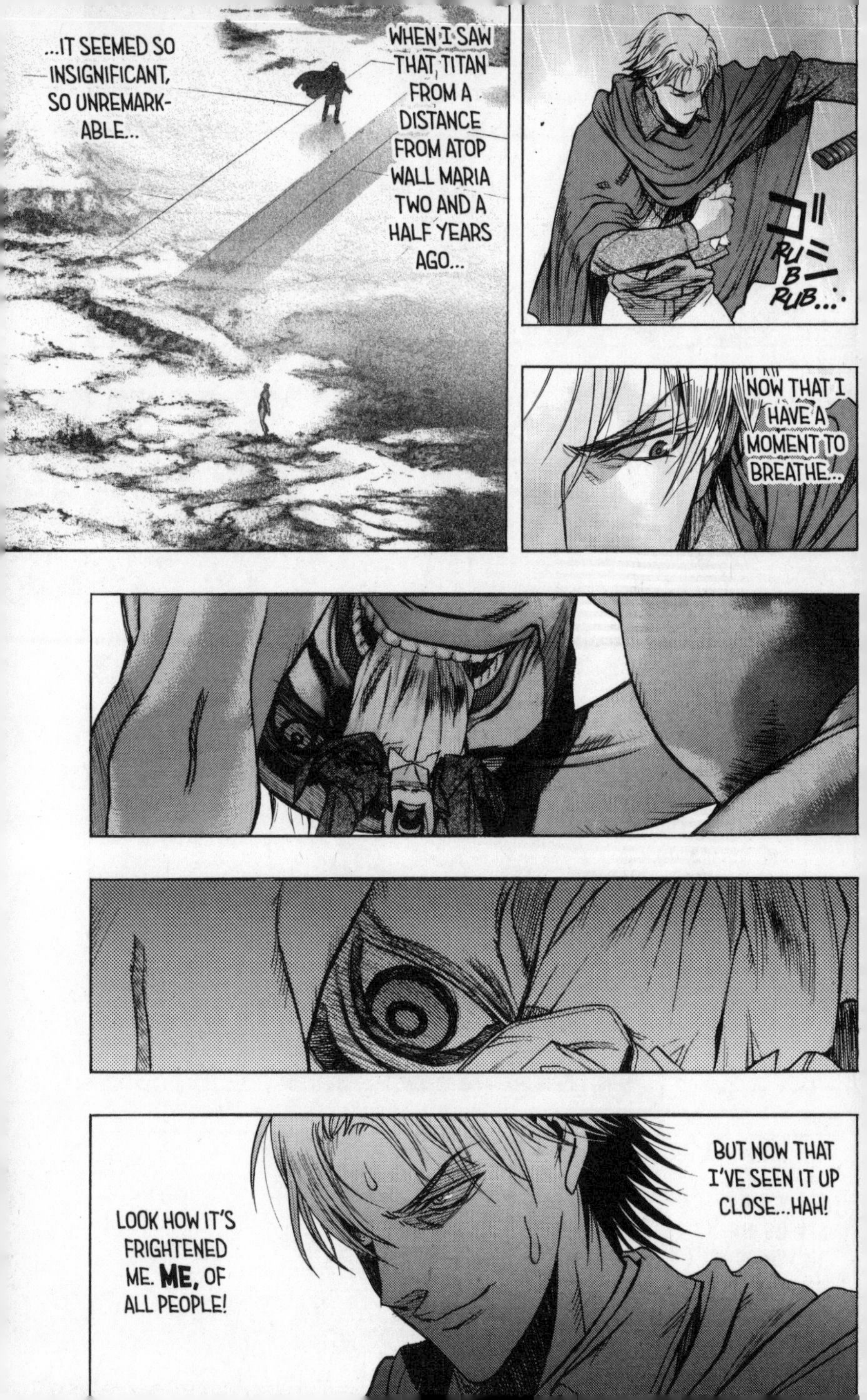
RUB RUB...
NOW THAT I HAVE A MOMENT TO BREATHE...
WHEN I SAW THAT TITAN FROM A DISTANCE FROM ATOP WALL MARIA TWO AND A HALF YEARS AGO...
...IT SEEMED SO INSIGNIFICANT, SO UNREMARKABLE...
BUT NOW THAT I'VE SEEN IT UP CLOSE...HAH!
LOOK HOW IT'S FRIGHTENED ME. **ME,** OF ALL PEOPLE!

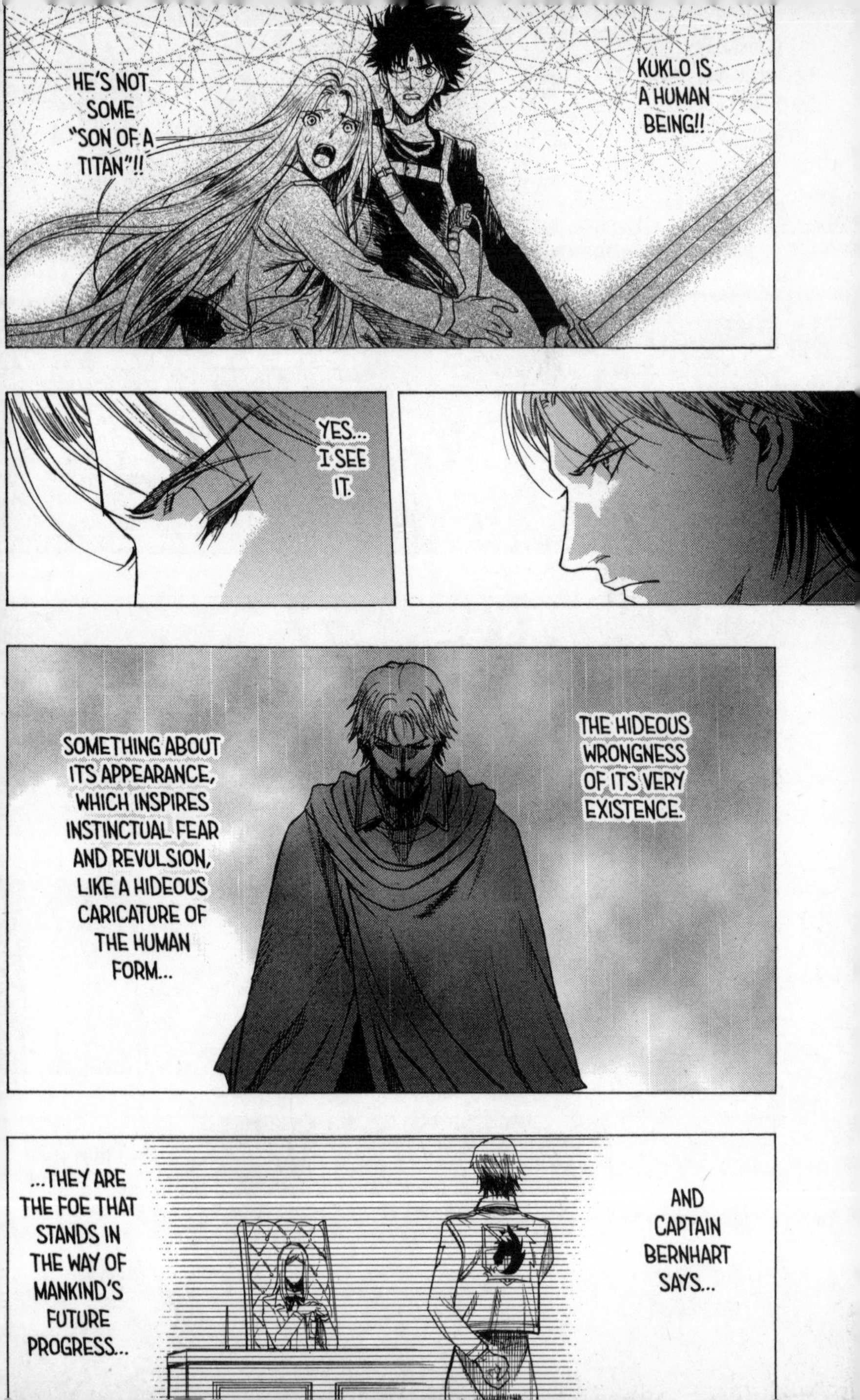
KUKLO IS A HUMAN BEING!!
HE'S NOT SOME "SON OF A TITAN"!!
YES... I SEE IT.
THE HIDEOUS WRONGNESS OF ITS VERY EXISTENCE.
SOMETHING ABOUT ITS APPEARANCE, WHICH INSPIRES INSTINCTUAL FEAR AND REVULSION, LIKE A HIDEOUS CARICATURE OF THE HUMAN FORM...
AND CAPTAIN BERNHART SAYS...
...THEY ARE THE FOE THAT STANDS IN THE WAY OF MANKIND'S FUTURE PROGRESS...

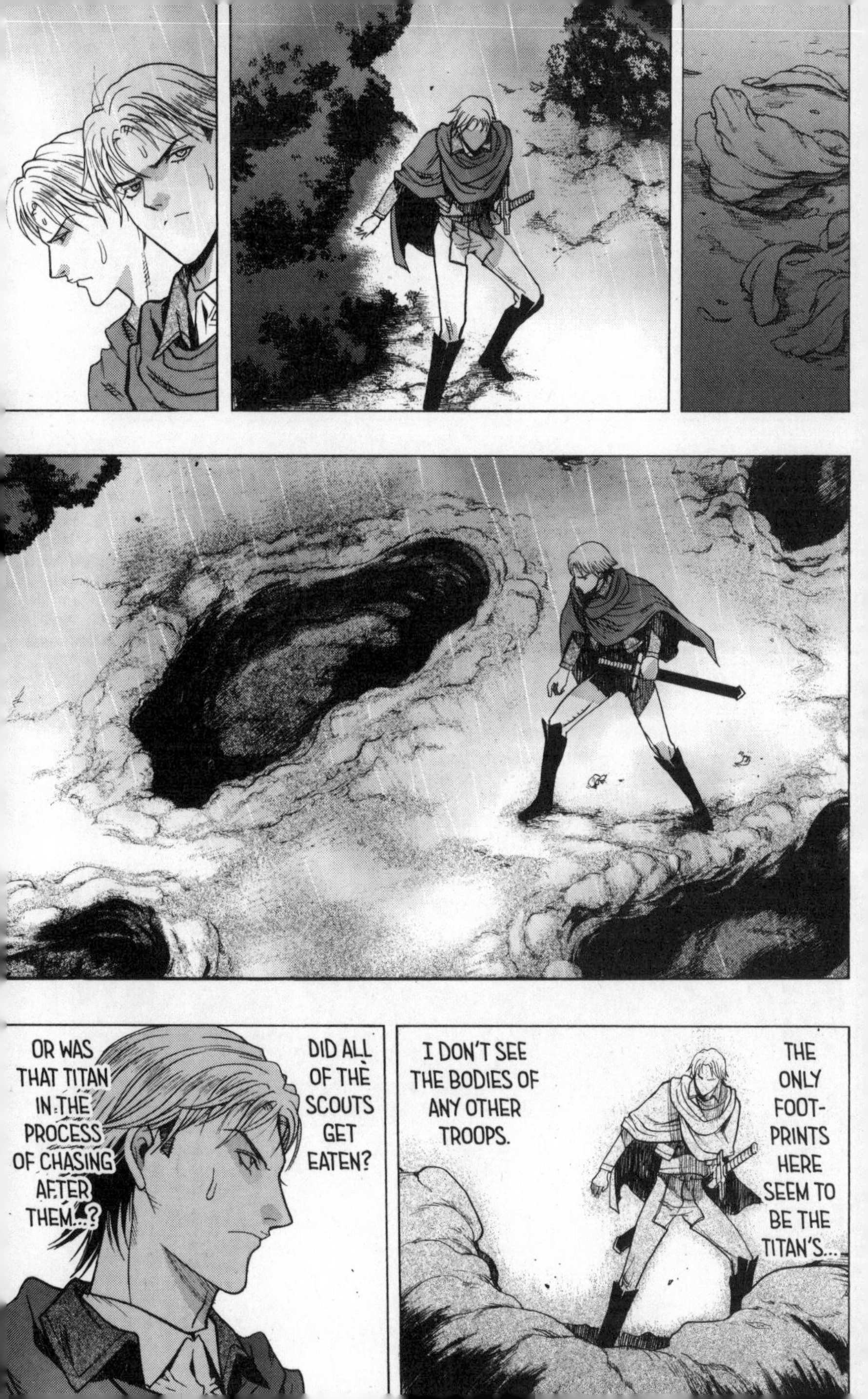
THE ONLY FOOT-PRINTS HERE SEEM TO BE THE TITAN'S...
I DON'T SEE THE BODIES OF ANY OTHER TROOPS.
DID ALL OF THE SCOUTS GET EATEN?
OR WAS THAT TITAN IN THE PROCESS OF CHASING AFTER THEM...?

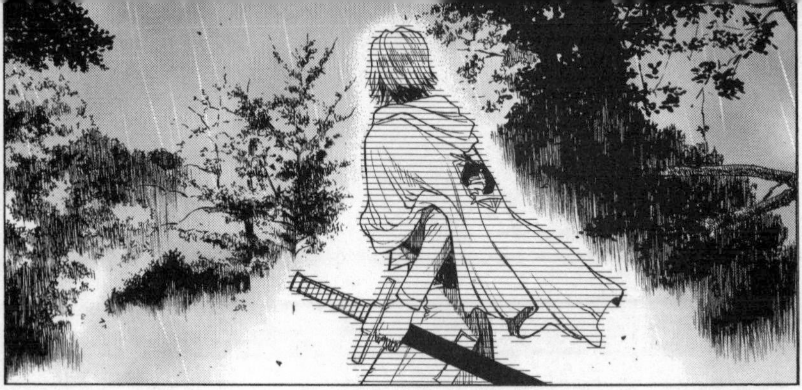

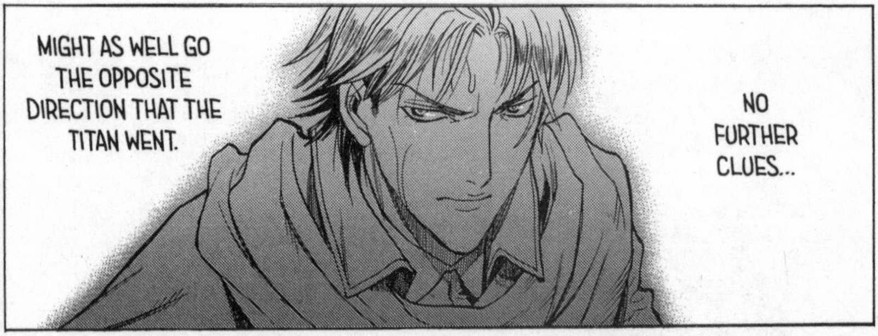
NO FURTHER CLUES...
MIGHT AS WELL GO THE OPPOSITE DIRECTION THAT THE TITAN WENT.

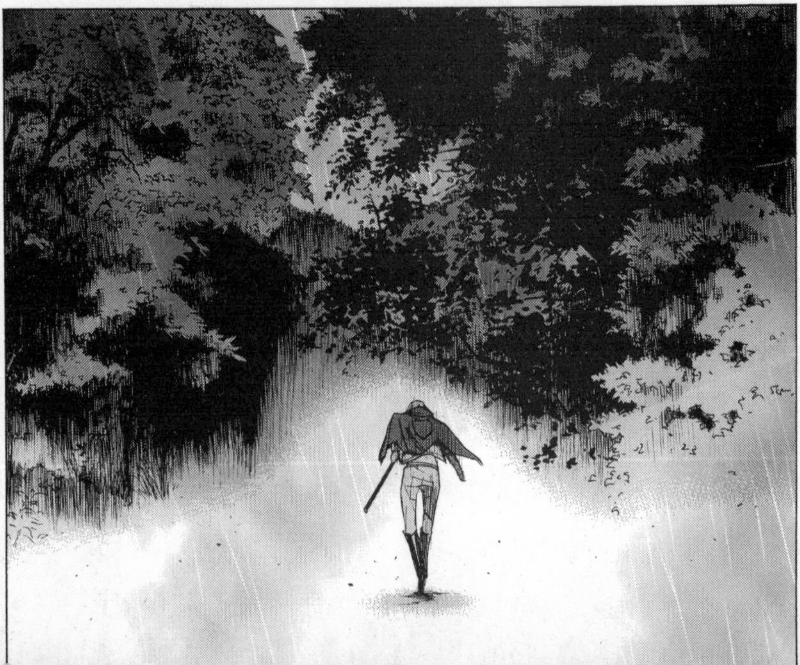

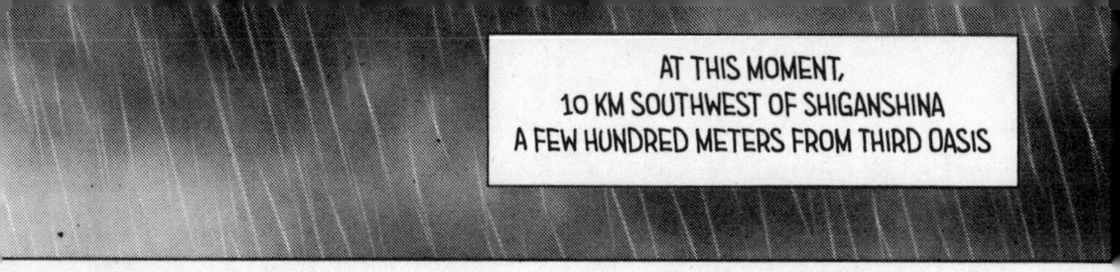
AT THIS MOMENT,
10 KM SOUTHWEST OF SHIGANSHINA
A FEW HUNDRED METERS FROM THIRD OASIS

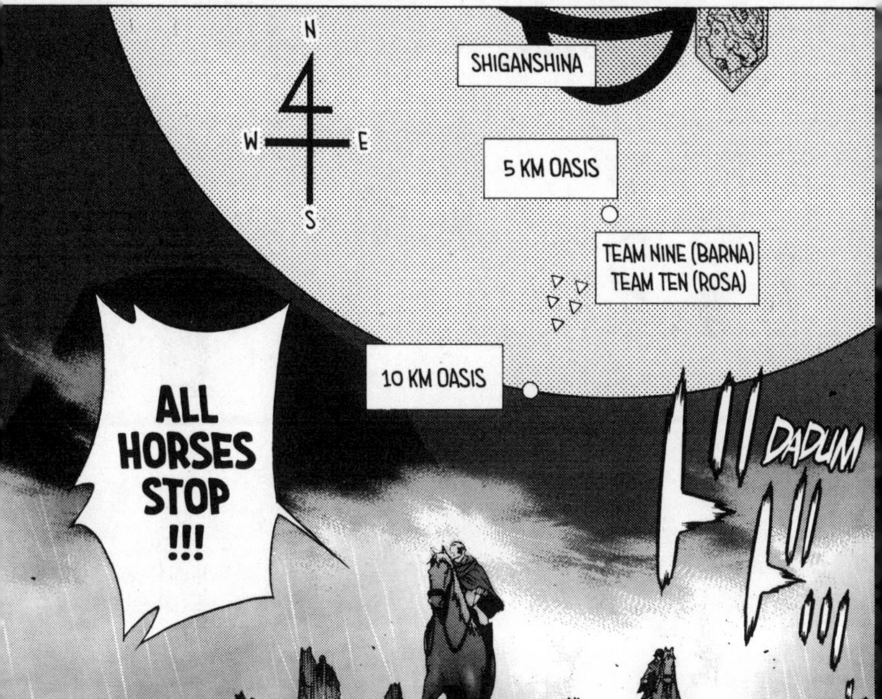
N
W
E
S
SHIGANSHINA
5 KM OASIS
TEAM NINE (BARNA)
TEAM TEN (ROSA)
10 KM OASIS
ALL HORSES STOP !!!
DADUM

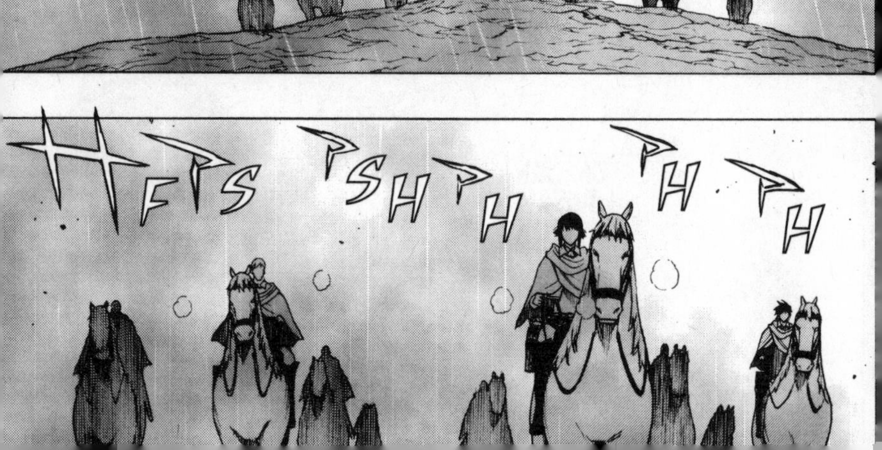
HFPS
PSH
PH
PH
PH

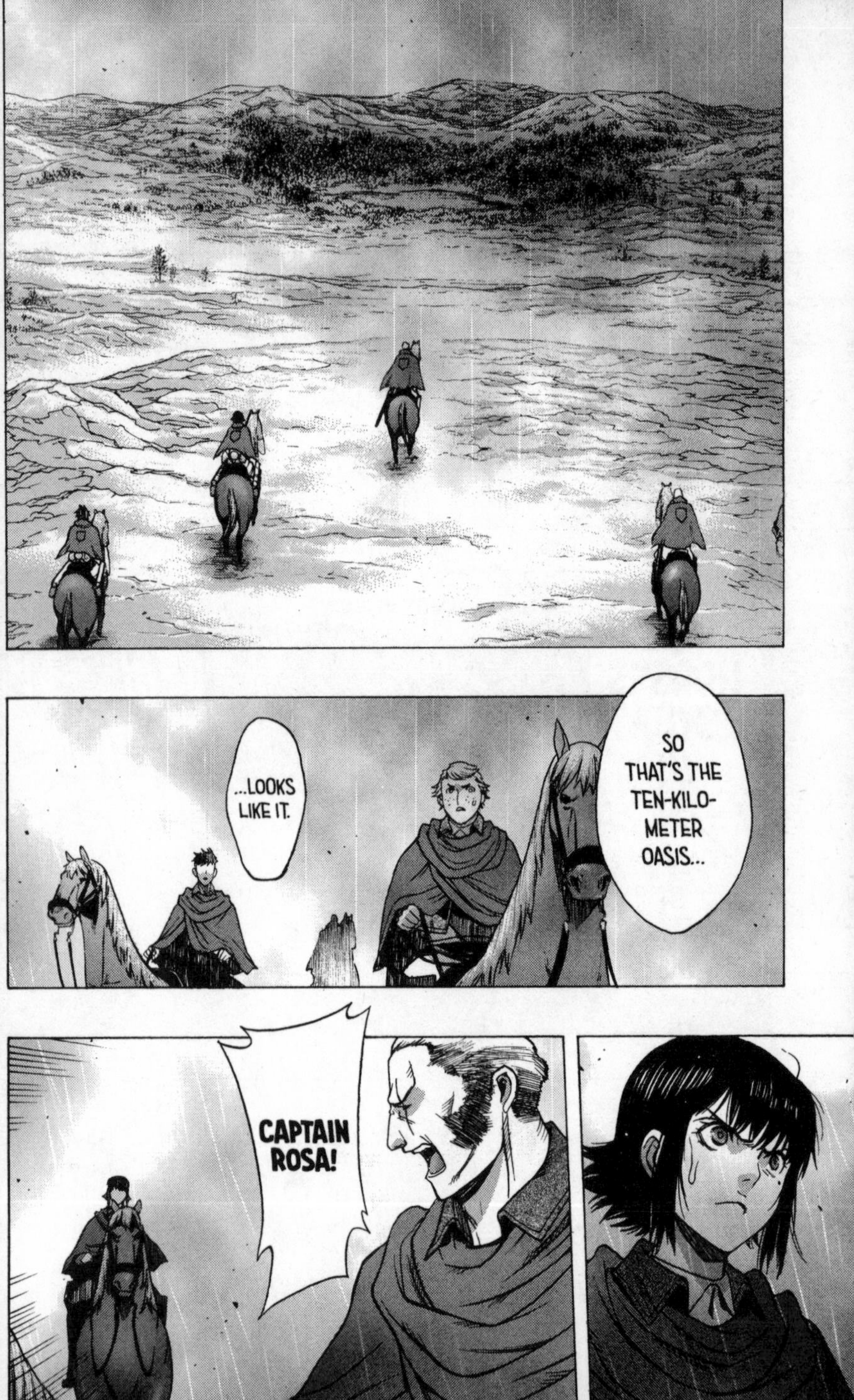
SO THAT'S THE TEN-KILO-METER OASIS...
...LOOKS LIKE IT.
CAPTAIN ROSA!

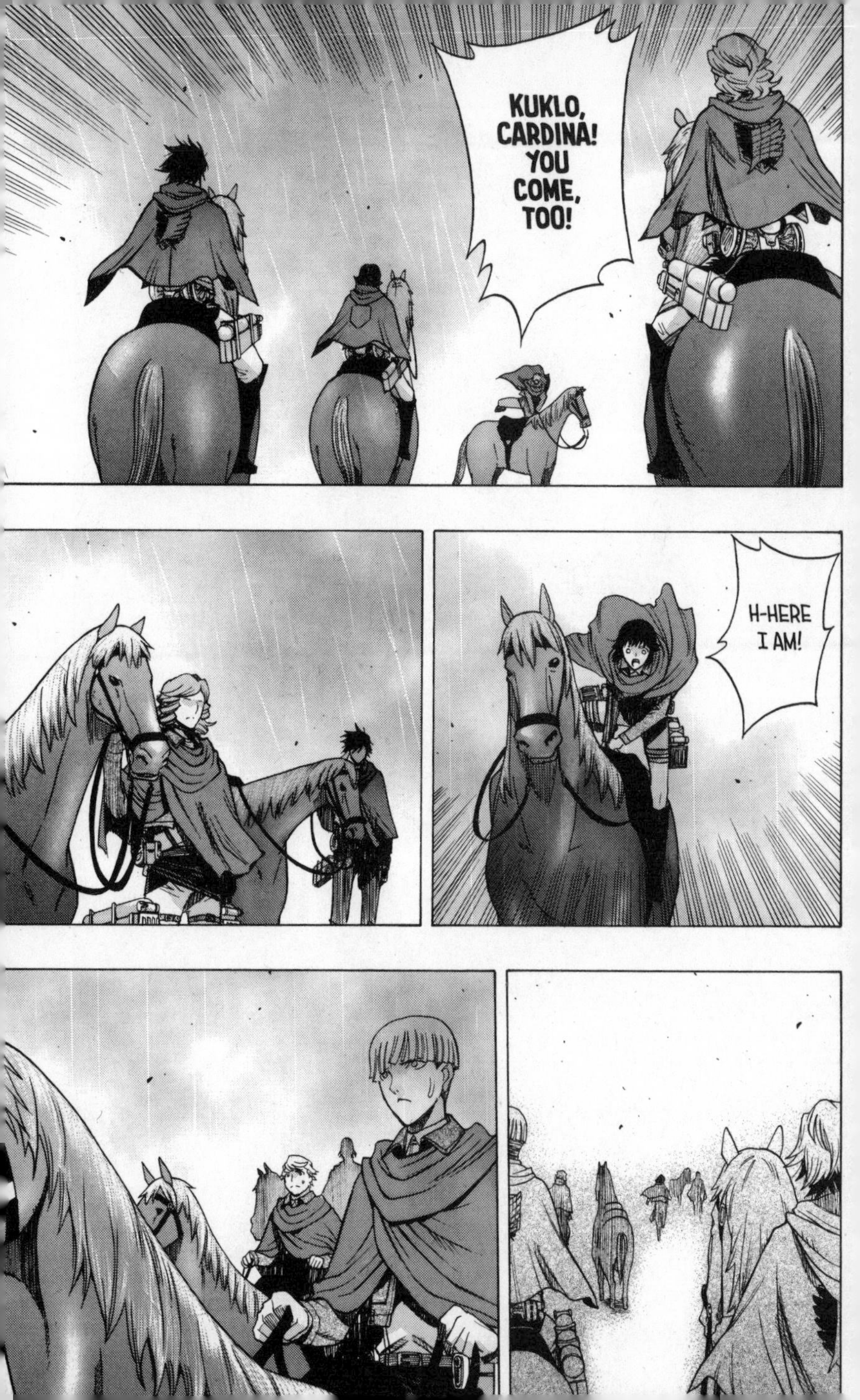
KUKLO, CARDINA! YOU COME, TOO!
H-HERE I AM!

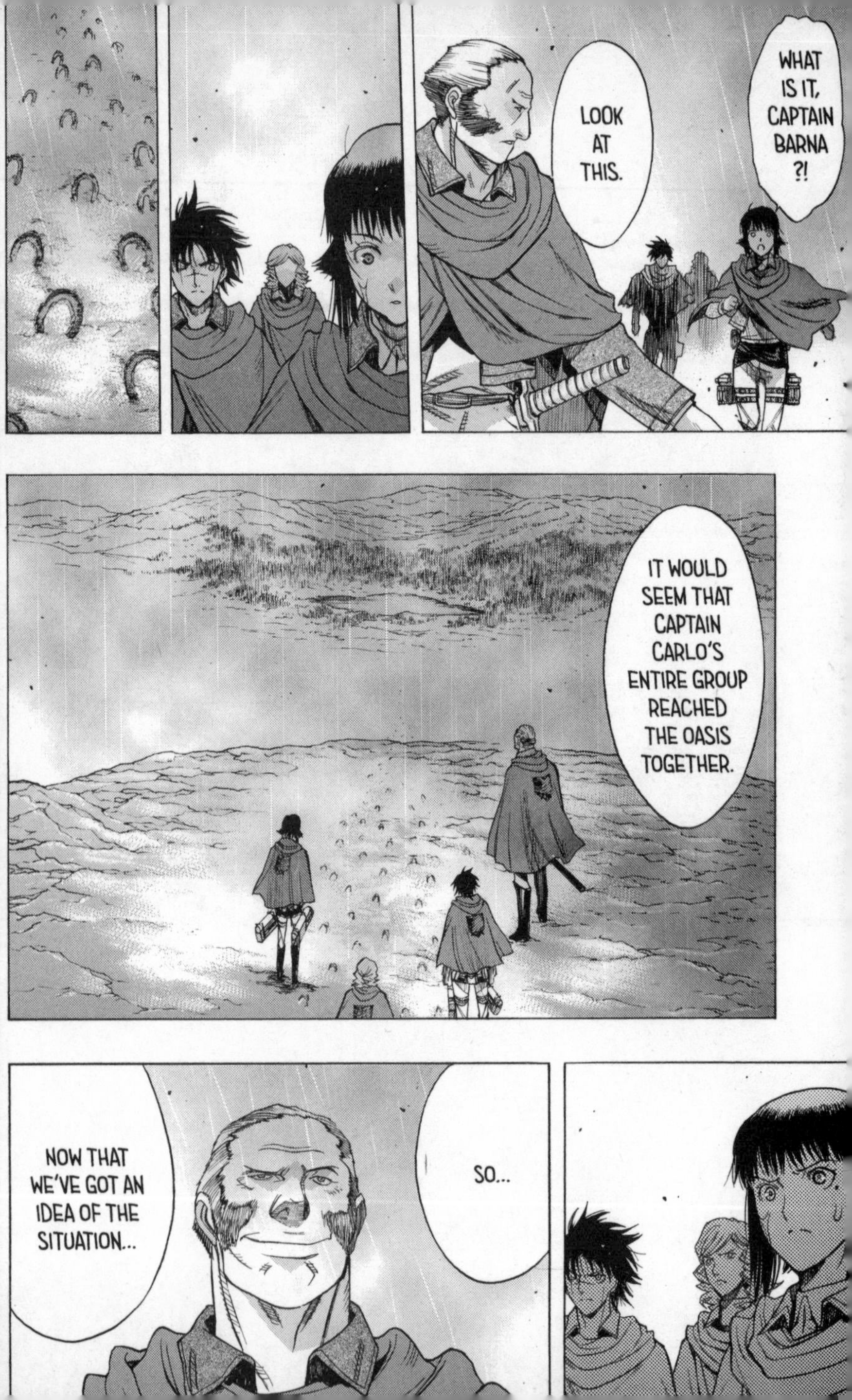
WHAT IS IT, CAPTAIN BARNA?!
LOOK AT THIS.
IT WOULD SEEM THAT CAPTAIN CARLO'S ENTIRE GROUP REACHED THE OASIS TOGETHER.
NOW THAT WE'VE GOT AN IDEA OF THE SITUATION...
SO...

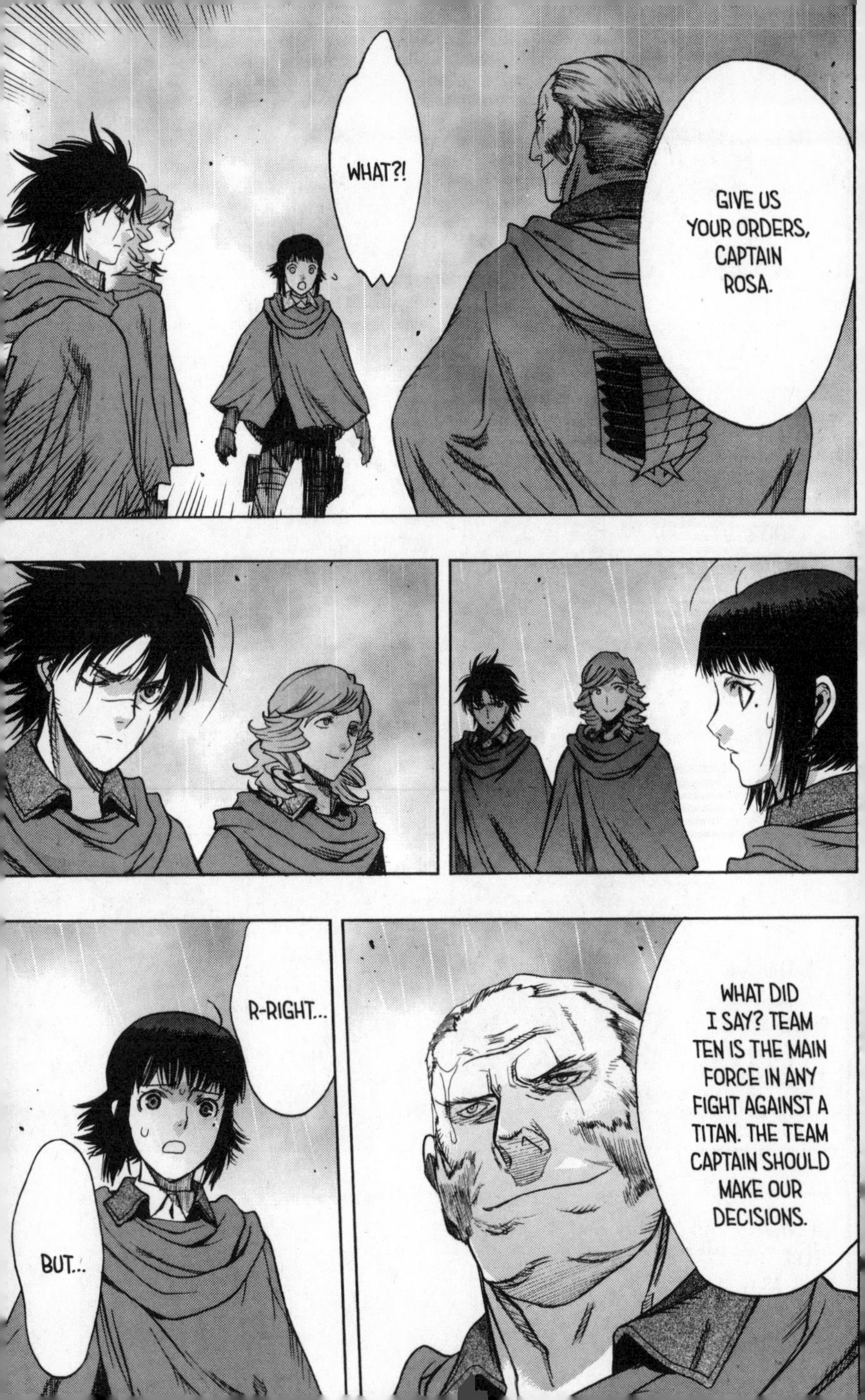
GIVE US YOUR ORDERS, CAPTAIN ROSA.
WHAT?!
WHAT DID I SAY? TEAM TEN IS THE MAIN FORCE IN ANY FIGHT AGAINST A TITAN. THE TEAM CAPTAIN SHOULD MAKE OUR DECISIONS.
R-RIGHT...
BUT...

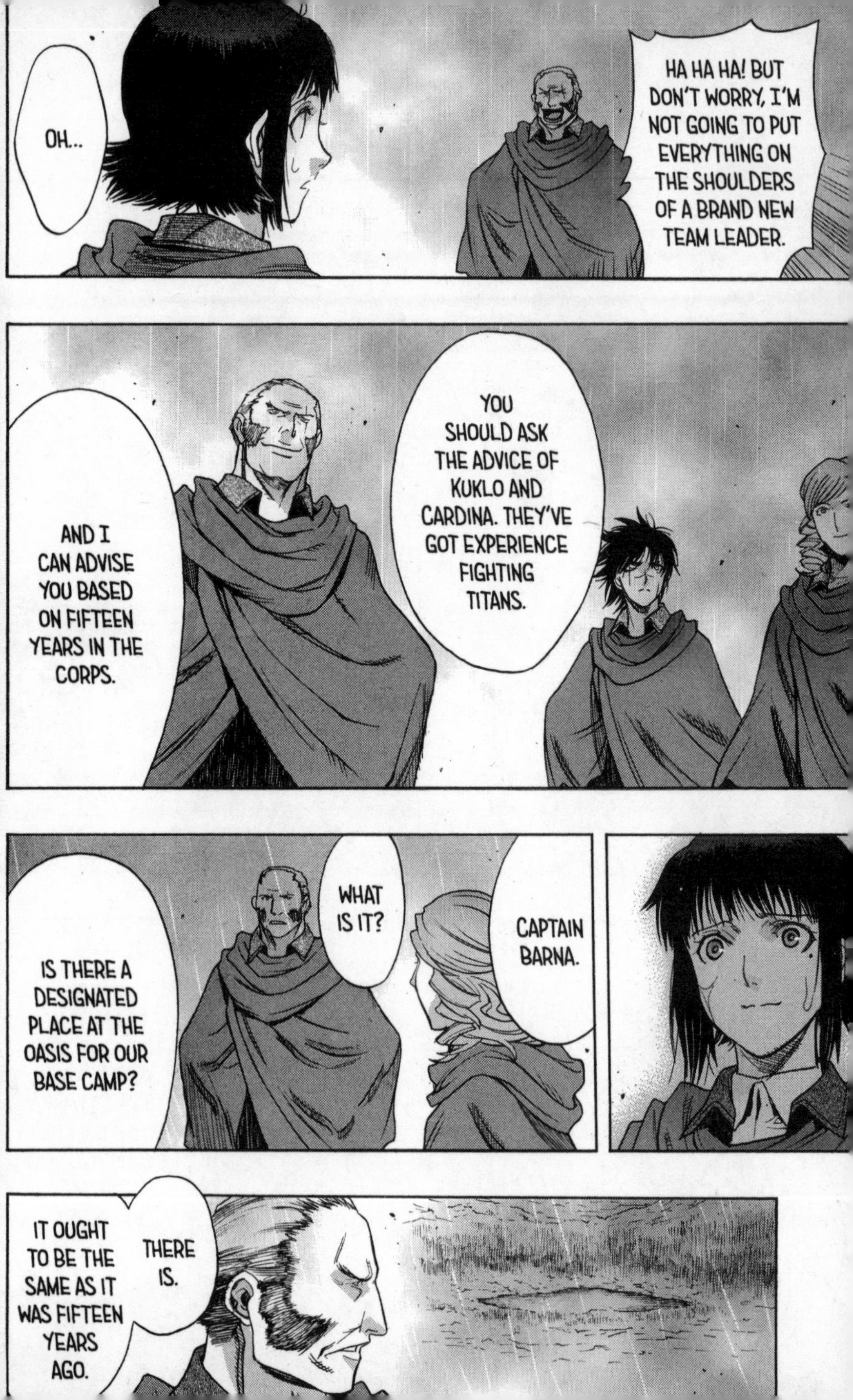
HA HA HA! BUT DON'T WORRY, I'M NOT GOING TO PUT EVERYTHING ON THE SHOULDERS OF A BRAND NEW TEAM LEADER.
OH...
YOU SHOULD ASK THE ADVICE OF KUKLO AND CARDINA. THEY'VE GOT EXPERIENCE FIGHTING TITANS.
AND I CAN ADVISE YOU BASED ON FIFTEEN YEARS IN THE CORPS.
CAPTAIN BARNA.
WHAT IS IT?
IS THERE A DESIGNATED PLACE AT THE OASIS FOR OUR BASE CAMP?
THERE IS.
IT OUGHT TO BE THE SAME AS IT WAS FIFTEEN YEARS AGO.

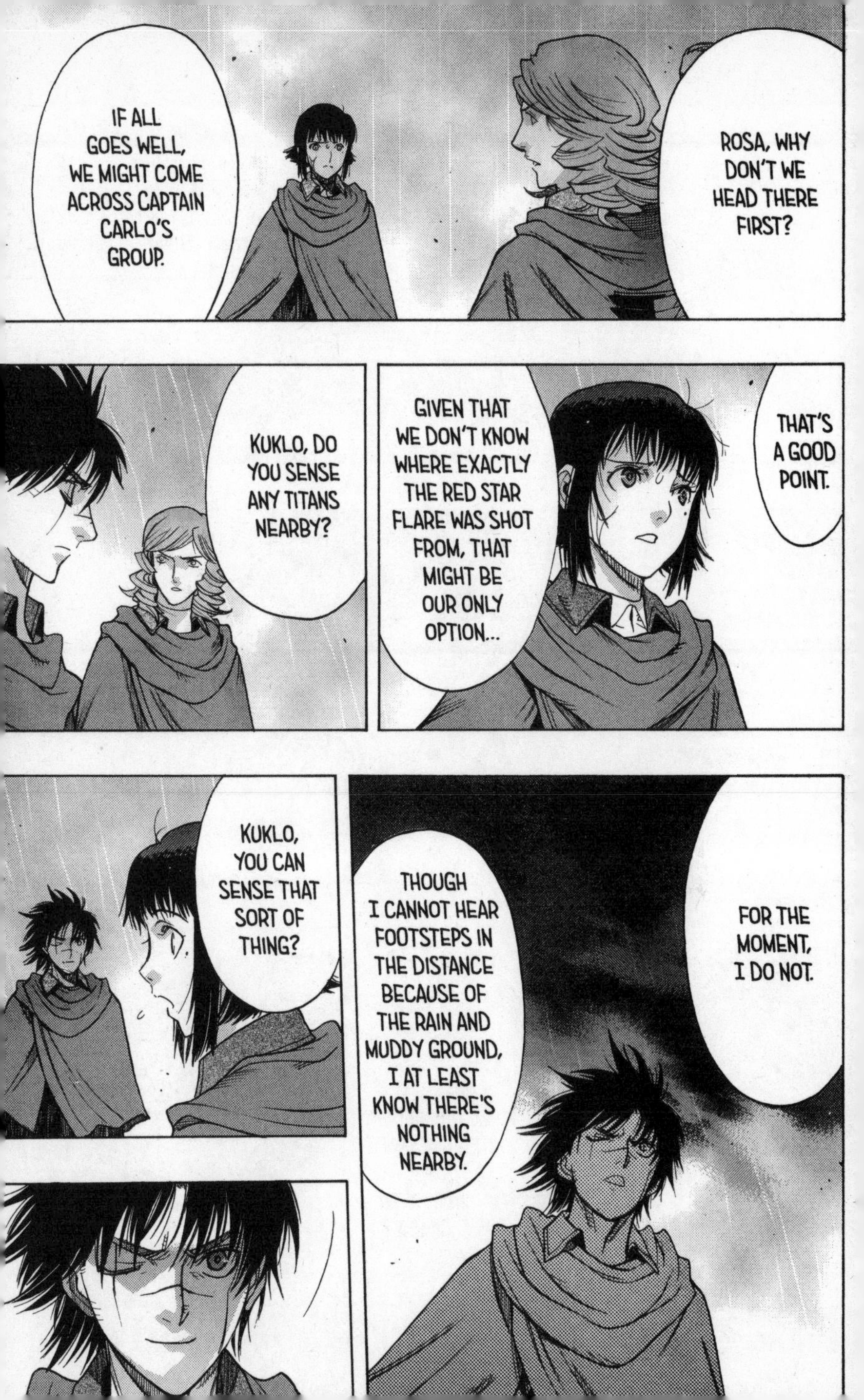
ROSA, WHY DON'T WE HEAD THERE FIRST?
IF ALL GOES WELL, WE MIGHT COME ACROSS CAPTAIN CARLO'S GROUP.
THAT'S A GOOD POINT.
GIVEN THAT WE DON'T KNOW WHERE EXACTLY THE RED STAR FLARE WAS SHOT FROM, THAT MIGHT BE OUR ONLY OPTION...
KUKLO, DO YOU SENSE ANY TITANS NEARBY?
FOR THE MOMENT, I DO NOT.
KUKLO, YOU CAN SENSE THAT SORT OF THING?
THOUGH I CANNOT HEAR FOOTSTEPS IN THE DISTANCE BECAUSE OF THE RAIN AND MUDDY GROUND, I AT LEAST KNOW THERE'S NOTHING NEARBY.

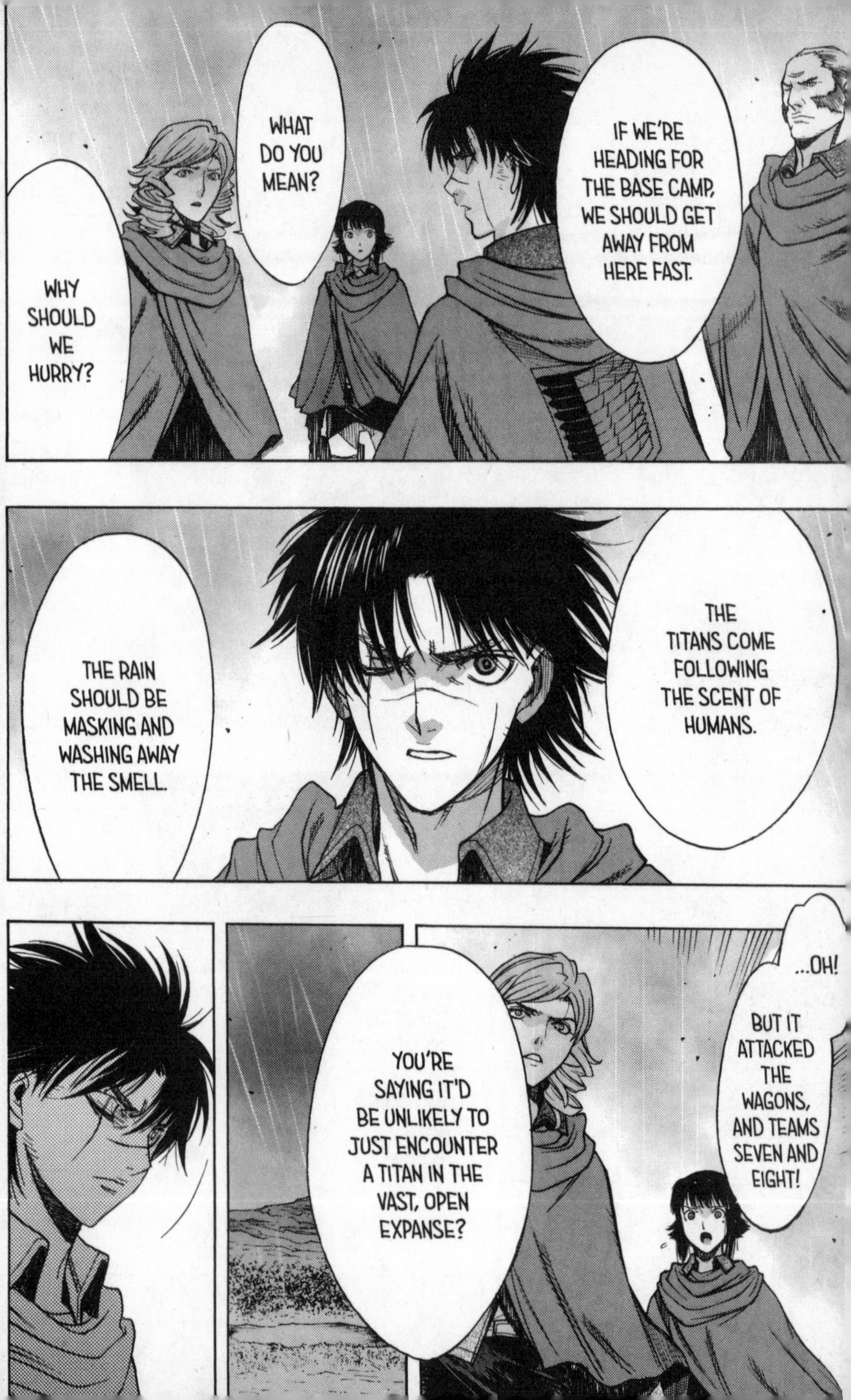
IF WE'RE HEADING FOR THE BASE CAMP, WE SHOULD GET AWAY FROM HERE FAST.
WHAT DO YOU MEAN?
WHY SHOULD WE HURRY?
THE TITANS COME FOLLOWING THE SCENT OF HUMANS.
THE RAIN SHOULD BE MASKING AND WASHING AWAY THE SMELL.
YOU'RE SAYING IT'D BE UNLIKELY TO JUST ENCOUNTER A TITAN IN THE VAST, OPEN EXPANSE?
...OH!
BUT IT ATTACKED THE WAGONS, AND TEAMS SEVEN AND EIGHT!

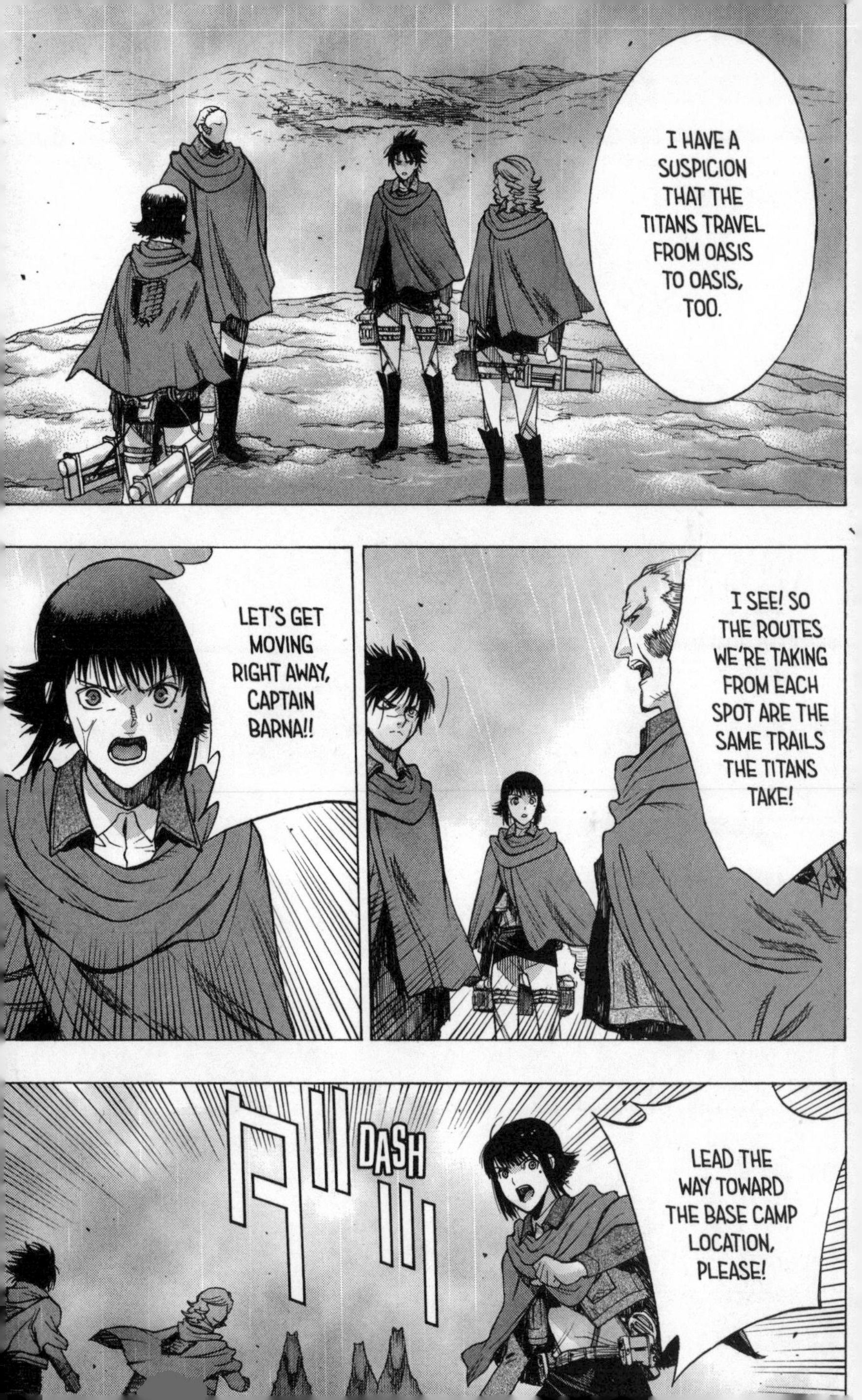
I HAVE A SUSPICION THAT THE TITANS TRAVEL FROM OASIS TO OASIS, TOO.
I SEE! SO THE ROUTES WE'RE TAKING FROM EACH SPOT ARE THE SAME TRAILS THE TITANS TAKE!
LET'S GET MOVING RIGHT AWAY, CAPTAIN BARNA!!
LEAD THE WAY TOWARD THE BASE CAMP LOCATION, PLEASE!
DASH

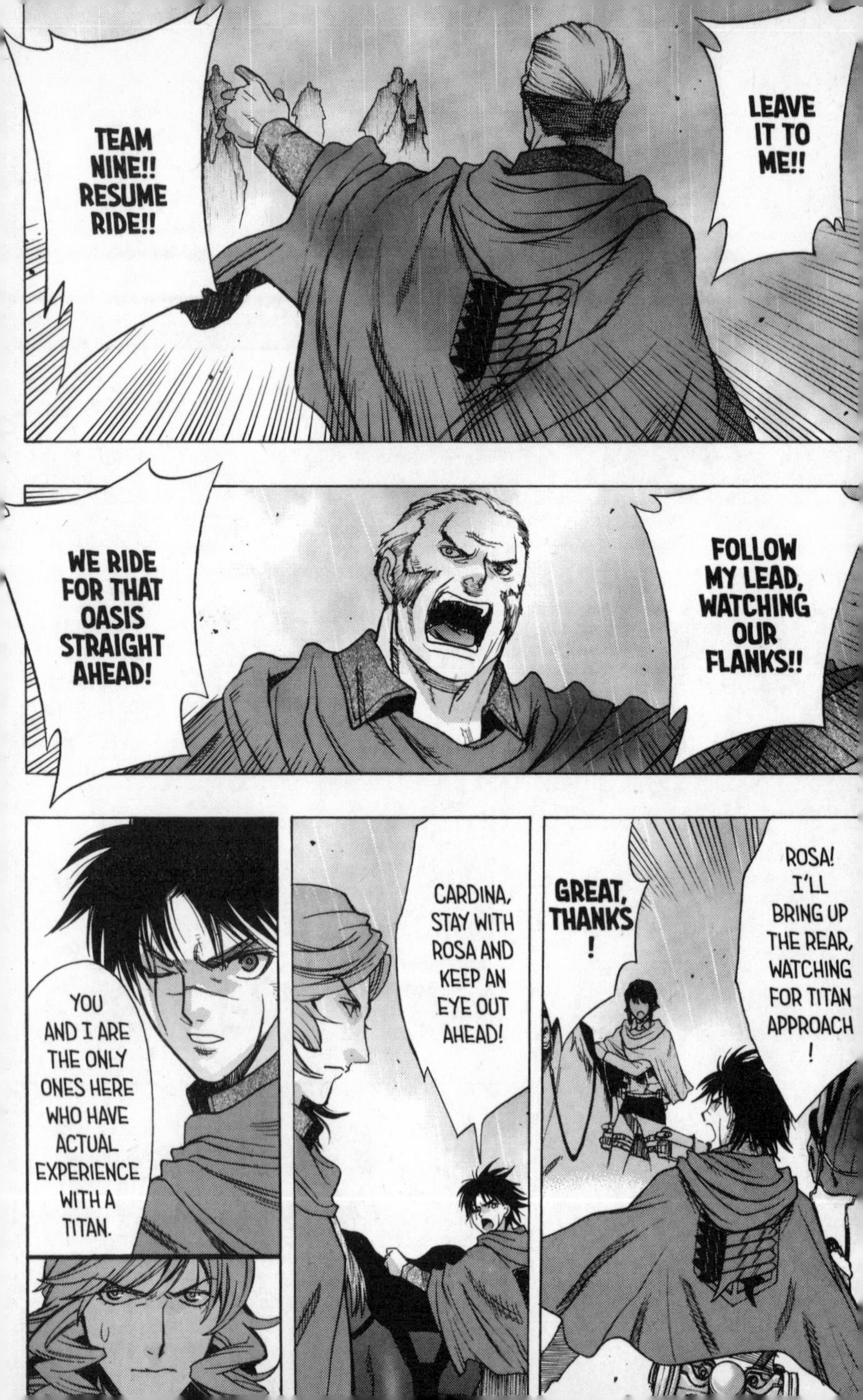
LEAVE IT TO ME!!
TEAM NINE!! RESUME RIDE!!
FOLLOW MY LEAD, WATCHING OUR FLANKS!!
WE RIDE FOR THAT OASIS STRAIGHT AHEAD!
ROSA! I'LL BRING UP THE REAR, WATCHING FOR TITAN APPROACH!
GREAT, THANKS!
CARDINA, STAY WITH ROSA AND KEEP AN EYE OUT AHEAD!
YOU AND I ARE THE ONLY ONES HERE WHO HAVE ACTUAL EXPERIENCE WITH A TITAN.

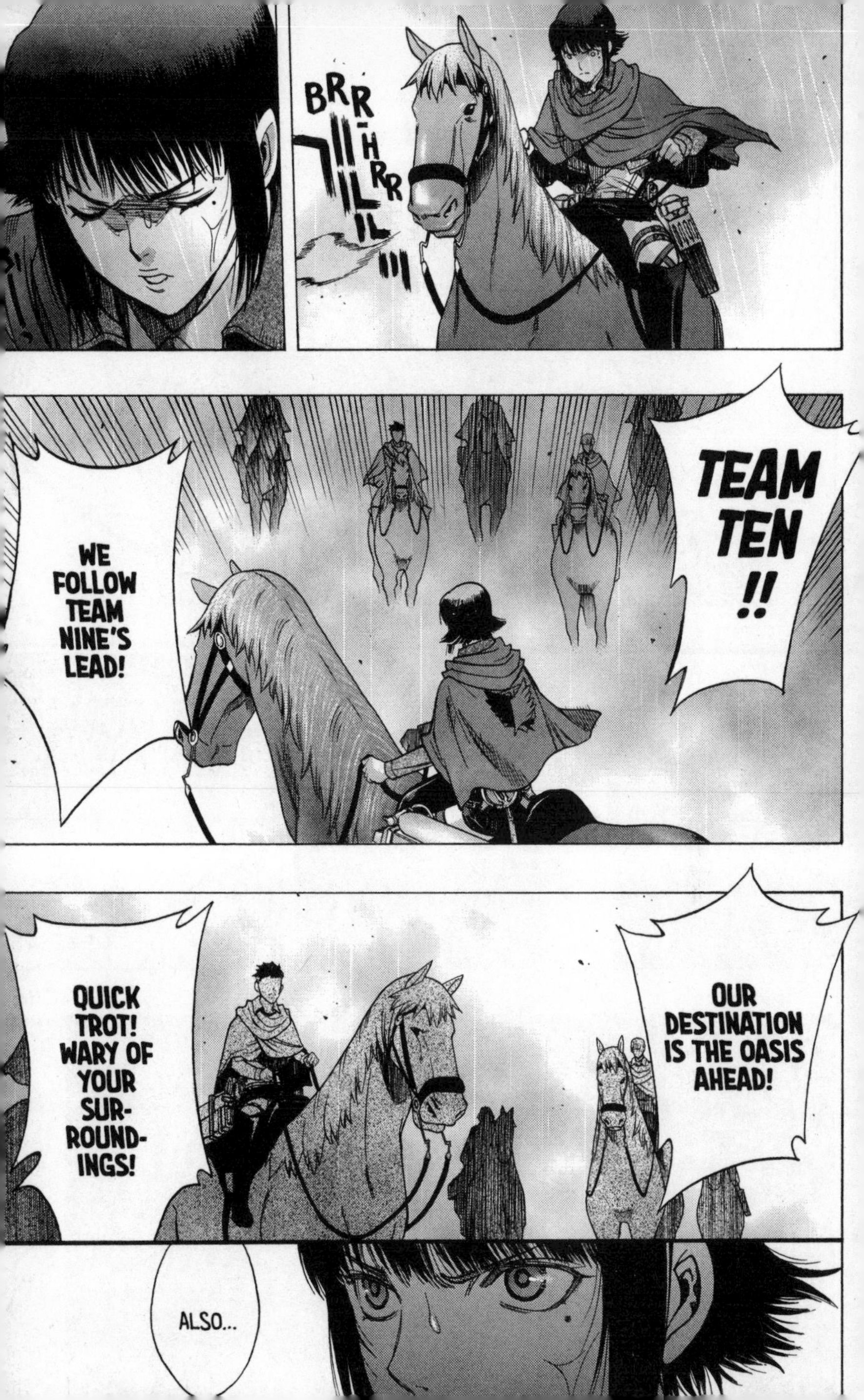
BRRR-HRR
TEAM TEN!!
WE FOLLOW TEAM NINE'S LEAD!
OUR DESTINATION IS THE OASIS AHEAD!
QUICK TROT! WARY OF YOUR SUR-ROUND-INGS!
ALSO...

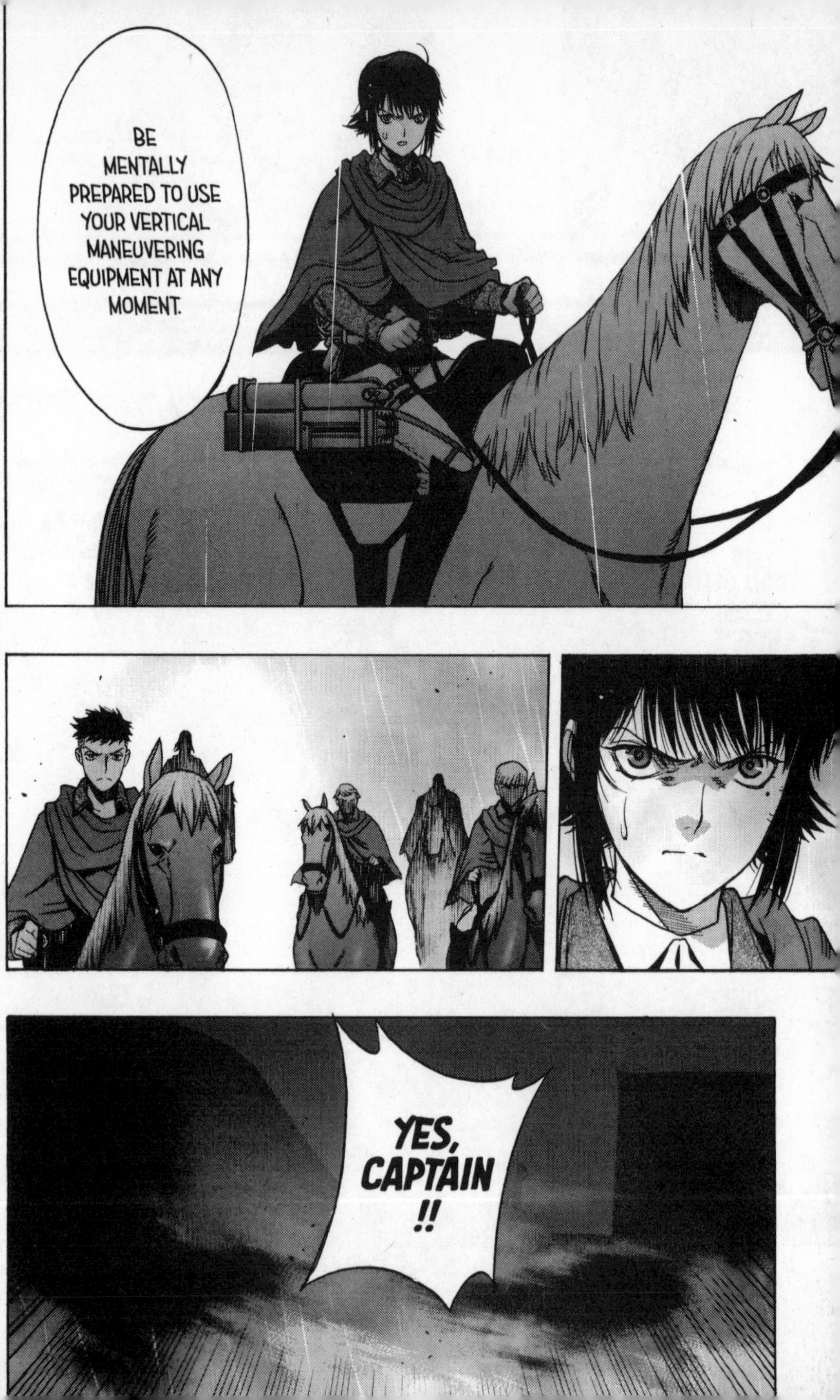
BE MENTALLY PREPARED TO USE YOUR VERTICAL MANEUVERING EQUIPMENT AT ANY MOMENT.
YES, CAPTAIN !!

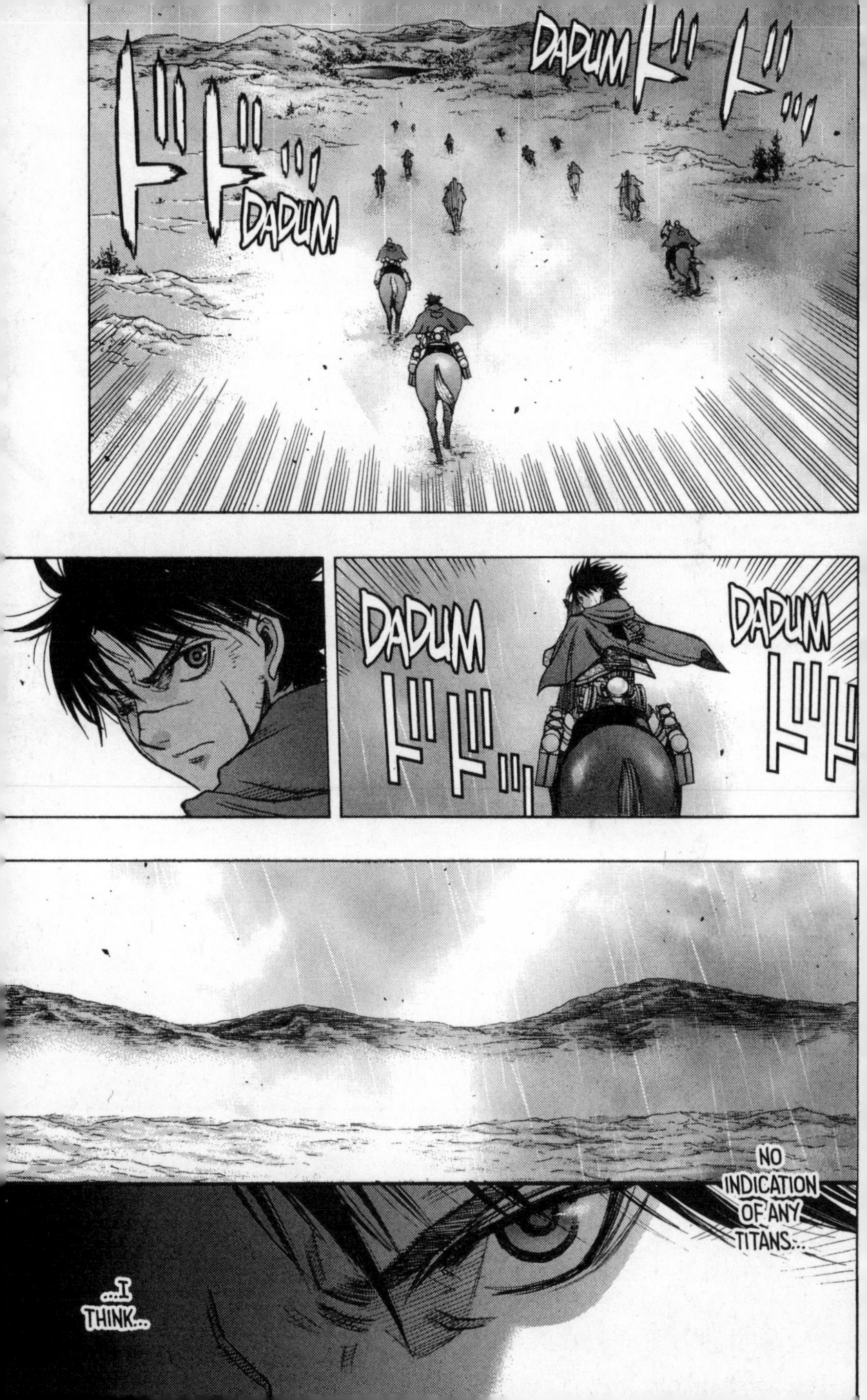
DADUM
DADUM
DADUM
DADUM
NO INDICATION OF ANY TITANS...
...I THINK...

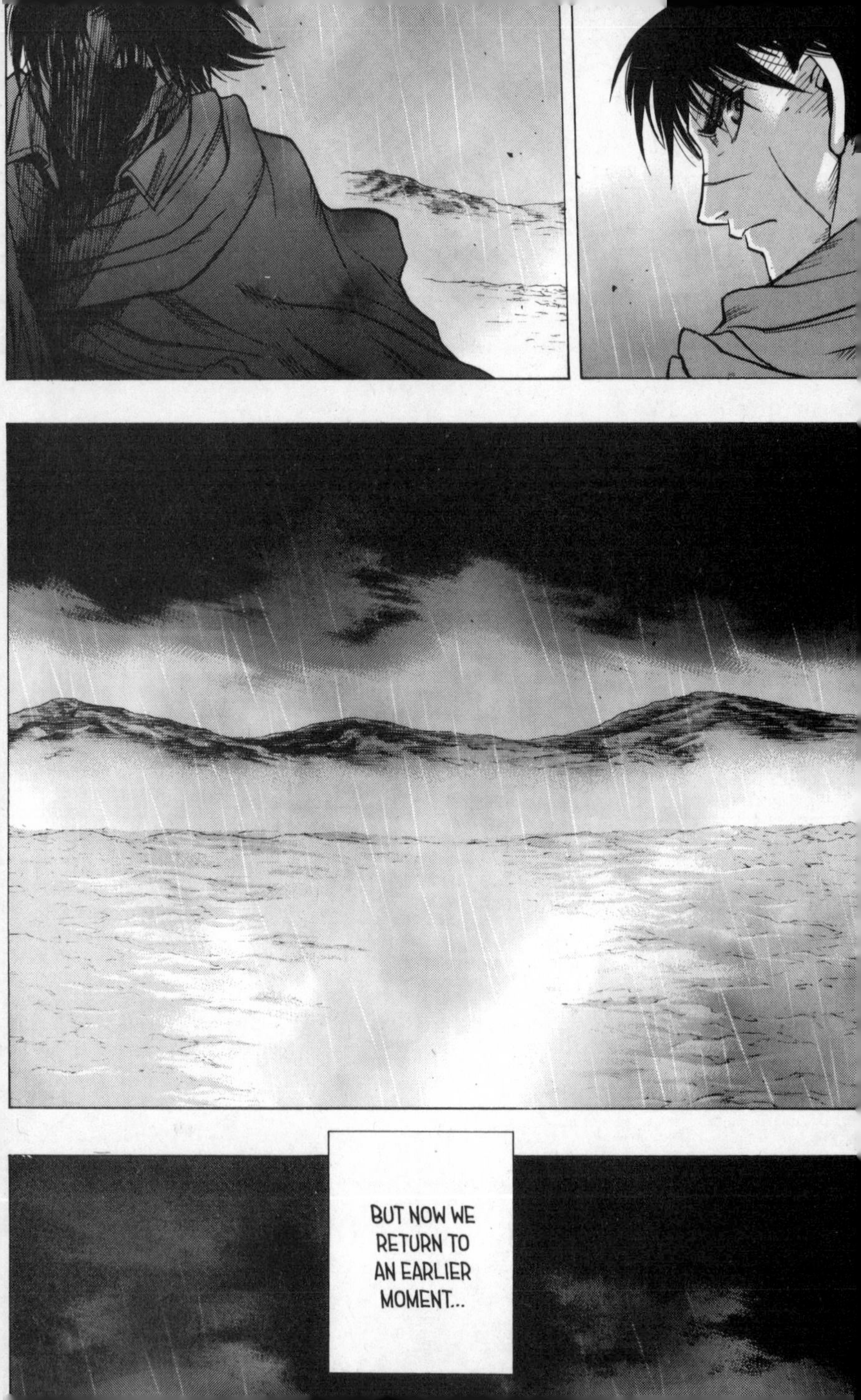
BUT NOW WE RETURN TO AN EARLIER MOMENT...

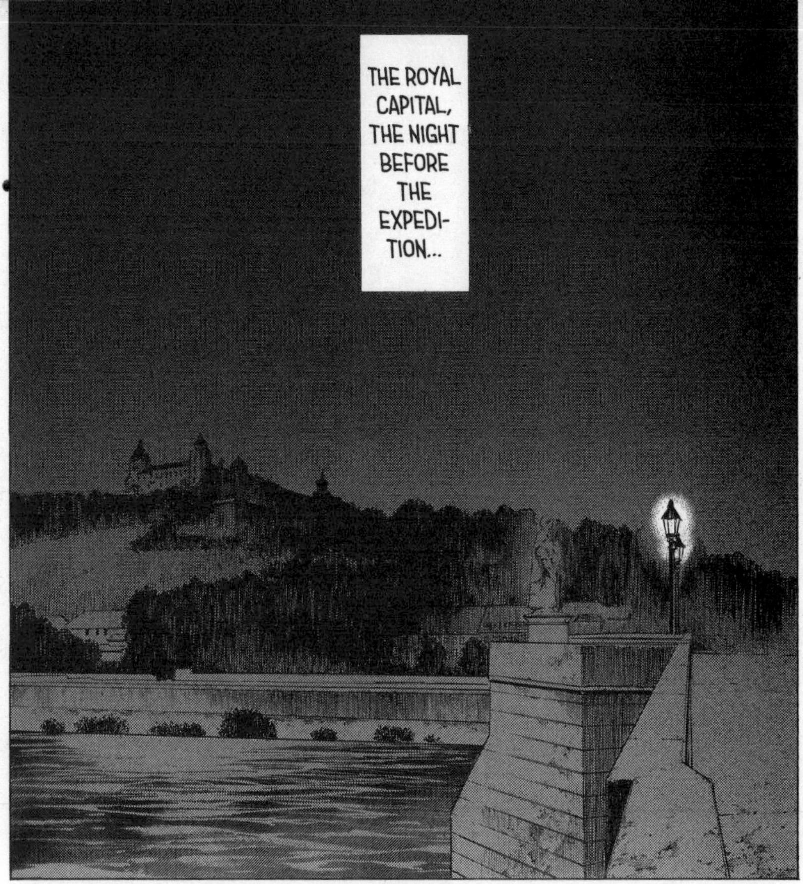
THE ROYAL CAPITAL, THE NIGHT BEFORE THE EXPEDI- TION...

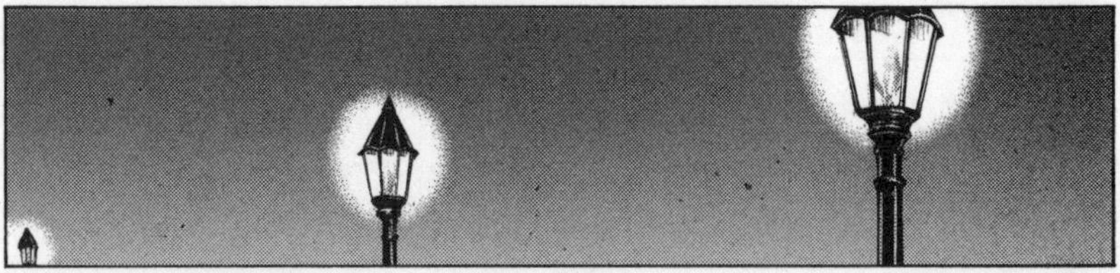

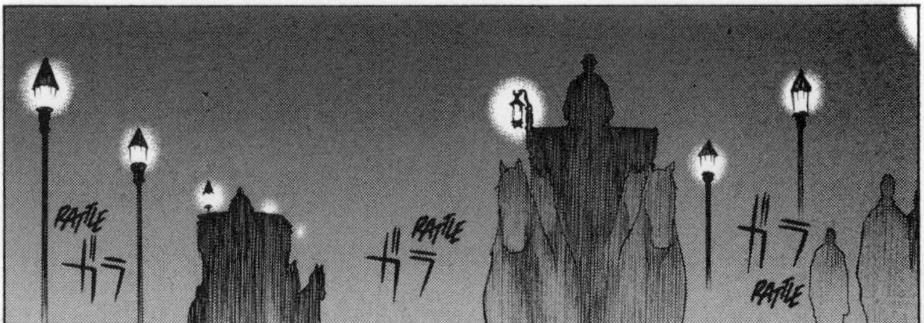
ガラ
RATTLE
ガラ
RATTLE
ガラ
RATTLE

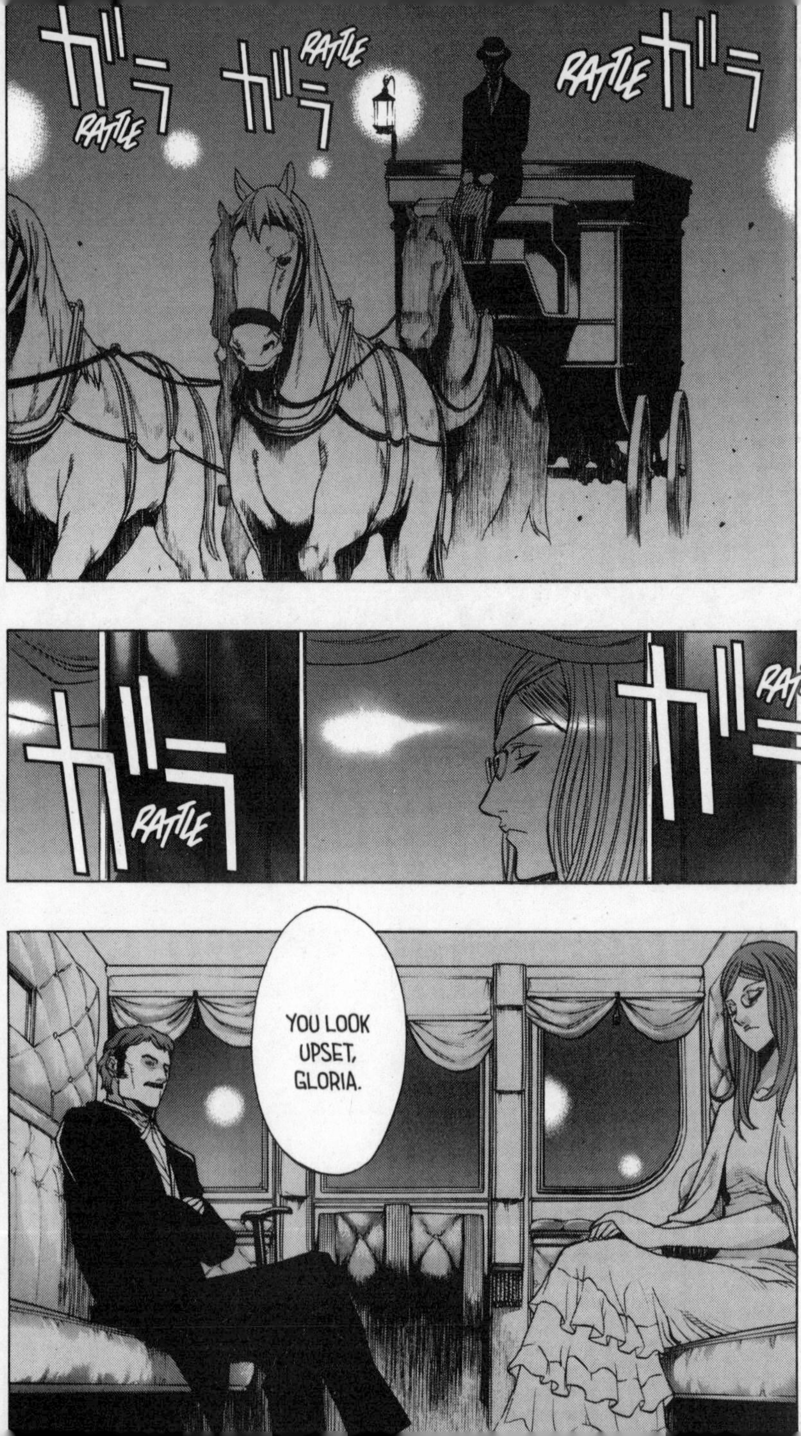

ガラ RATTLE
ガラ RATTLE
ガラ RATTLE
ガラ RATTLE
ガラ RATTLE
YOU LOOK UPSET, GLORIA.

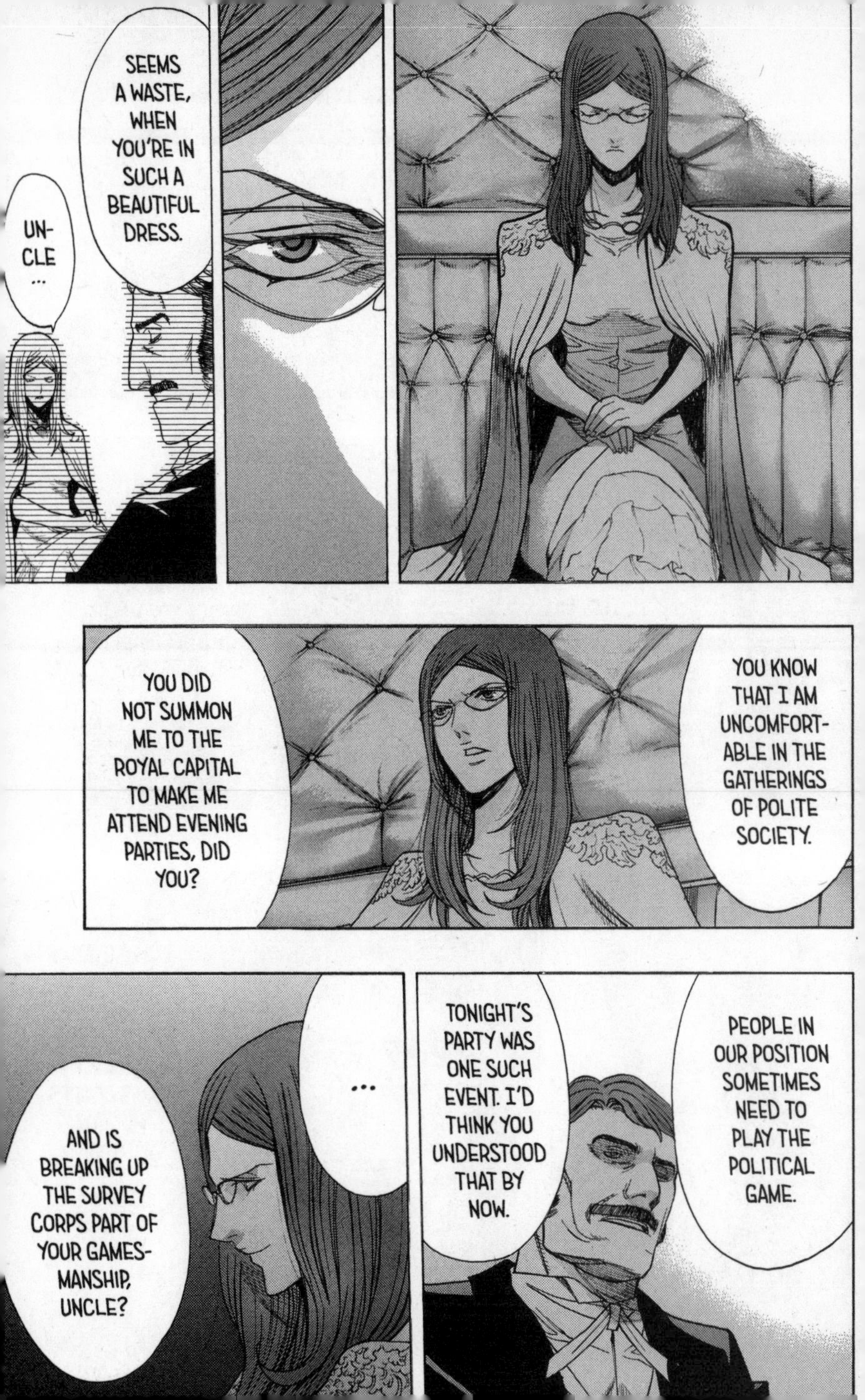
SEEMS A WASTE, WHEN YOU'RE IN SUCH A BEAUTIFUL DRESS.
UN-CLE ...
YOU KNOW THAT I AM UNCOMFORT-ABLE IN THE GATHERINGS OF POLITE SOCIETY.
YOU DID NOT SUMMON ME TO THE ROYAL CAPITAL TO MAKE ME ATTEND EVENING PARTIES, DID YOU?
PEOPLE IN OUR POSITION SOMETIMES NEED TO PLAY THE POLITICAL GAME.
TONIGHT'S PARTY WAS ONE SUCH EVENT. I'D THINK YOU UNDERSTOOD THAT BY NOW.
...
AND IS BREAKING UP THE SURVEY CORPS PART OF YOUR GAMES-MANSHIP, UNCLE?

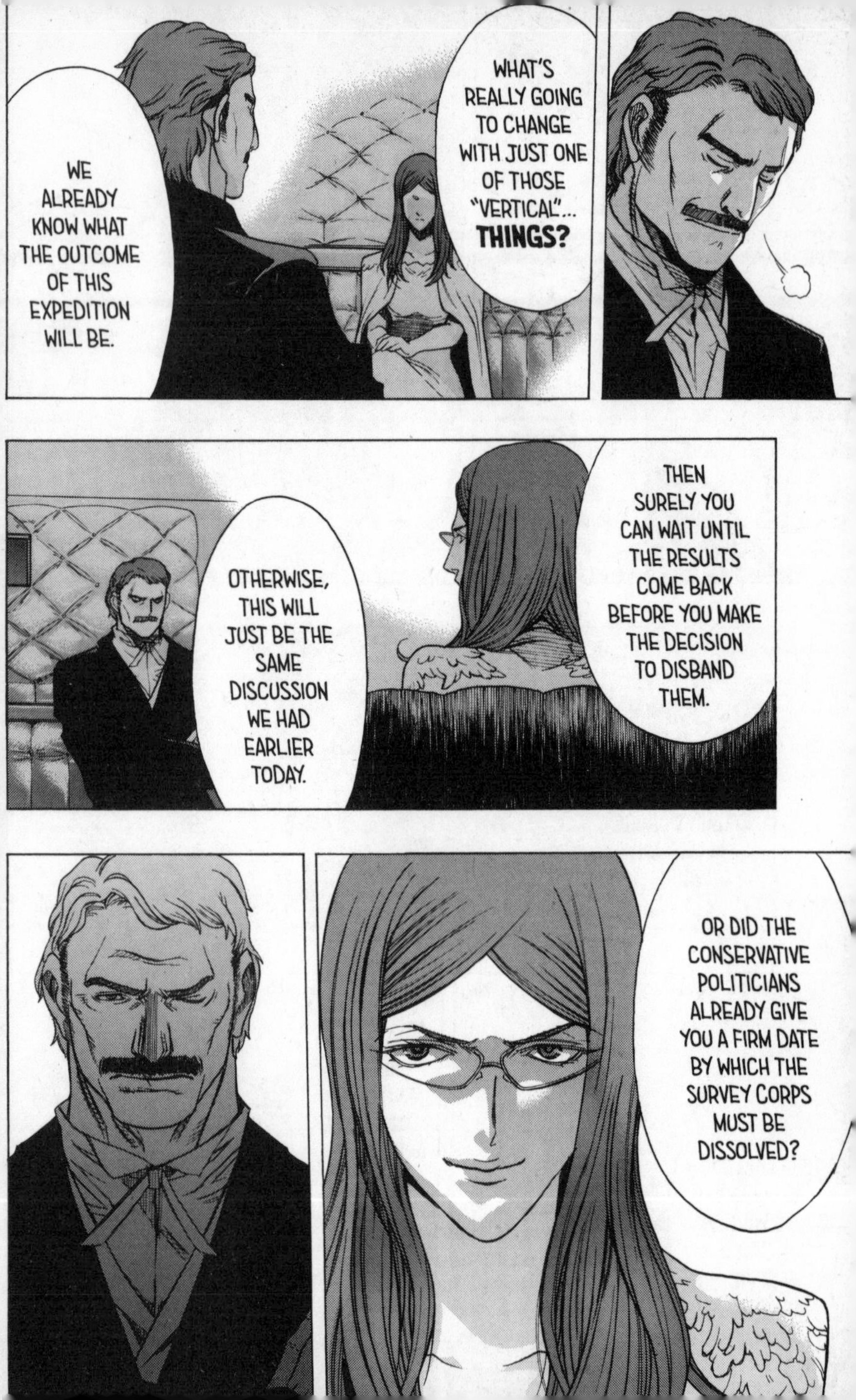
WHAT'S REALLY GOING TO CHANGE WITH JUST ONE OF THOSE "VERTICAL"... **THINGS?**
WE ALREADY KNOW WHAT THE OUTCOME OF THIS EXPEDITION WILL BE.
THEN SURELY YOU CAN WAIT UNTIL THE RESULTS COME BACK BEFORE YOU MAKE THE DECISION TO DISBAND THEM.
OTHERWISE, THIS WILL JUST BE THE SAME DISCUSSION WE HAD EARLIER TODAY.
OR DID THE CONSERVATIVE POLITICIANS ALREADY GIVE YOU A FIRM DATE BY WHICH THE SURVEY CORPS MUST BE DISSOLVED?

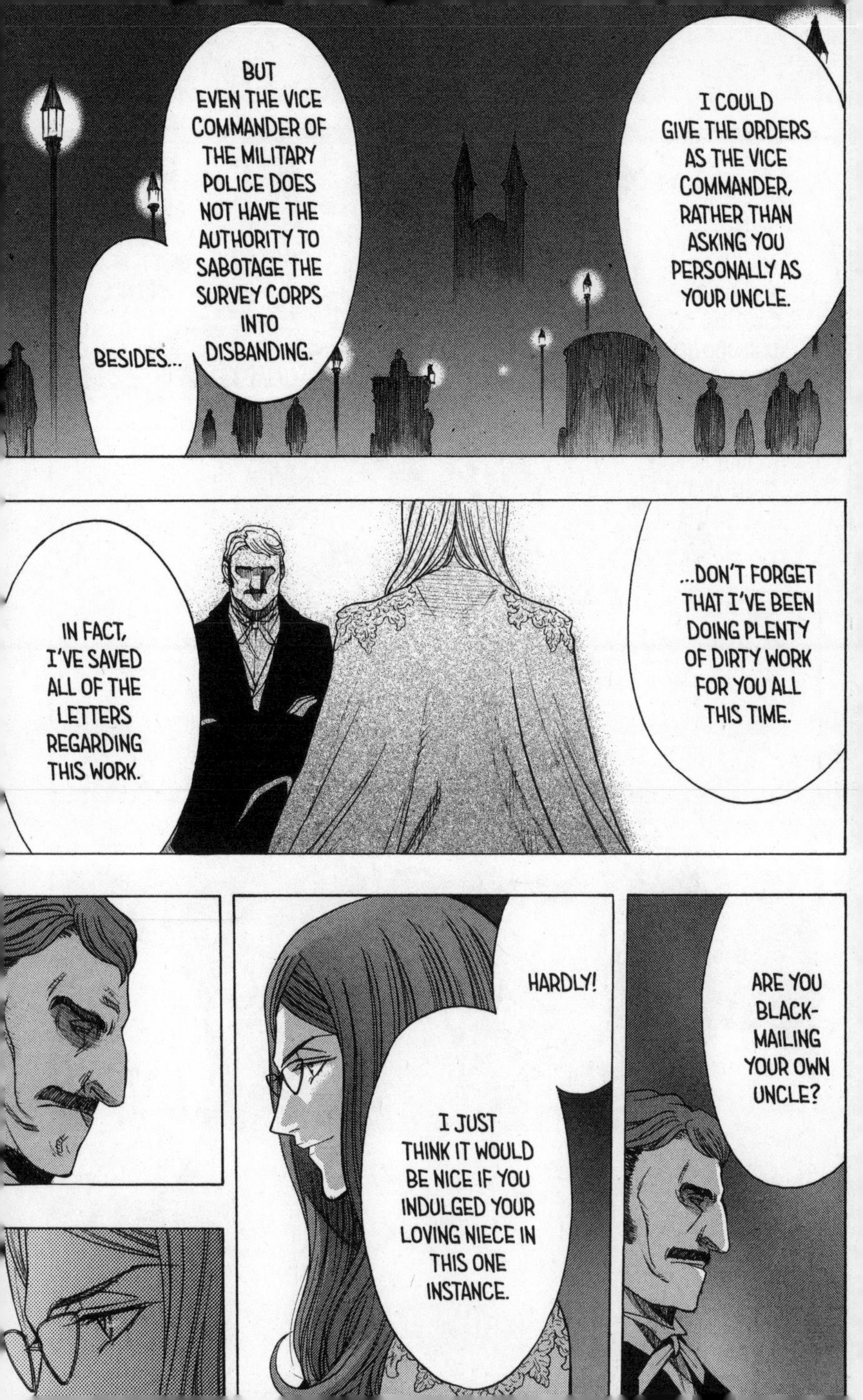
I COULD GIVE THE ORDERS AS THE VICE COMMANDER, RATHER THAN ASKING YOU PERSONALLY AS YOUR UNCLE.
BUT EVEN THE VICE COMMANDER OF THE MILITARY POLICE DOES NOT HAVE THE AUTHORITY TO SABOTAGE THE SURVEY CORPS INTO DISBANDING.
BESIDES...
...DON'T FORGET THAT I'VE BEEN DOING PLENTY OF DIRTY WORK FOR YOU ALL THIS TIME.
IN FACT, I'VE SAVED ALL OF THE LETTERS REGARDING THIS WORK.
ARE YOU BLACK-MAILING YOUR OWN UNCLE?
HARDLY!
I JUST THINK IT WOULD BE NICE IF YOU INDULGED YOUR LOVING NIECE IN THIS ONE INSTANCE.

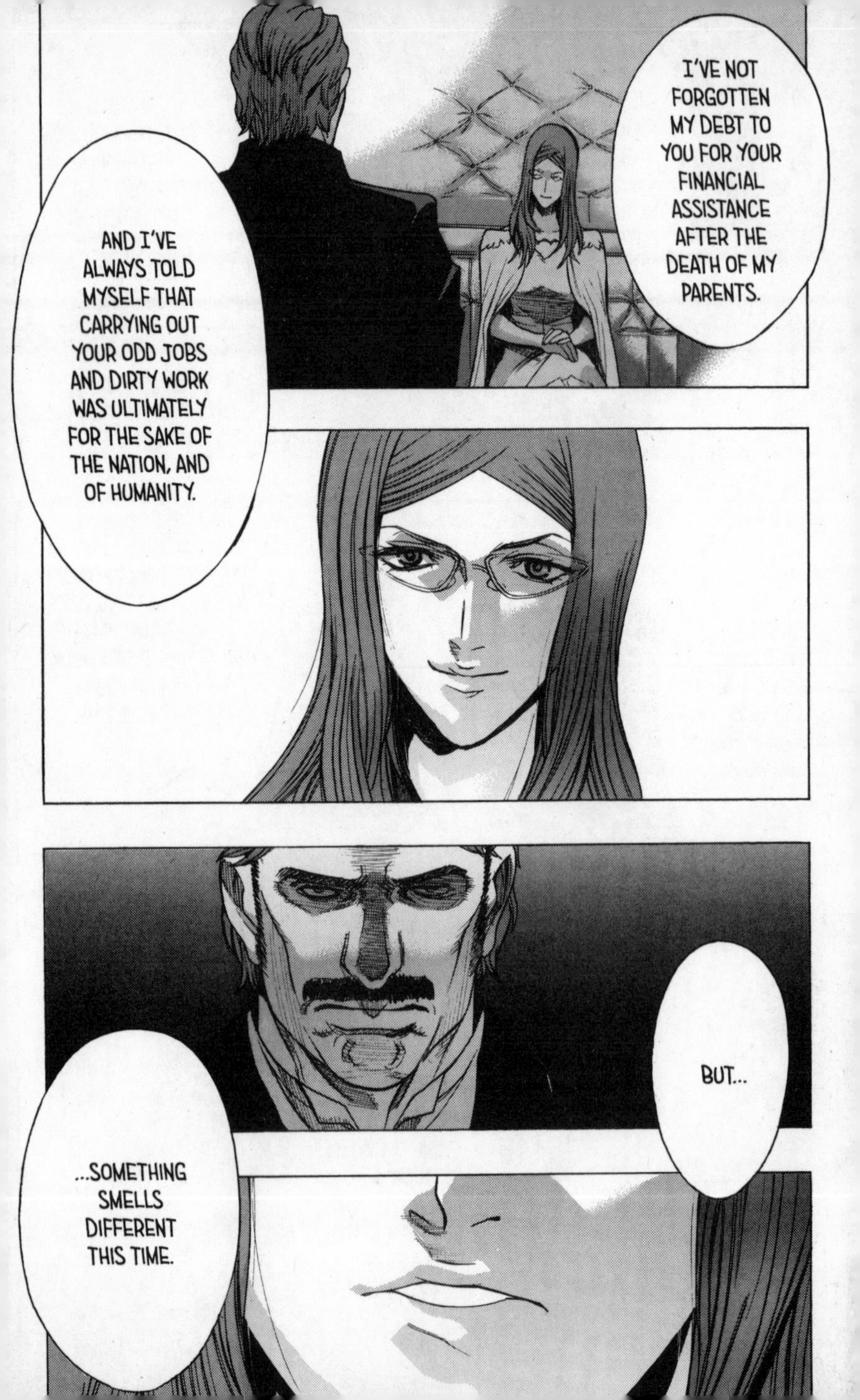
I'VE NOT FORGOTTEN MY DEBT TO YOU FOR YOUR FINANCIAL ASSISTANCE AFTER THE DEATH OF MY PARENTS.
AND I'VE ALWAYS TOLD MYSELF THAT CARRYING OUT YOUR ODD JOBS AND DIRTY WORK WAS ULTIMATELY FOR THE SAKE OF THE NATION, AND OF HUMANITY.
BUT...
...SOMETHING SMELLS DIFFERENT THIS TIME.

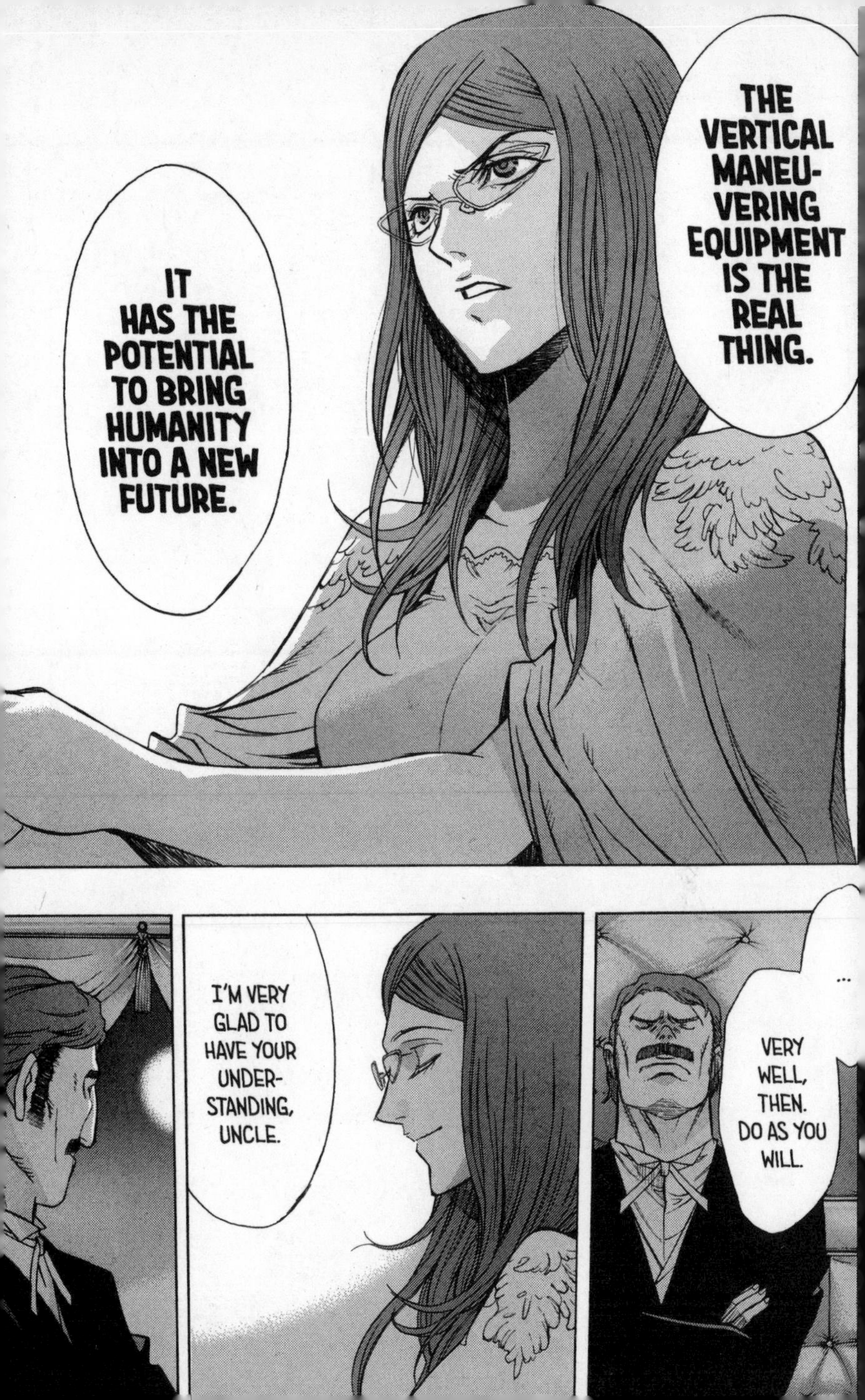
THE VERTICAL MANEU-VERING EQUIPMENT IS THE REAL THING.
IT HAS THE POTENTIAL TO BRING HUMANITY INTO A NEW FUTURE.
...
VERY WELL, THEN. DO AS YOU WILL.
I'M VERY GLAD TO HAVE YOUR UNDER-STANDING, UNCLE.

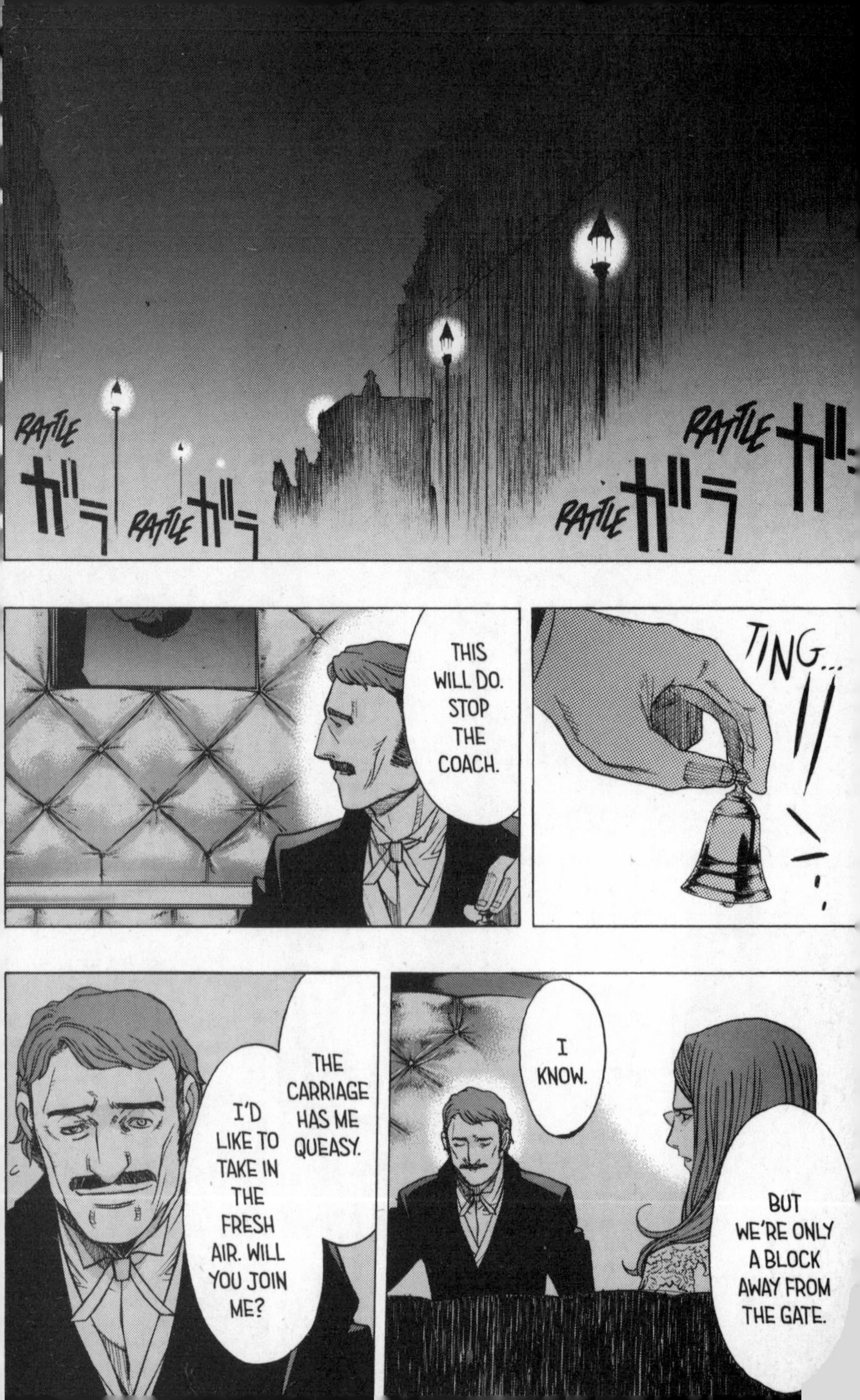
RATTLE ガ
RATTLE ガラ
RATTLE ガラ
RATTLE ガラ
TING...
THIS WILL DO. STOP THE COACH.
BUT WE'RE ONLY A BLOCK AWAY FROM THE GATE.
I KNOW.
THE CARRIAGE HAS ME QUEASY.
I'D LIKE TO TAKE IN THE FRESH AIR. WILL YOU JOIN ME?

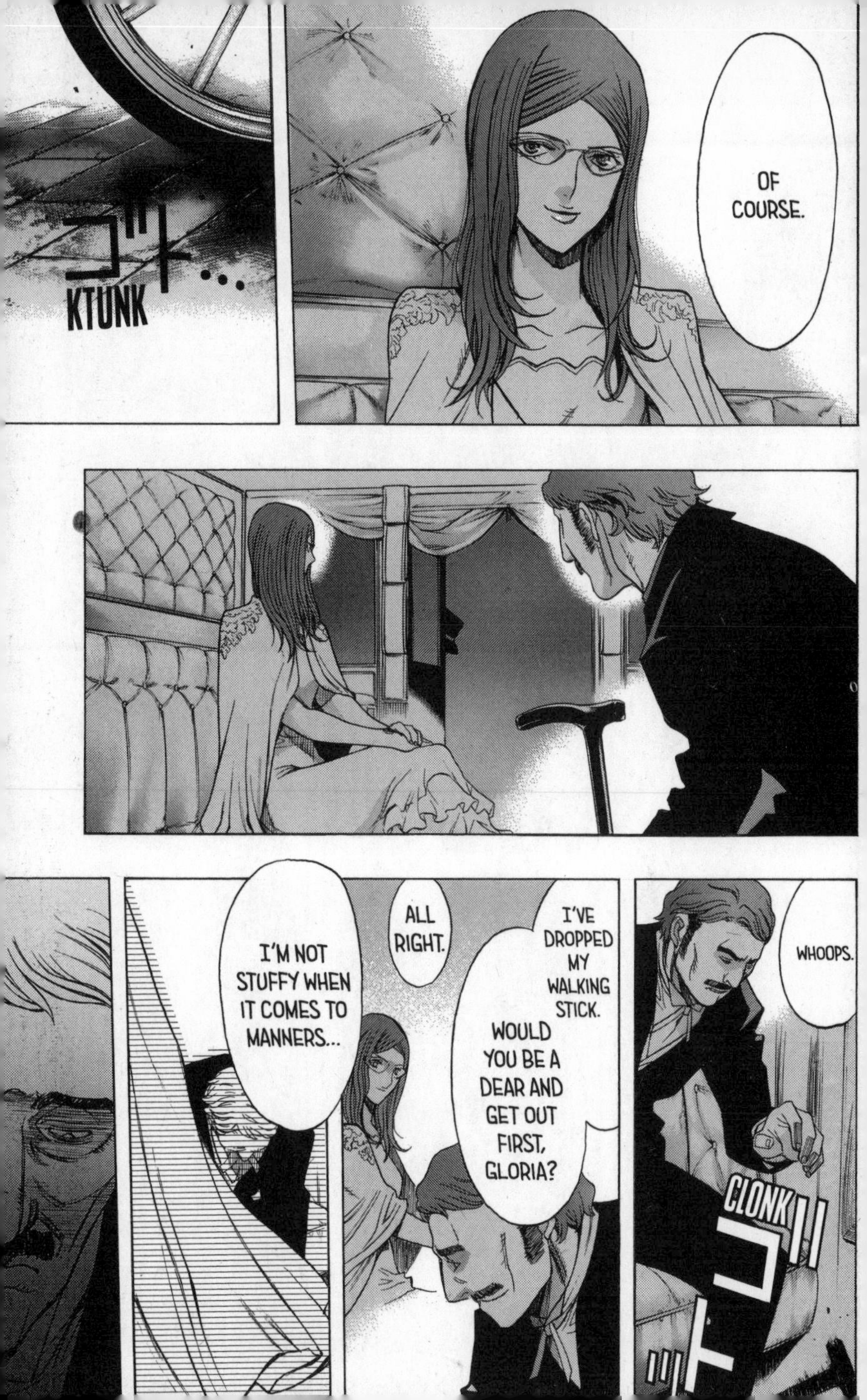
OF COURSE.
KTUNK
WHOOPS.
CLONK
I'VE DROPPED MY WALKING STICK.
WOULD YOU BE A DEAR AND GET OUT FIRST, GLORIA?
ALL RIGHT.
I'M NOT STUFFY WHEN IT COMES TO MANNERS...

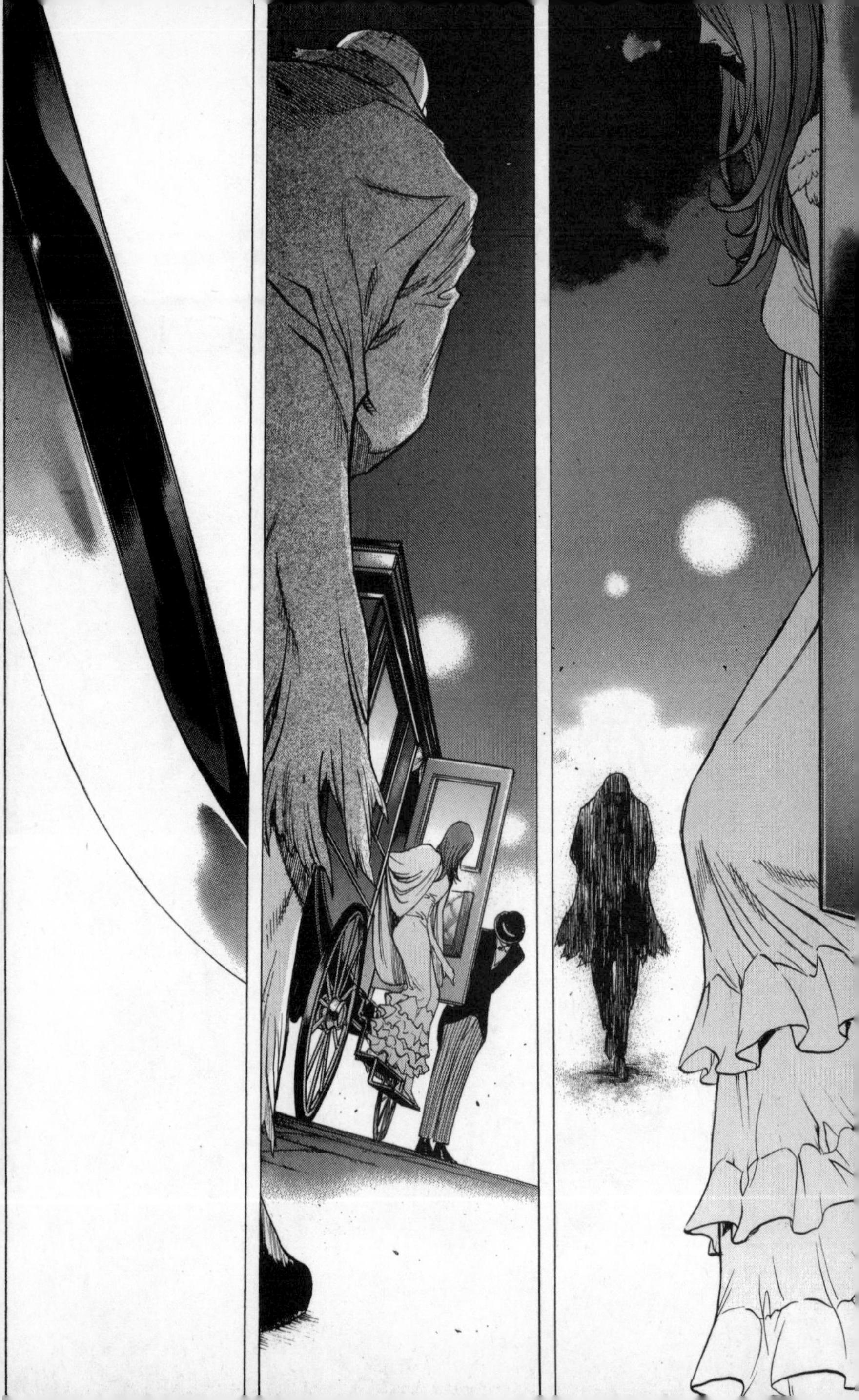

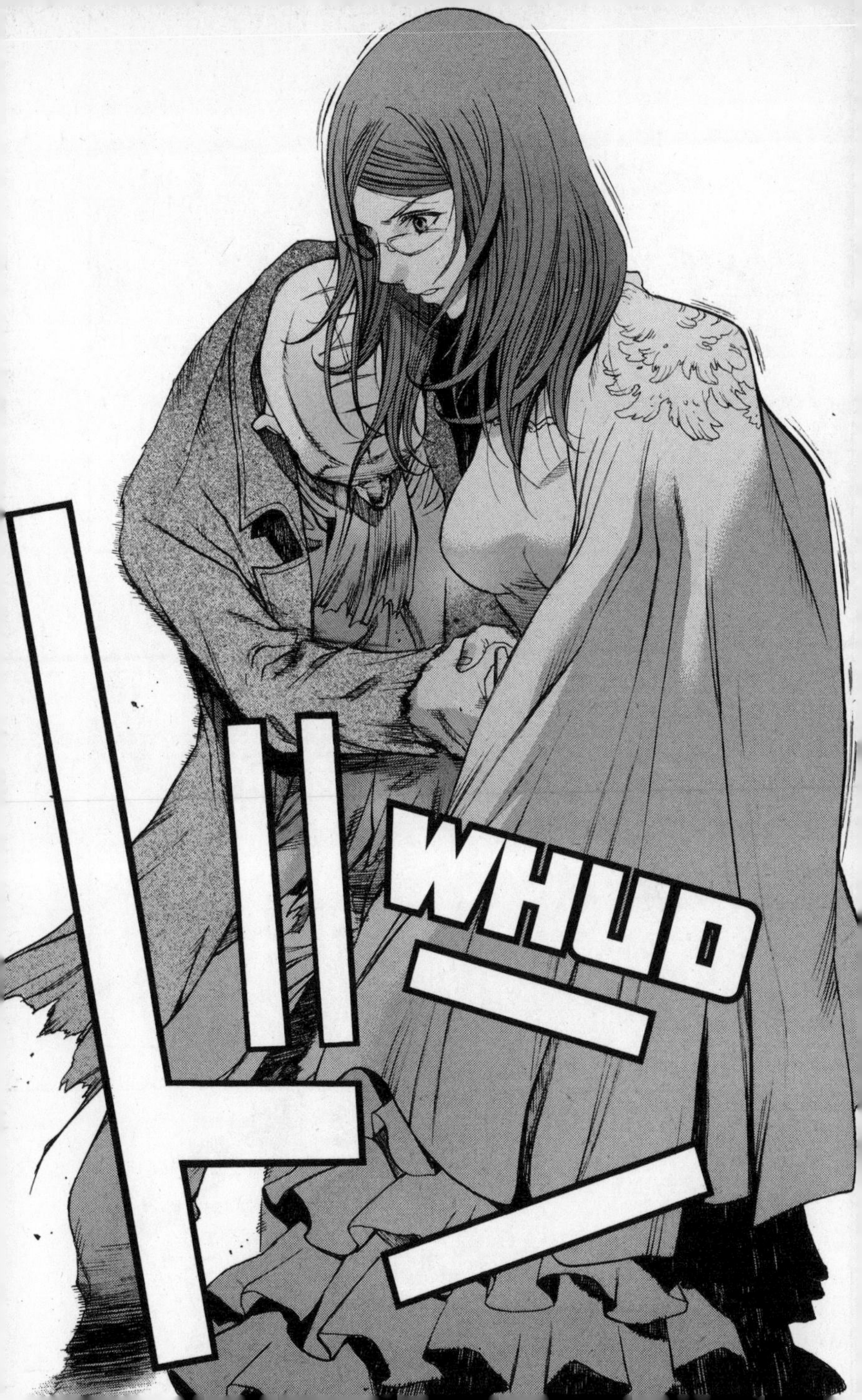
WHUD

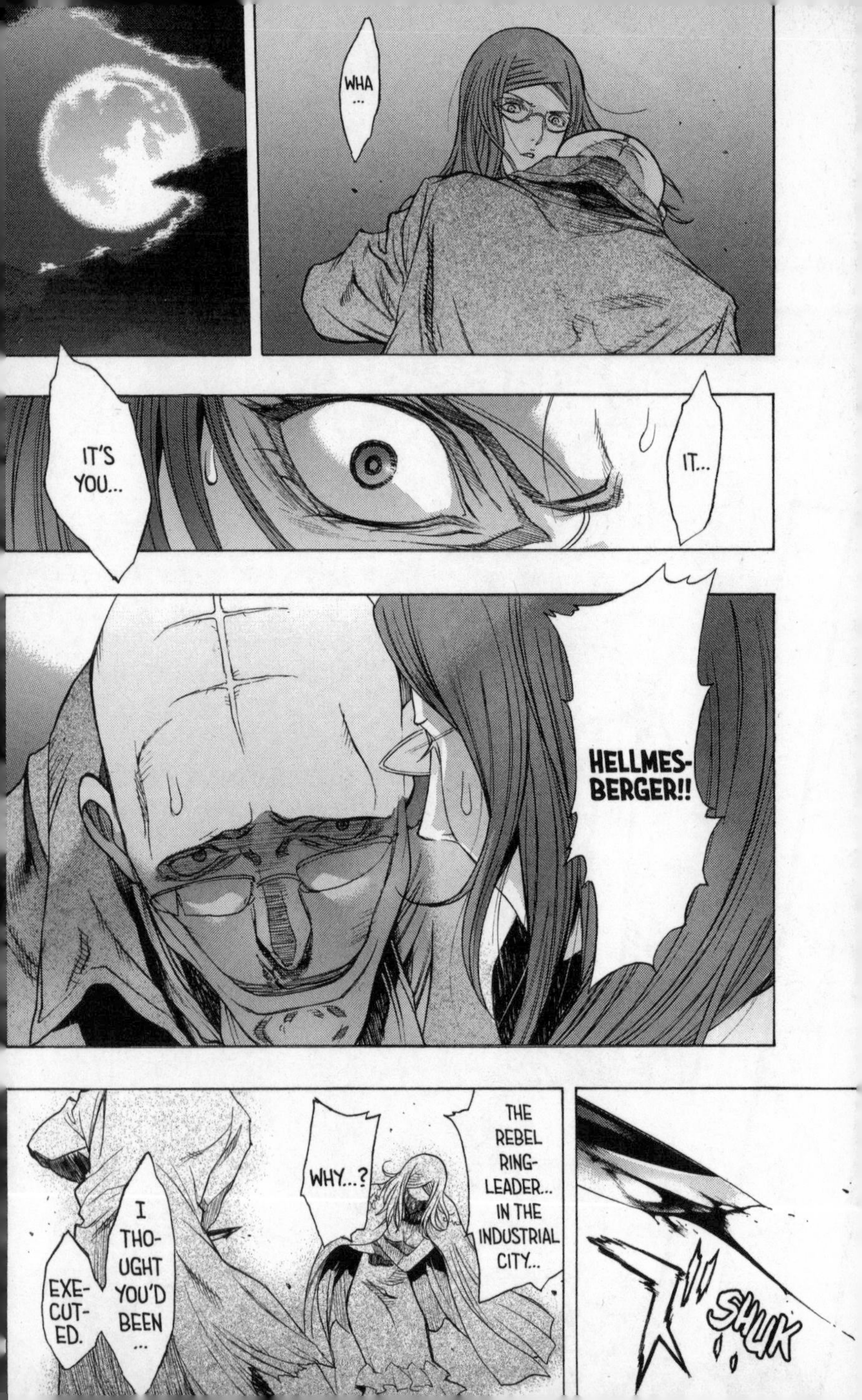
WHA...
IT...
IT'S YOU...
HELLMES-BERGER!!
SHUK
THE REBEL RING-LEADER... IN THE INDUSTRIAL CITY...
WHY...?
I THO-UGHT YOU'D BEEN...
EXE-CUT-ED.

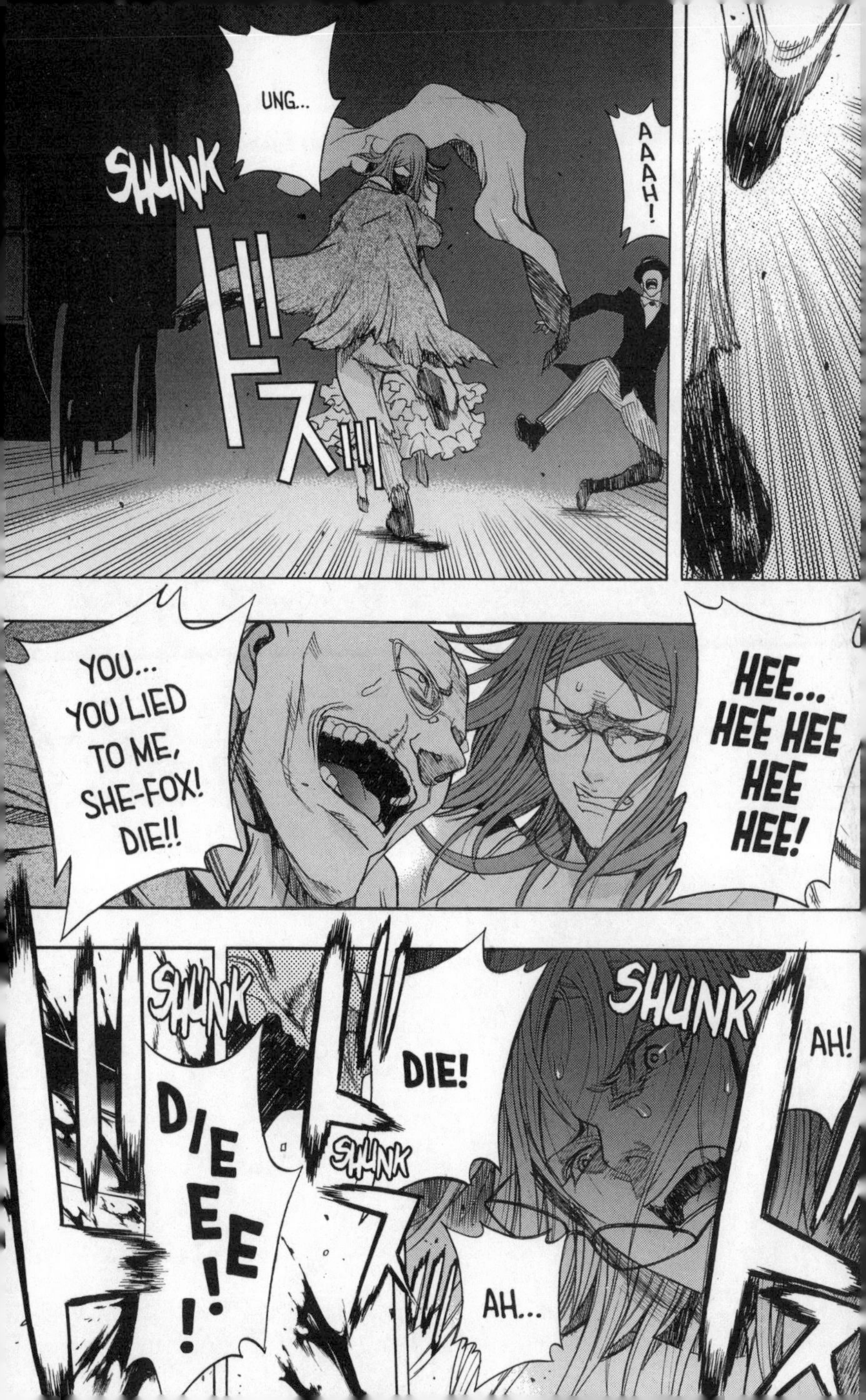
AAAAH!
UNG...
SHUNK
ドス
HEE... HEE HEE HEE HEE!
YOU... YOU LIED TO ME, SHE-FOX! DIE!!
SHUNK
AH!
SHUNK
DIE!
SHUNK
DIEEE!!
AH...

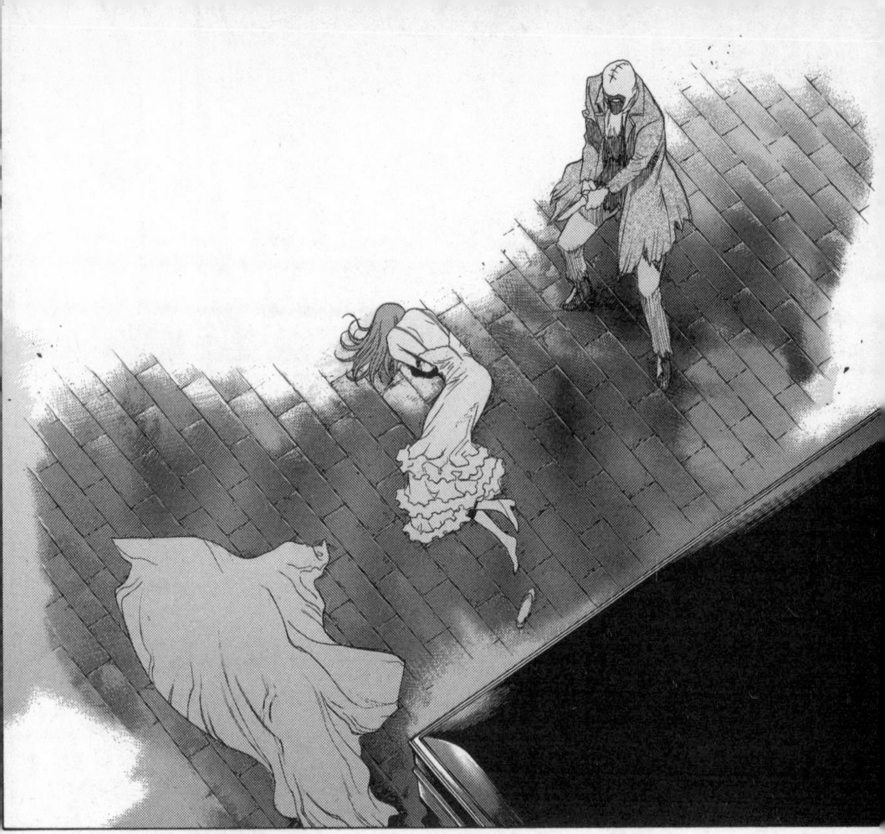
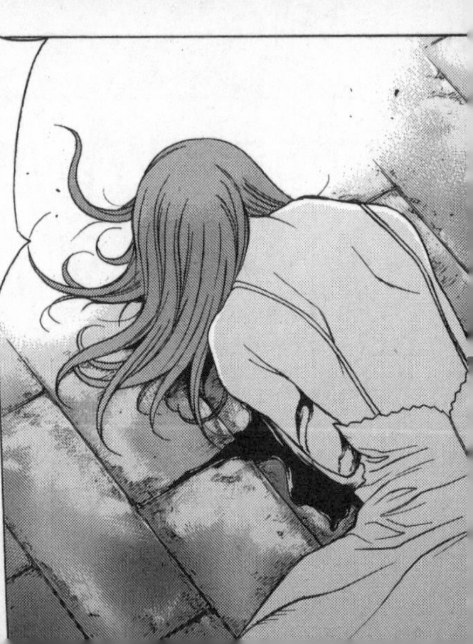
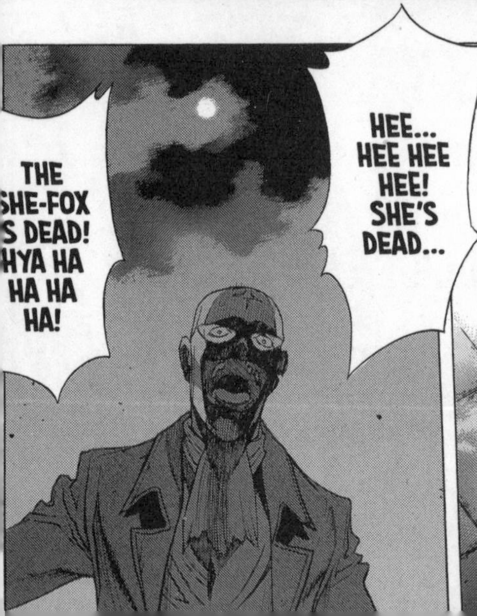
HEE... HEE HEE HEE! SHE'S DEAD...
THE SHE-FOX S DEAD! HYA HA HA HA HA!

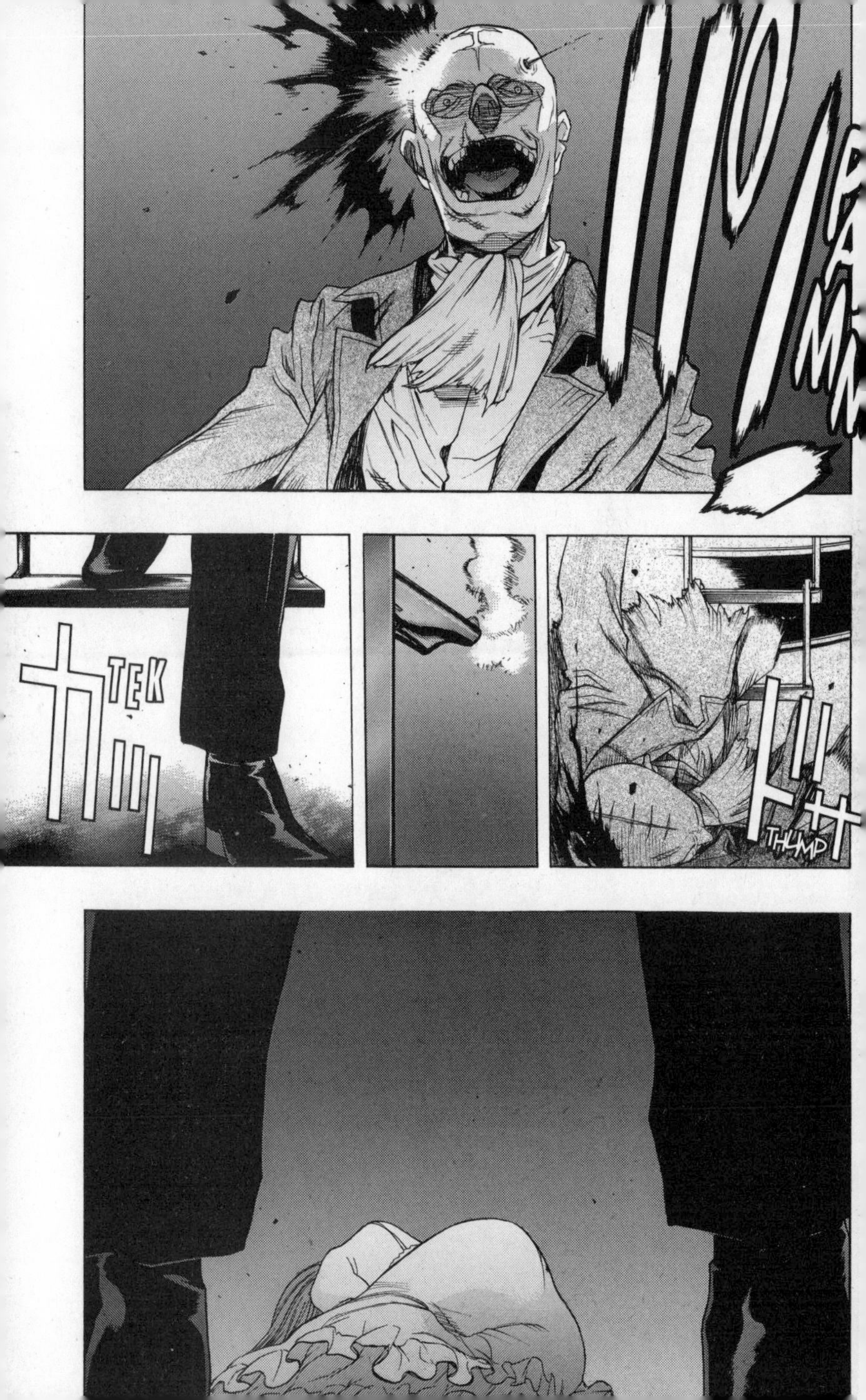
PAM
THUMP
TEK

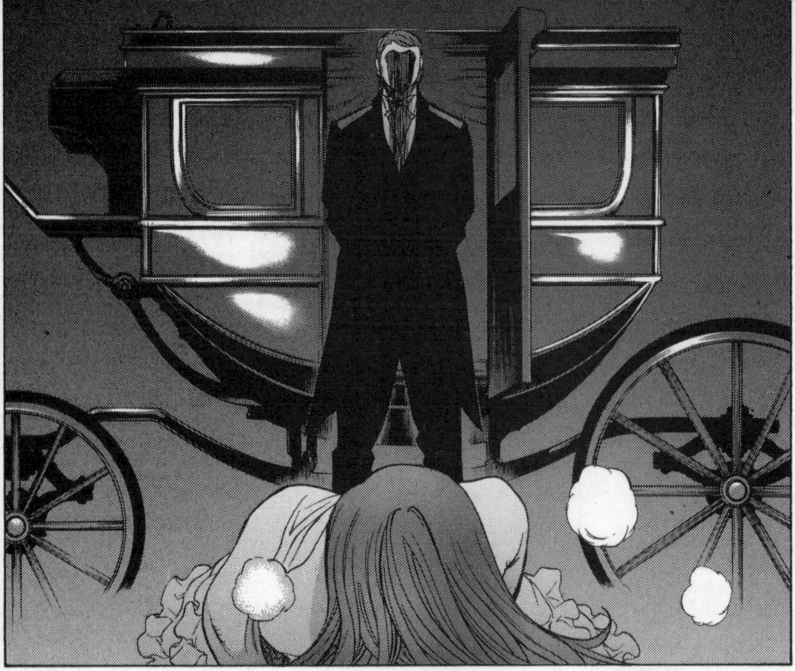

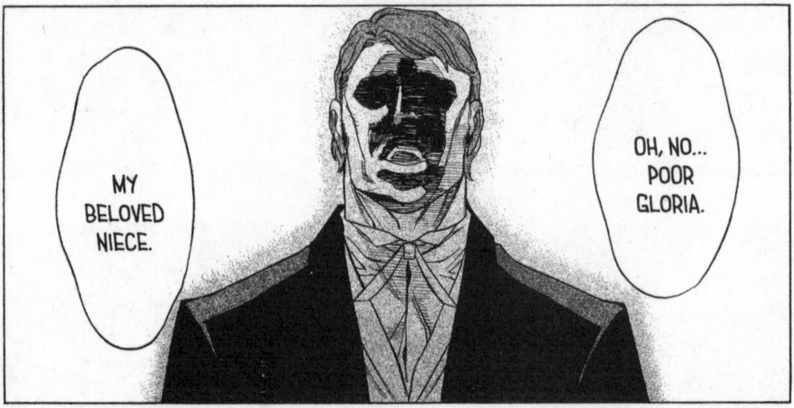
OH, NO... POOR GLORIA.
MY BELOVED NIECE.

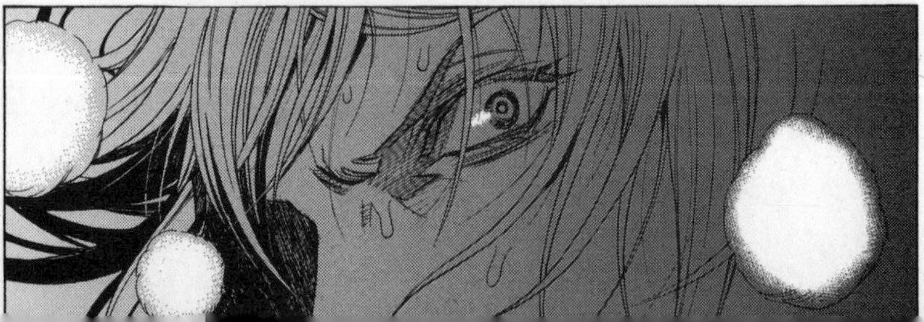

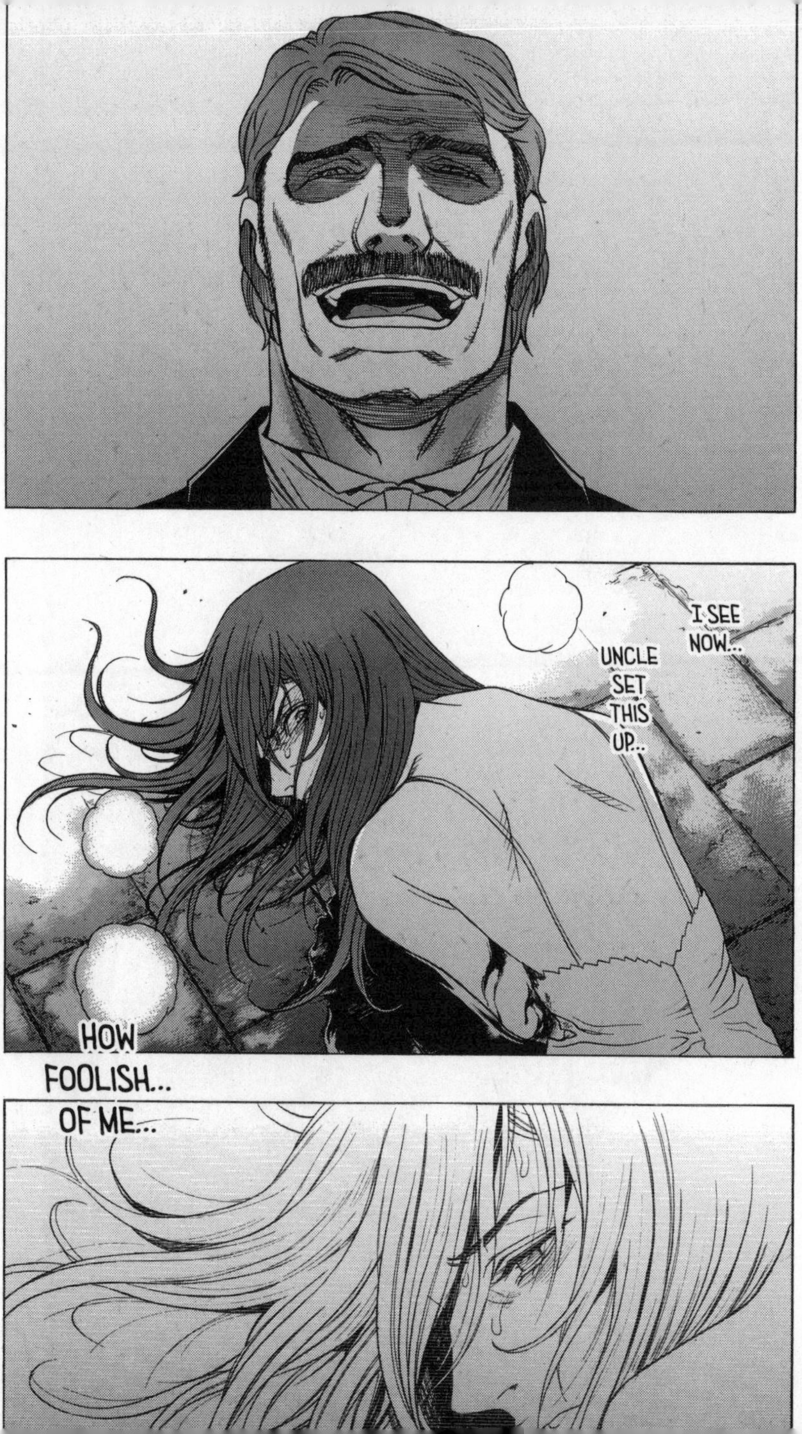
I SEE NOW...
UNCLE SET THIS UP...
HOW FOOLISH... OF ME...

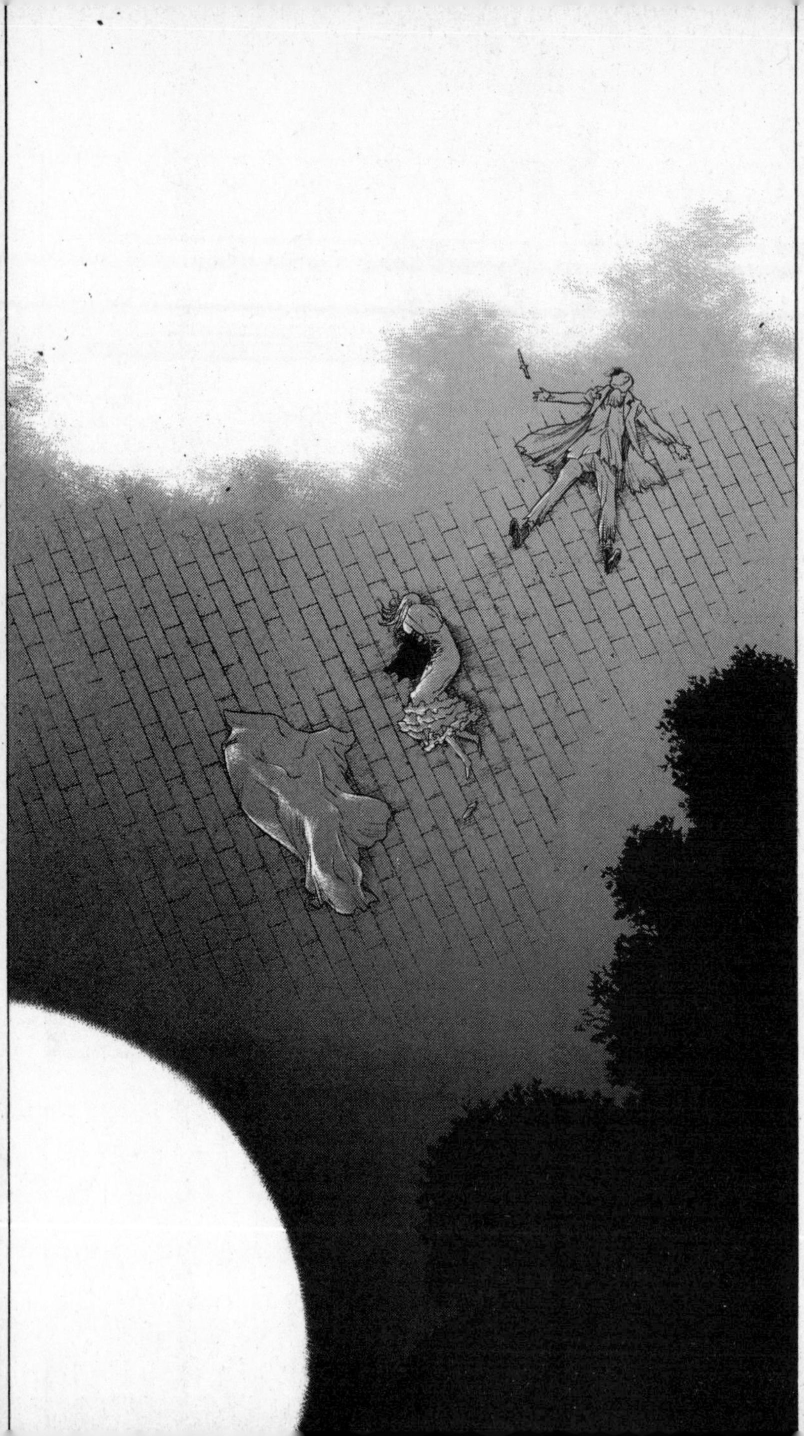

Chapter 61: Fell Blade in the Royal Capital

ATTACK on TITAN
BEFORE THE FALL

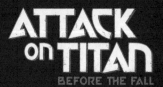

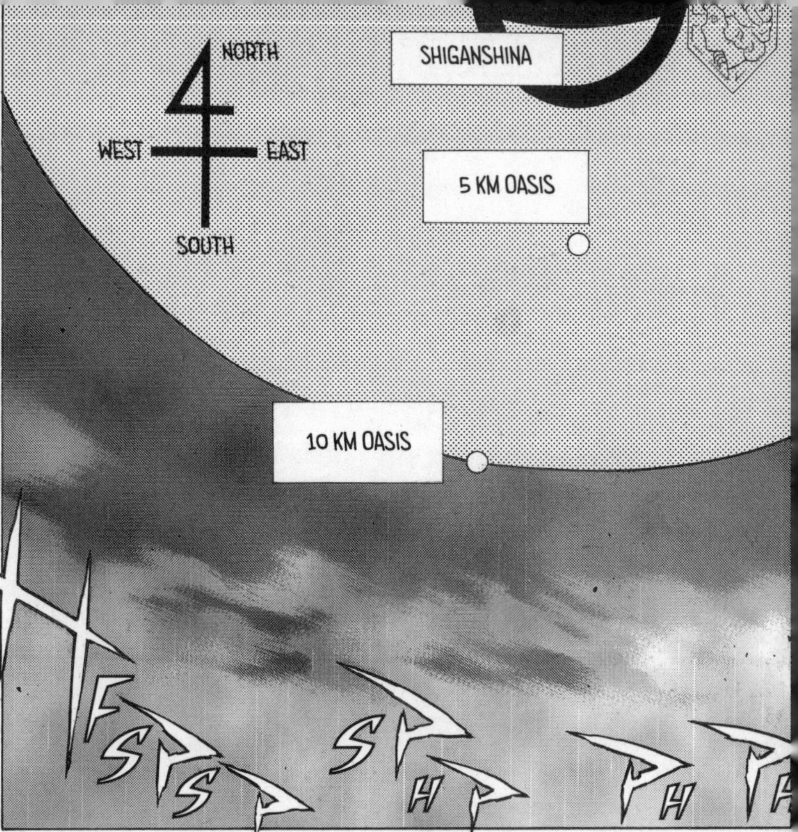
NORTH
WEST
EAST
SOUTH
SHIGANSHINA
5 KM OASIS
10 KM OASIS
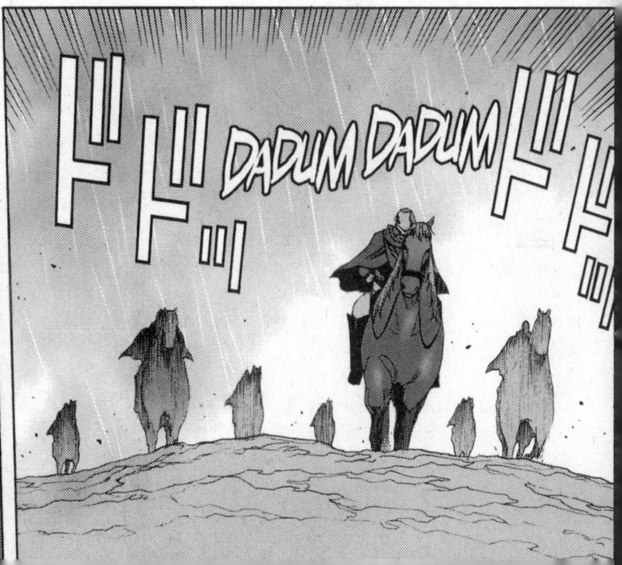
DADUM DADUM
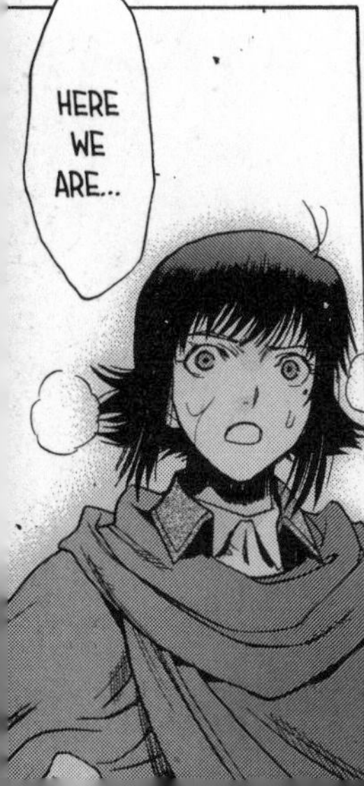
HERE WE ARE...

Chapter 62: The Cost of Victory

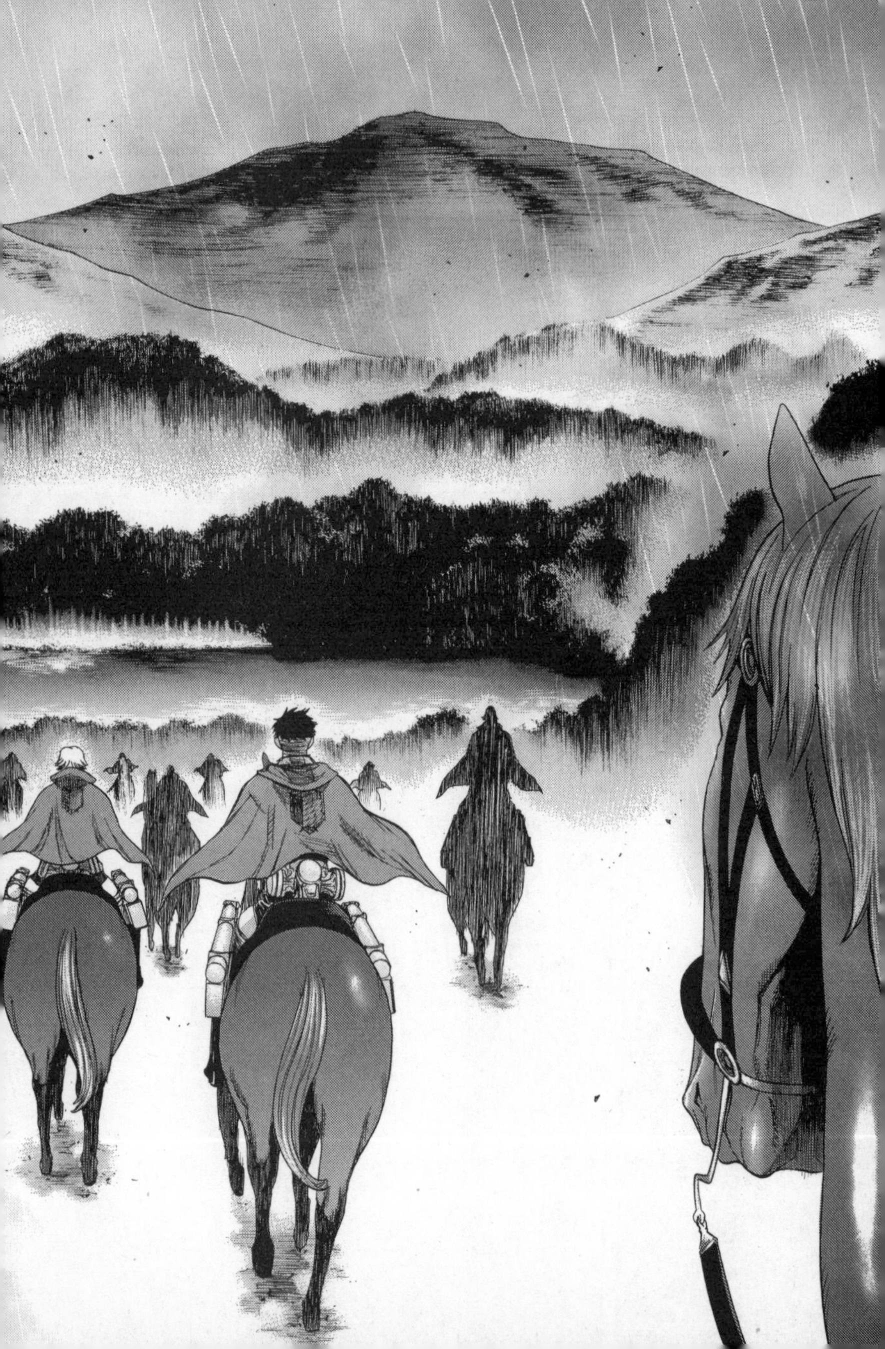

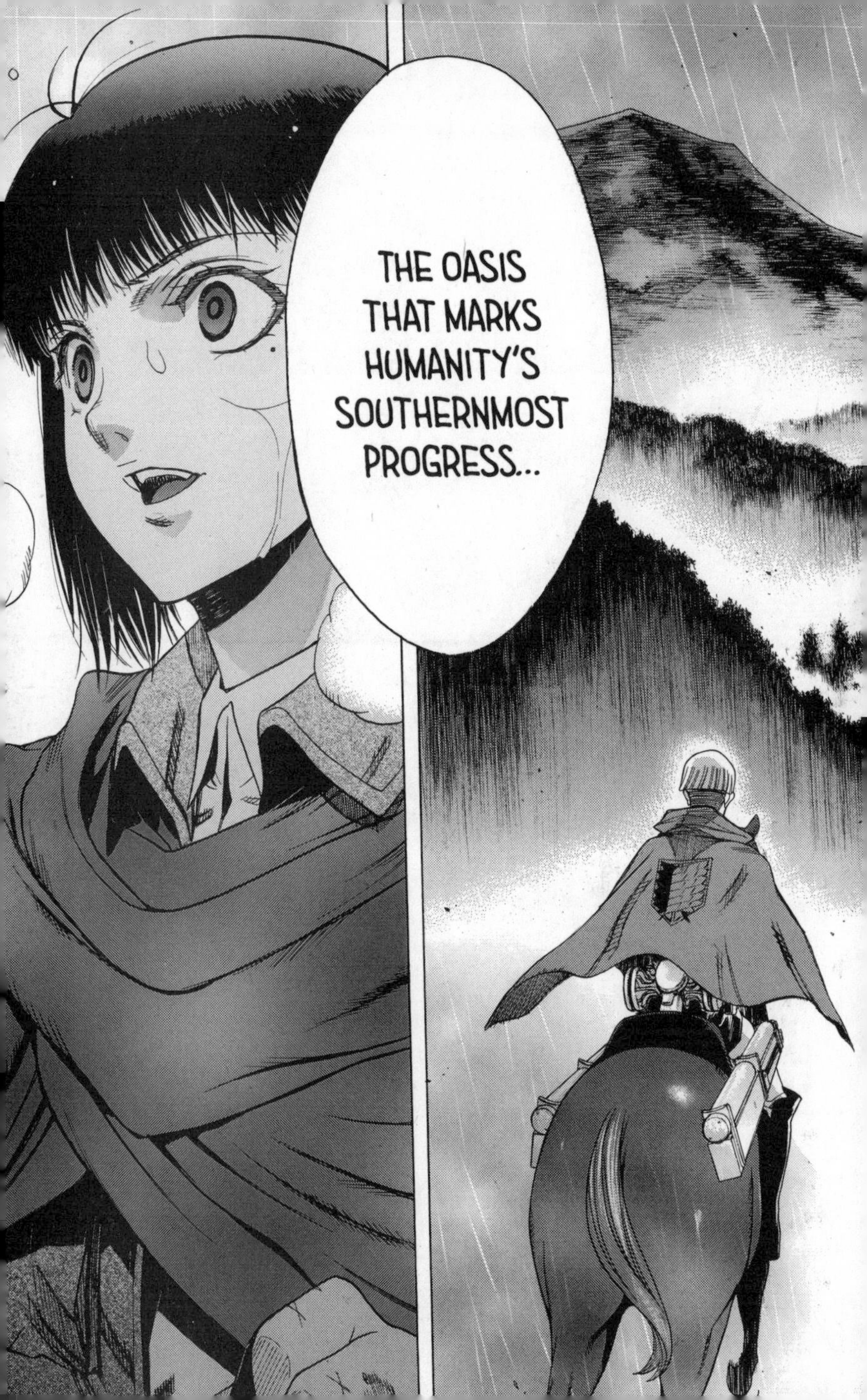
THE OASIS THAT MARKS HUMANITY'S SOUTHERNMOST PROGRESS...

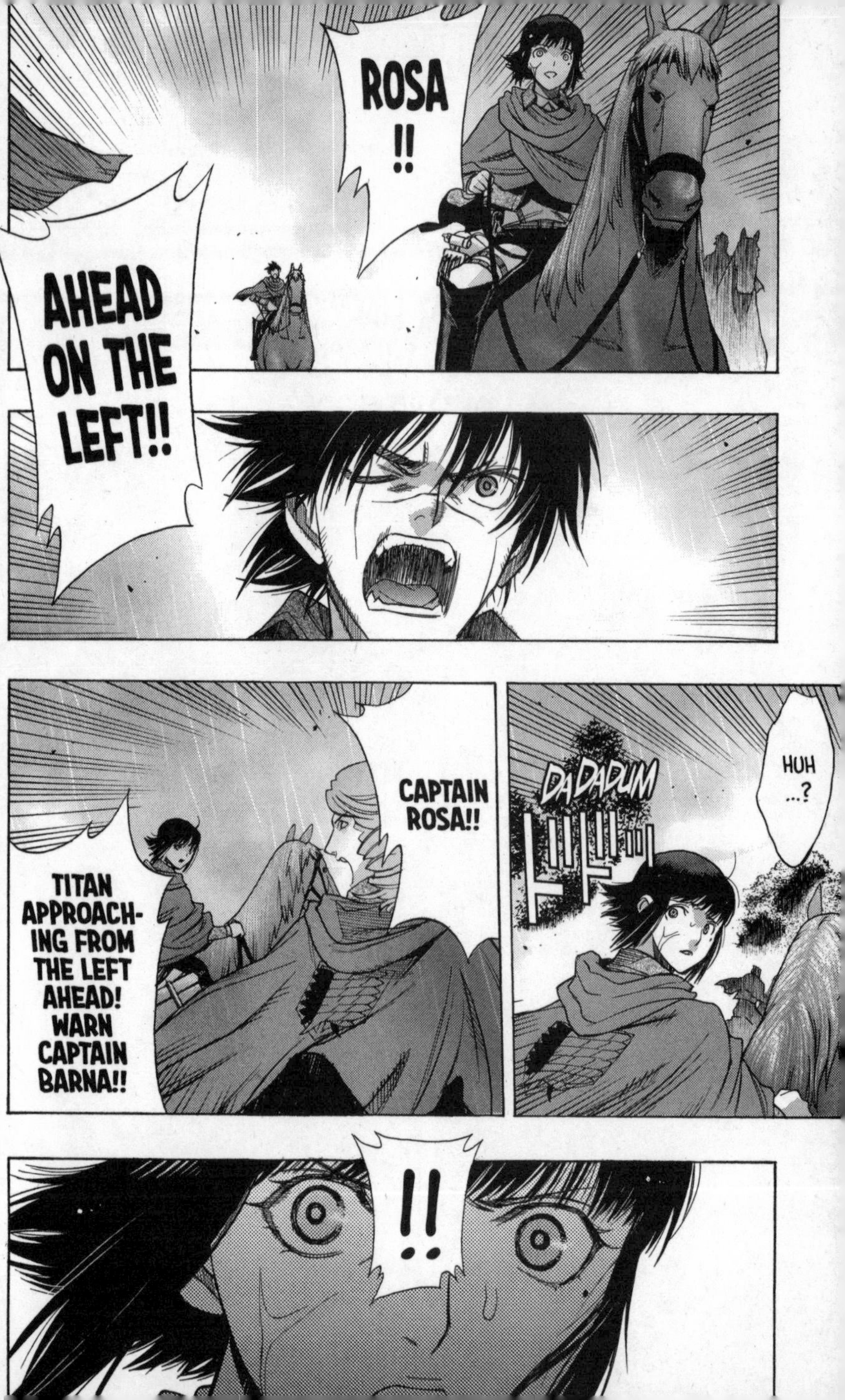
ROSA !!
AHEAD ON THE LEFT!!
DA DADUM
HUH ...?
CAPTAIN ROSA!!
TITAN APPROACHING FROM THE LEFT AHEAD! WARN CAPTAIN BARNA!!
!!

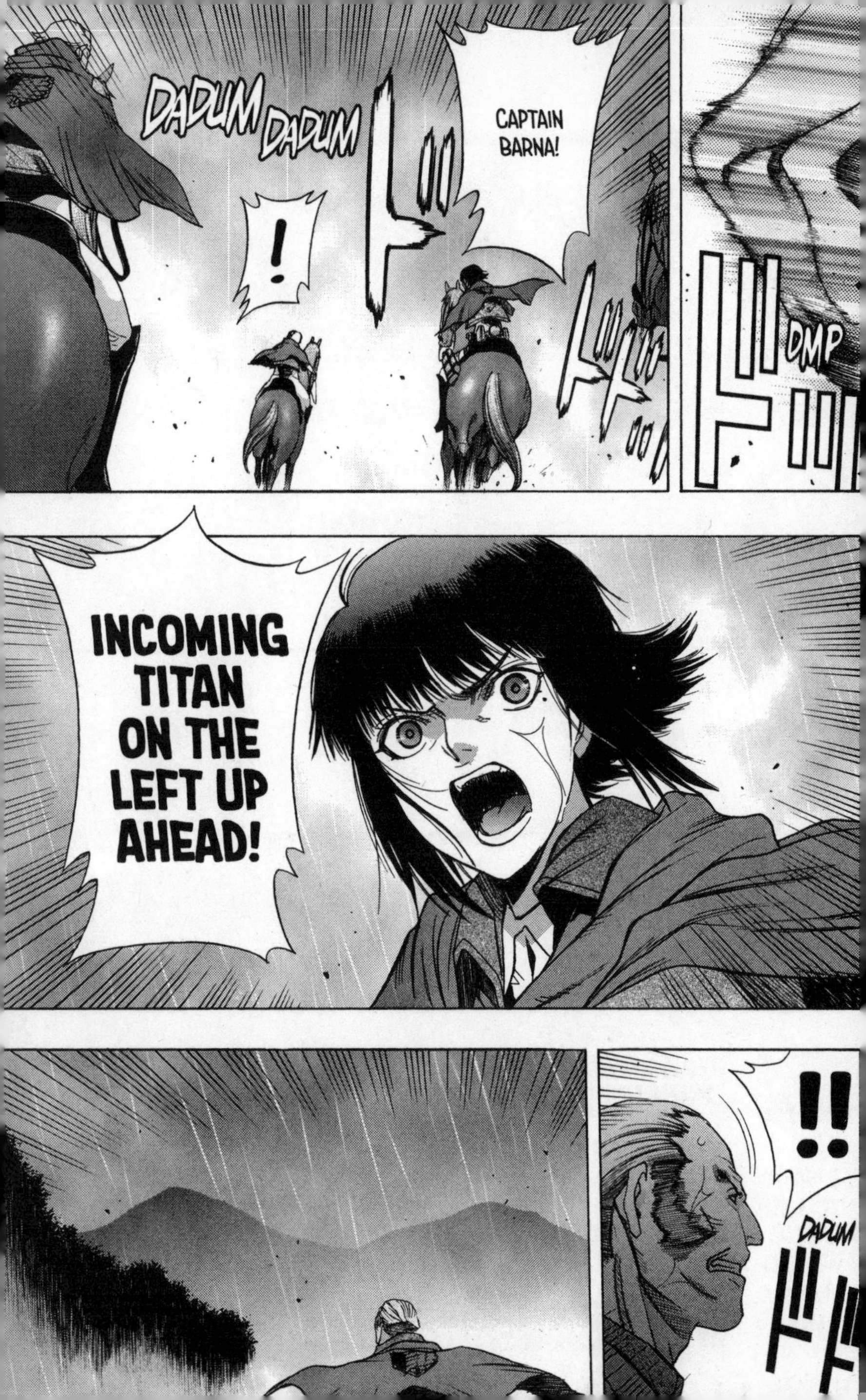
DMP
CAPTAIN BARNA!
DADUM DADUM
!
INCOMING TITAN ON THE LEFT UP AHEAD!
!!
DADUM

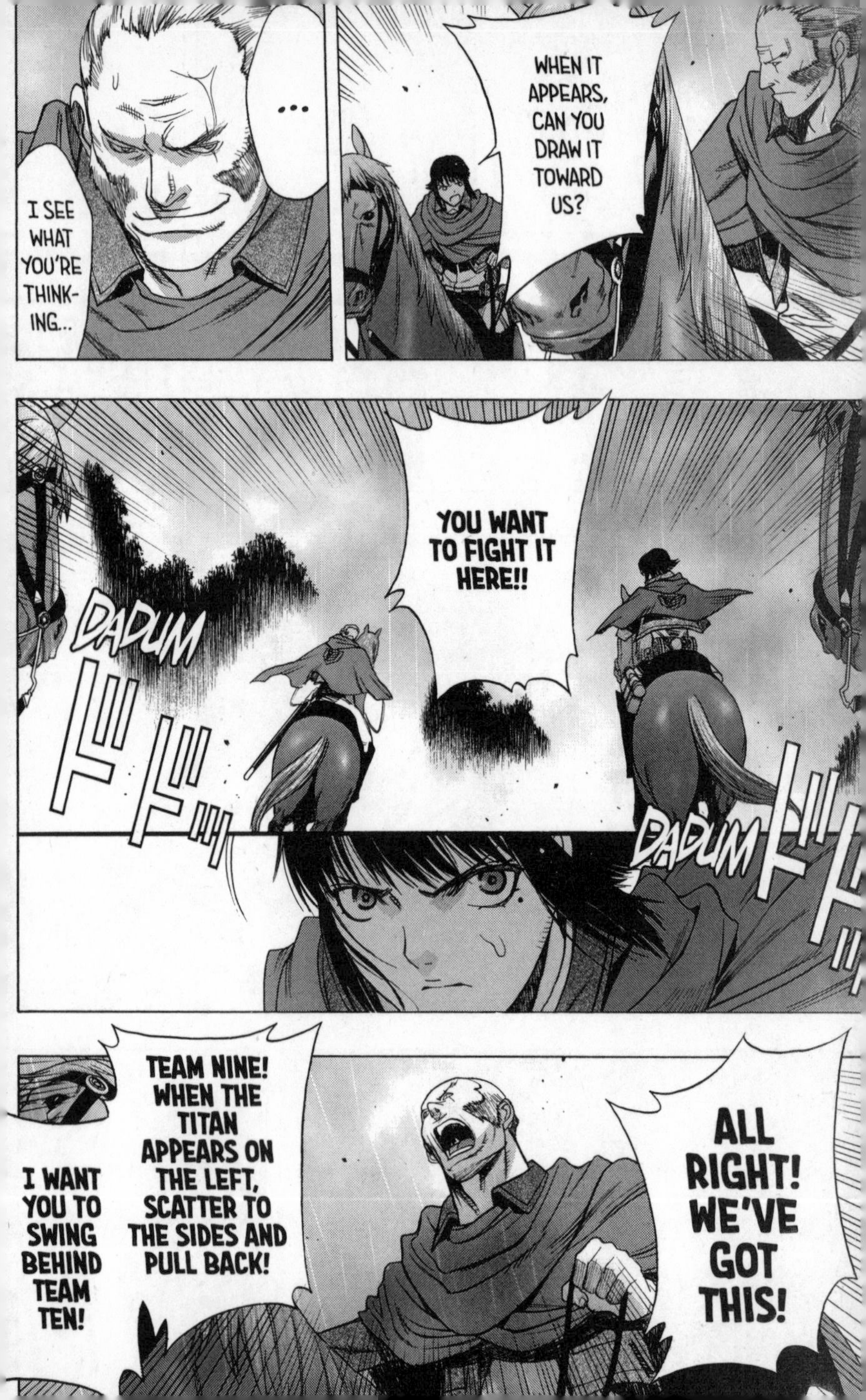

WHEN IT APPEARS, CAN YOU DRAW IT TOWARD US?
...
I SEE WHAT YOU'RE THINK-ING...
YOU WANT TO FIGHT IT HERE!!
DADUM
DADUM
ALL RIGHT! WE'VE GOT THIS!
TEAM NINE! WHEN THE TITAN APPEARS ON THE LEFT, SCATTER TO THE SIDES AND PULL BACK!
I WANT YOU TO SWING BEHIND TEAM TEN!

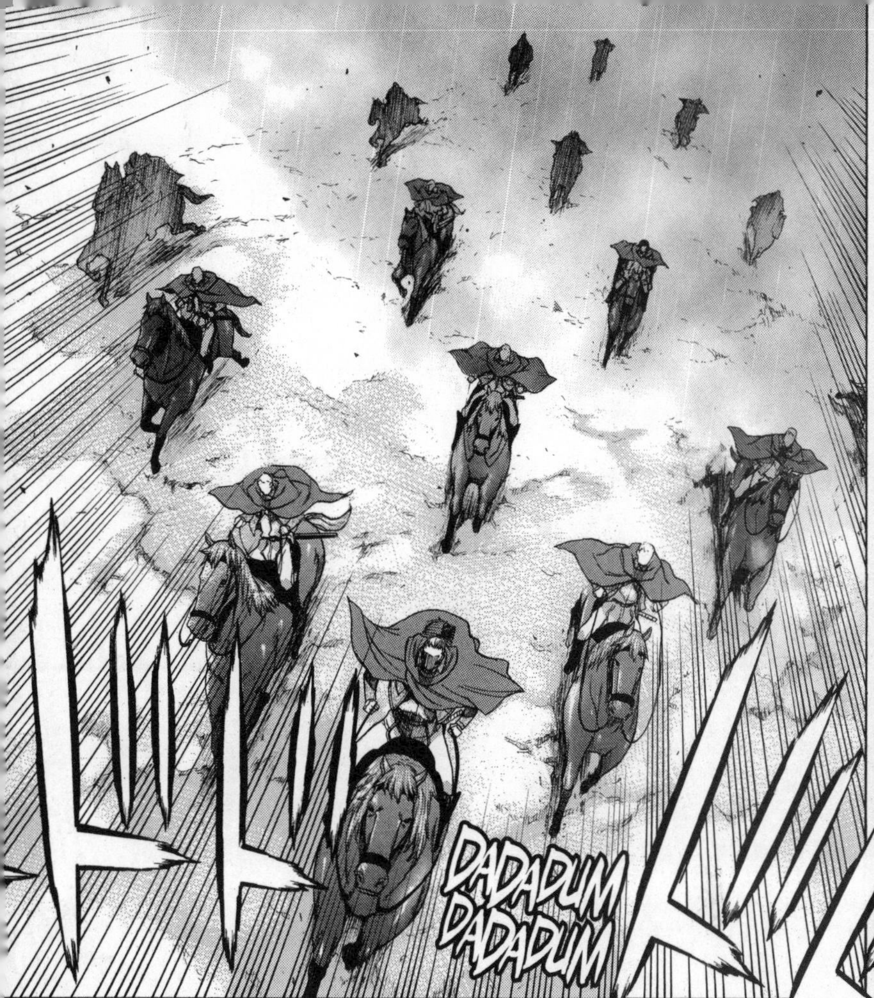
DADADUM
DADADUM
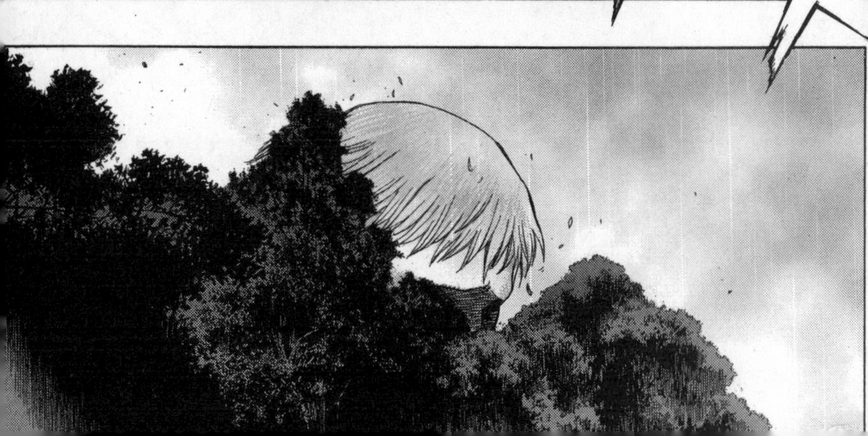

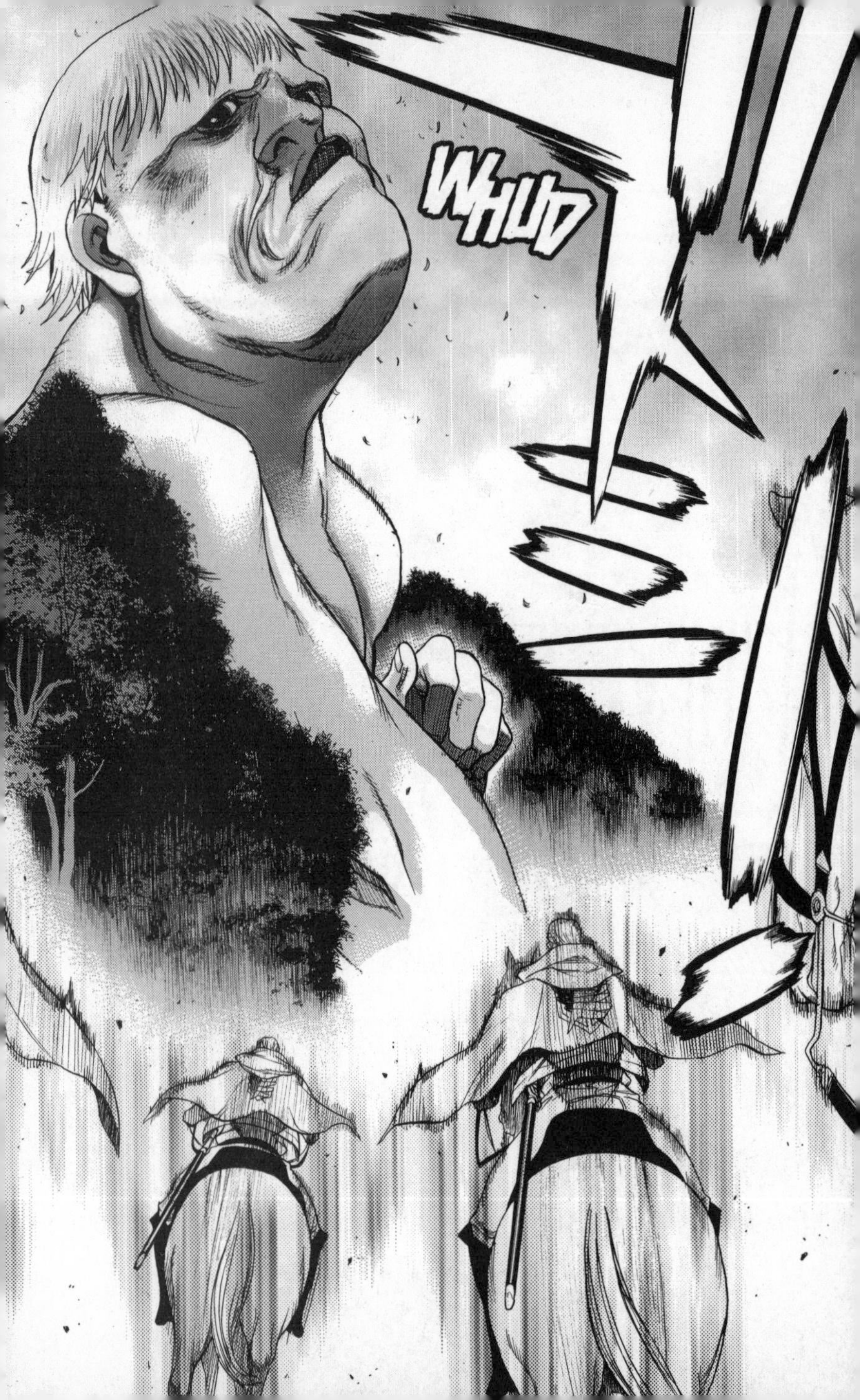
WHUD

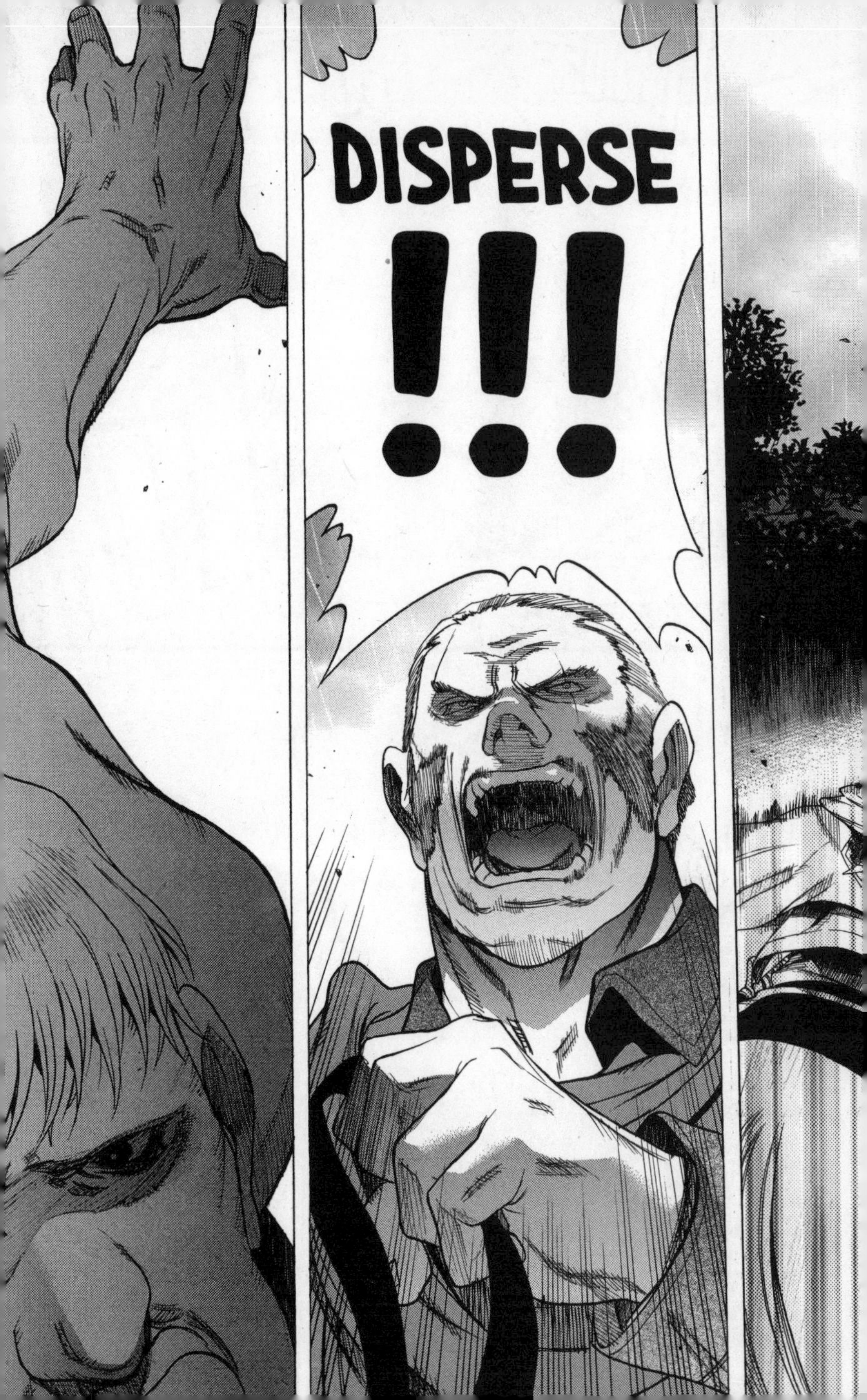
DISPERSE!!!

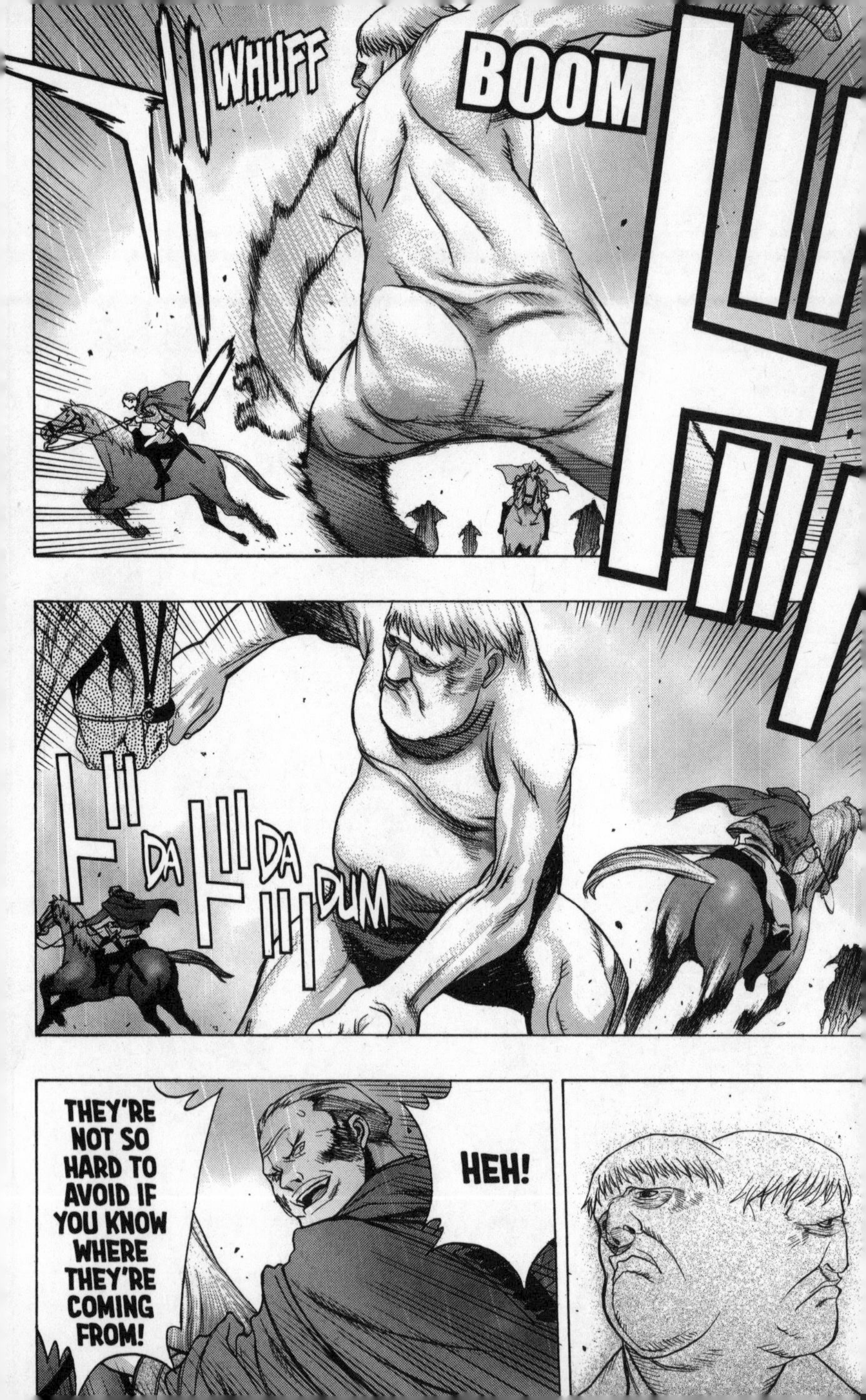
BOOM
WHUFF
DA DA DUM
HEH!
THEY'RE NOT SO HARD TO AVOID IF YOU KNOW WHERE THEY'RE COMING FROM!

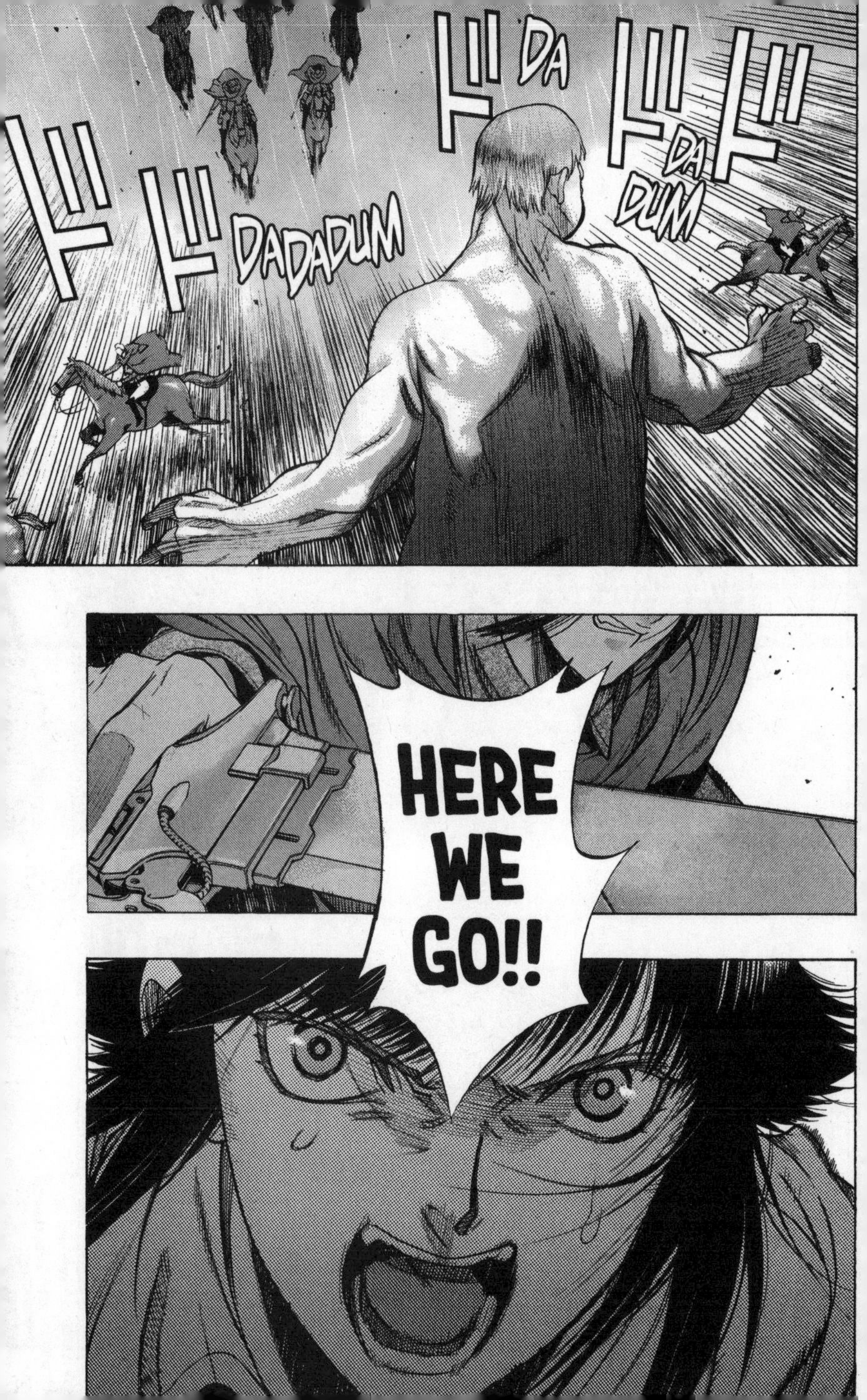
ドドド
DA
DA DUM
ドド
DADADUM
HERE WE GO!!

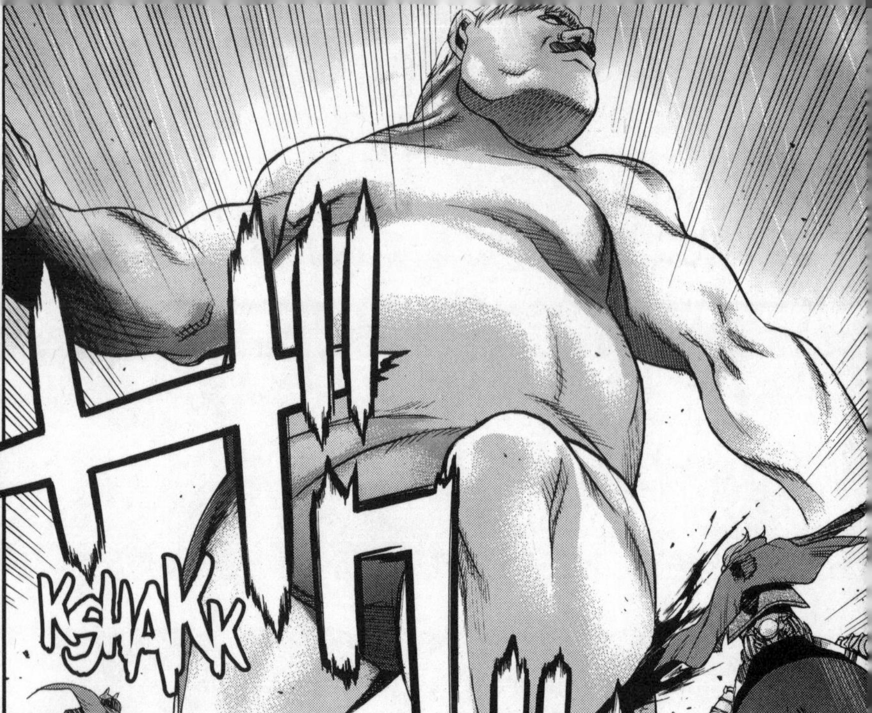
KSHAKK
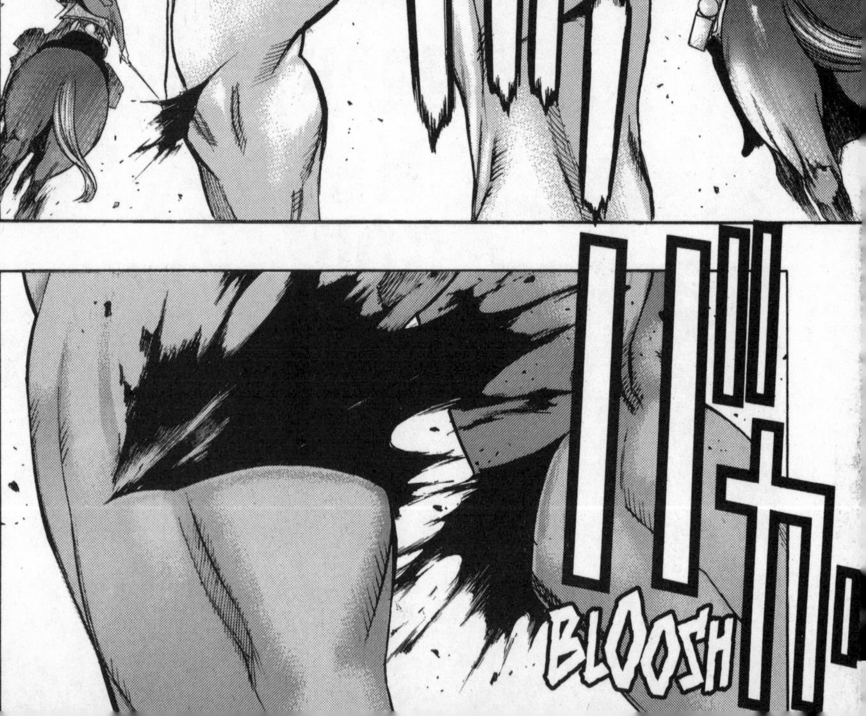
BLOOSH

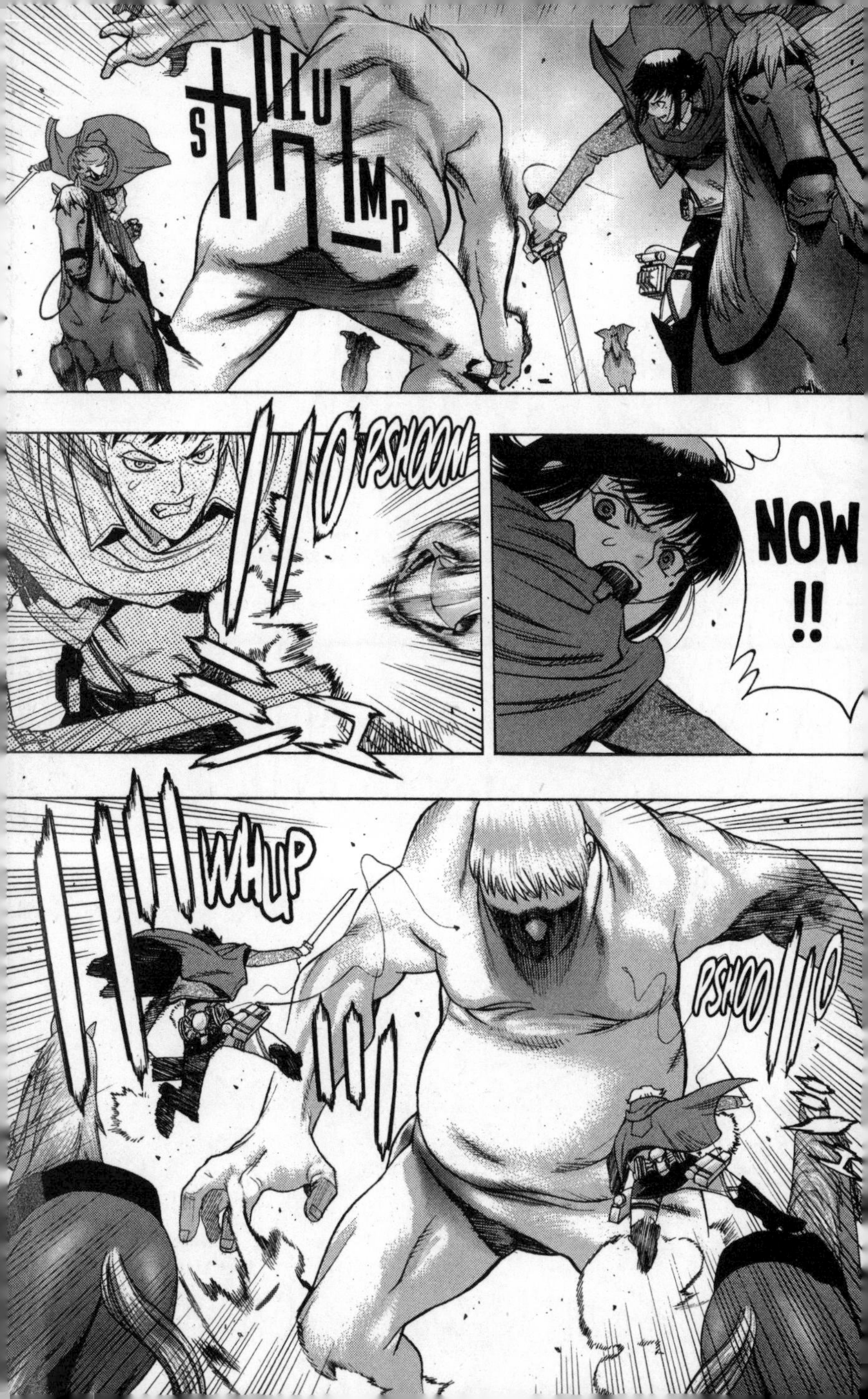
SHLUMP
NOW!!
PSHOOM
PSHOO
WHUP

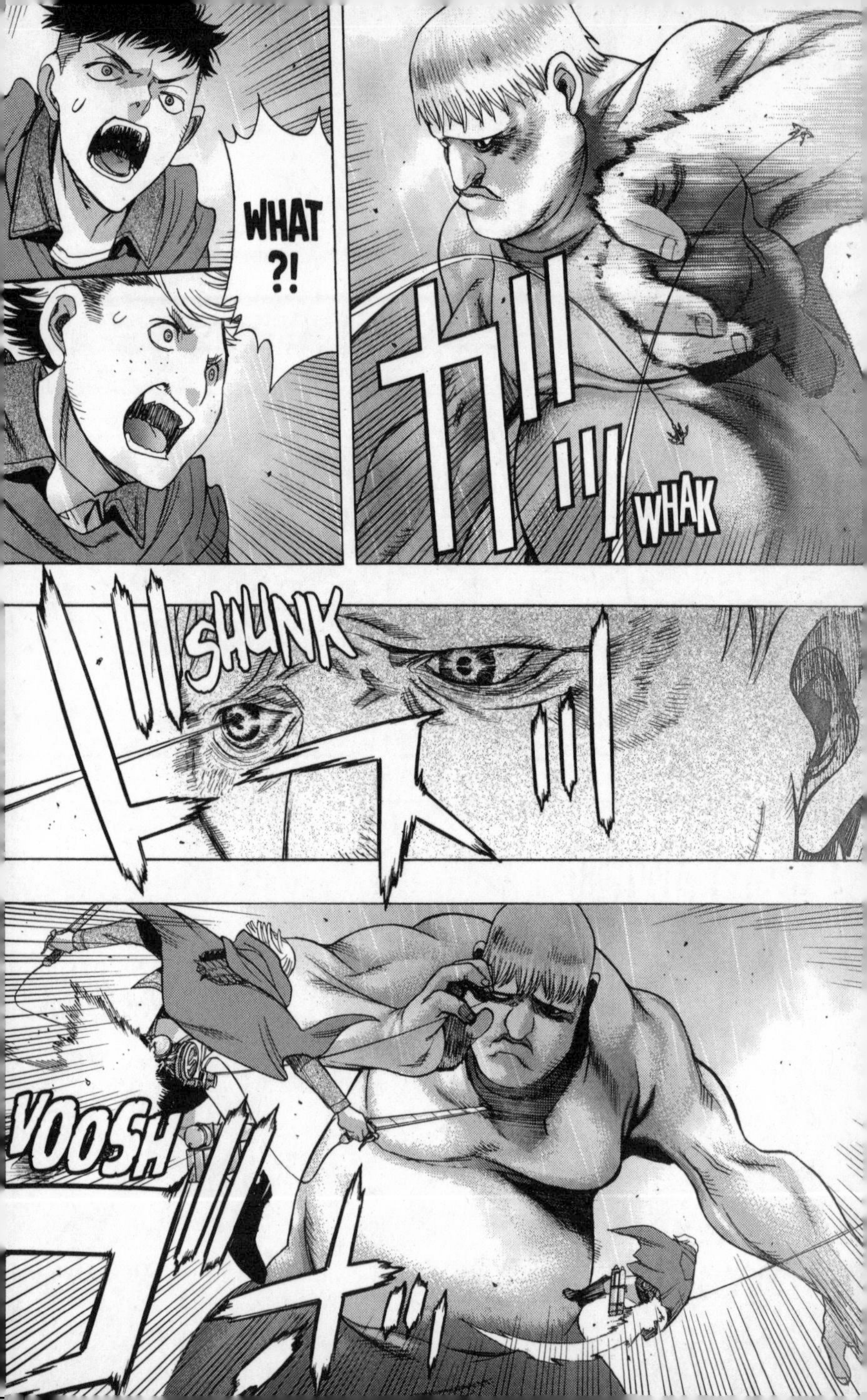
WHAK
WHAT ?!
SHUNK
VOOSH

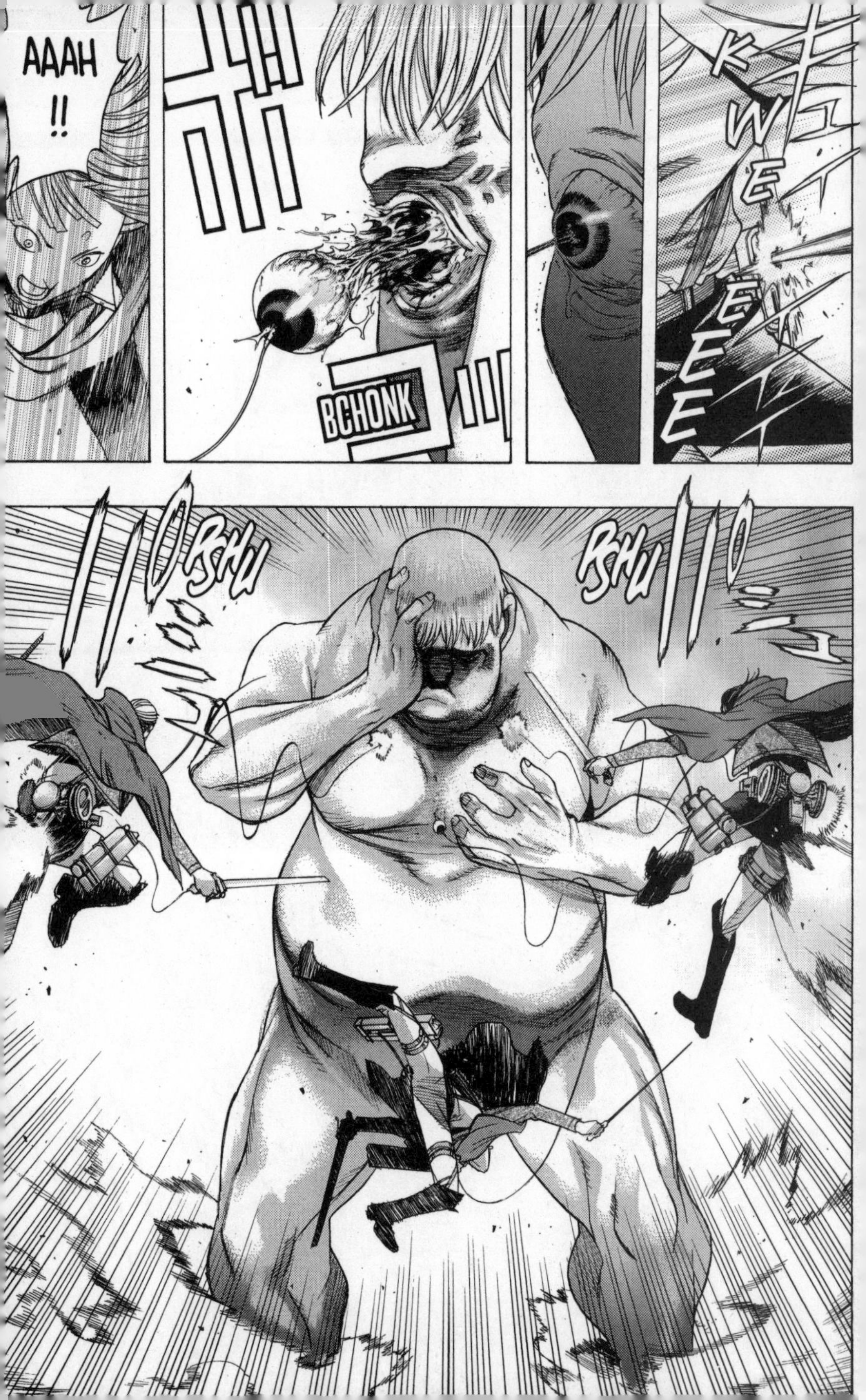
KWEEEEE
BCHONK
AAAH!!
PSHU
PSHU

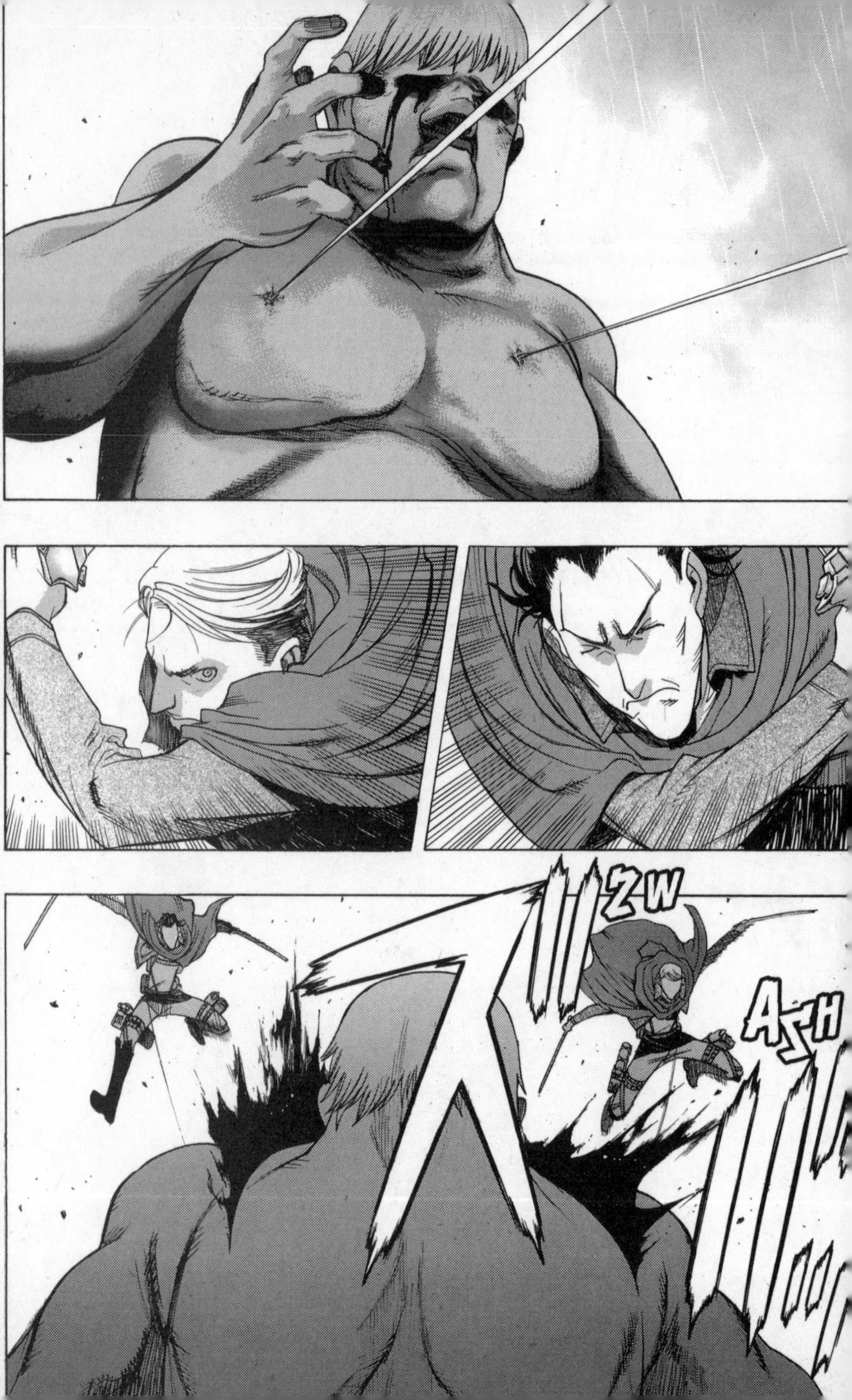
ZW
AZH

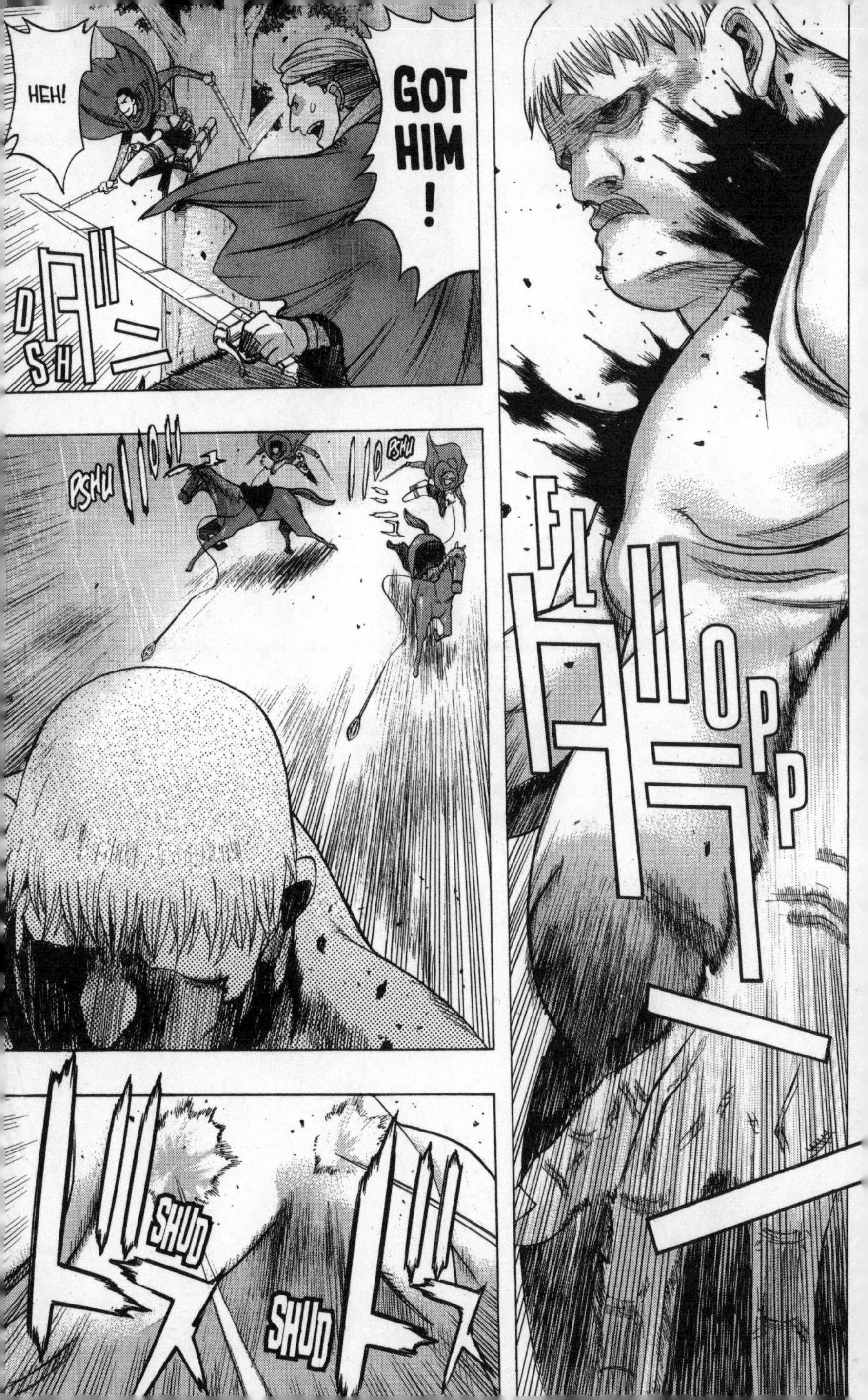
FLOPP
GOT HIM!
HEH!
DSH
PSHU
PSHU
SHUD
SHUD

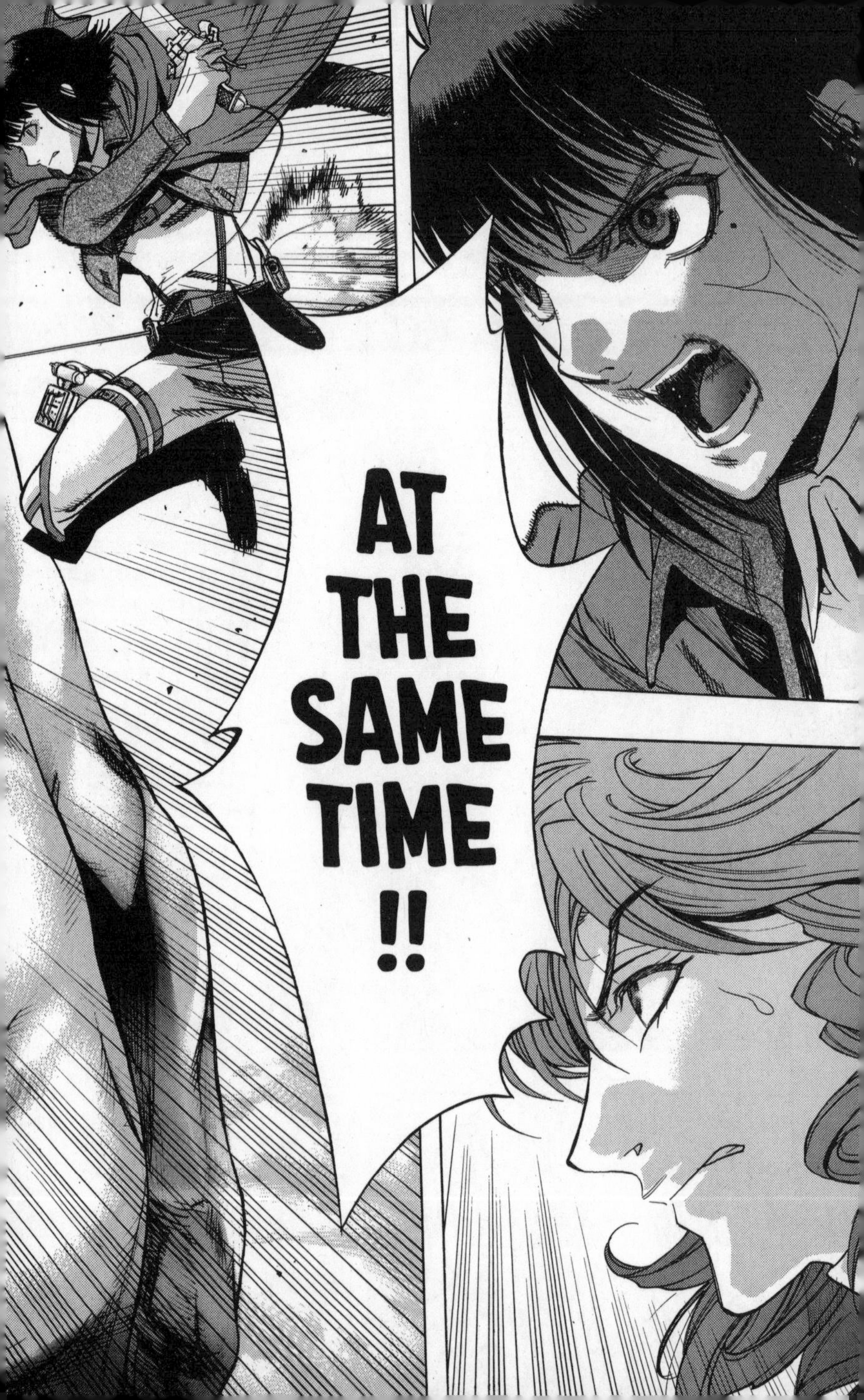
AT THE SAME TIME !!

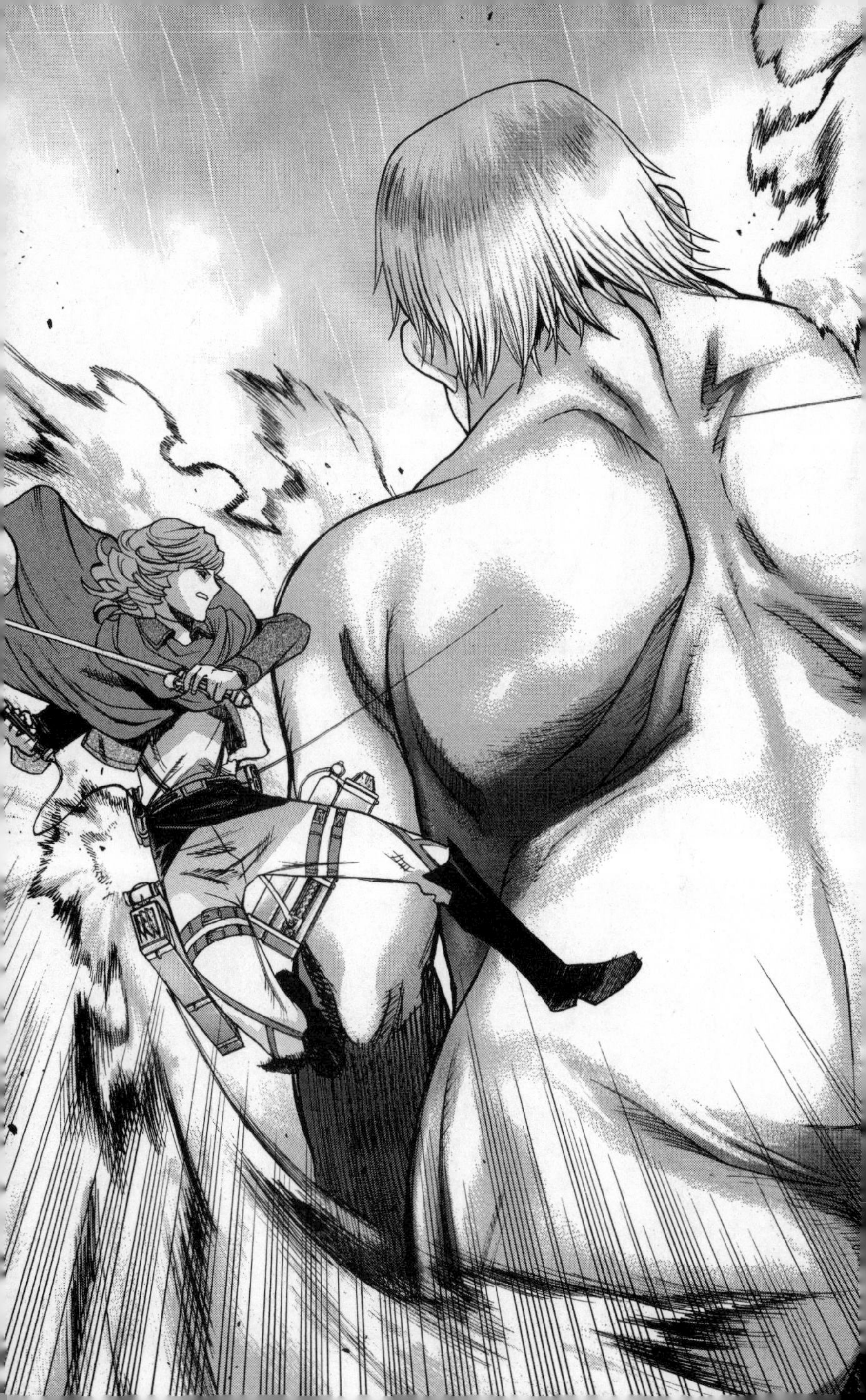

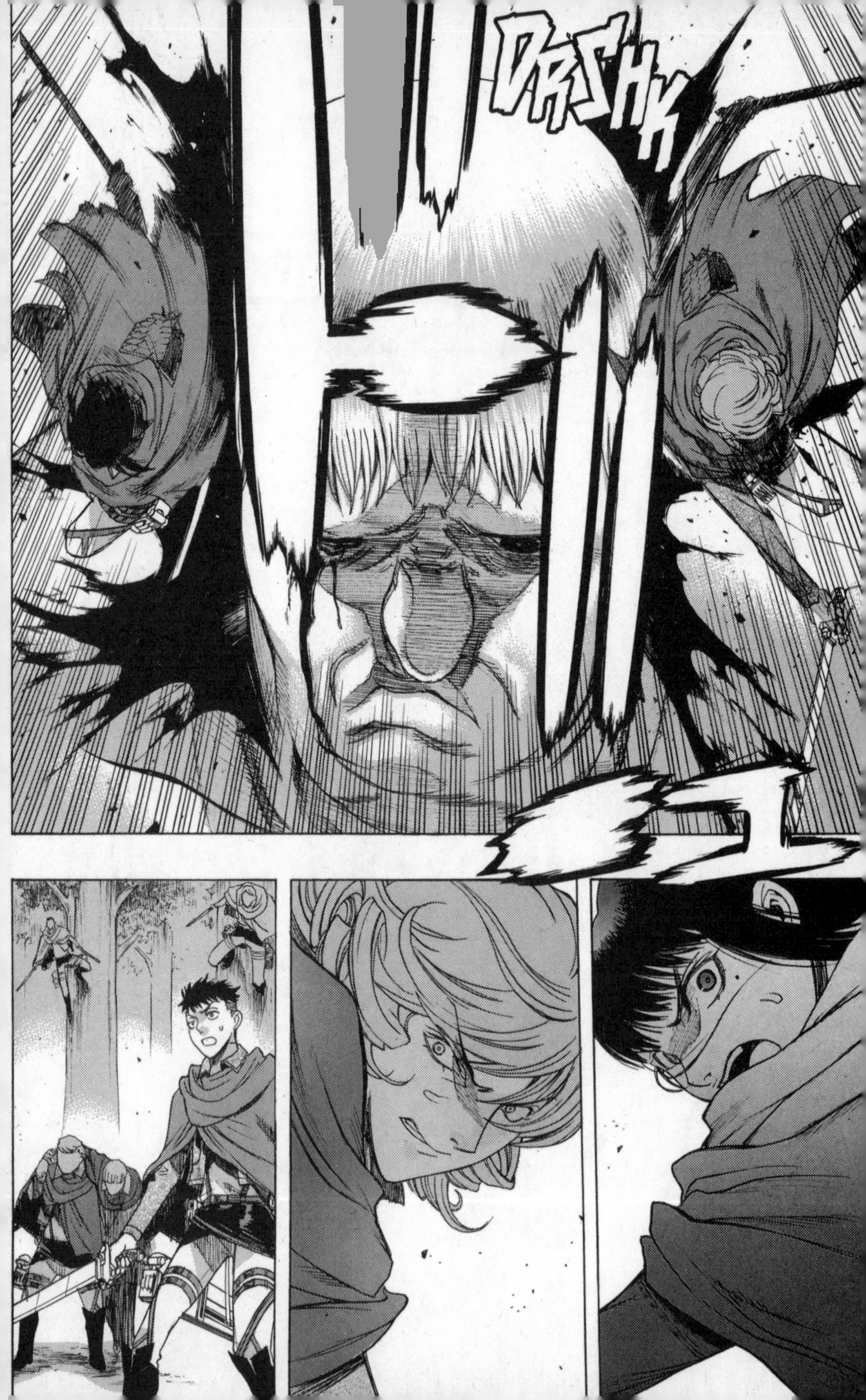
DRSHK

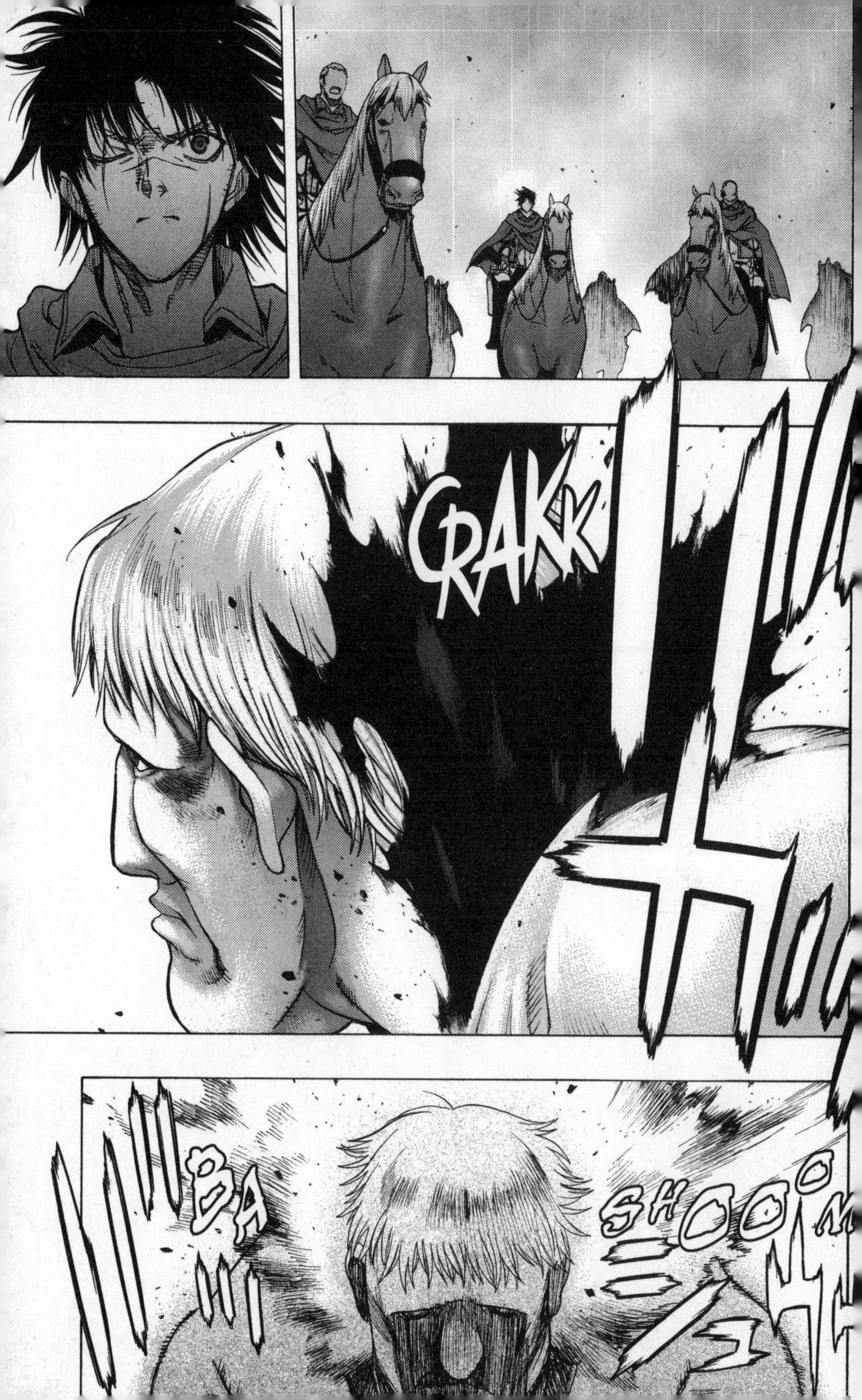
CRAKK
BA
SHOOOM

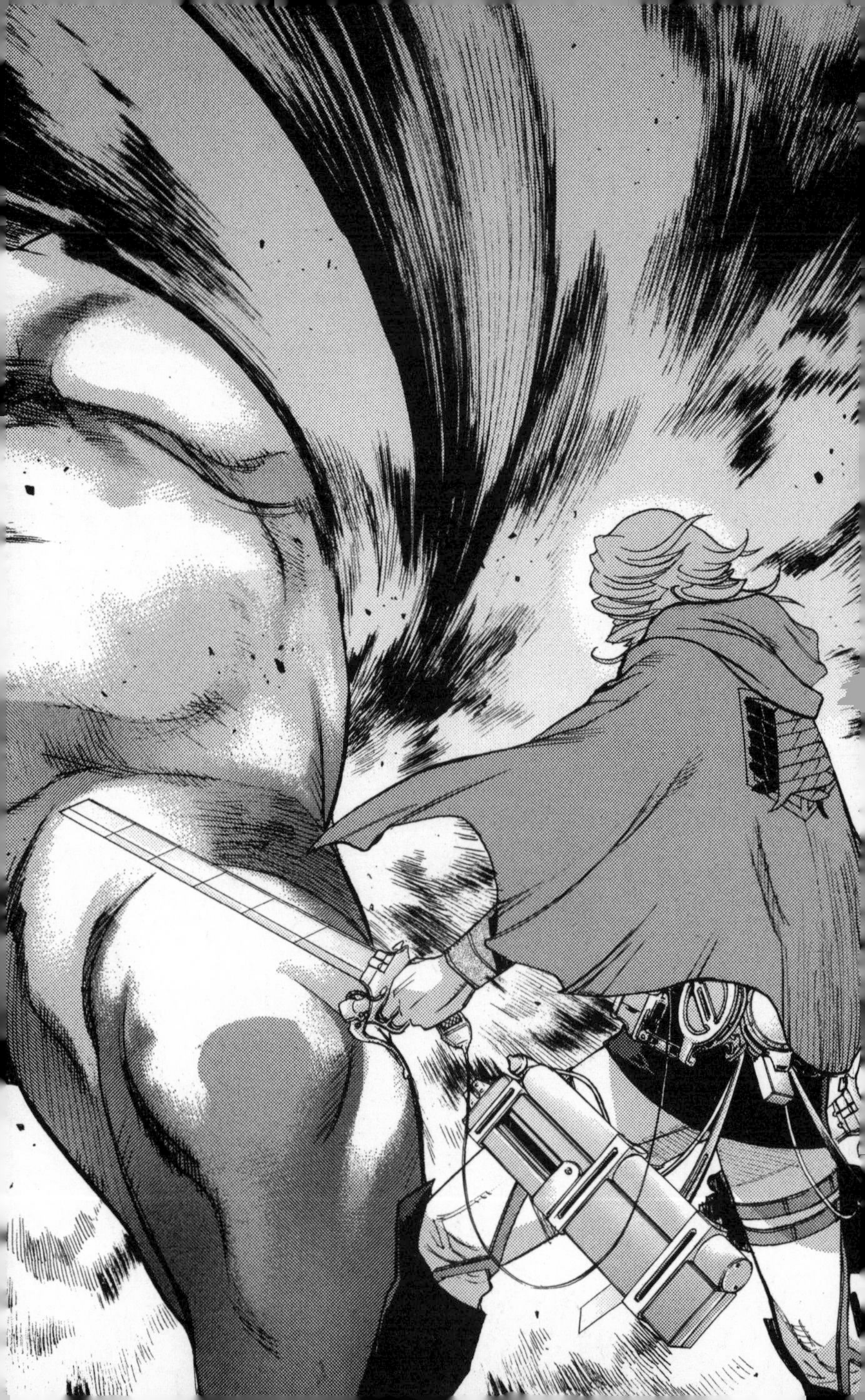

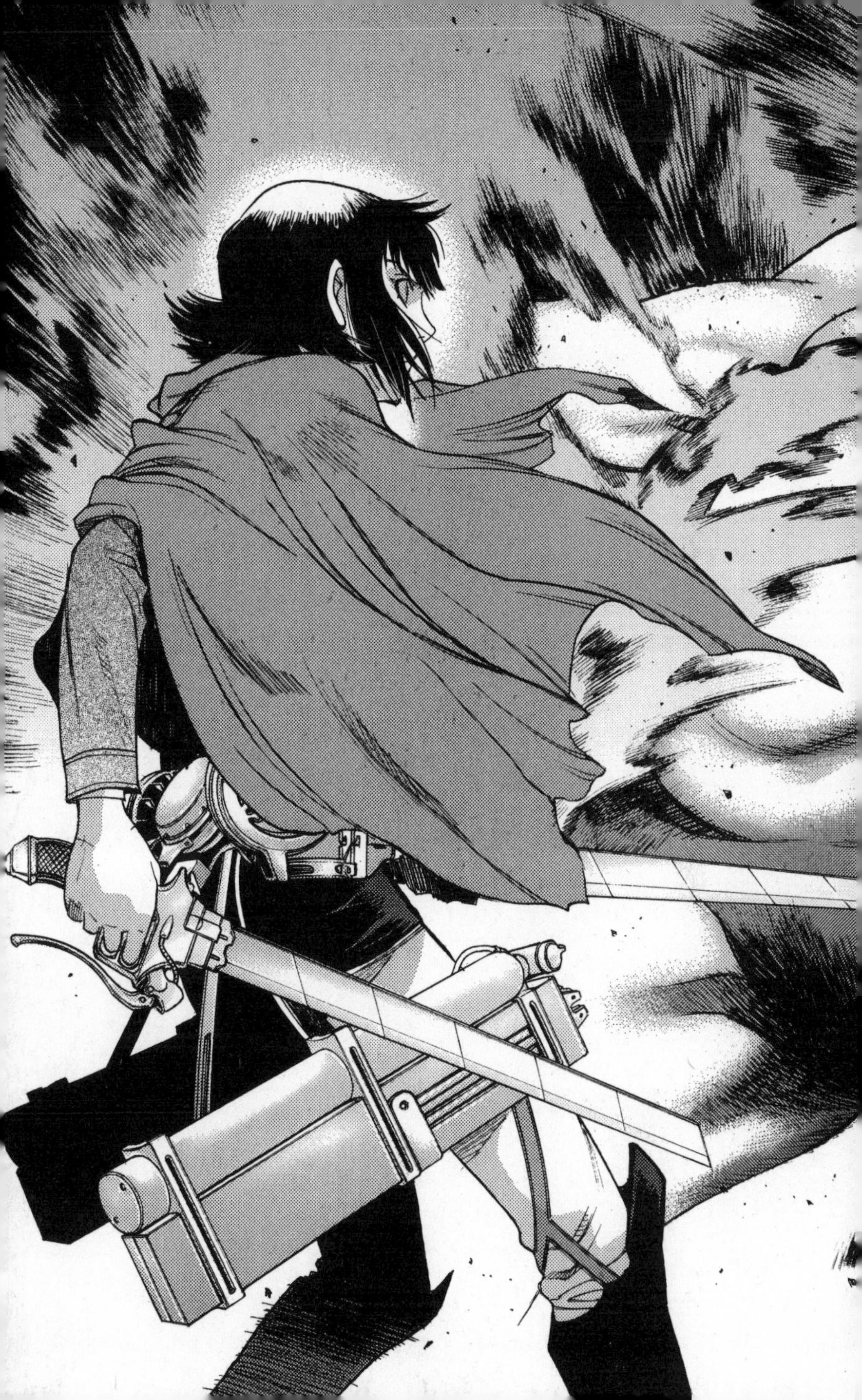

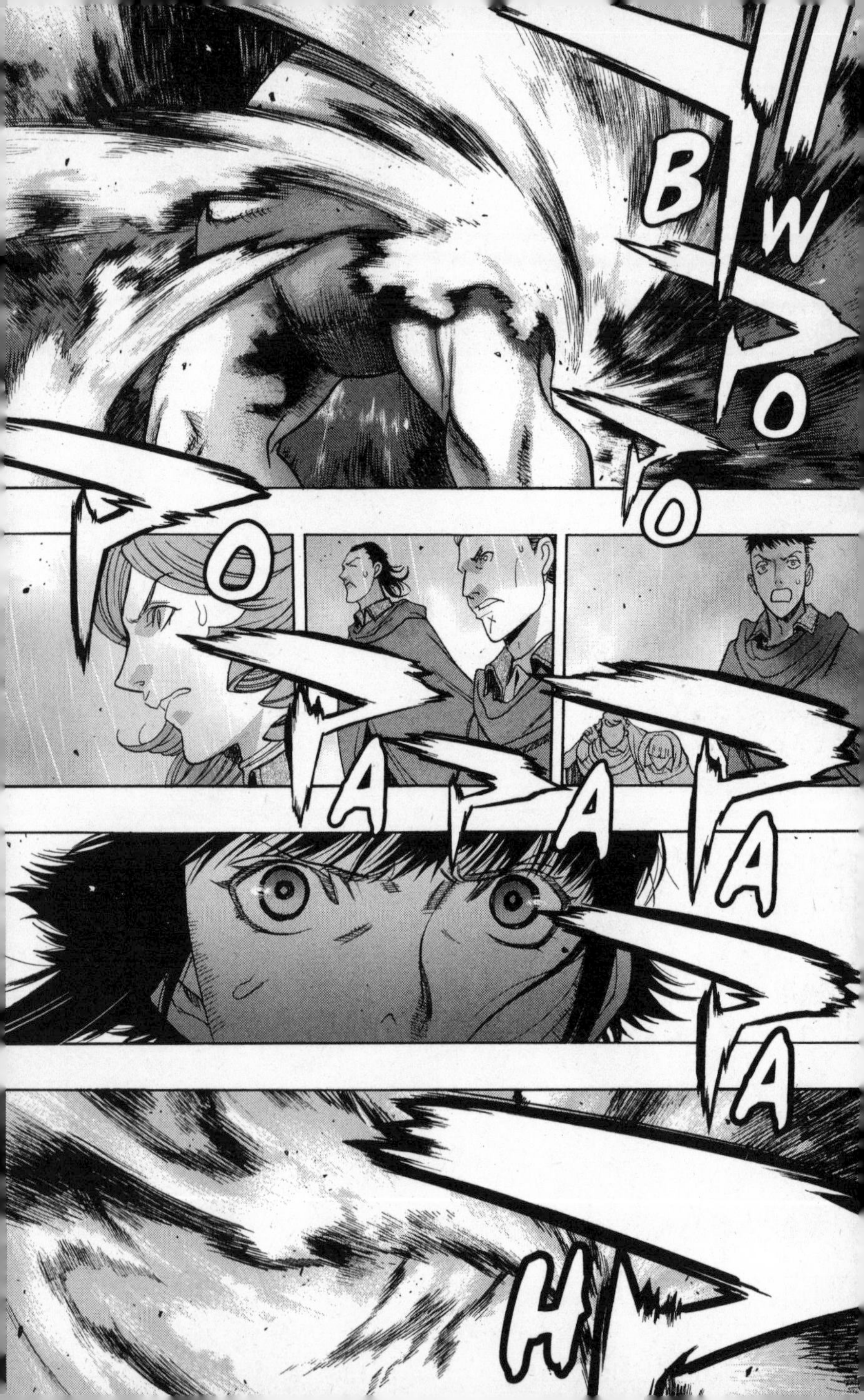
BWOOO
AAAAH

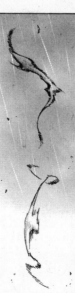

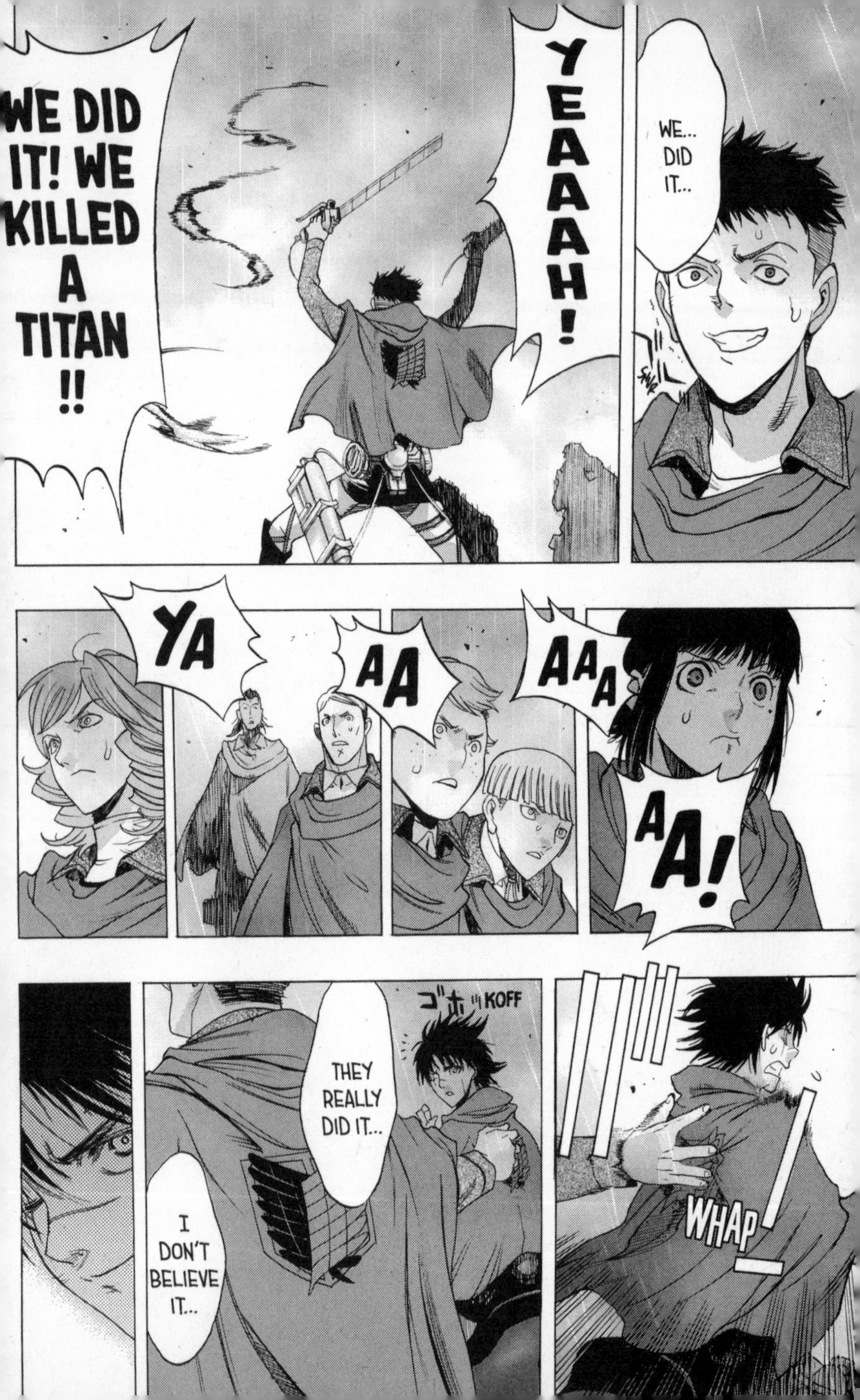

WE... DID IT...
YEAAAAH!
WE DID IT! WE KILLED A TITAN!!
AAA
AA!
AA
YA
WHAP
ゴホッ KOFF
THEY REALLY DID IT...
I DON'T BELIEVE IT...

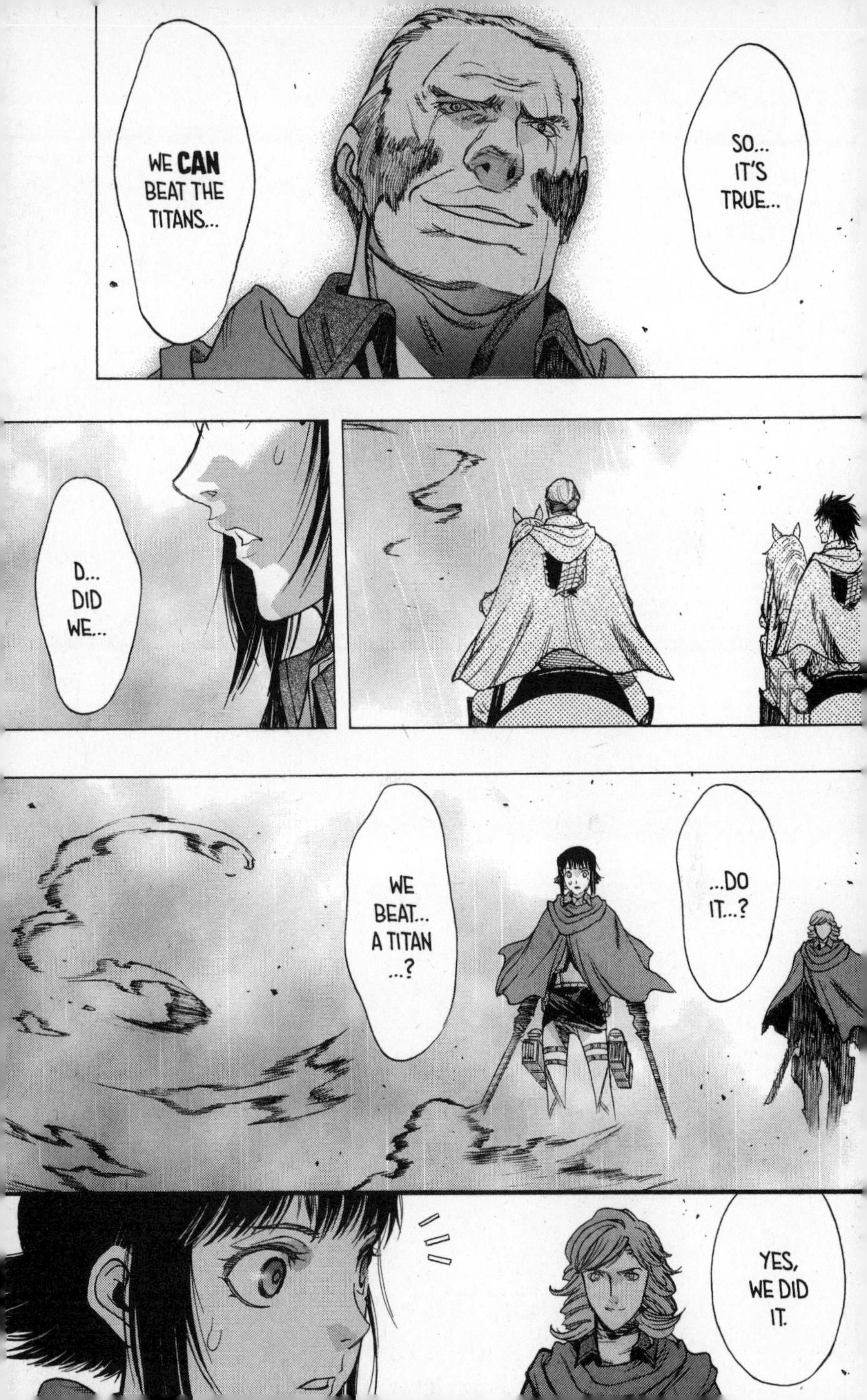
SO... IT'S TRUE...
WE **CAN** BEAT THE TITANS...
D... DID WE...
...DO IT...?
WE BEAT... A TITAN ...?
YES, WE DID IT.

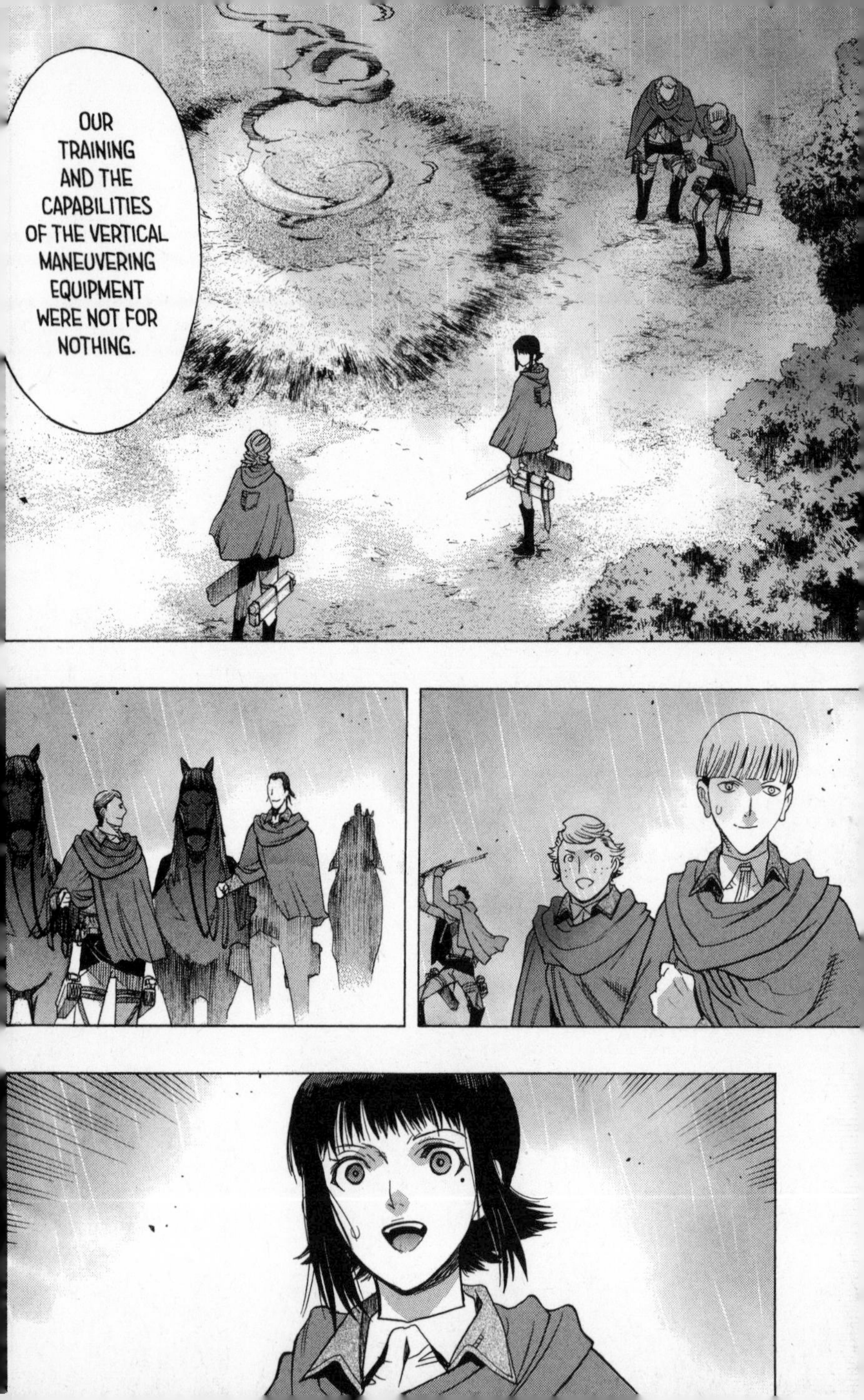
OUR TRAINING AND THE CAPABILITIES OF THE VERTICAL MANEUVERING EQUIPMENT WERE NOT FOR NOTHING.

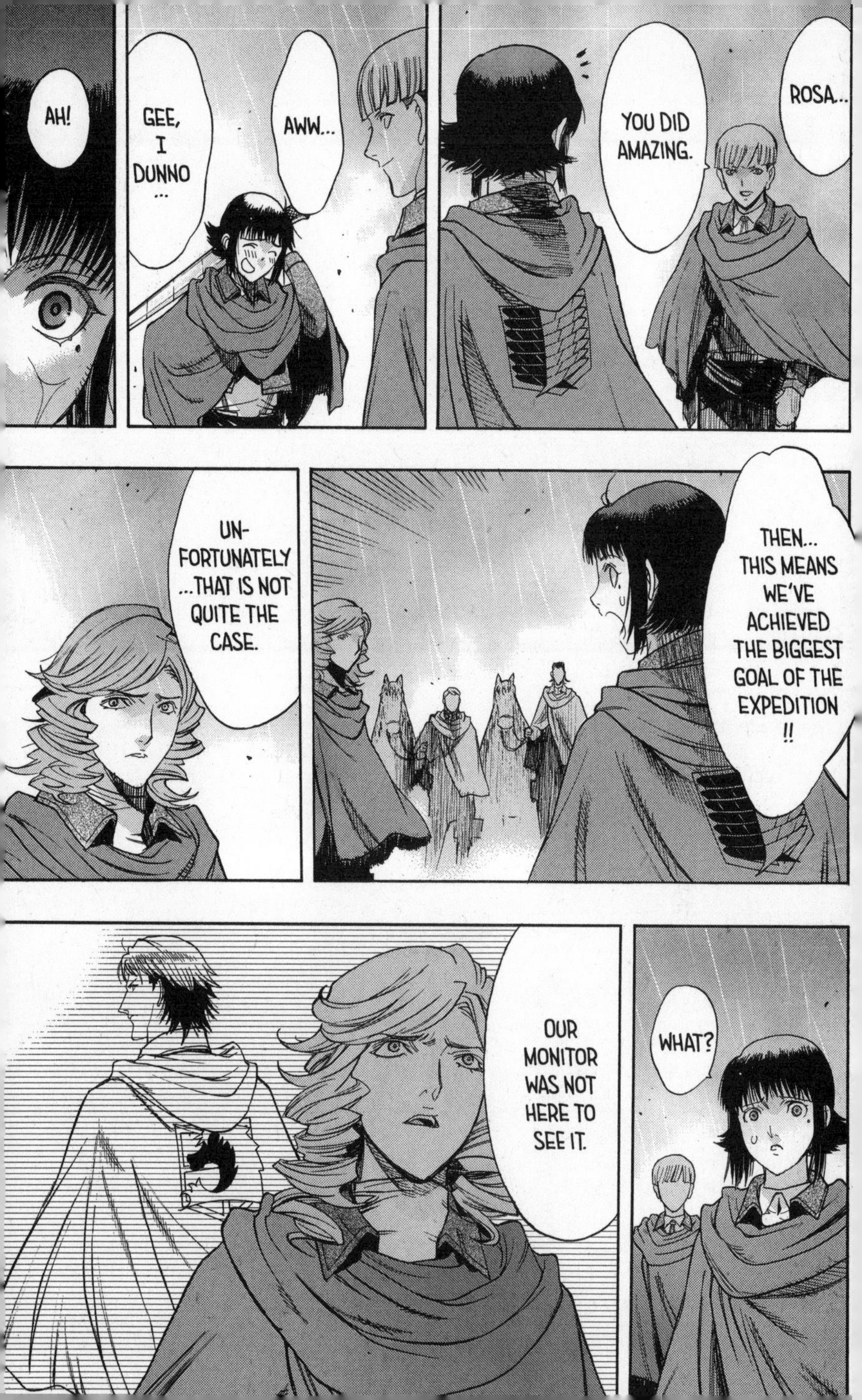
ROSA...
YOU DID AMAZING.
AWW...
GEE, I DUNNO ...
AH!
THEN... THIS MEANS WE'VE ACHIEVED THE BIGGEST GOAL OF THE EXPEDITION !!
UN-FORTUNATELY ...THAT IS NOT QUITE THE CASE.
WHAT?
OUR MONITOR WAS NOT HERE TO SEE IT.

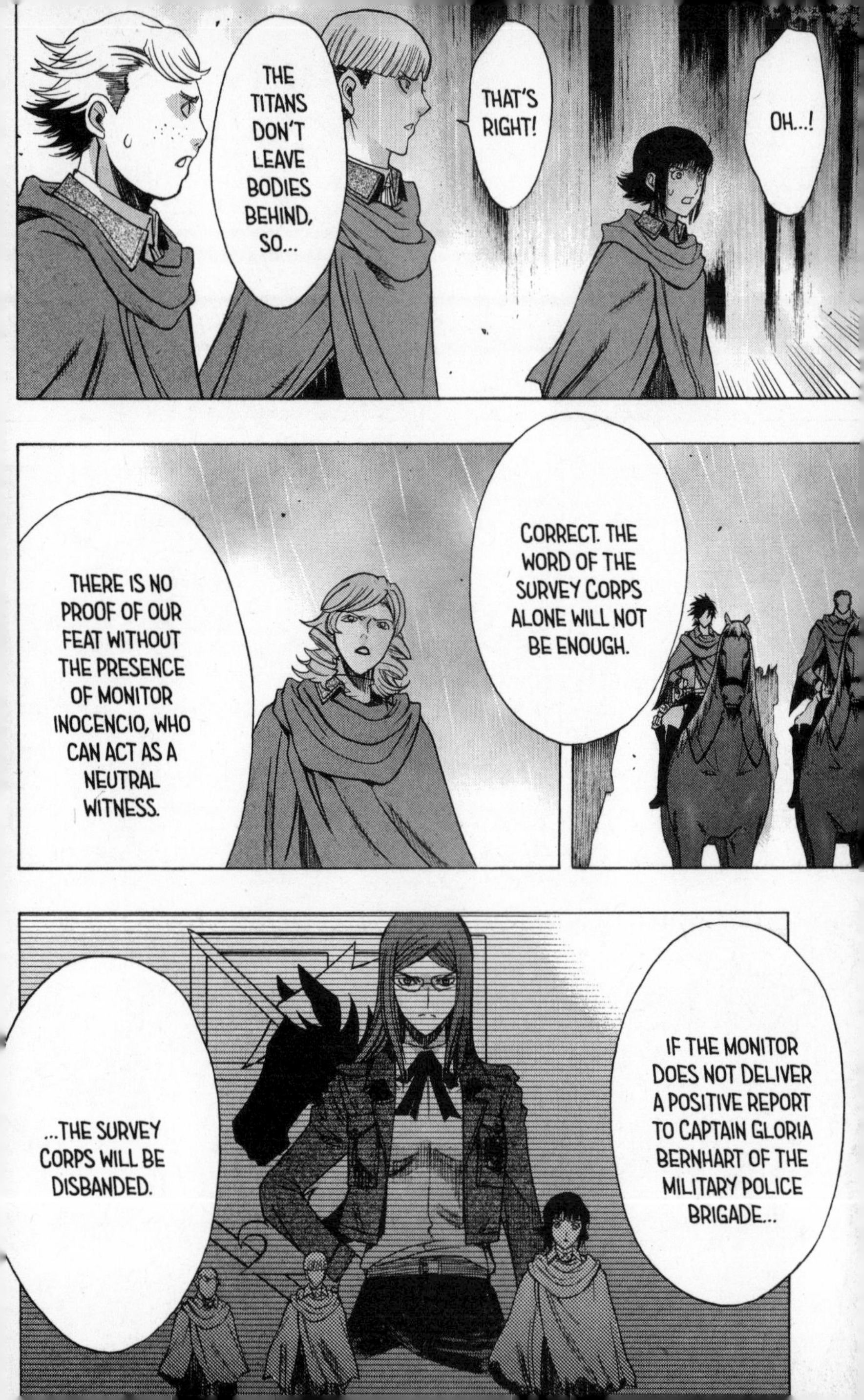
OH...!
THAT'S RIGHT!
THE TITANS DON'T LEAVE BODIES BEHIND, SO...
CORRECT. THE WORD OF THE SURVEY CORPS ALONE WILL NOT BE ENOUGH.
THERE IS NO PROOF OF OUR FEAT WITHOUT THE PRESENCE OF MONITOR INOCENCIO, WHO CAN ACT AS A NEUTRAL WITNESS.
IF THE MONITOR DOES NOT DELIVER A POSITIVE REPORT TO CAPTAIN GLORIA BERNHART OF THE MILITARY POLICE BRIGADE...
...THE SURVEY CORPS WILL BE DISBANDED.

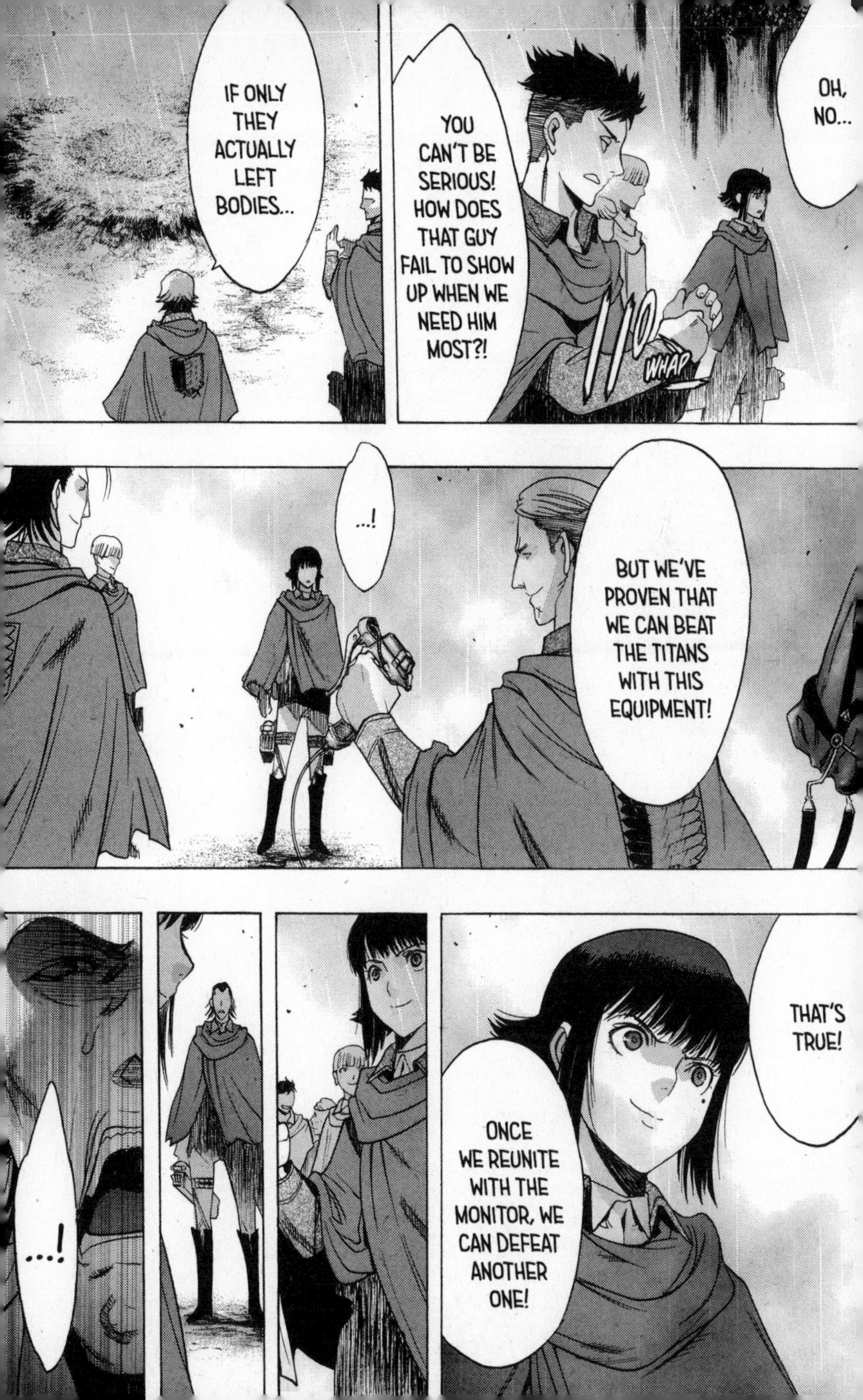
OH, NO...
YOU CAN'T BE SERIOUS! HOW DOES THAT GUY FAIL TO SHOW UP WHEN WE NEED HIM MOST?!
WHAP
IF ONLY THEY ACTUALLY LEFT BODIES...
BUT WE'VE PROVEN THAT WE CAN BEAT THE TITANS WITH THIS EQUIPMENT!
...!
THAT'S TRUE!
ONCE WE REUNITE WITH THE MONITOR, WE CAN DEFEAT ANOTHER ONE!
...!

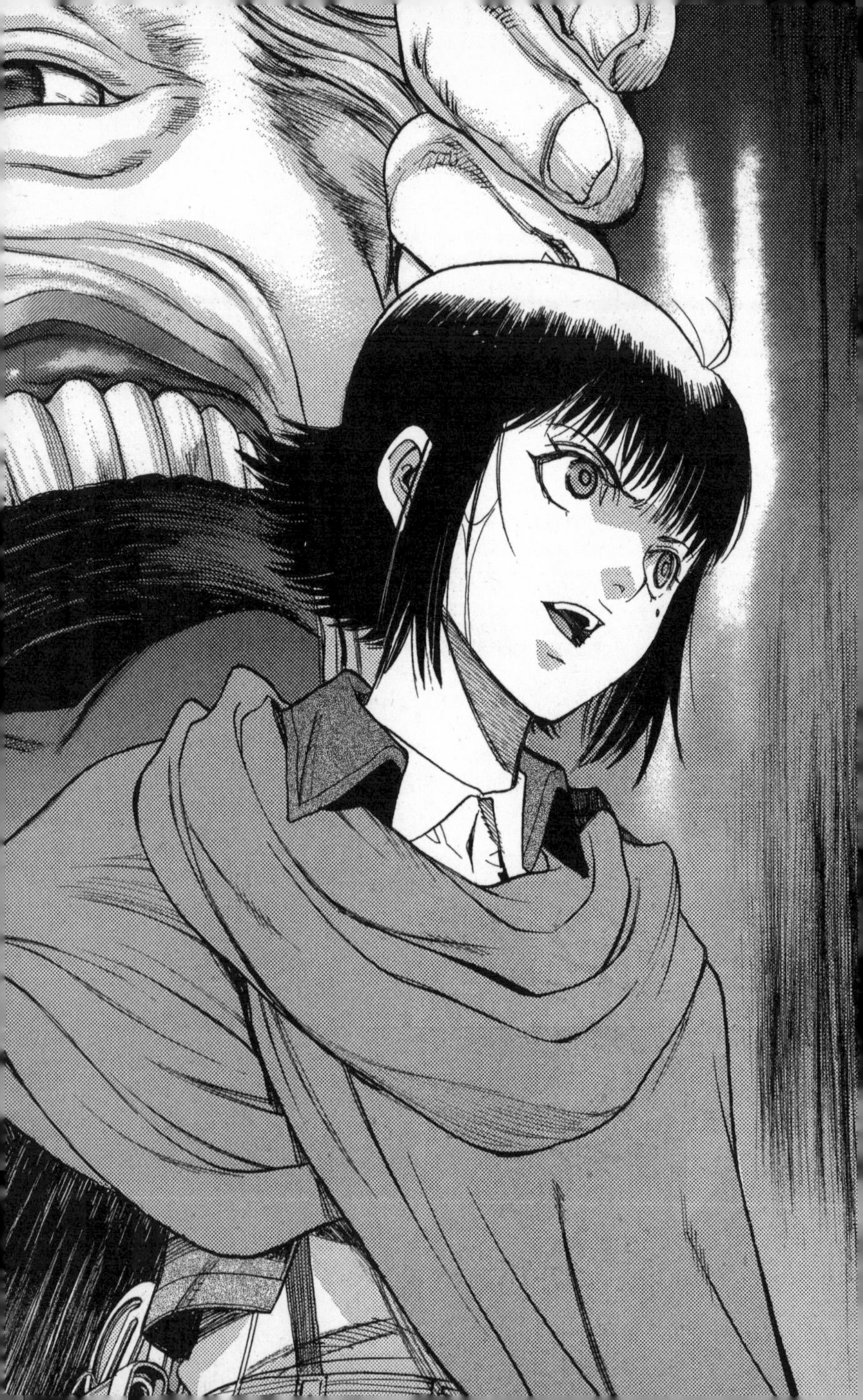

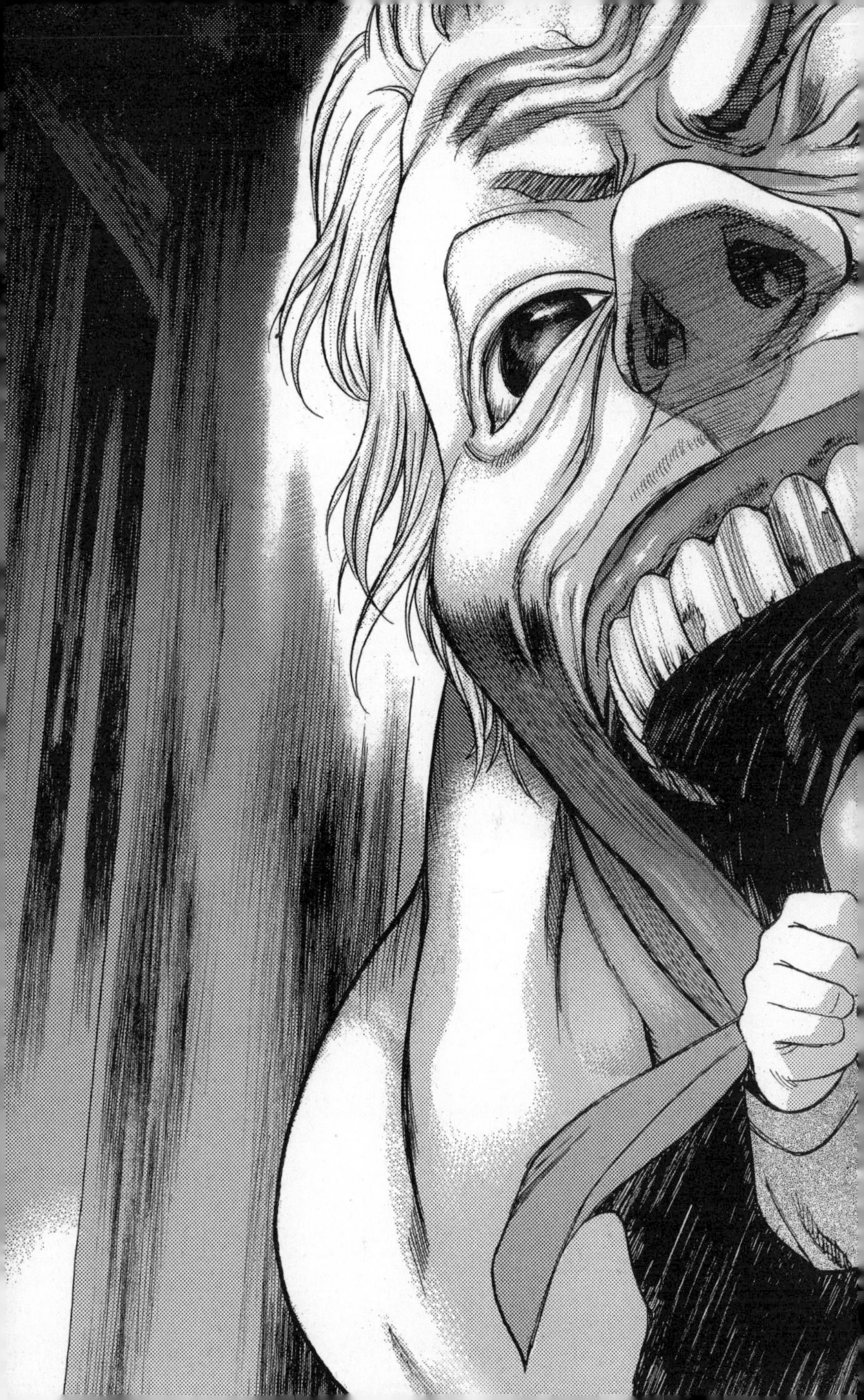

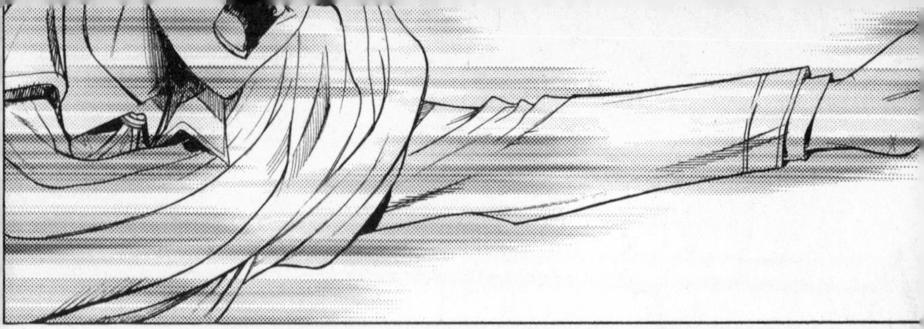
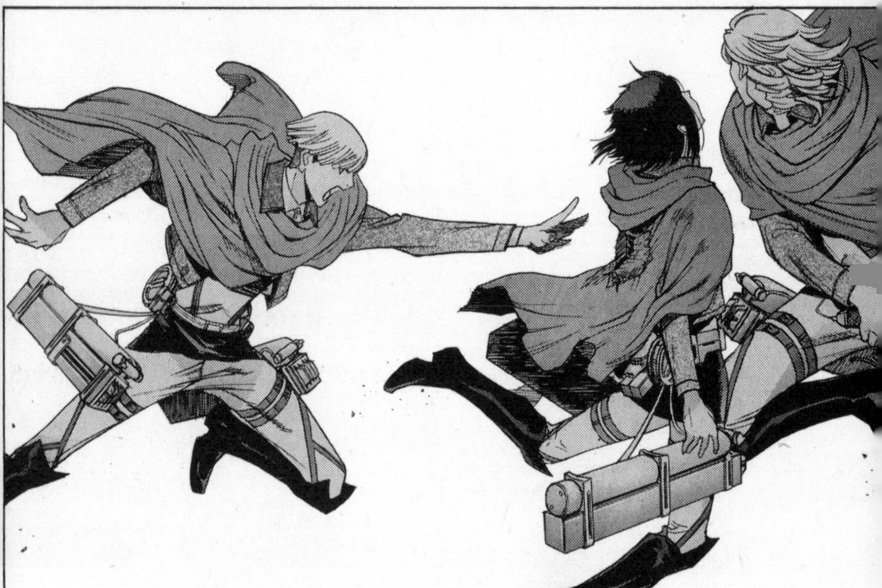
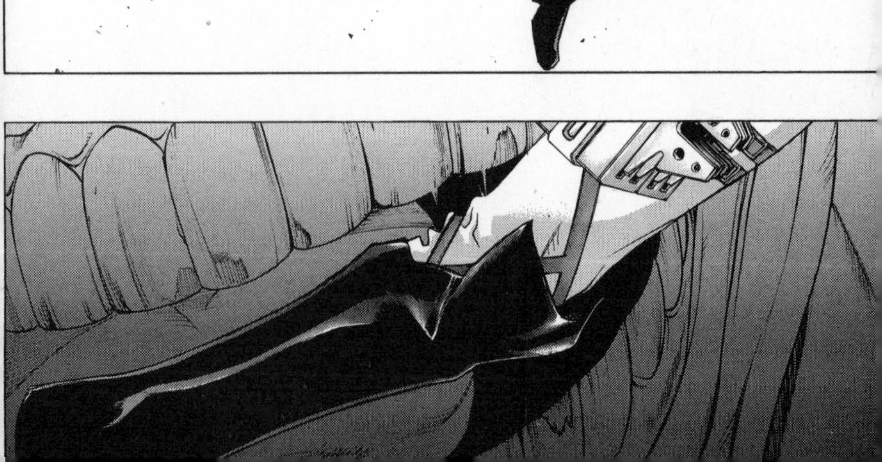

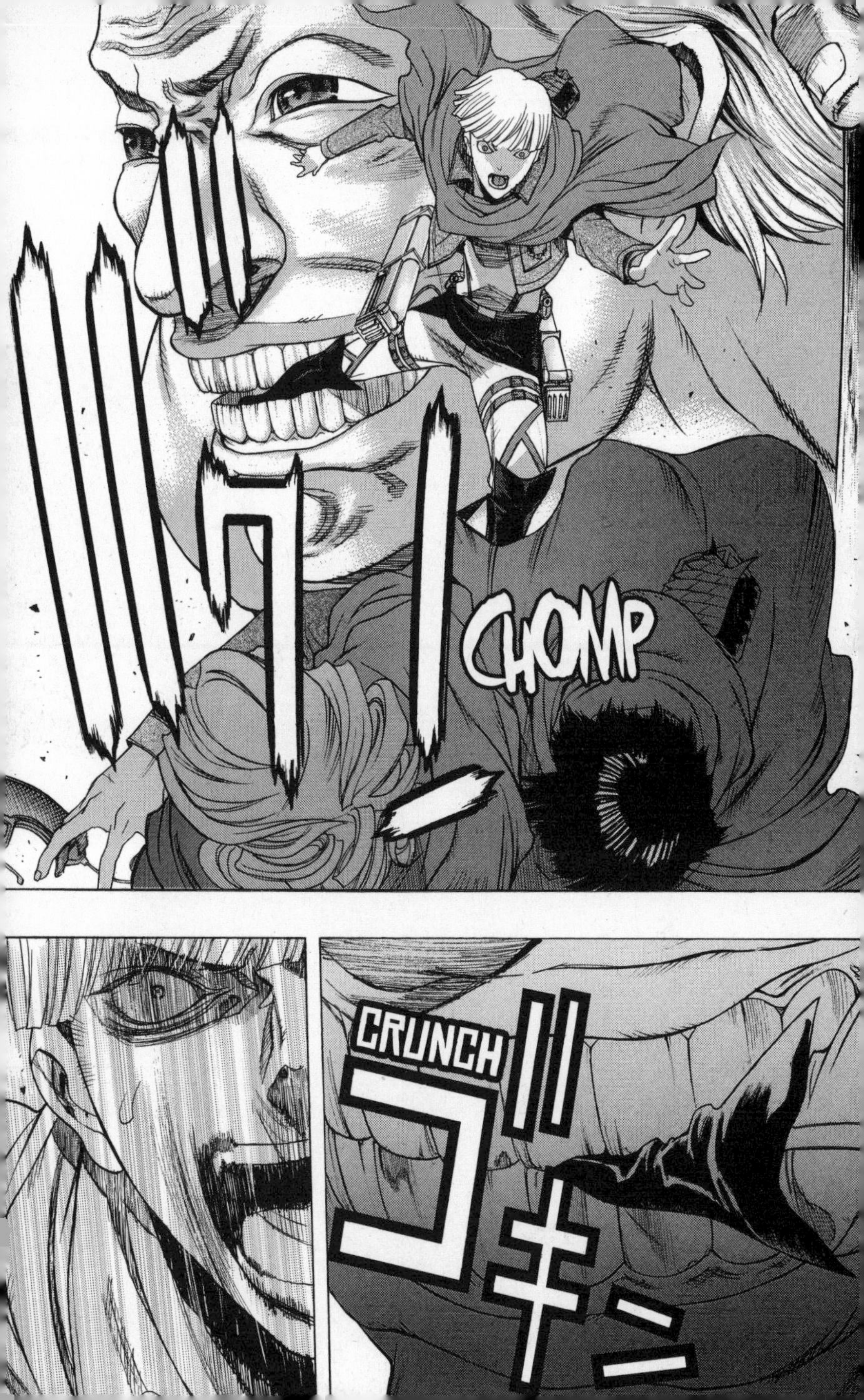
CHOMP
CRUNCH

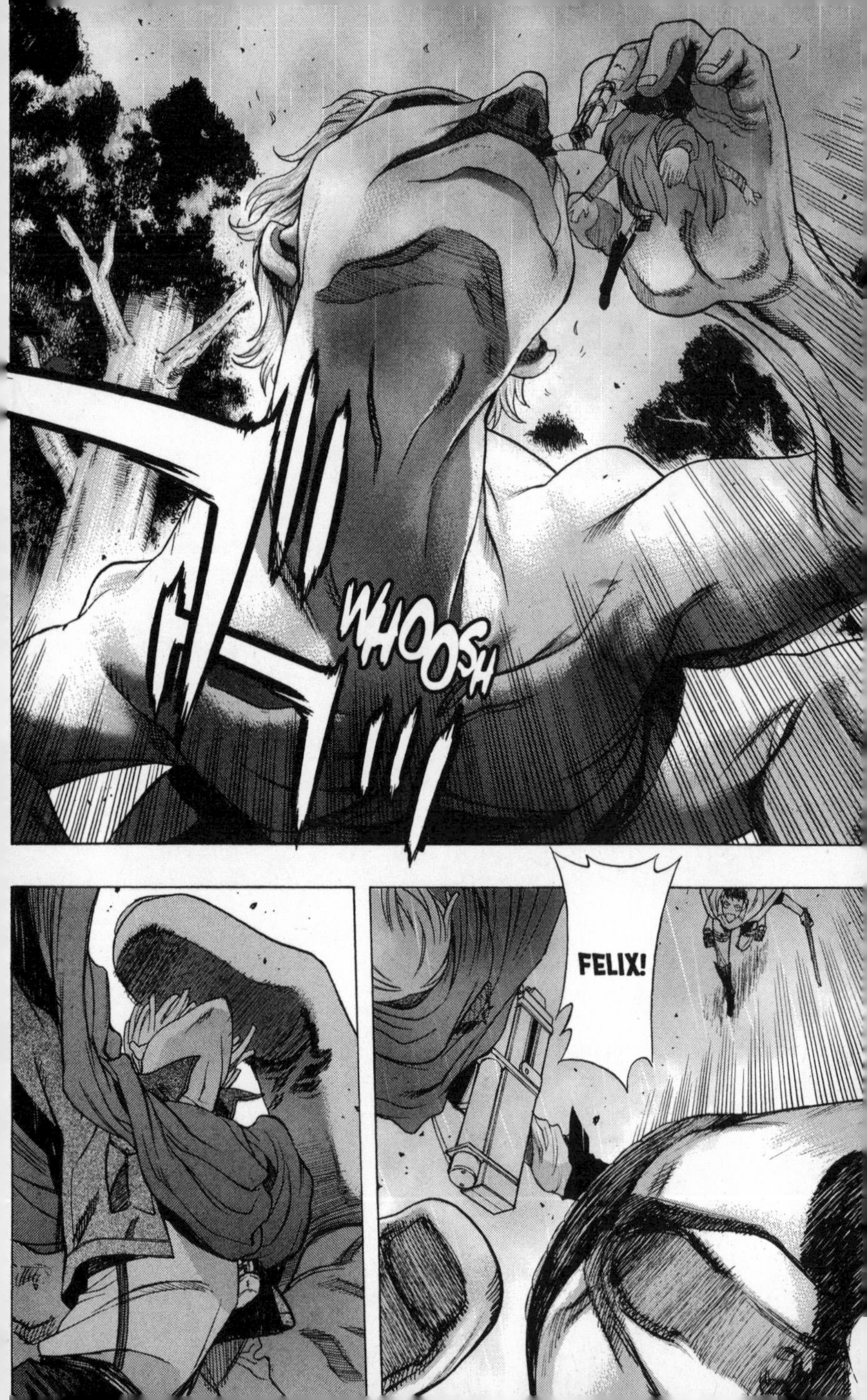
WHOOSH
FELIX!

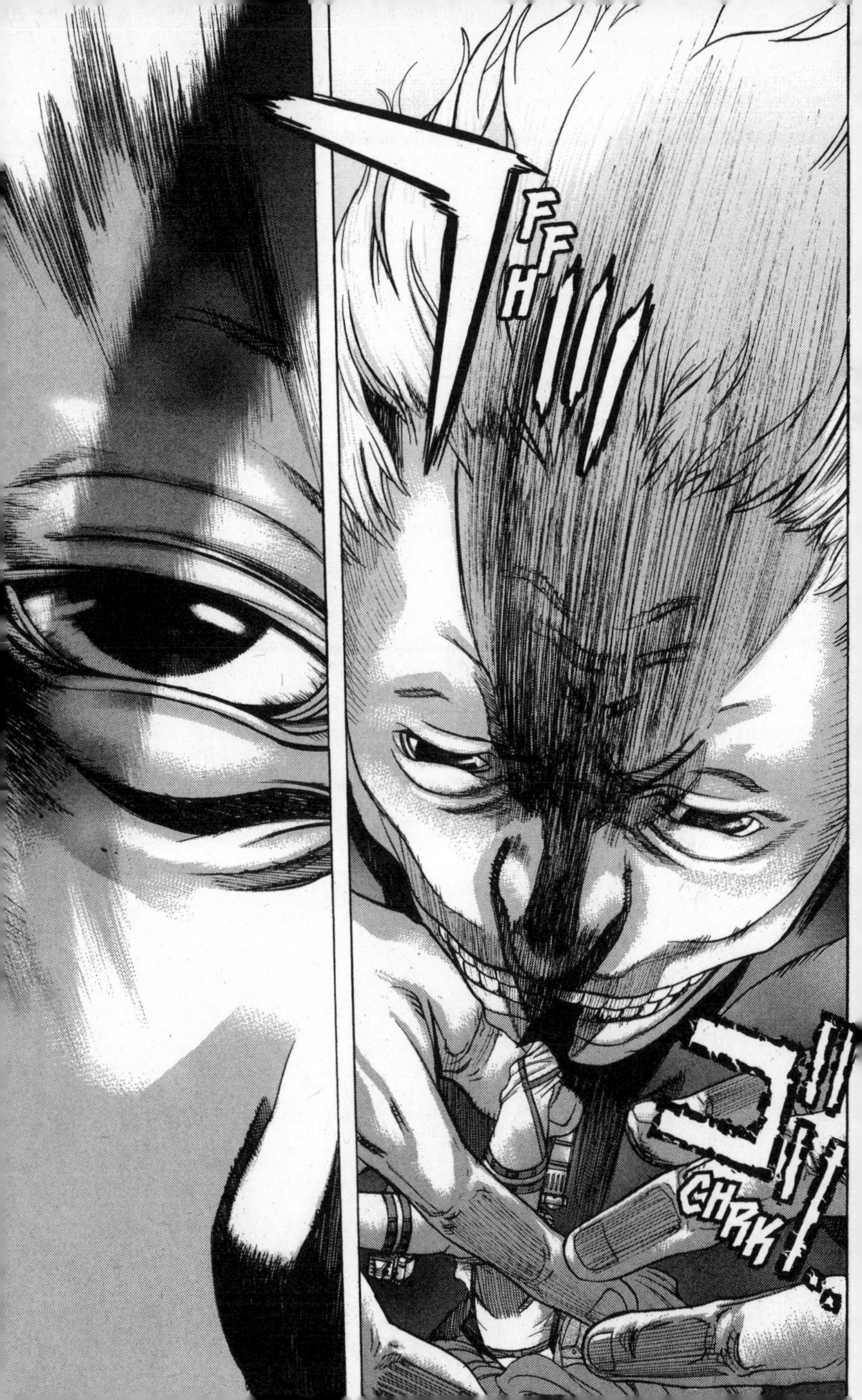
FFH
CHRK!

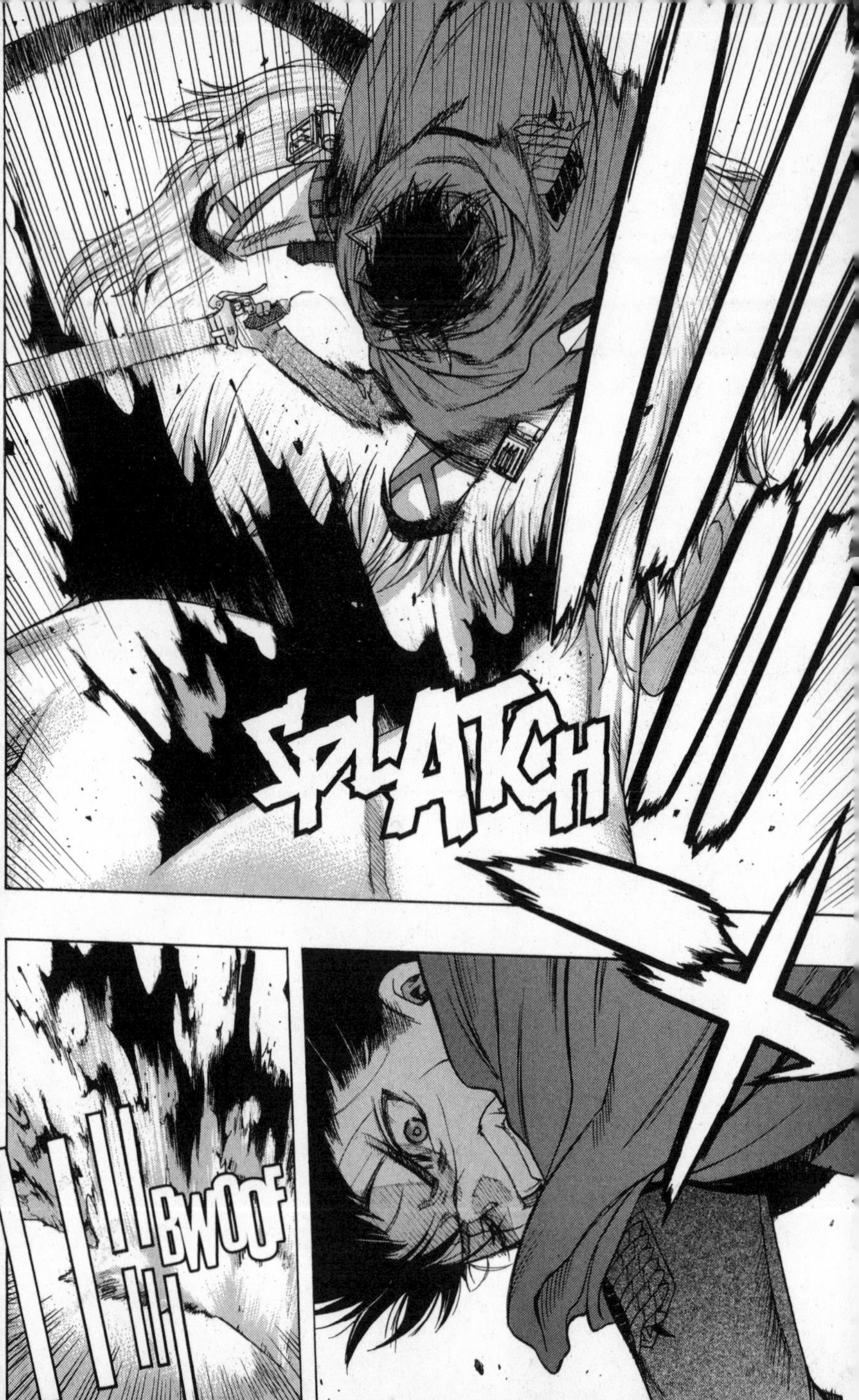
SPLATCH
BWOOF

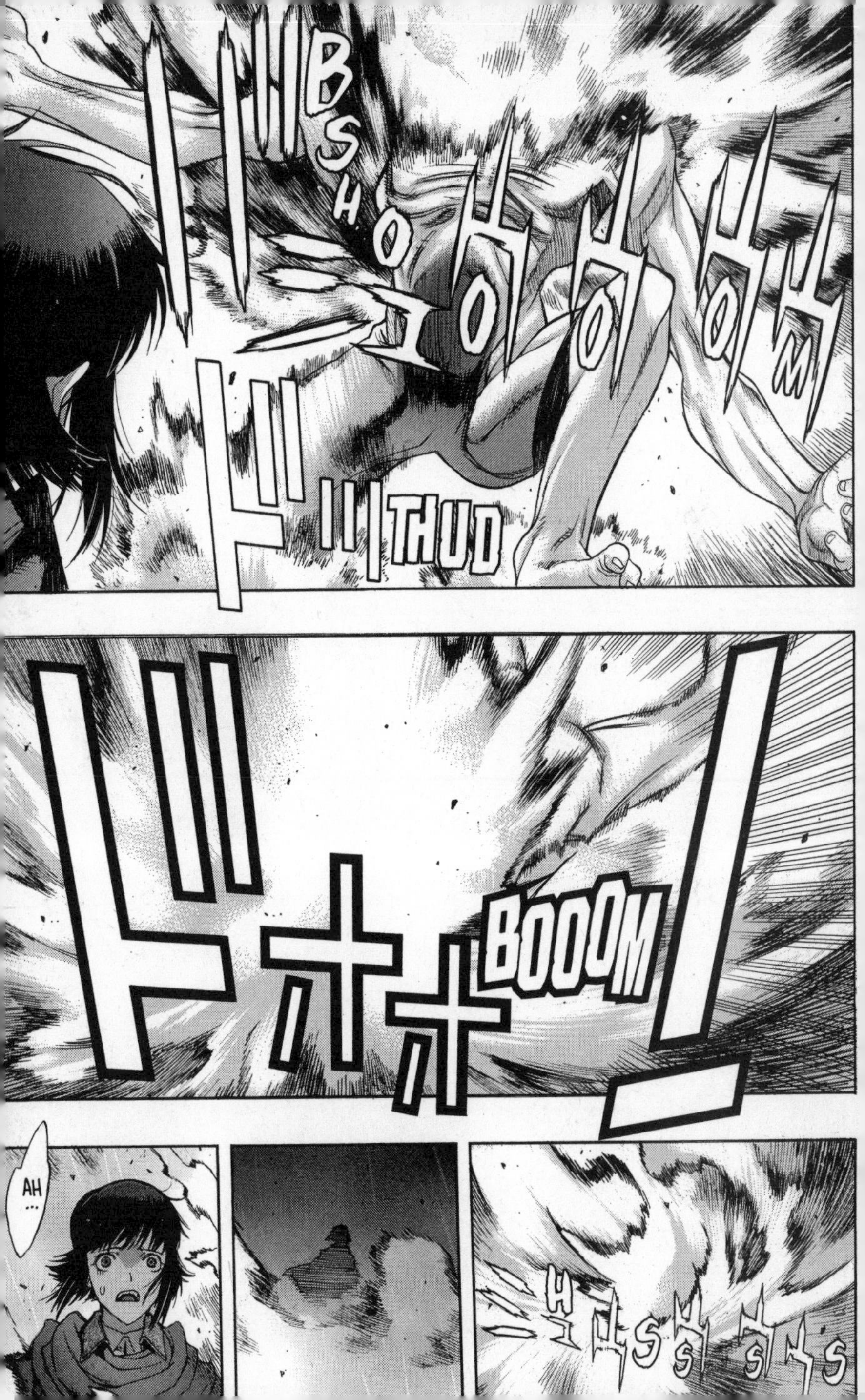
BSHOOOOM
THUD
BOOOM
HISSSS
AH...

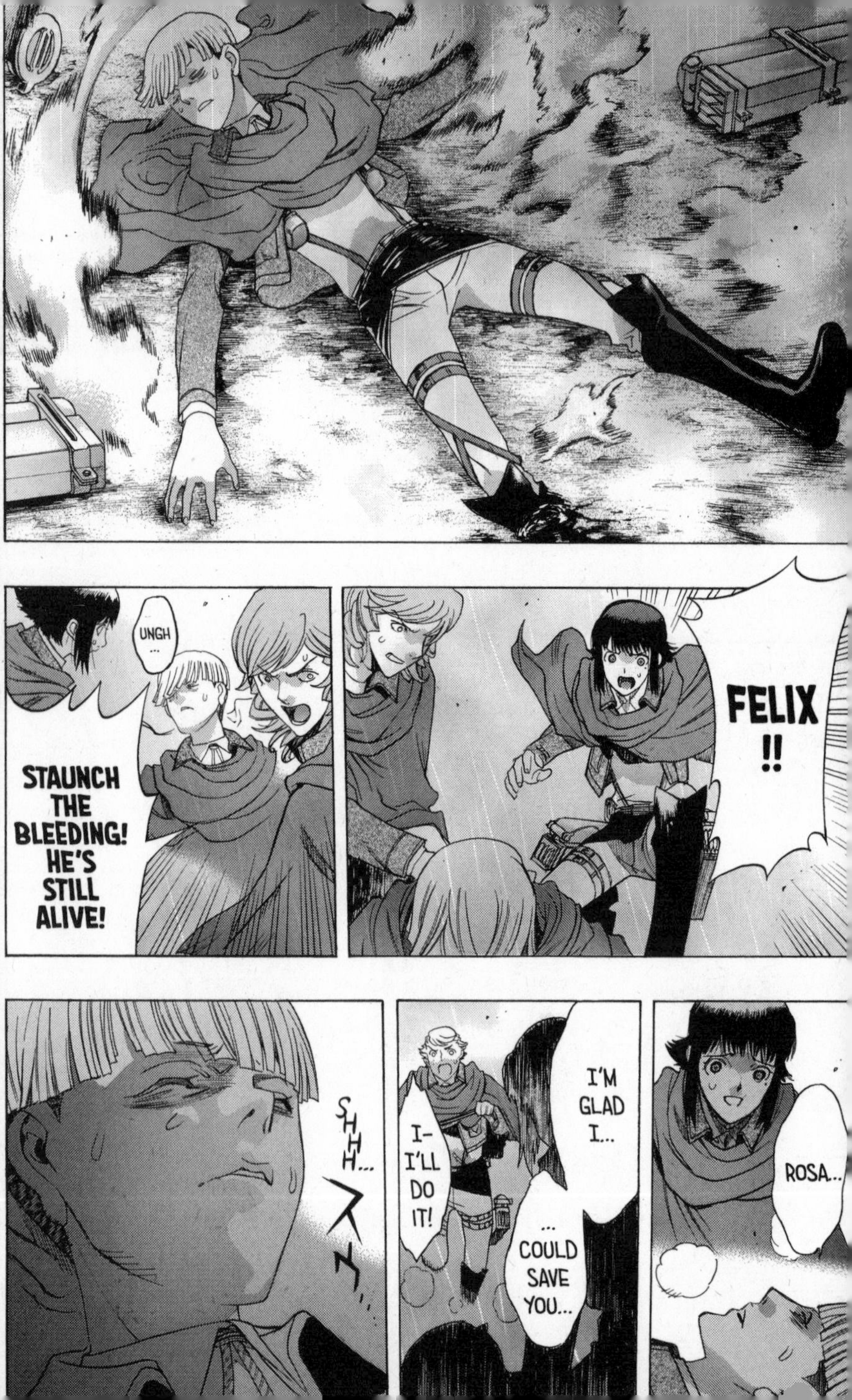
FELIX !!
UNGH ...
STAUNCH THE BLEEDING! HE'S STILL ALIVE!
ROSA...
I'M GLAD I...
... COULD SAVE YOU...
I- I'LL DO IT!
SHHH...

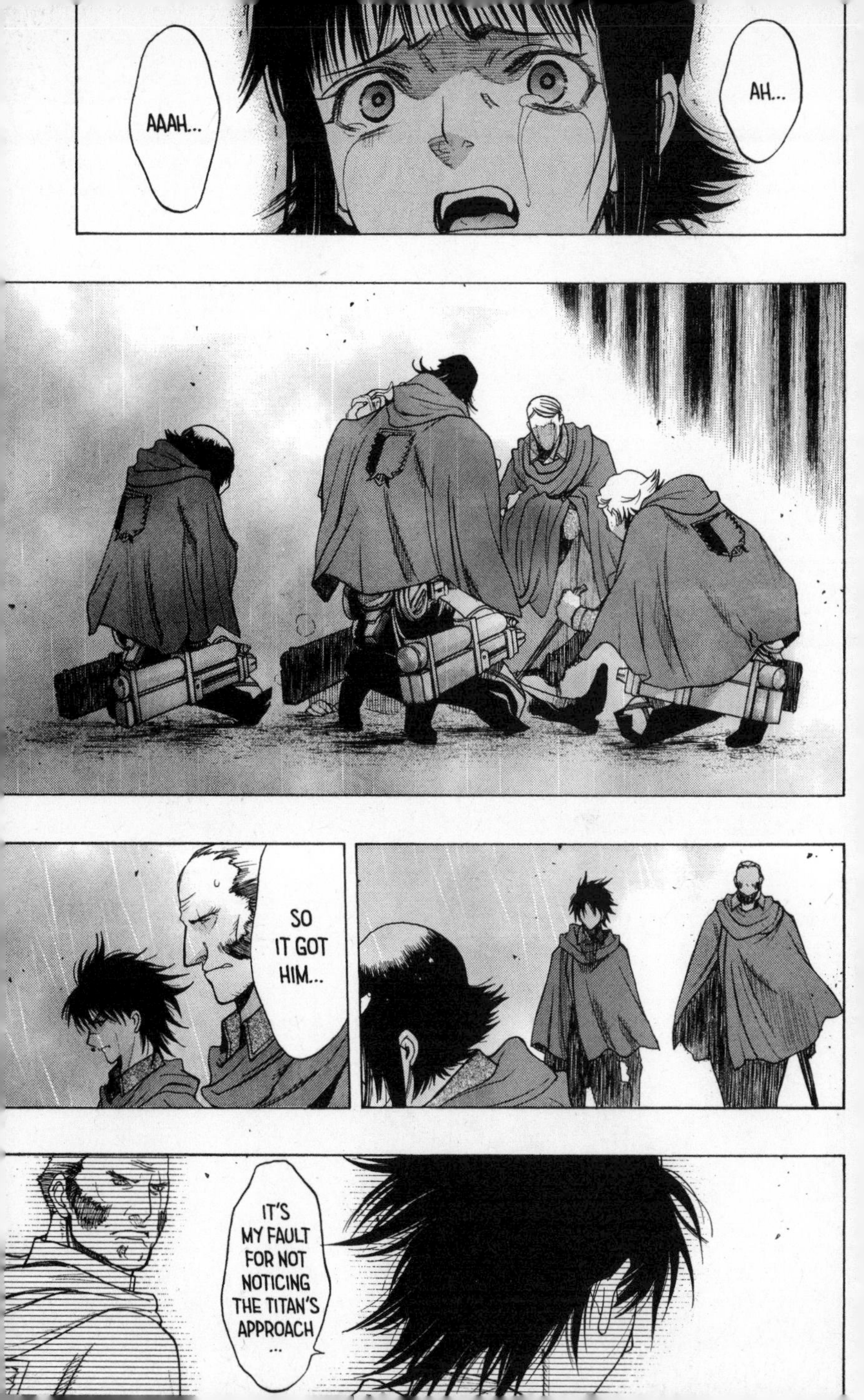
AH...
AAAH...
SO IT GOT HIM...
IT'S MY FAULT FOR NOT NOTICING THE TITAN'S APPROACH ...

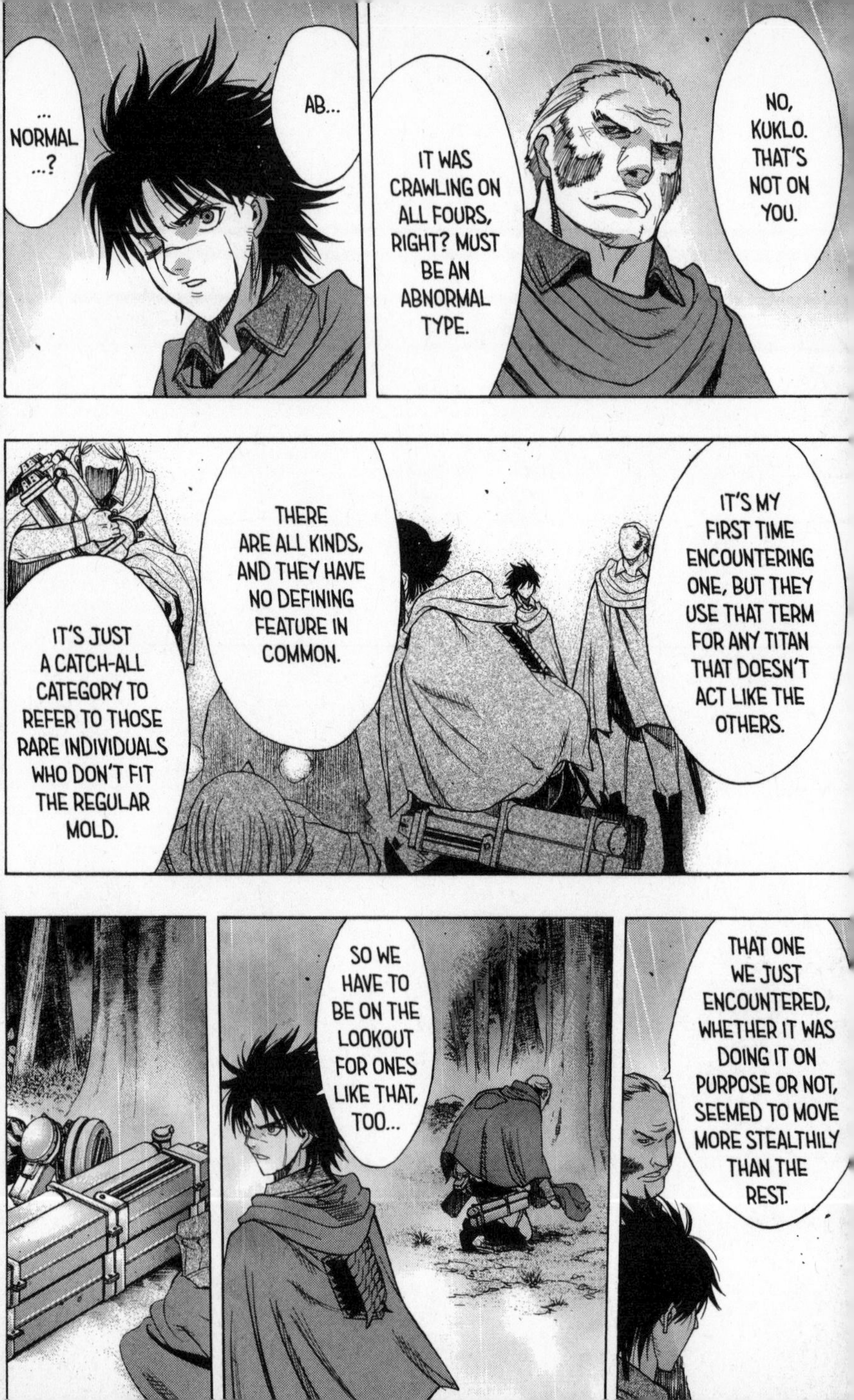
NO, KUKLO. THAT'S NOT ON YOU.
IT WAS CRAWLING ON ALL FOURS, RIGHT? MUST BE AN ABNORMAL TYPE.
AB...
... NORMAL ...?
IT'S MY FIRST TIME ENCOUNTERING ONE, BUT THEY USE THAT TERM FOR ANY TITAN THAT DOESN'T ACT LIKE THE OTHERS.
THERE ARE ALL KINDS, AND THEY HAVE NO DEFINING FEATURE IN COMMON.
IT'S JUST A CATCH-ALL CATEGORY TO REFER TO THOSE RARE INDIVIDUALS WHO DON'T FIT THE REGULAR MOLD.
THAT ONE WE JUST ENCOUNTERED, WHETHER IT WAS DOING IT ON PURPOSE OR NOT, SEEMED TO MOVE MORE STEALTHILY THAN THE REST.
SO WE HAVE TO BE ON THE LOOKOUT FOR ONES LIKE THAT, TOO...

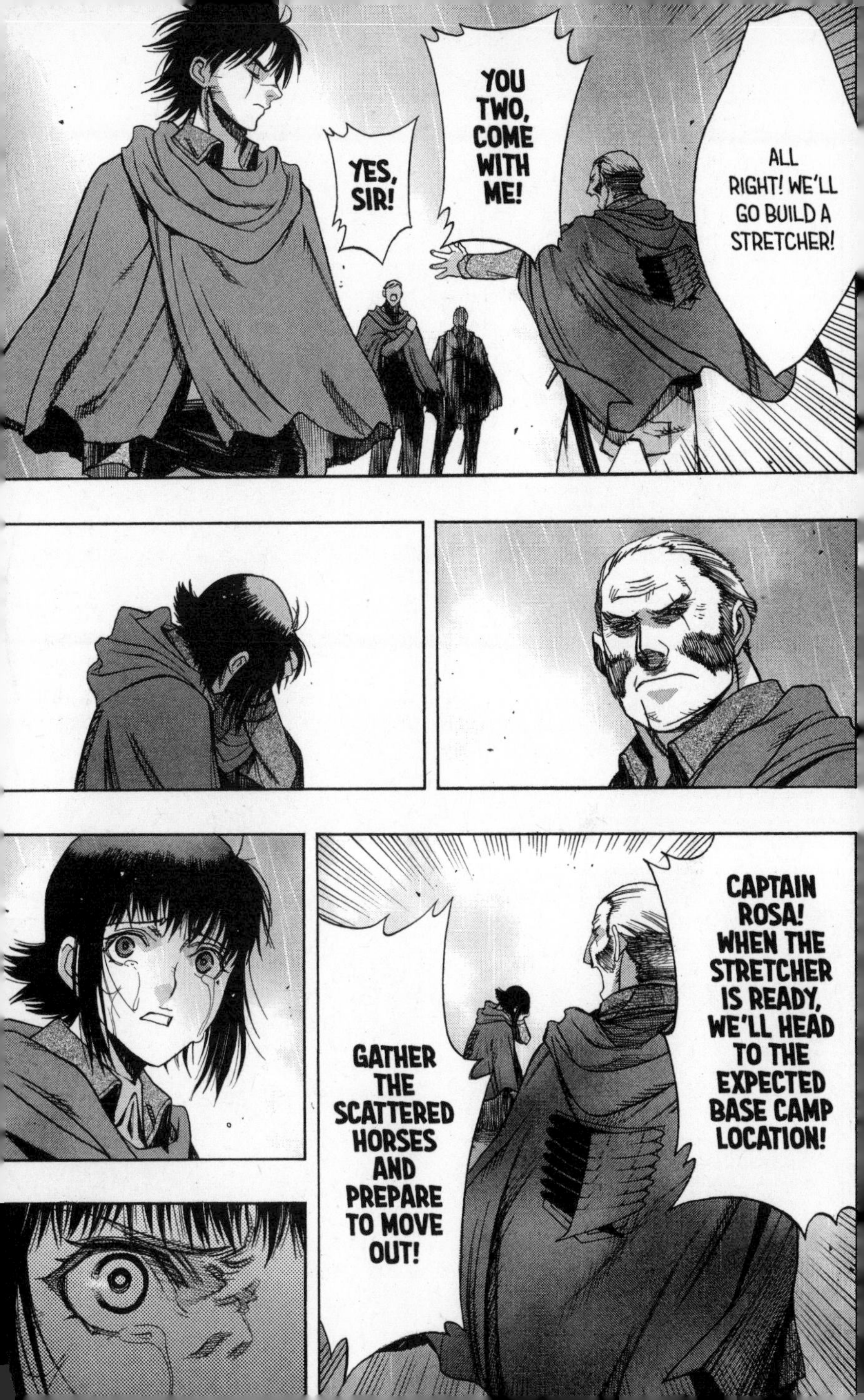
ALL RIGHT! WE'LL GO BUILD A STRETCHER!
YOU TWO, COME WITH ME!
YES, SIR!
CAPTAIN ROSA! WHEN THE STRETCHER IS READY, WE'LL HEAD TO THE EXPECTED BASE CAMP LOCATION!
GATHER THE SCATTERED HORSES AND PREPARE TO MOVE OUT!

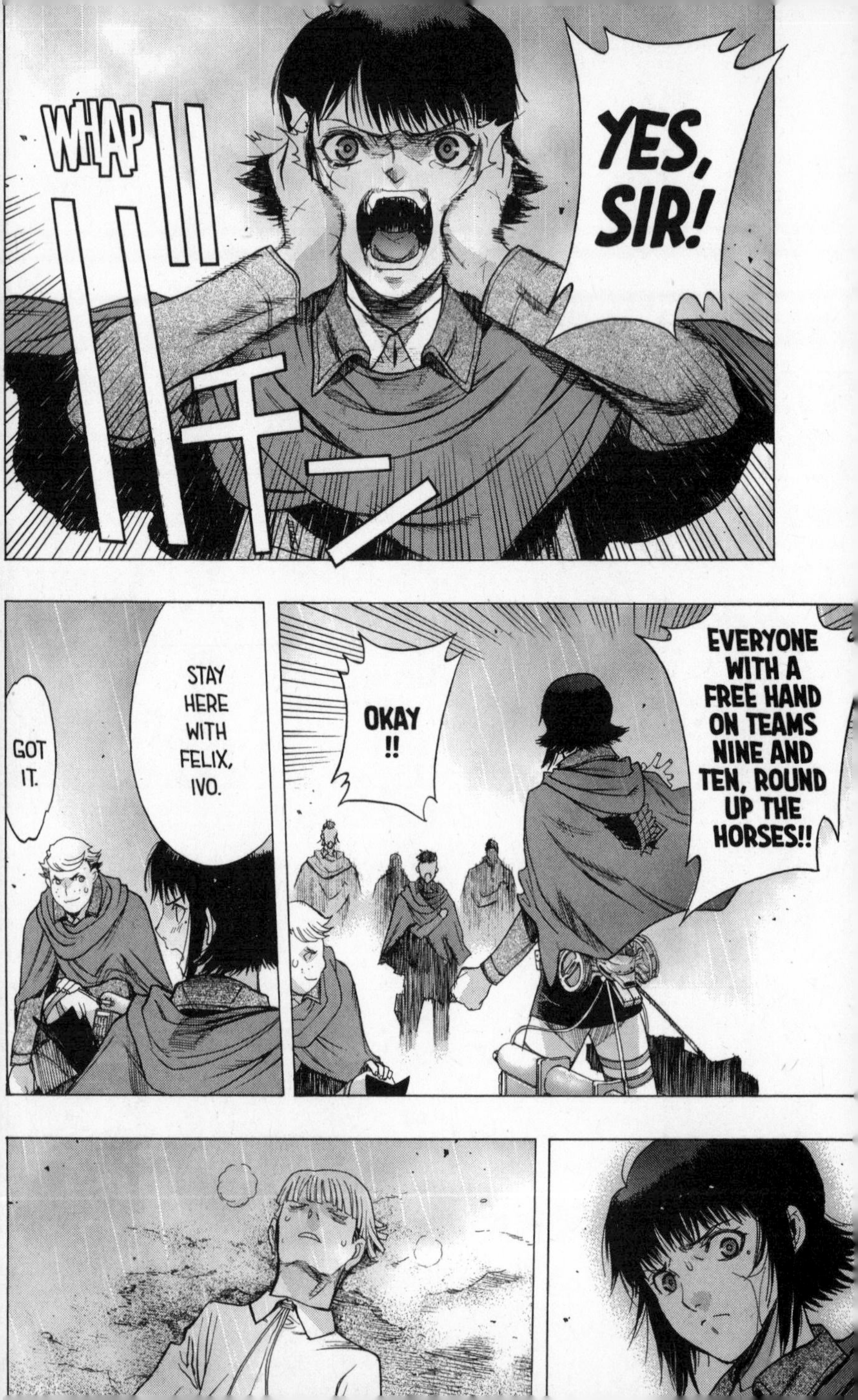
YES, SIR!
WHAP!!
EVERYONE WITH A FREE HAND ON TEAMS NINE AND TEN, ROUND UP THE HORSES!!
OKAY !!
STAY HERE WITH FELIX, IVO.
GOT IT.

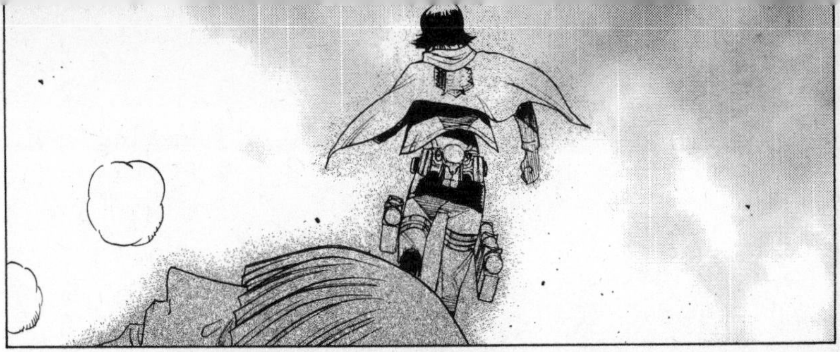

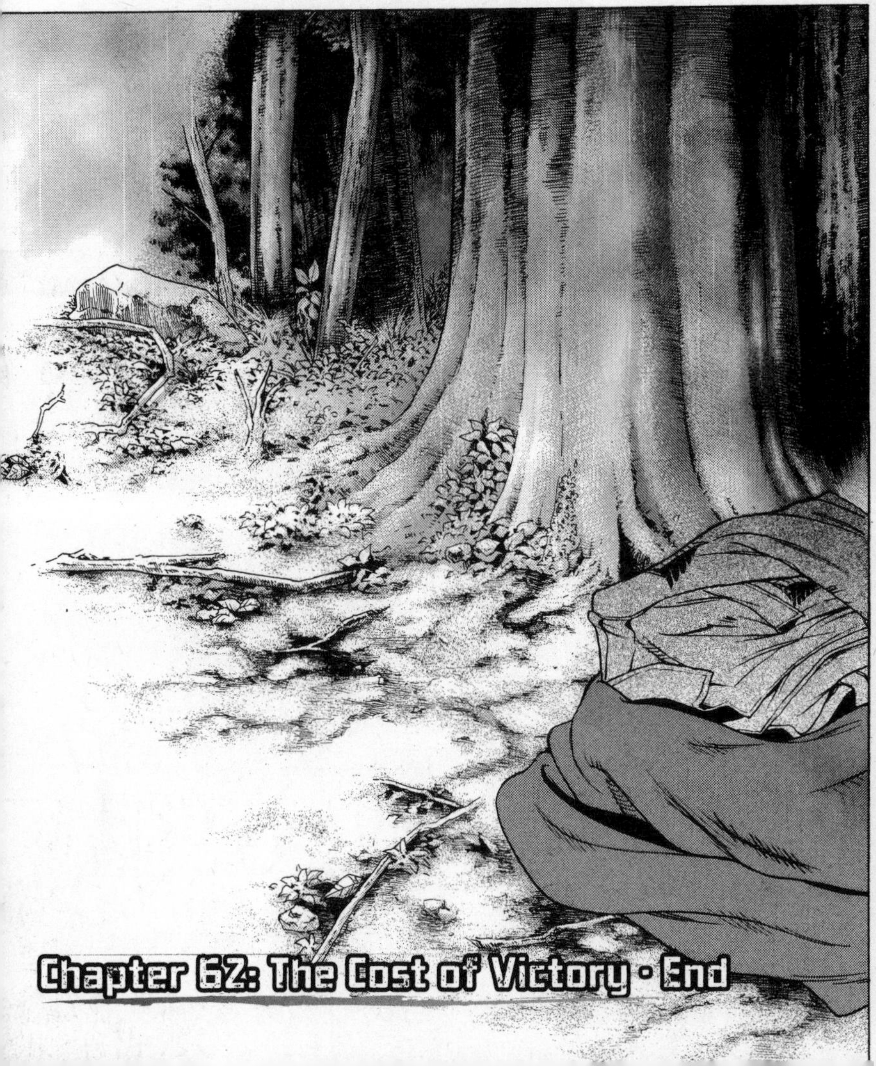
Chapter 62: The Cost of Victory • End

ATTACK on TITAN

BEFORE THE FALL

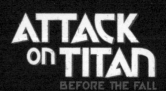

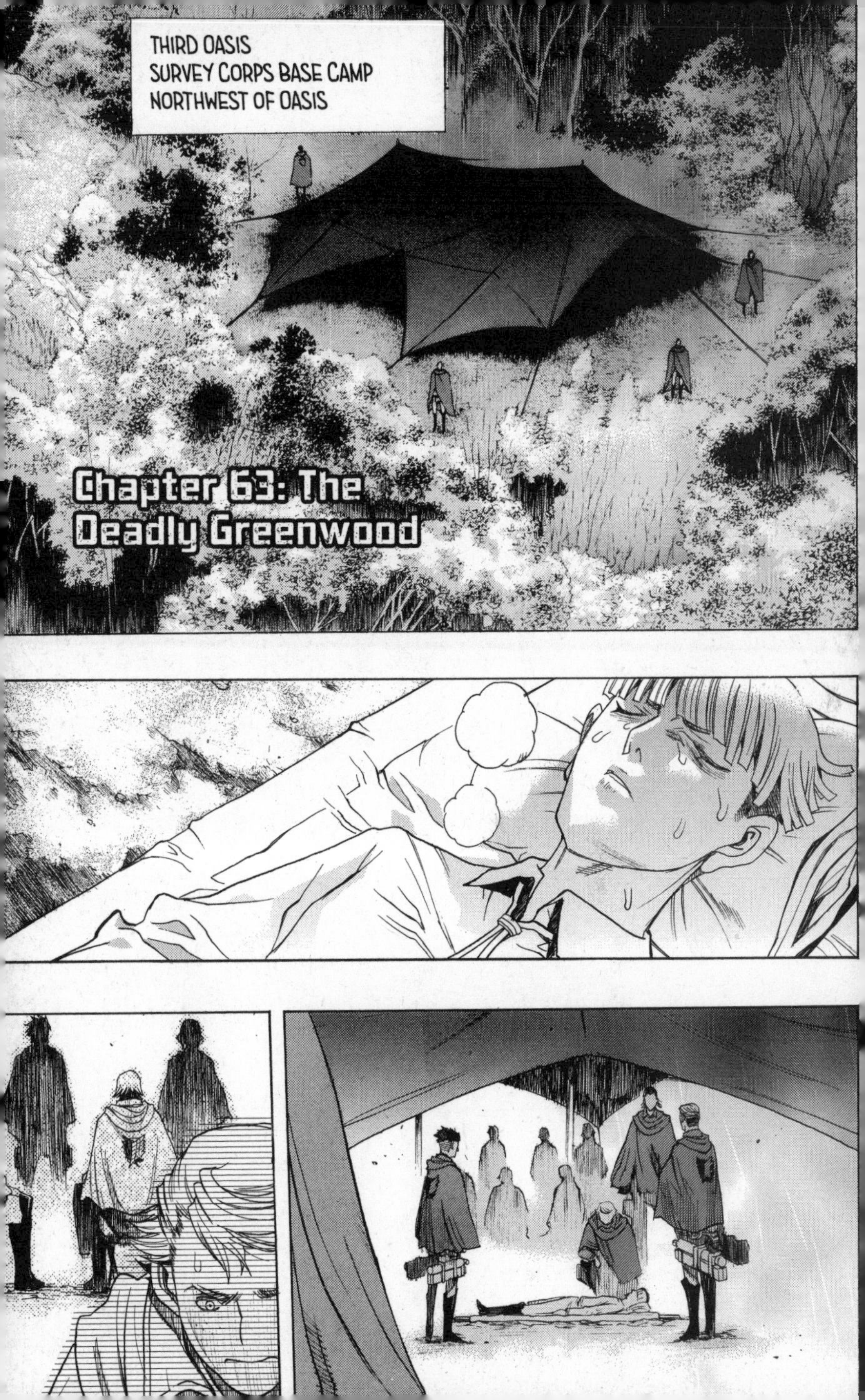
THIRD OASIS
SURVEY CORPS BASE CAMP
NORTHWEST OF OASIS
Chapter 63: The Deadly Greenwood

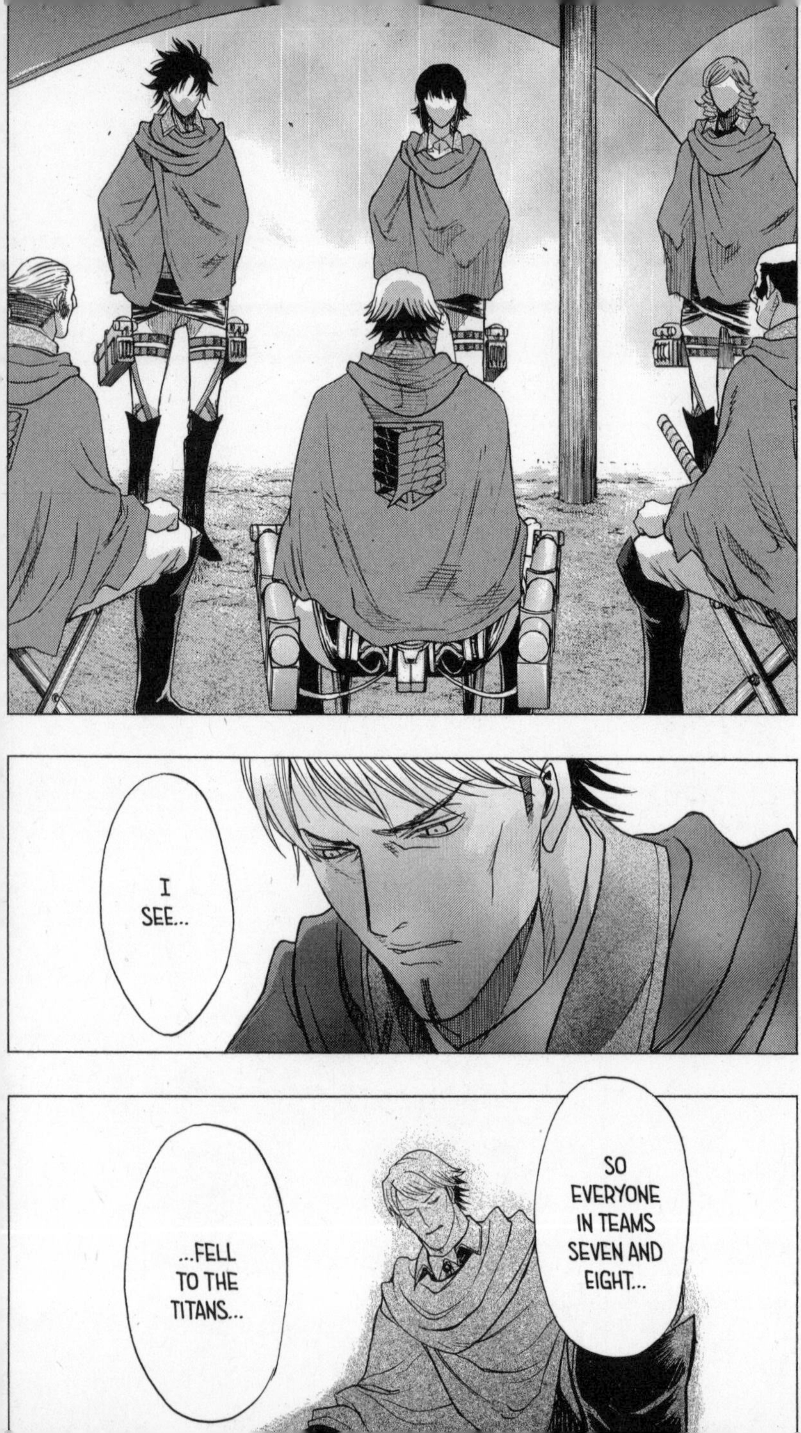
I SEE...
SO EVERYONE IN TEAMS SEVEN AND EIGHT...
...FELL TO THE TITANS...

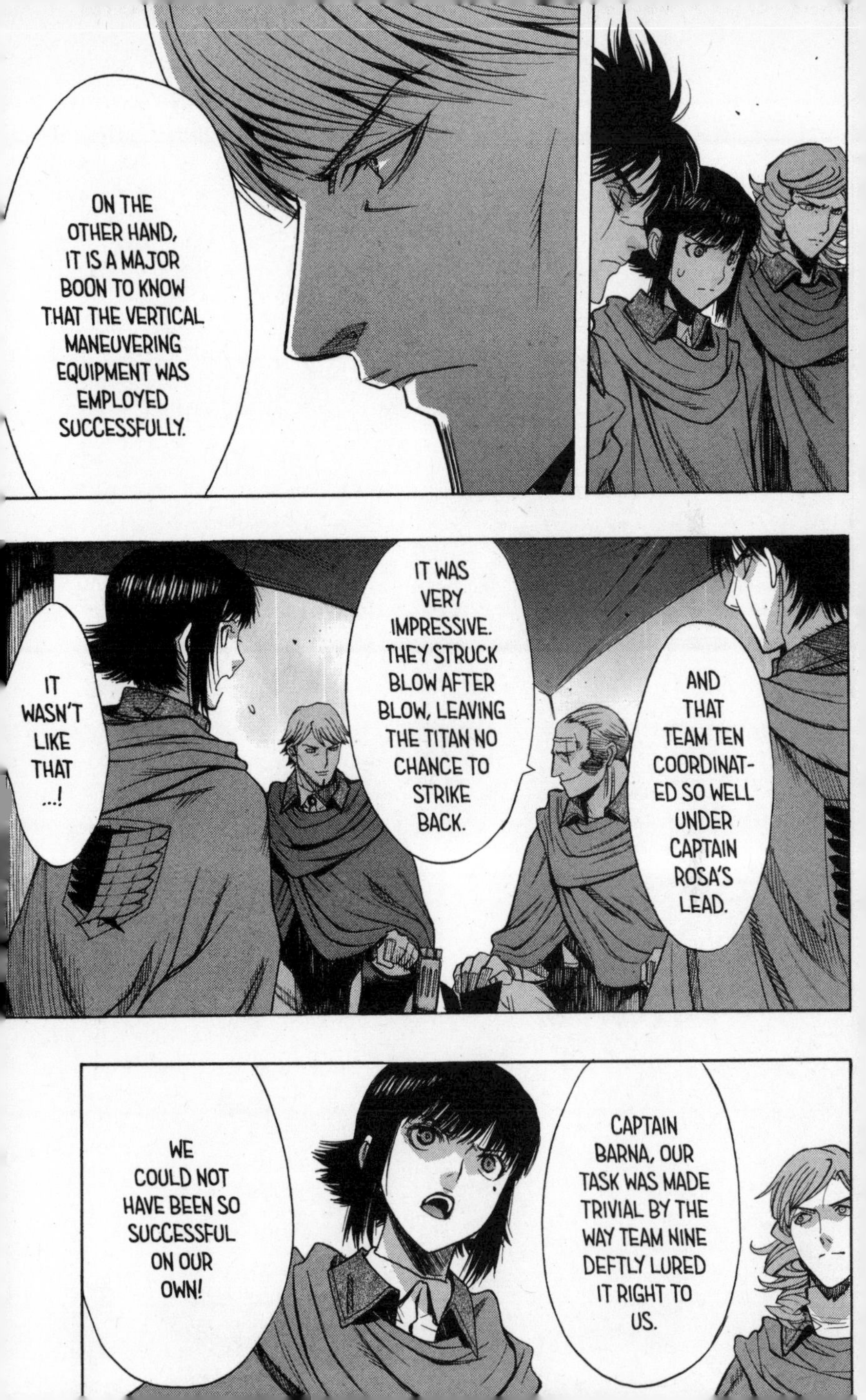
ON THE OTHER HAND, IT IS A MAJOR BOON TO KNOW THAT THE VERTICAL MANEUVERING EQUIPMENT WAS EMPLOYED SUCCESSFULLY.
IT WAS VERY IMPRESSIVE. THEY STRUCK BLOW AFTER BLOW, LEAVING THE TITAN NO CHANCE TO STRIKE BACK.
AND THAT TEAM TEN COORDINAT-ED SO WELL UNDER CAPTAIN ROSA'S LEAD.
IT WASN'T LIKE THAT ...!
CAPTAIN BARNA, OUR TASK WAS MADE TRIVIAL BY THE WAY TEAM NINE DEFTLY LURED IT RIGHT TO US.
WE COULD NOT HAVE BEEN SO SUCCESSFUL ON OUR OWN!

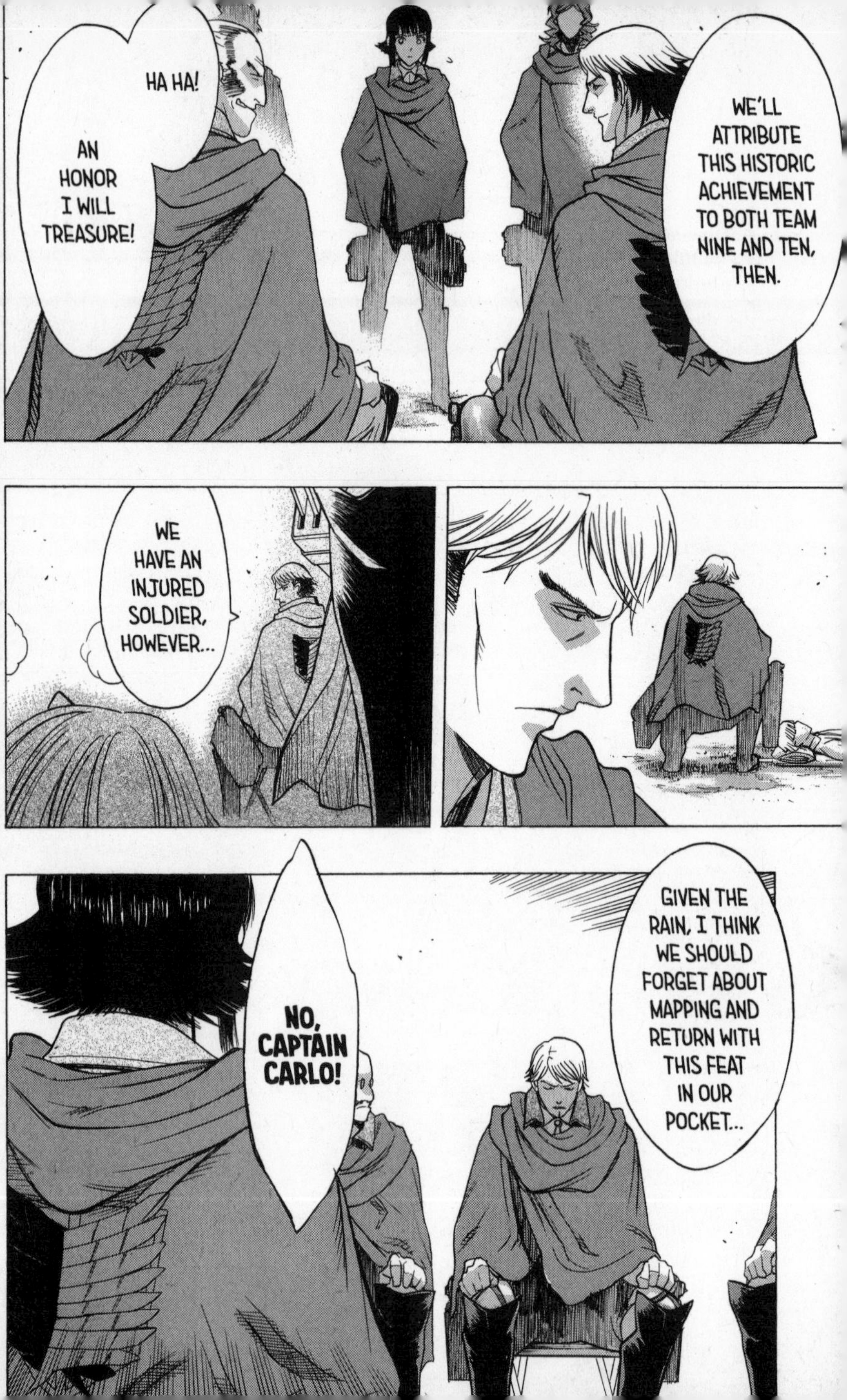
WE'LL ATTRIBUTE THIS HISTORIC ACHIEVEMENT TO BOTH TEAM NINE AND TEN, THEN.
HA HA!
AN HONOR I WILL TREASURE!
WE HAVE AN INJURED SOLDIER, HOWEVER...
GIVEN THE RAIN, I THINK WE SHOULD FORGET ABOUT MAPPING AND RETURN WITH THIS FEAT IN OUR POCKET...
NO, CAPTAIN CARLO!

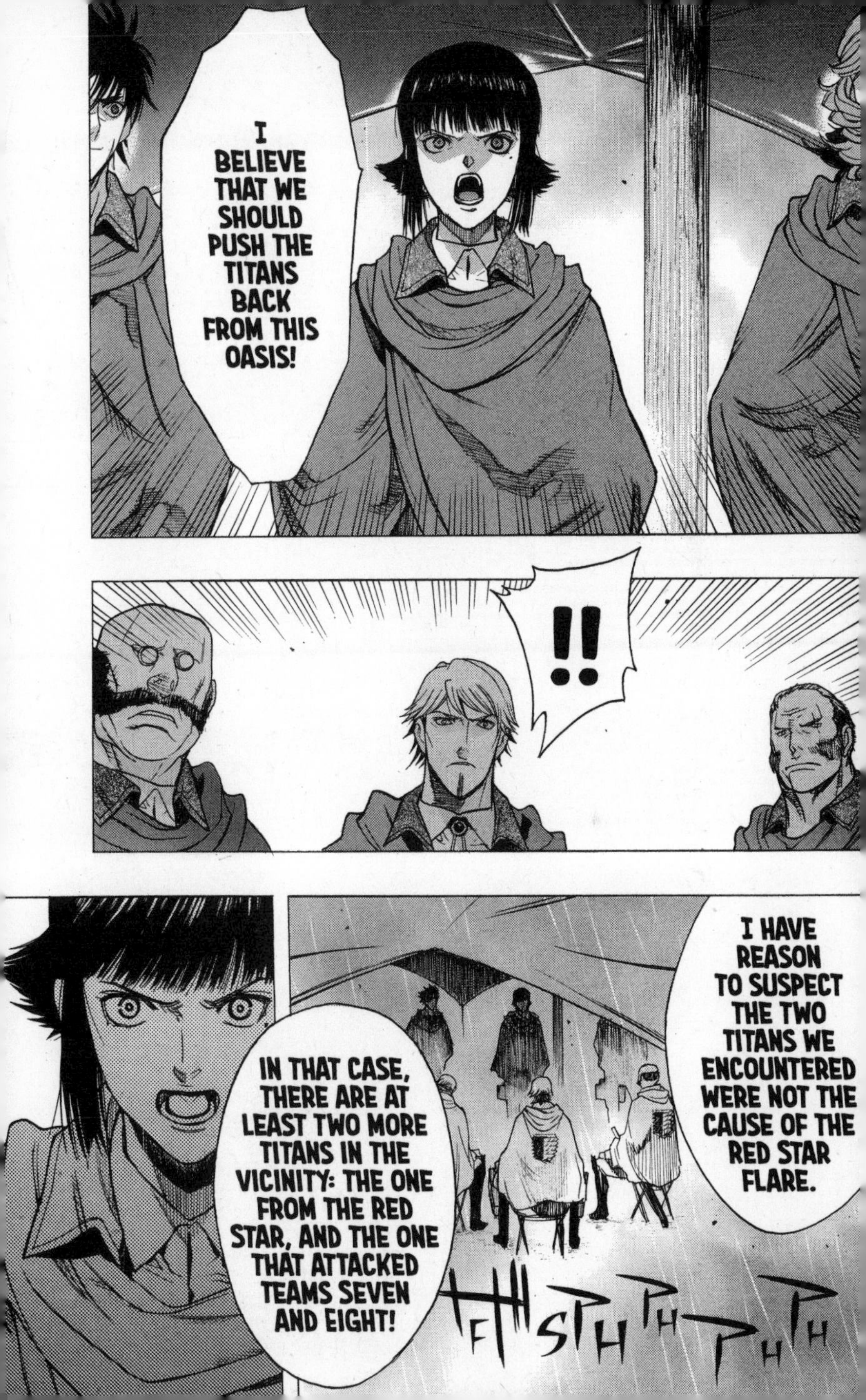
I BELIEVE THAT WE SHOULD PUSH THE TITANS BACK FROM THIS OASIS!
!!
I HAVE REASON TO SUSPECT THE TWO TITANS WE ENCOUNTERED WERE NOT THE CAUSE OF THE RED STAR FLARE.
IN THAT CASE, THERE ARE AT LEAST TWO MORE TITANS IN THE VICINITY: THE ONE FROM THE RED STAR, AND THE ONE THAT ATTACKED TEAMS SEVEN AND EIGHT!

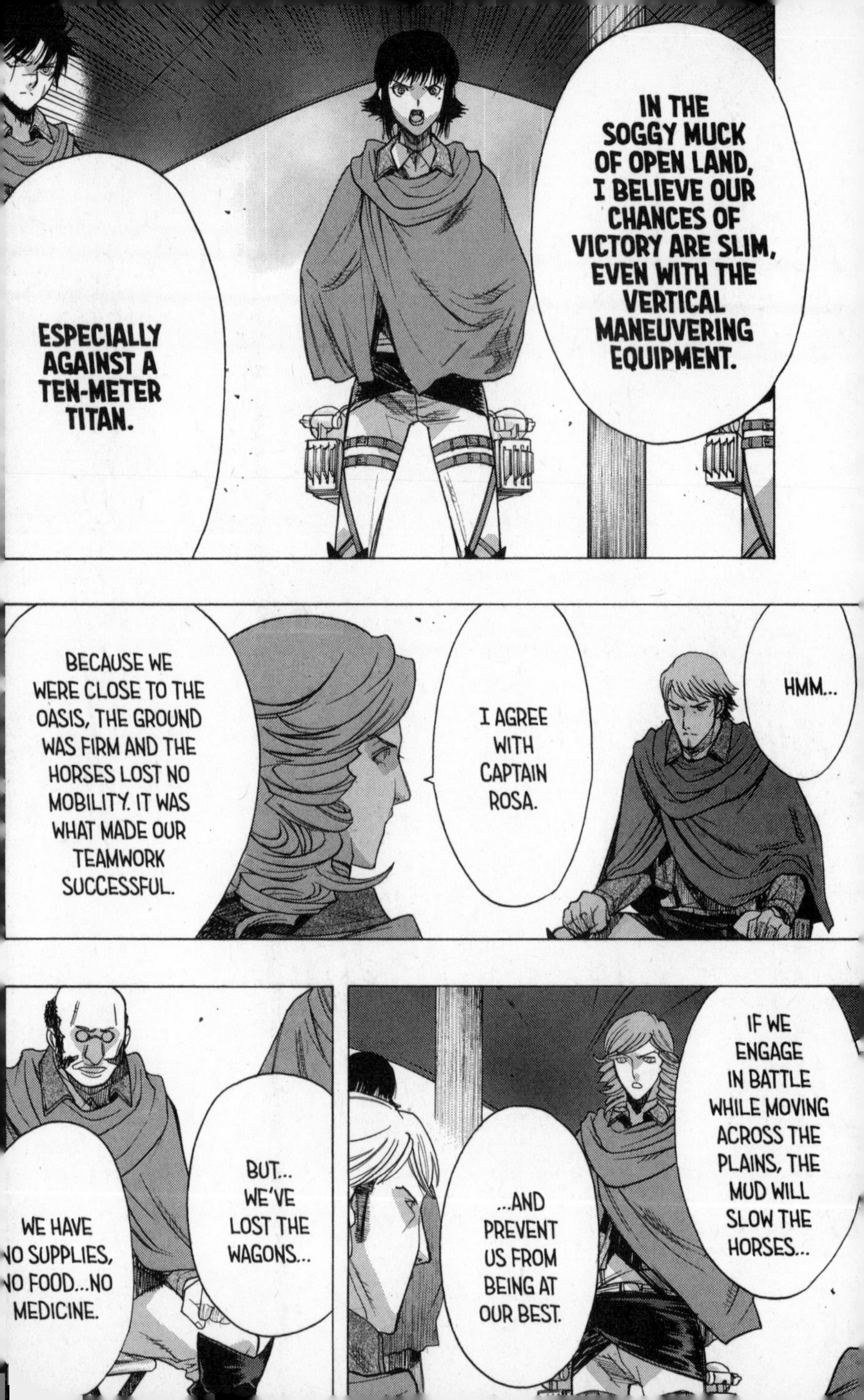
IN THE SOGGY MUCK OF OPEN LAND, I BELIEVE OUR CHANCES OF VICTORY ARE SLIM, EVEN WITH THE VERTICAL MANEUVERING EQUIPMENT.
ESPECIALLY AGAINST A TEN-METER TITAN.
HMM...
I AGREE WITH CAPTAIN ROSA.
BECAUSE WE WERE CLOSE TO THE OASIS, THE GROUND WAS FIRM AND THE HORSES LOST NO MOBILITY. IT WAS WHAT MADE OUR TEAMWORK SUCCESSFUL.
IF WE ENGAGE IN BATTLE WHILE MOVING ACROSS THE PLAINS, THE MUD WILL SLOW THE HORSES...
...AND PREVENT US FROM BEING AT OUR BEST.
BUT... WE'VE LOST THE WAGONS...
WE HAVE NO SUPPLIES, NO FOOD...NO MEDICINE.

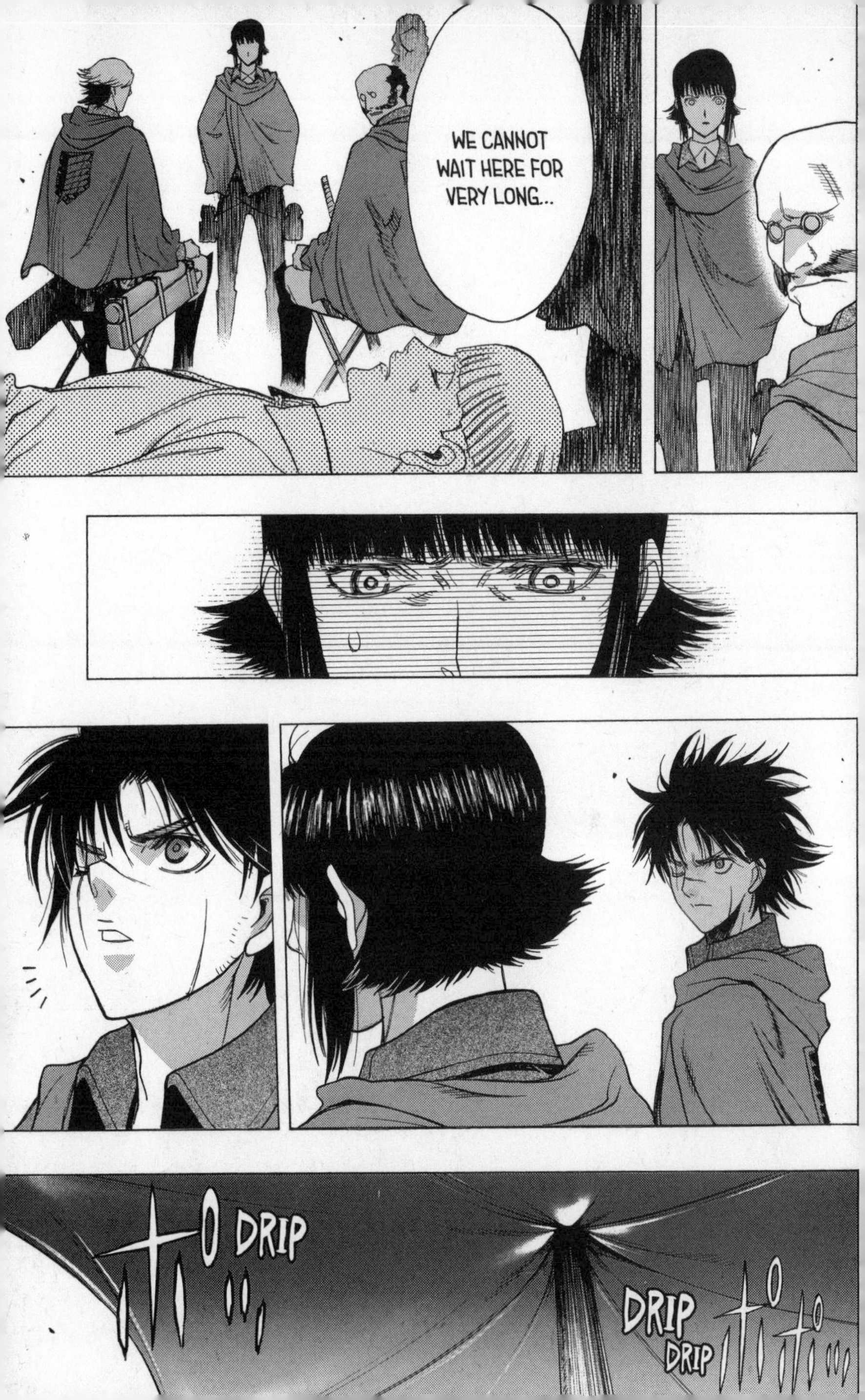
WE CANNOT WAIT HERE FOR VERY LONG...
DRIP
DRIP
DRIP

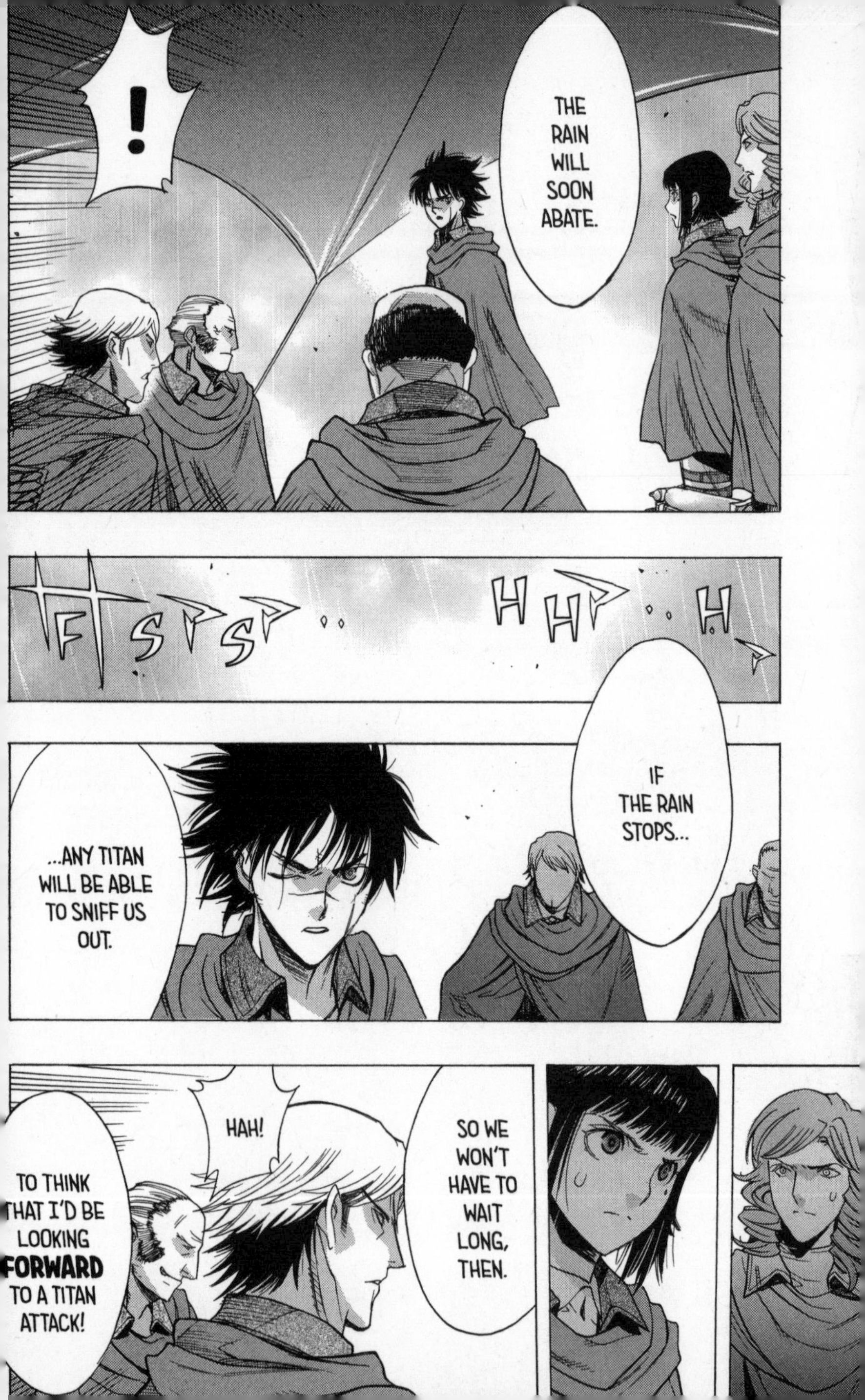
THE RAIN WILL SOON ABATE.
!
FSPSP.. HHP.. H.
IF THE RAIN STOPS...
...ANY TITAN WILL BE ABLE TO SNIFF US OUT.
SO WE WON'T HAVE TO WAIT LONG, THEN.
HAH!
TO THINK THAT I'D BE LOOKING **FORWARD** TO A TITAN ATTACK!

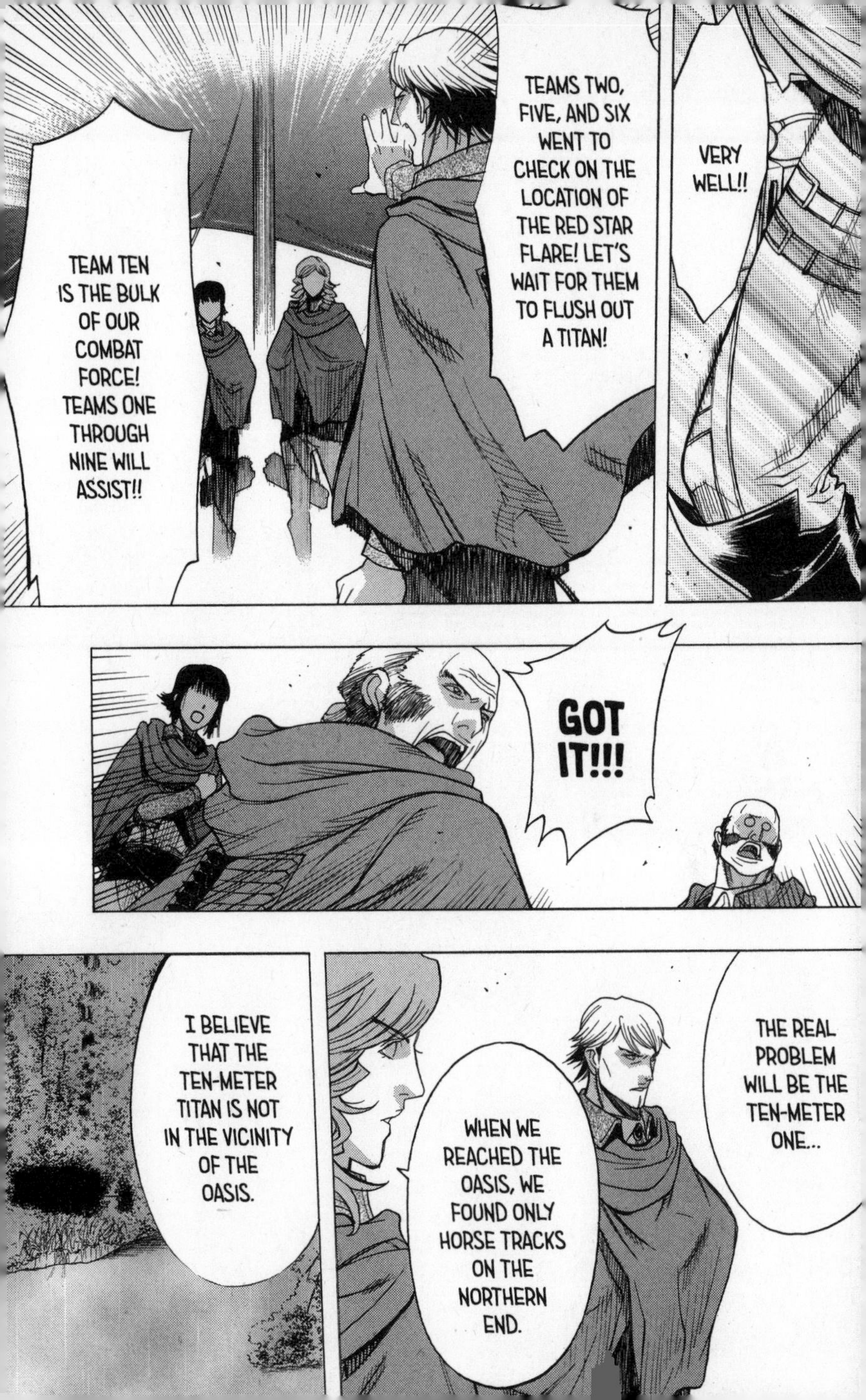
VERY WELL!!
TEAMS TWO, FIVE, AND SIX WENT TO CHECK ON THE LOCATION OF THE RED STAR FLARE! LET'S WAIT FOR THEM TO FLUSH OUT A TITAN!
TEAM TEN IS THE BULK OF OUR COMBAT FORCE! TEAMS ONE THROUGH NINE WILL ASSIST!!
GOT IT!!!
THE REAL PROBLEM WILL BE THE TEN-METER ONE...
WHEN WE REACHED THE OASIS, WE FOUND ONLY HORSE TRACKS ON THE NORTHERN END.
I BELIEVE THAT THE TEN-METER TITAN IS NOT IN THE VICINITY OF THE OASIS.

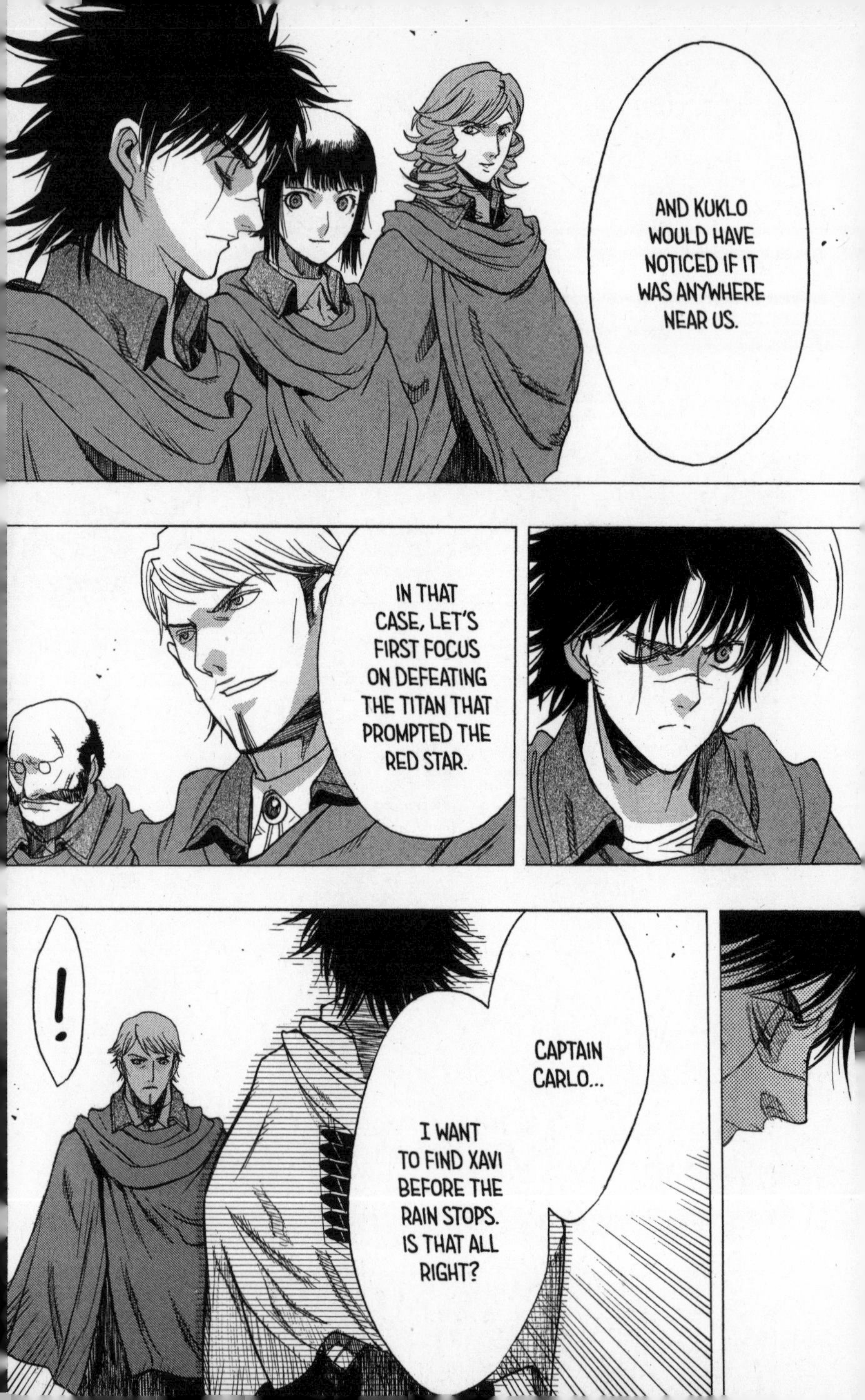
AND KUKLO WOULD HAVE NOTICED IF IT WAS ANYWHERE NEAR US.
IN THAT CASE, LET'S FIRST FOCUS ON DEFEATING THE TITAN THAT PROMPTED THE RED STAR.
CAPTAIN CARLO...
I WANT TO FIND XAVI BEFORE THE RAIN STOPS. IS THAT ALL RIGHT?
!

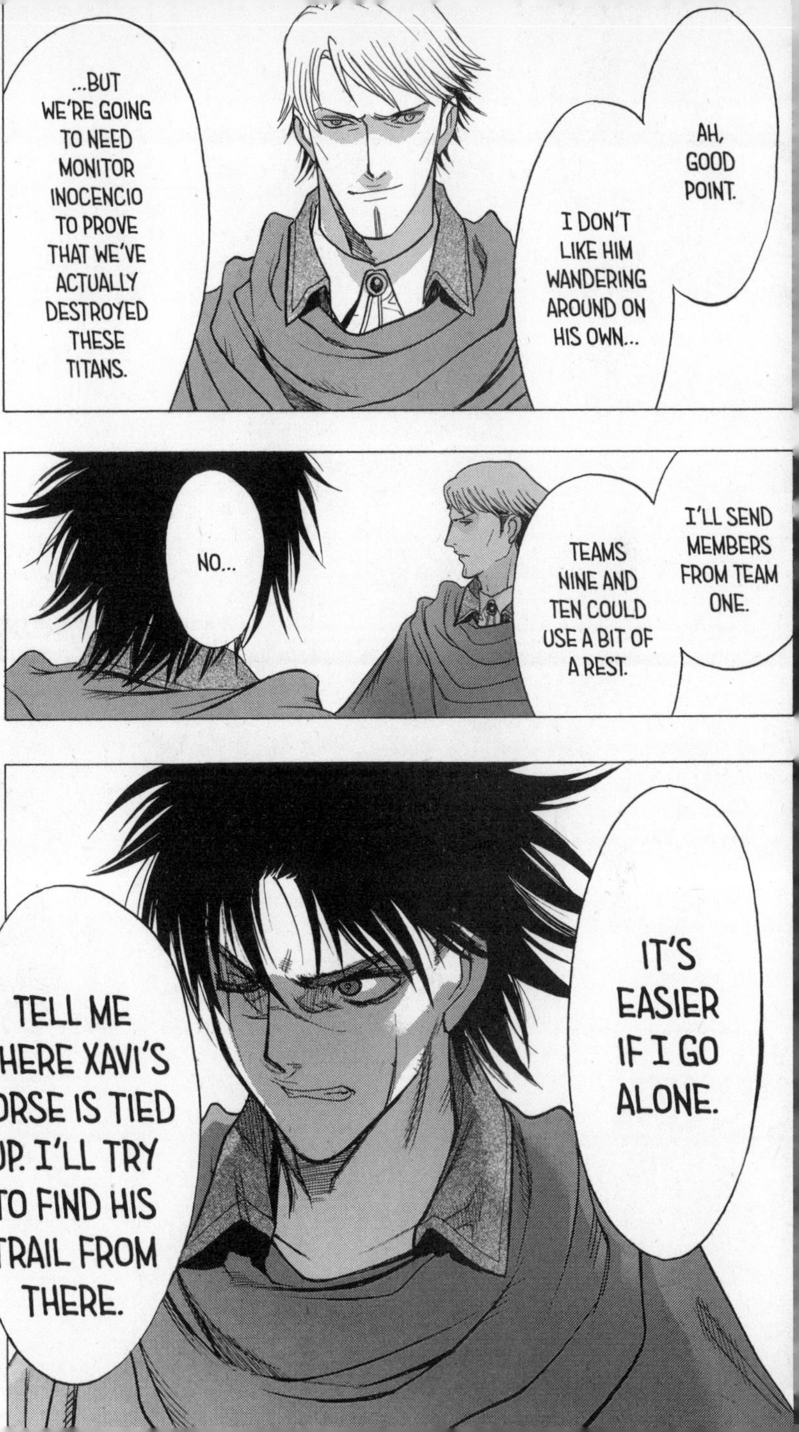
AH, GOOD POINT.
I DON'T LIKE HIM WANDERING AROUND ON HIS OWN...
...BUT WE'RE GOING TO NEED MONITOR INOCENCIO TO PROVE THAT WE'VE ACTUALLY DESTROYED THESE TITANS.
I'LL SEND MEMBERS FROM TEAM ONE.
TEAMS NINE AND TEN COULD USE A BIT OF A REST.
NO...
IT'S EASIER IF I GO ALONE.
TELL ME WHERE XAVI'S HORSE IS TIED UP. I'LL TRY TO FIND HIS TRAIL FROM THERE.

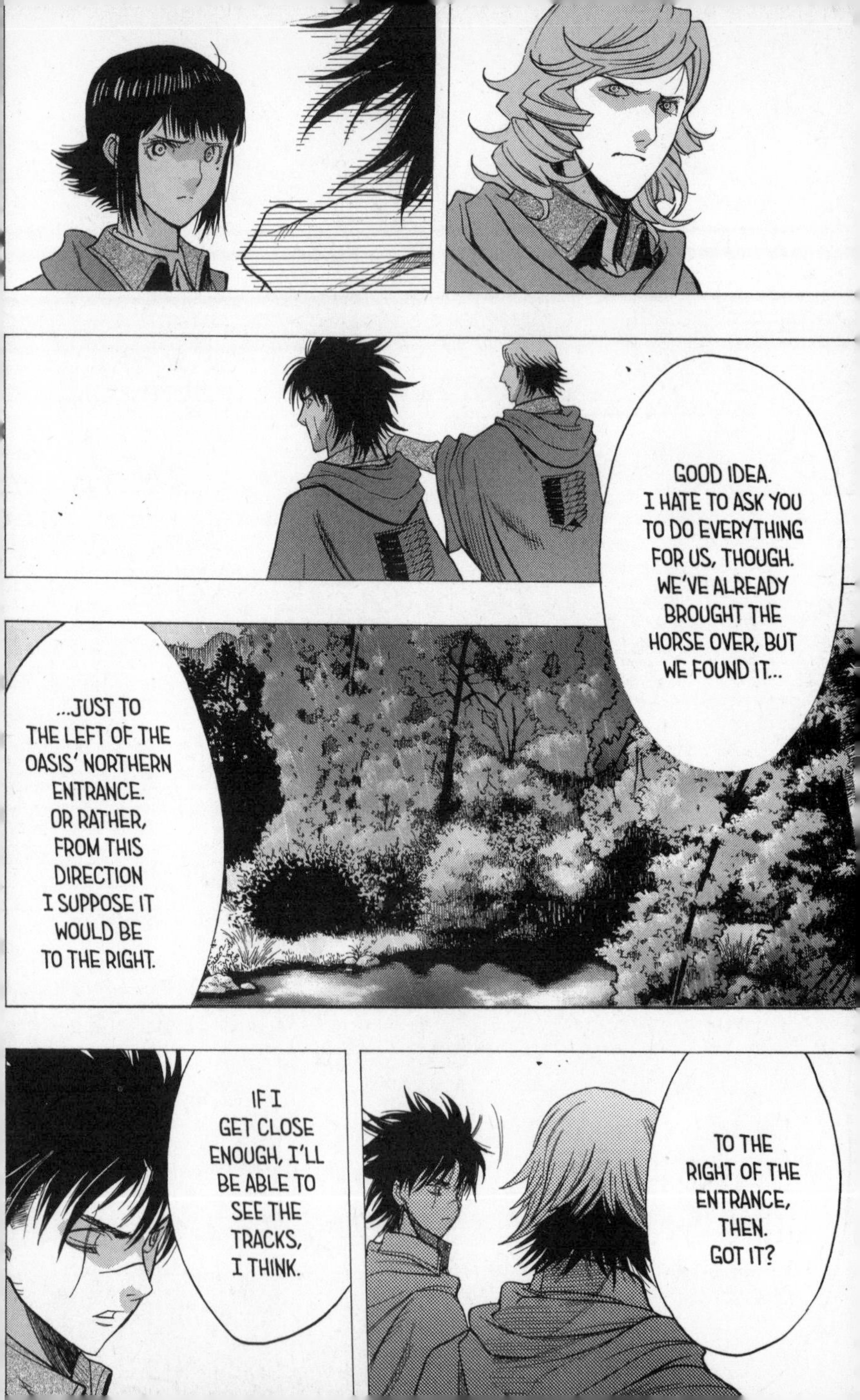
GOOD IDEA. I HATE TO ASK YOU TO DO EVERYTHING FOR US, THOUGH. WE'VE ALREADY BROUGHT THE HORSE OVER, BUT WE FOUND IT...
...JUST TO THE LEFT OF THE OASIS' NORTHERN ENTRANCE. OR RATHER, FROM THIS DIRECTION I SUPPOSE IT WOULD BE TO THE RIGHT.
TO THE RIGHT OF THE ENTRANCE, THEN. GOT IT?
IF I GET CLOSE ENOUGH, I'LL BE ABLE TO SEE THE TRACKS, I THINK.

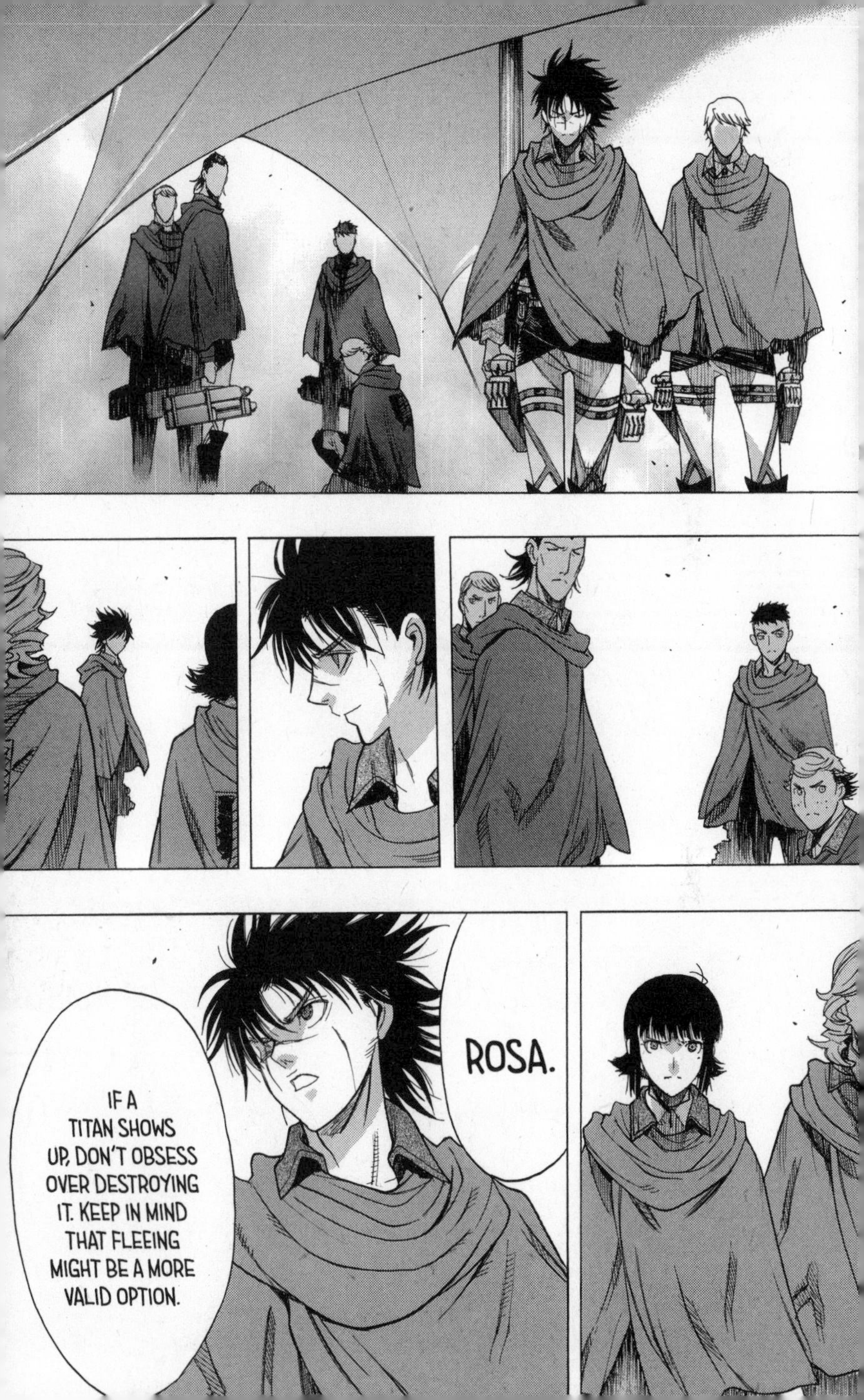
ROSA.
IF A TITAN SHOWS UP, DON'T OBSESS OVER DESTROYING IT. KEEP IN MIND THAT FLEEING MIGHT BE A MORE VALID OPTION.

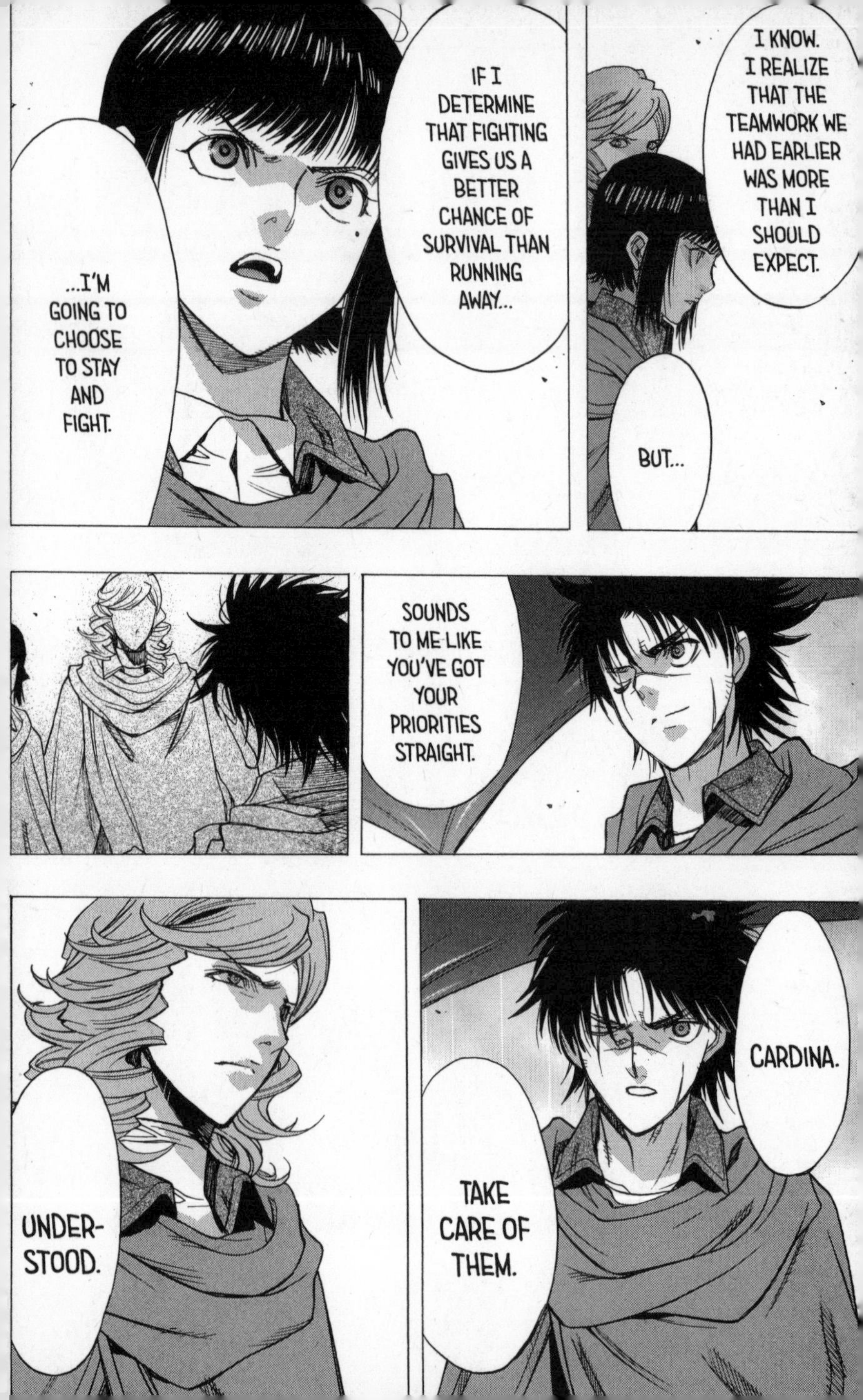
I KNOW. I REALIZE THAT THE TEAMWORK WE HAD EARLIER WAS MORE THAN I SHOULD EXPECT.
BUT...
IF I DETERMINE THAT FIGHTING GIVES US A BETTER CHANCE OF SURVIVAL THAN RUNNING AWAY...
...I'M GOING TO CHOOSE TO STAY AND FIGHT.
SOUNDS TO ME LIKE YOU'VE GOT YOUR PRIORITIES STRAIGHT.
CARDINA.
TAKE CARE OF THEM.
UNDER-STOOD.

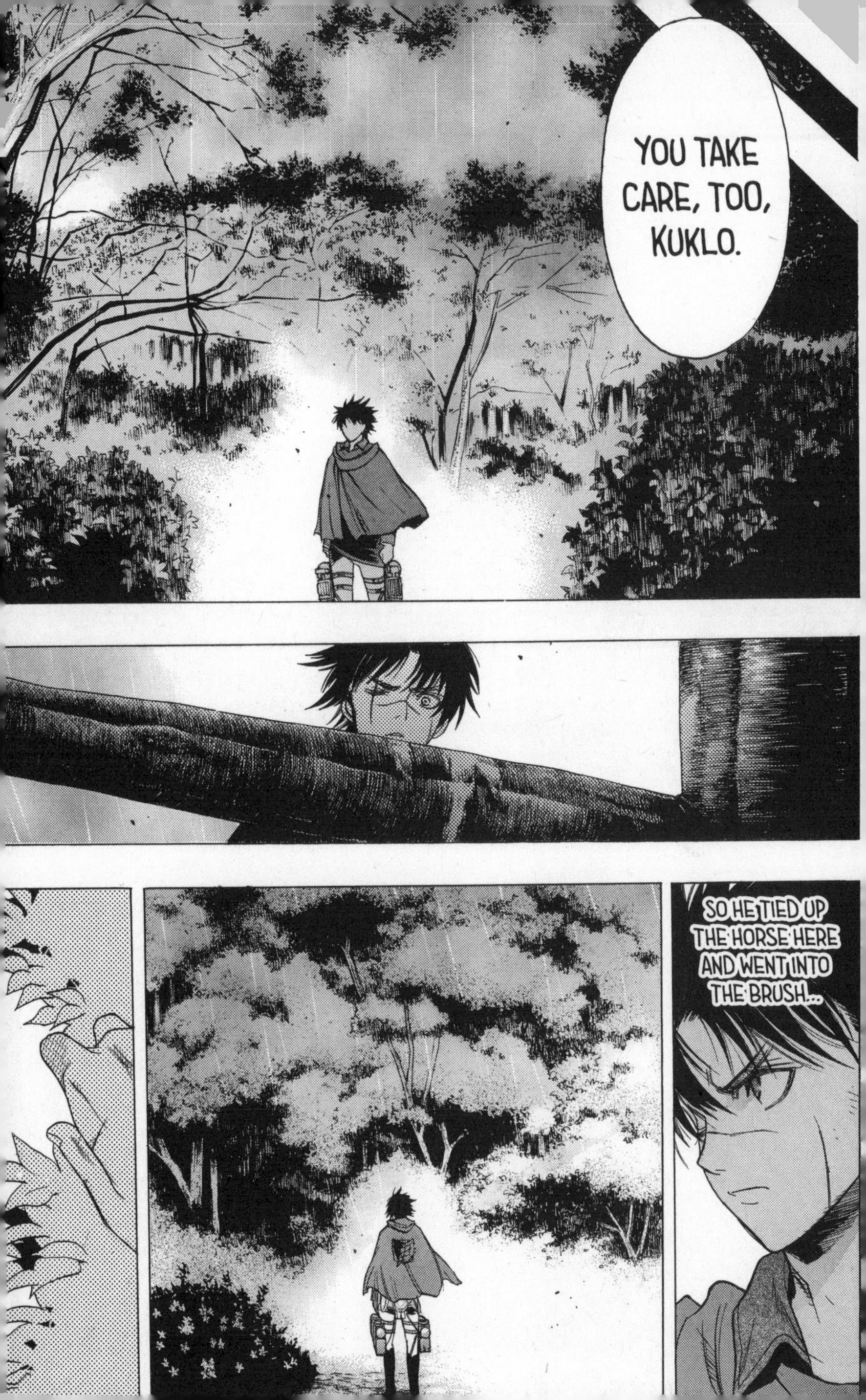
YOU TAKE CARE, TOO, KUKLO.
SO HE TIED UP THE HORSE HERE AND WENT INTO THE BRUSH...

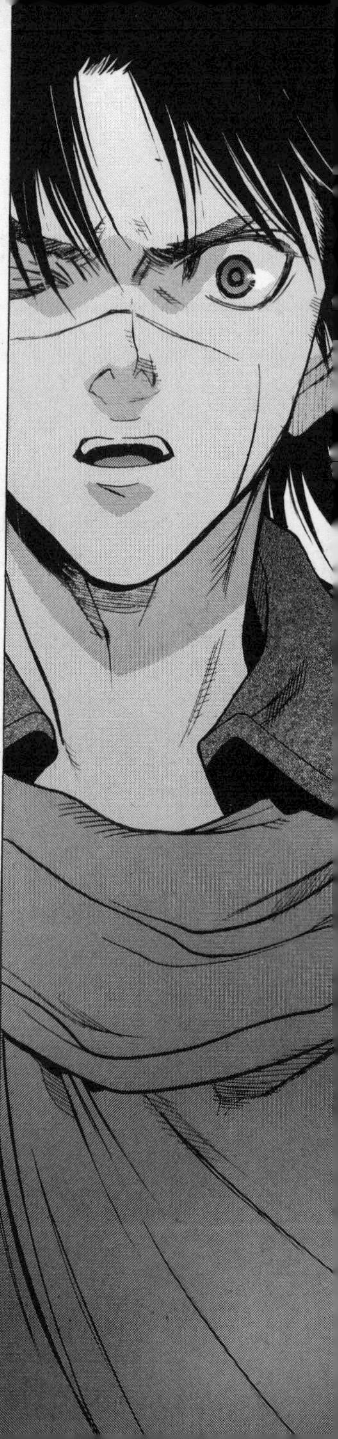
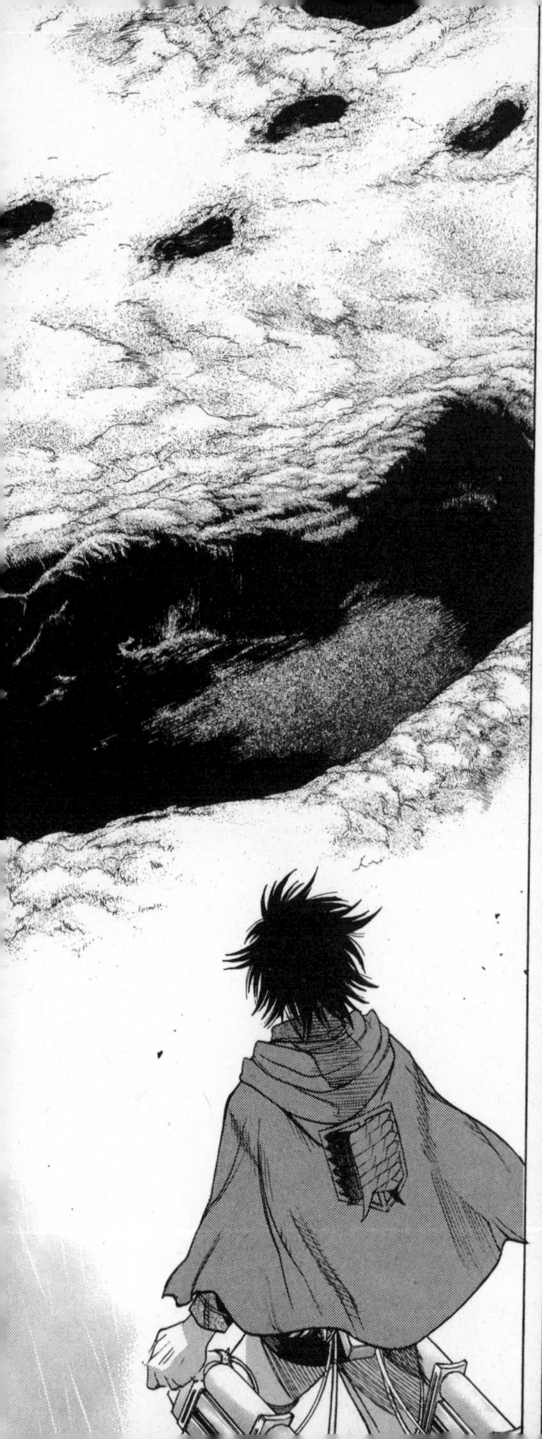

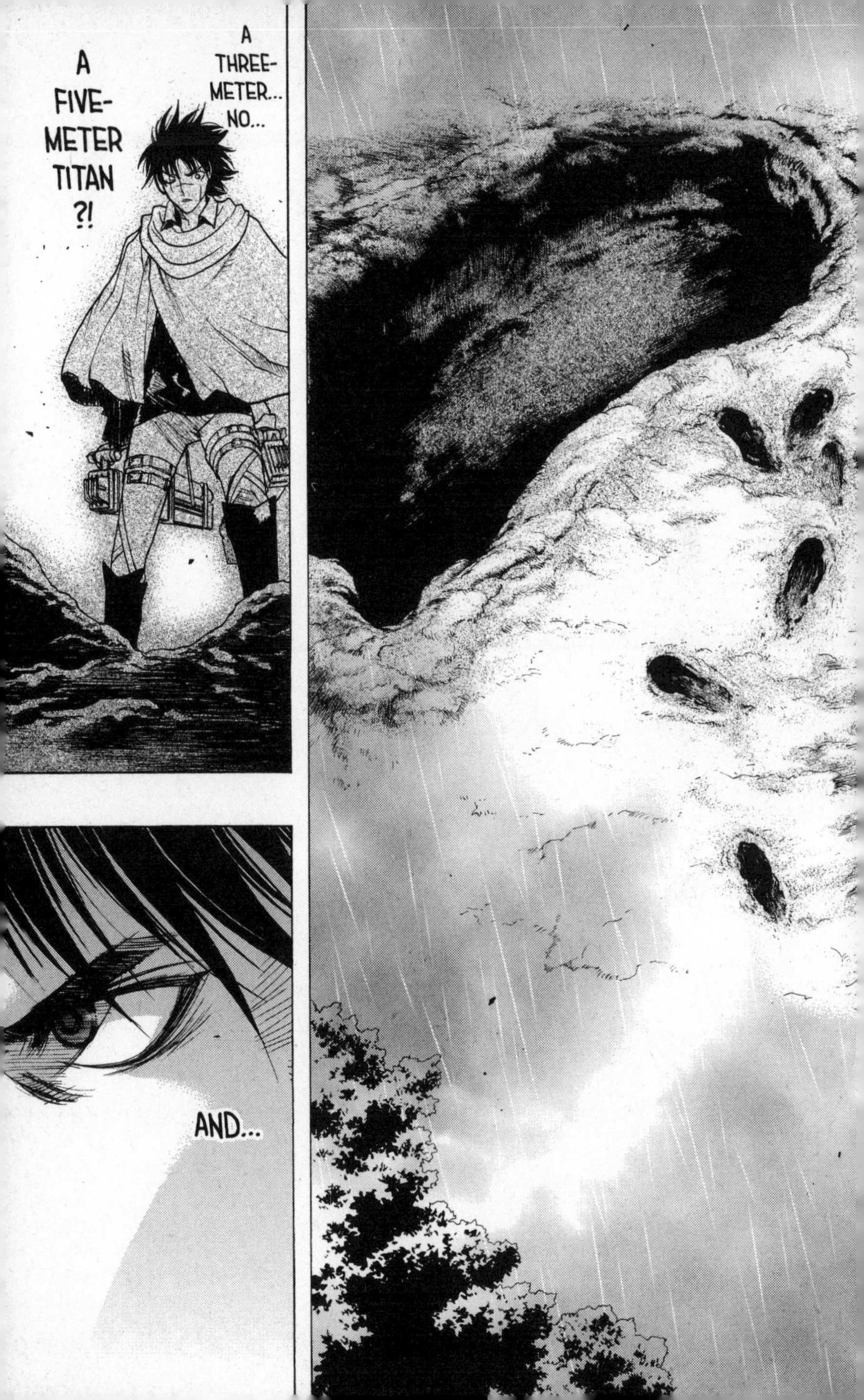
A THREE-METER... NO...
A FIVE-METER TITAN ?!
AND...

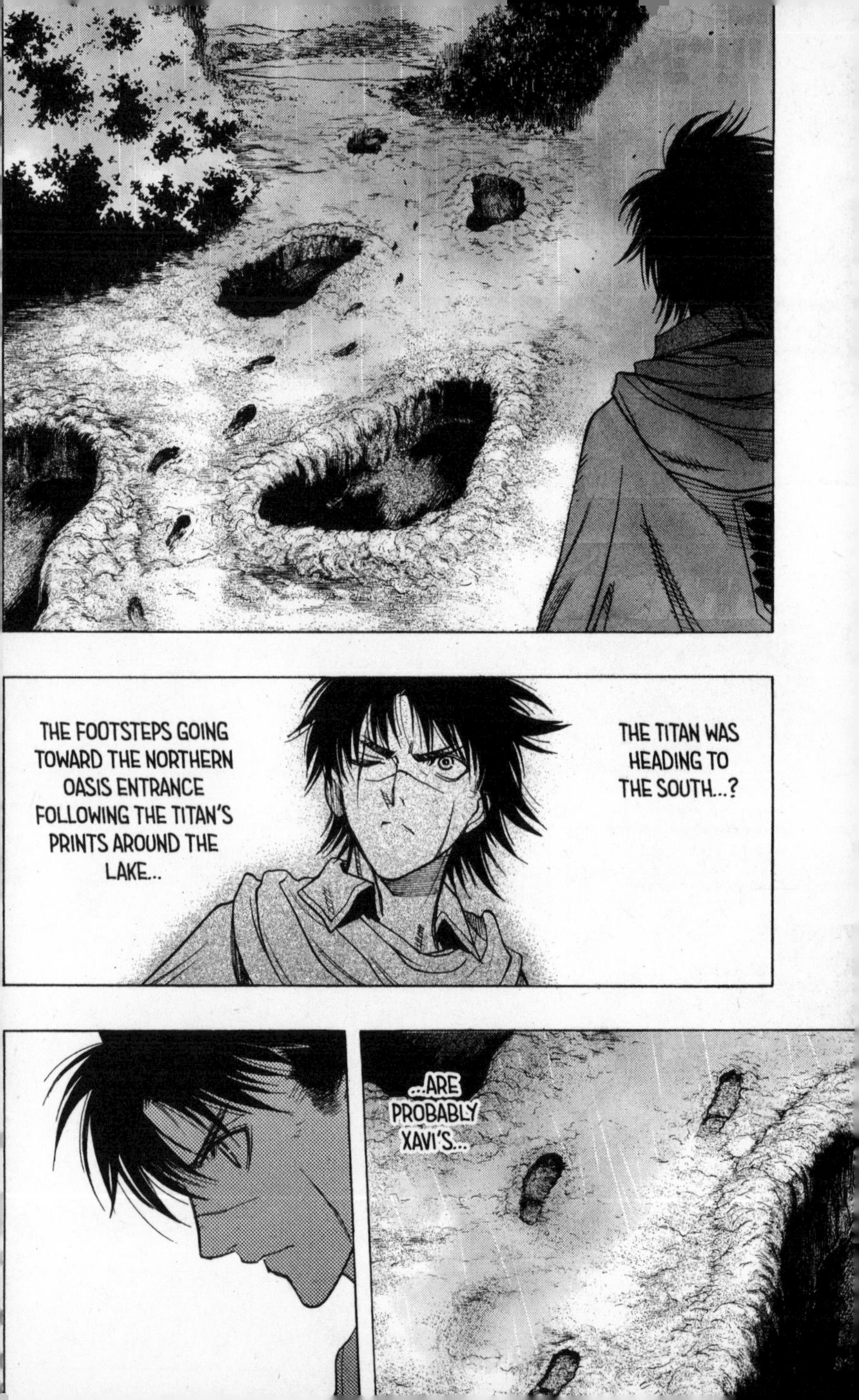
THE TITAN WAS HEADING TO THE SOUTH...?
THE FOOTSTEPS GOING TOWARD THE NORTHERN OASIS ENTRANCE FOLLOWING THE TITAN'S PRINTS AROUND THE LAKE...
...ARE PROBABLY XAVI'S...

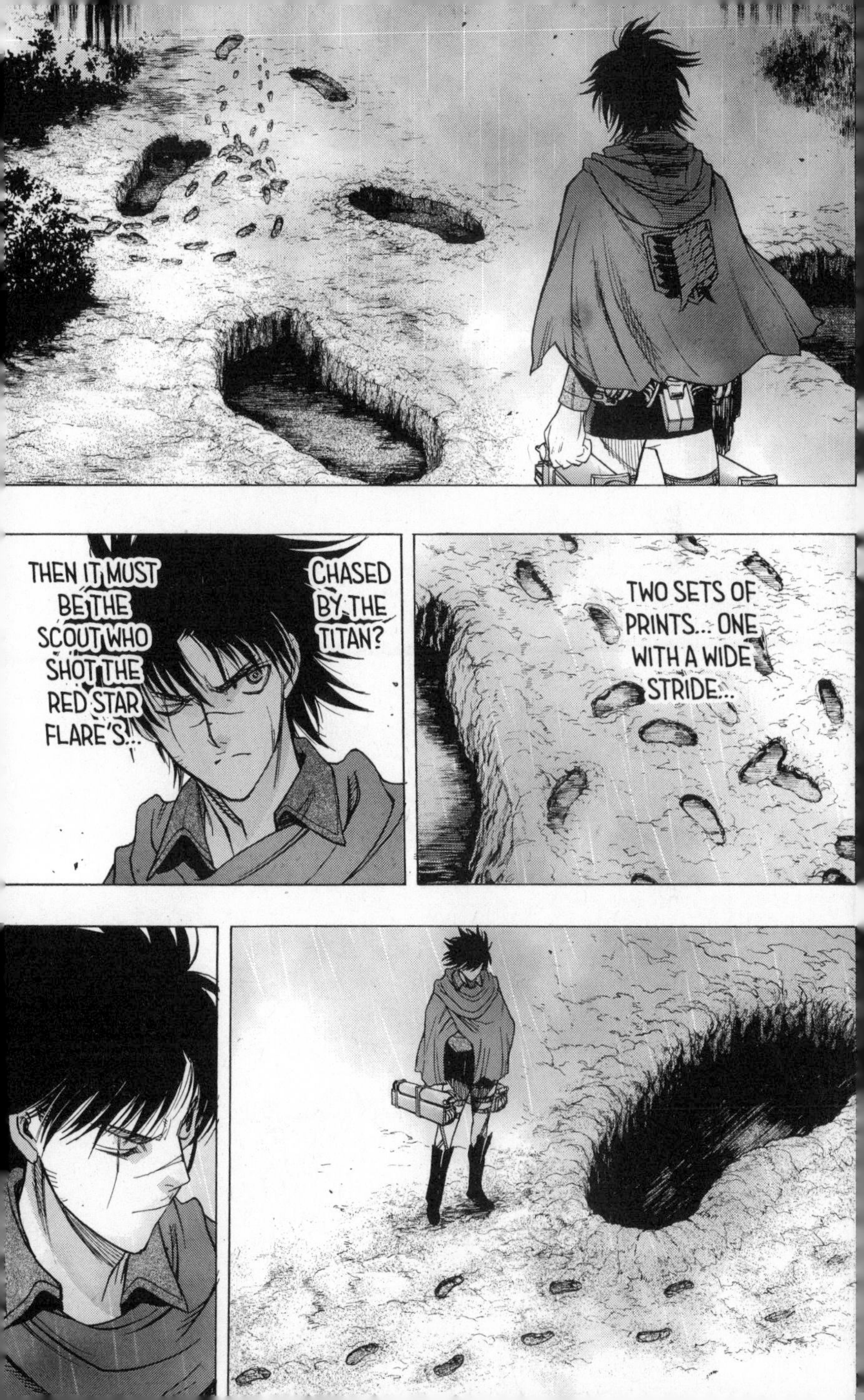
TWO SETS OF PRINTS... ONE WITH A WIDE STRIDE...
CHASED BY THE TITAN?
THEN IT MUST BE THE SCOUT WHO SHOT THE RED STAR FLARE'S...

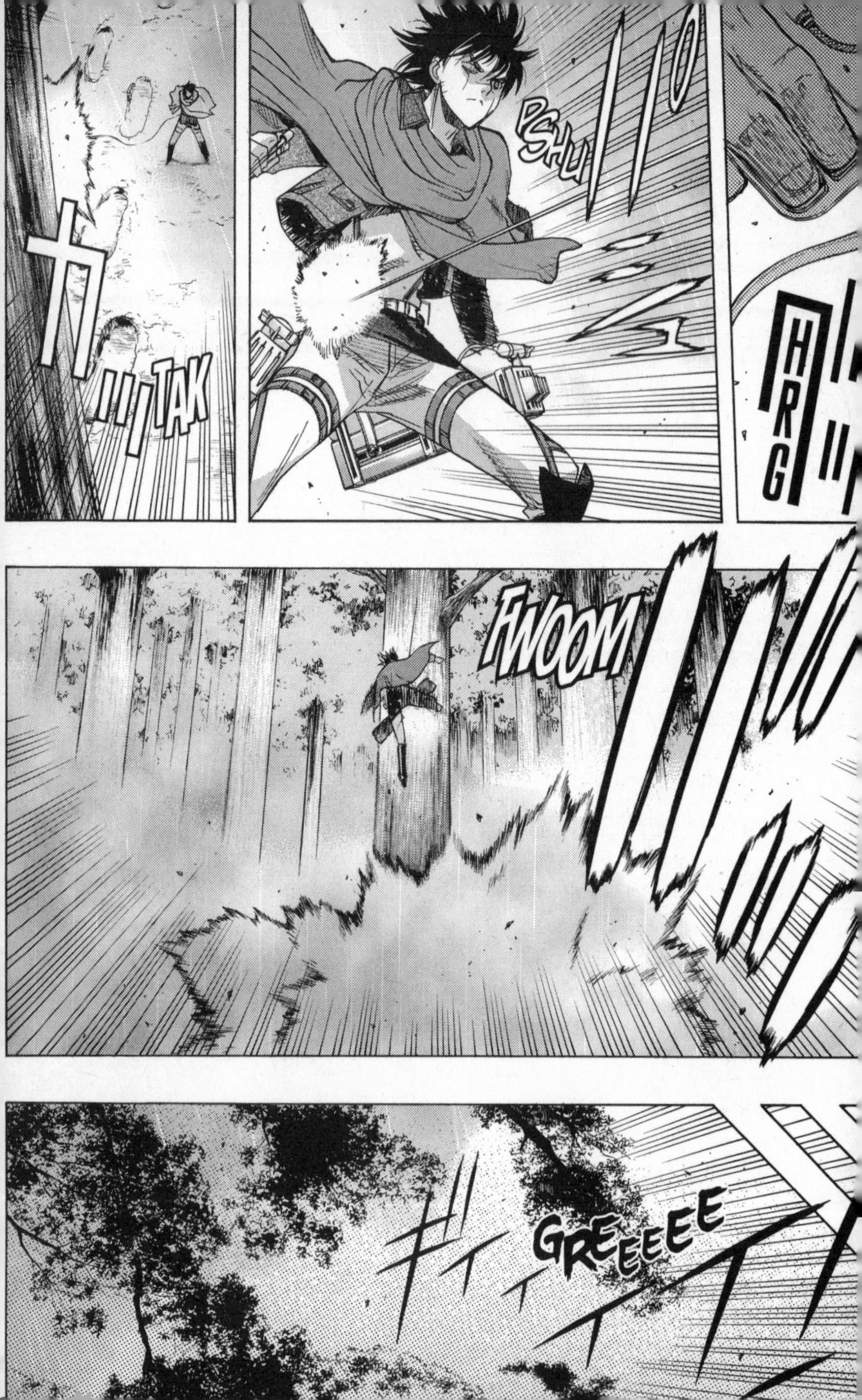
HRG
PSHU
TAK
FWOOM
GREEEEE

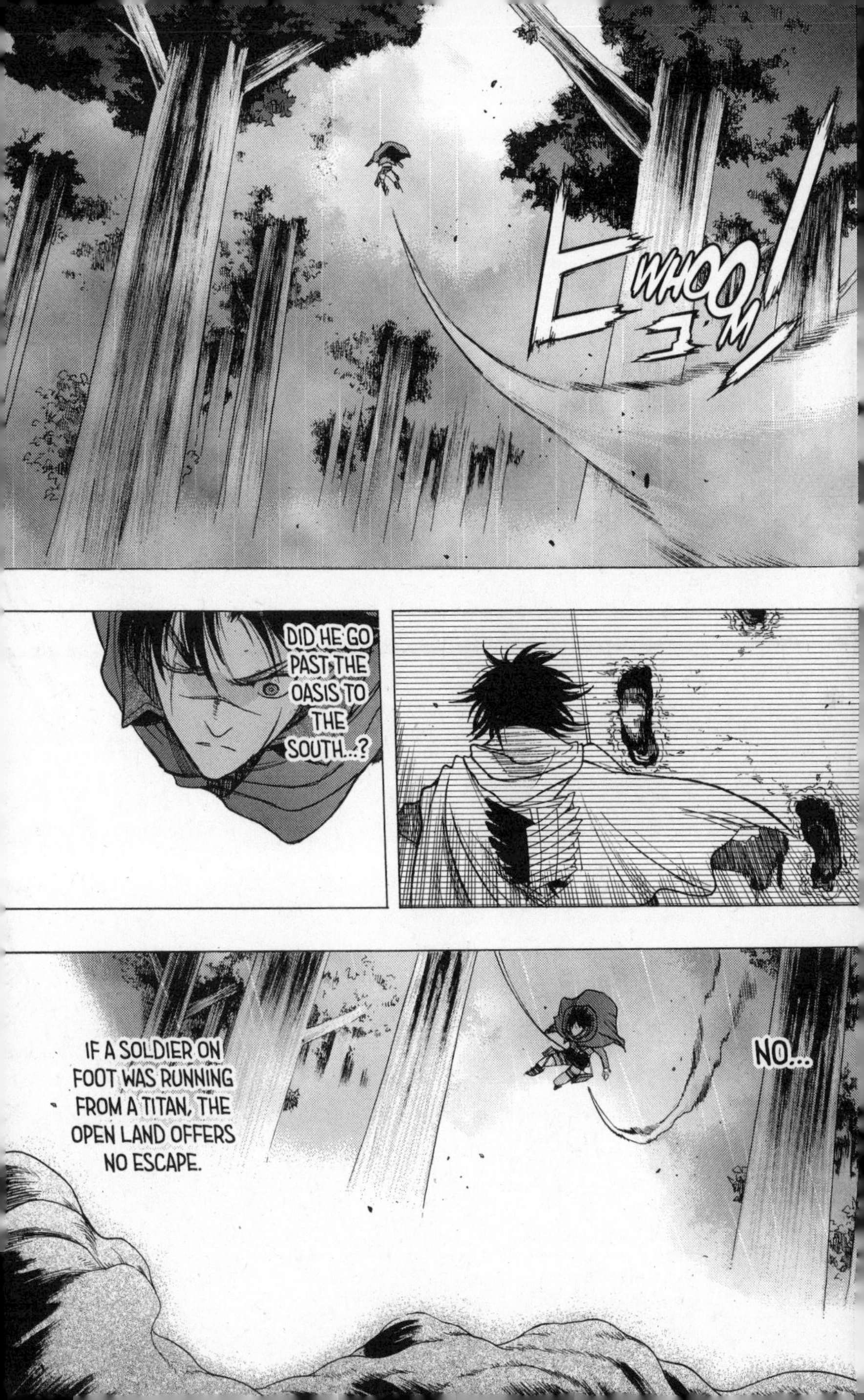
WHOOM
DID HE GO PAST THE OASIS TO THE SOUTH...?
NO...
IF A SOLDIER ON FOOT WAS RUNNING FROM A TITAN, THE OPEN LAND OFFERS NO ESCAPE.

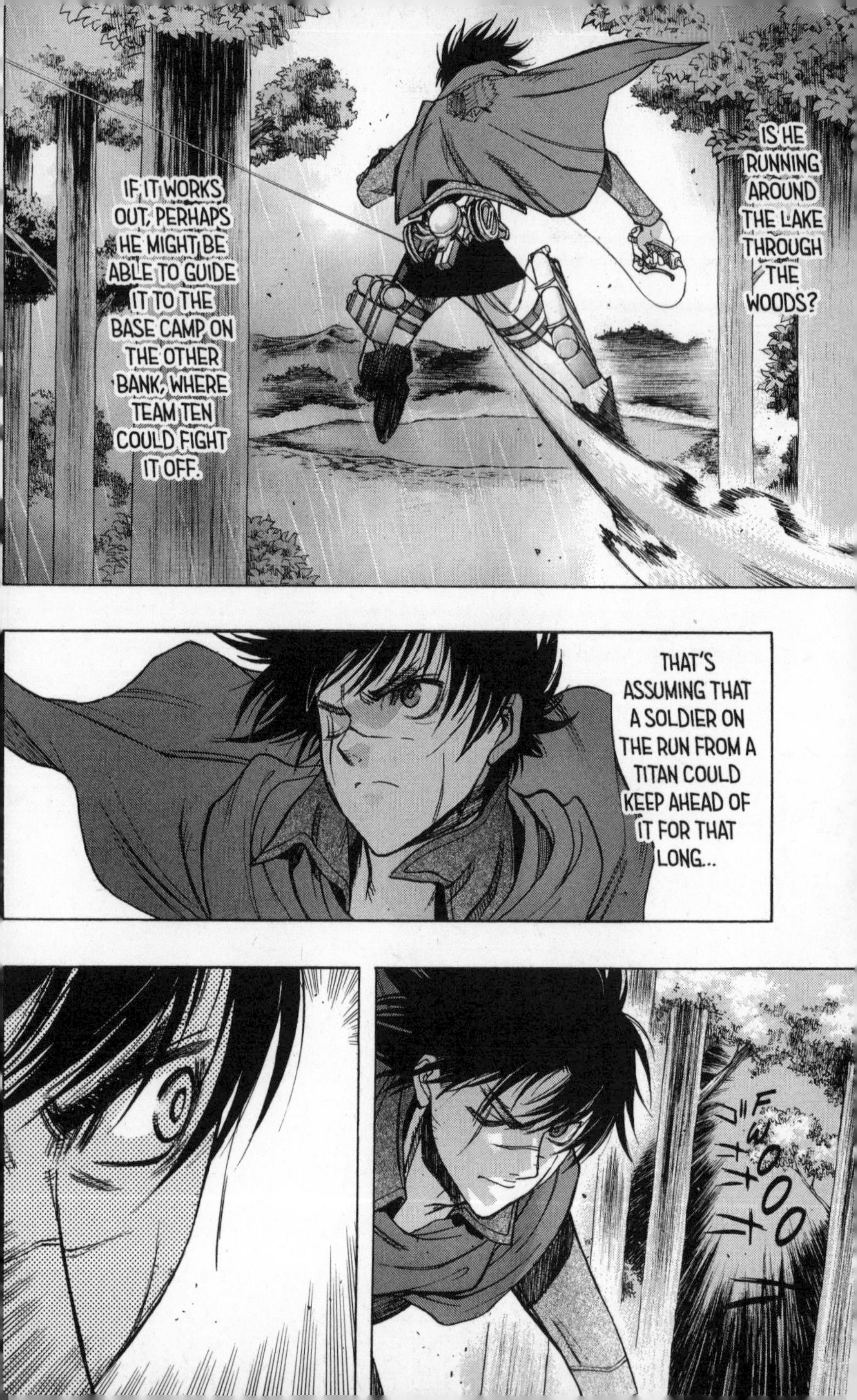
IS HE RUNNING AROUND THE LAKE THROUGH THE WOODS?
IF IT WORKS OUT, PERHAPS HE MIGHT BE ABLE TO GUIDE IT TO THE BASE CAMP ON THE OTHER BANK, WHERE TEAM TEN COULD FIGHT IT OFF.
THAT'S ASSUMING THAT A SOLDIER ON THE RUN FROM A TITAN COULD KEEP AHEAD OF IT FOR THAT LONG...
FWOOO

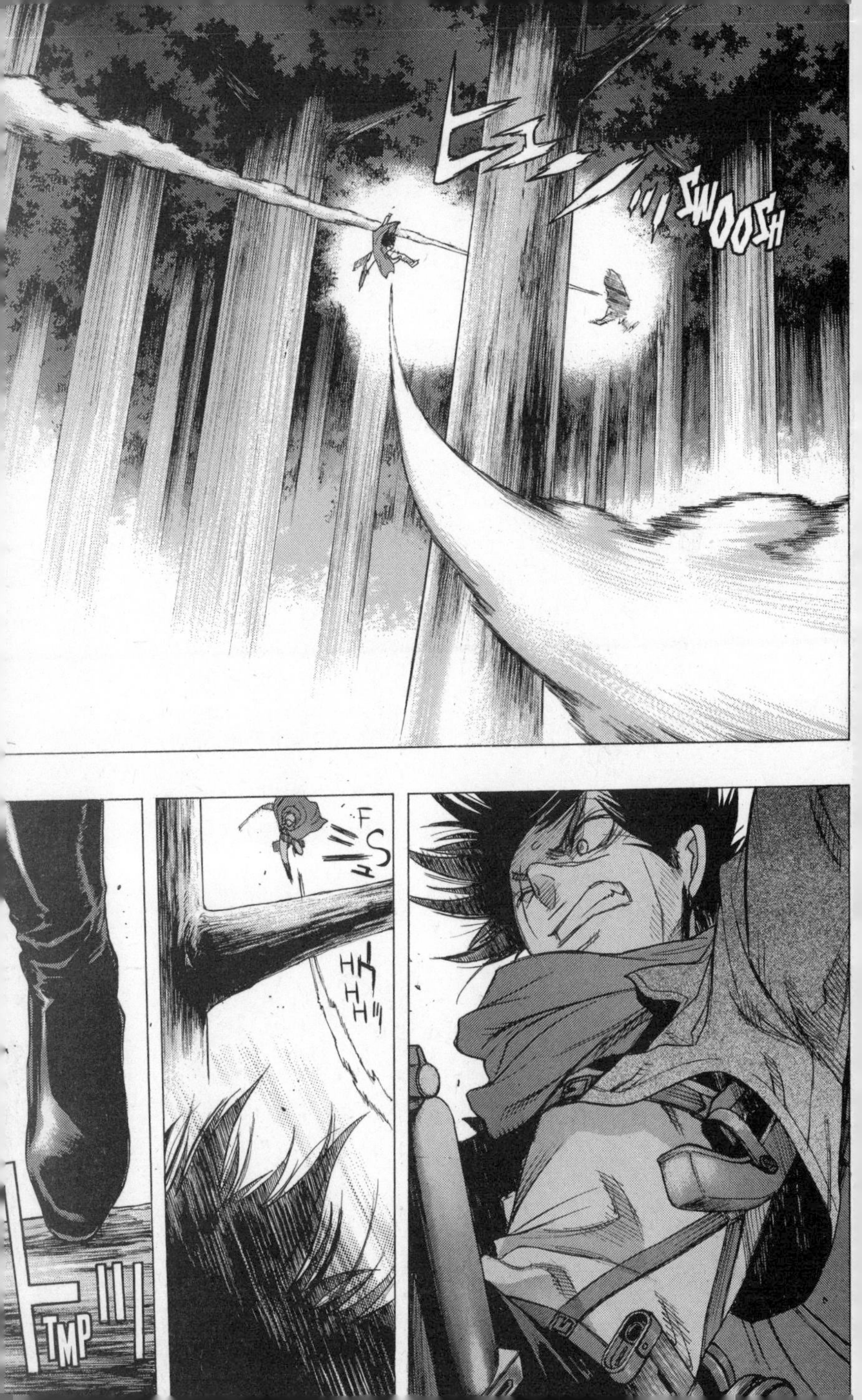
SWOOSH
FSH
TMP

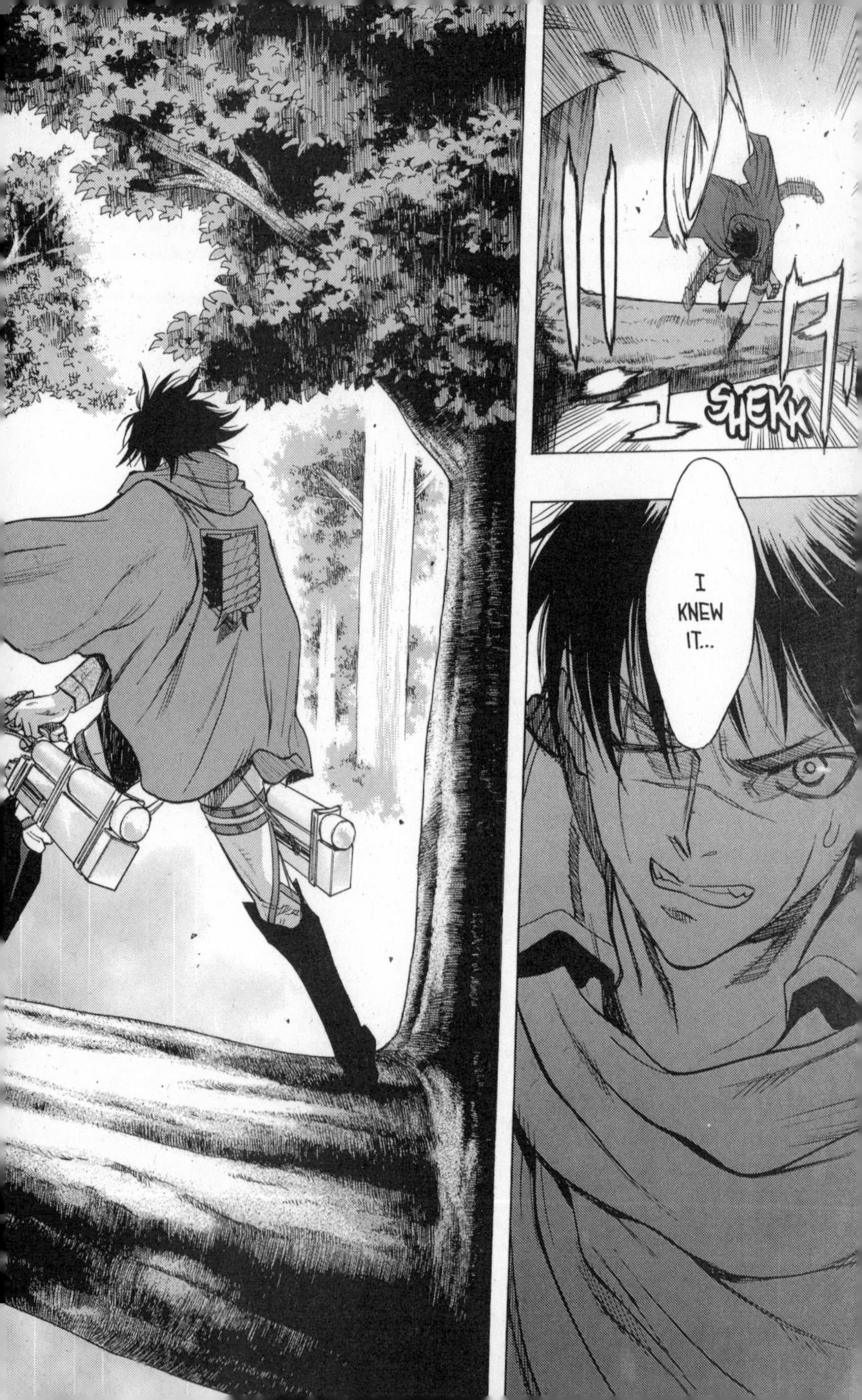
SHEKK
I KNEW IT...

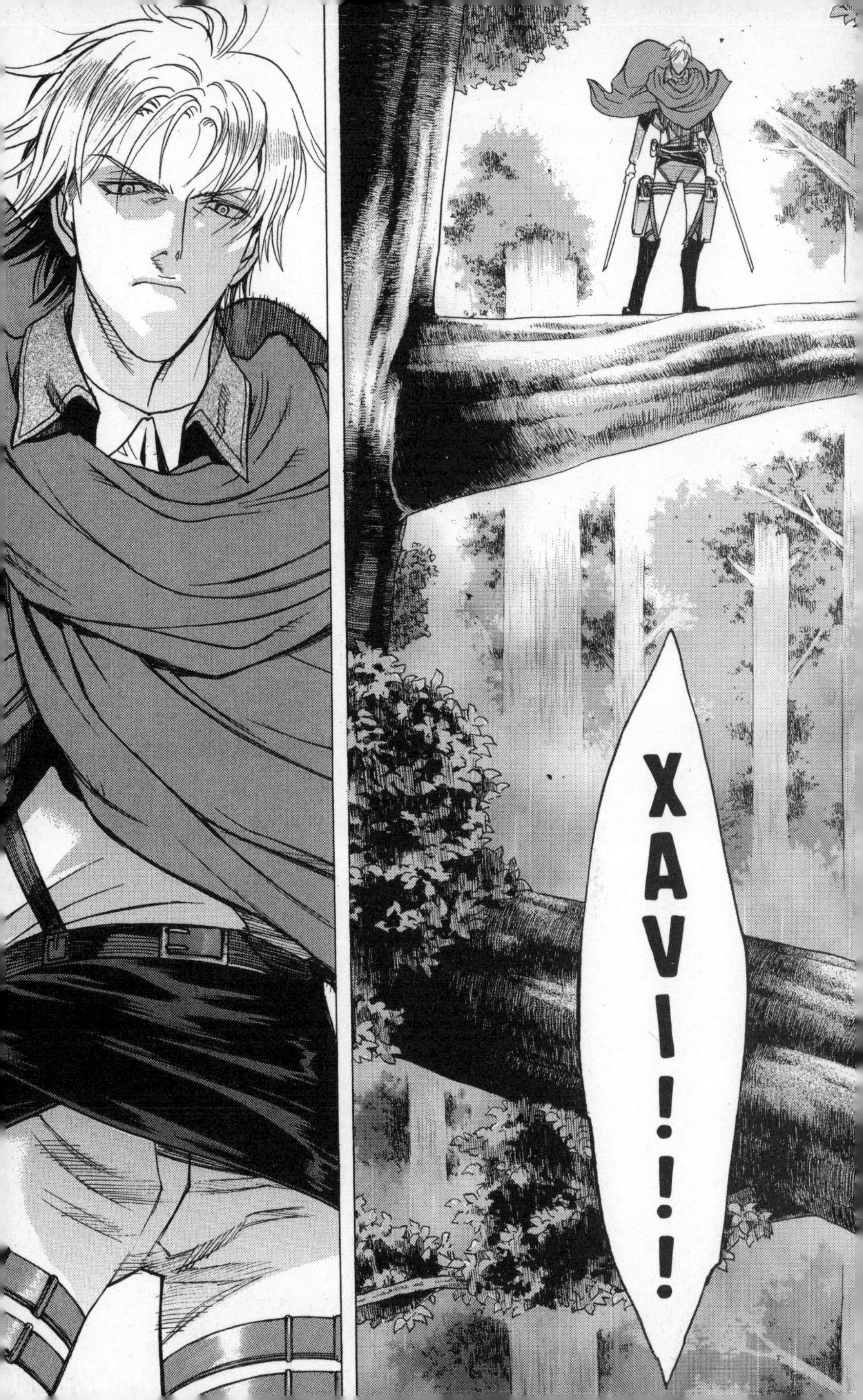
XAVI!!!!

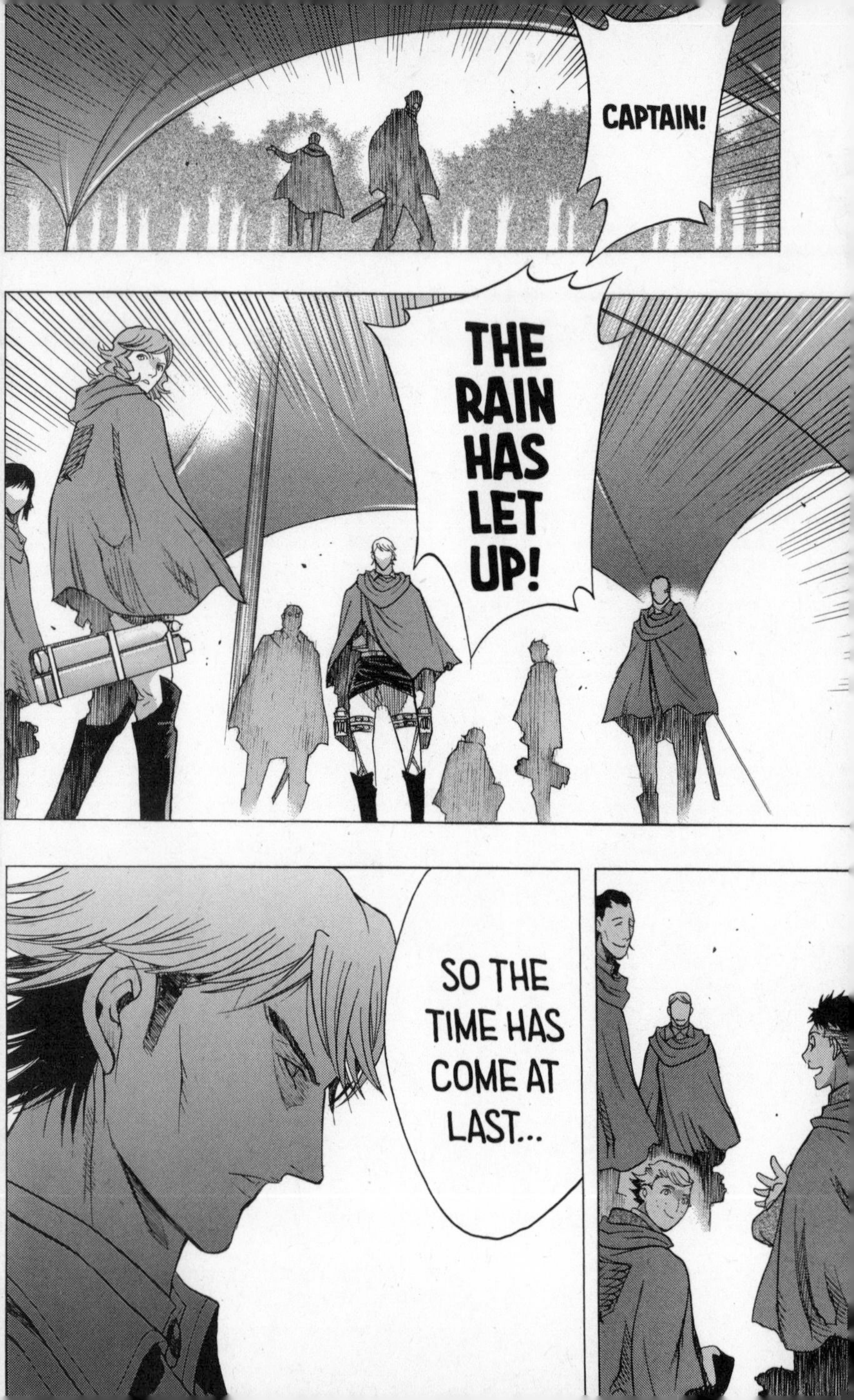
CAPTAIN!
THE RAIN HAS LET UP!
SO THE TIME HAS COME AT LAST...

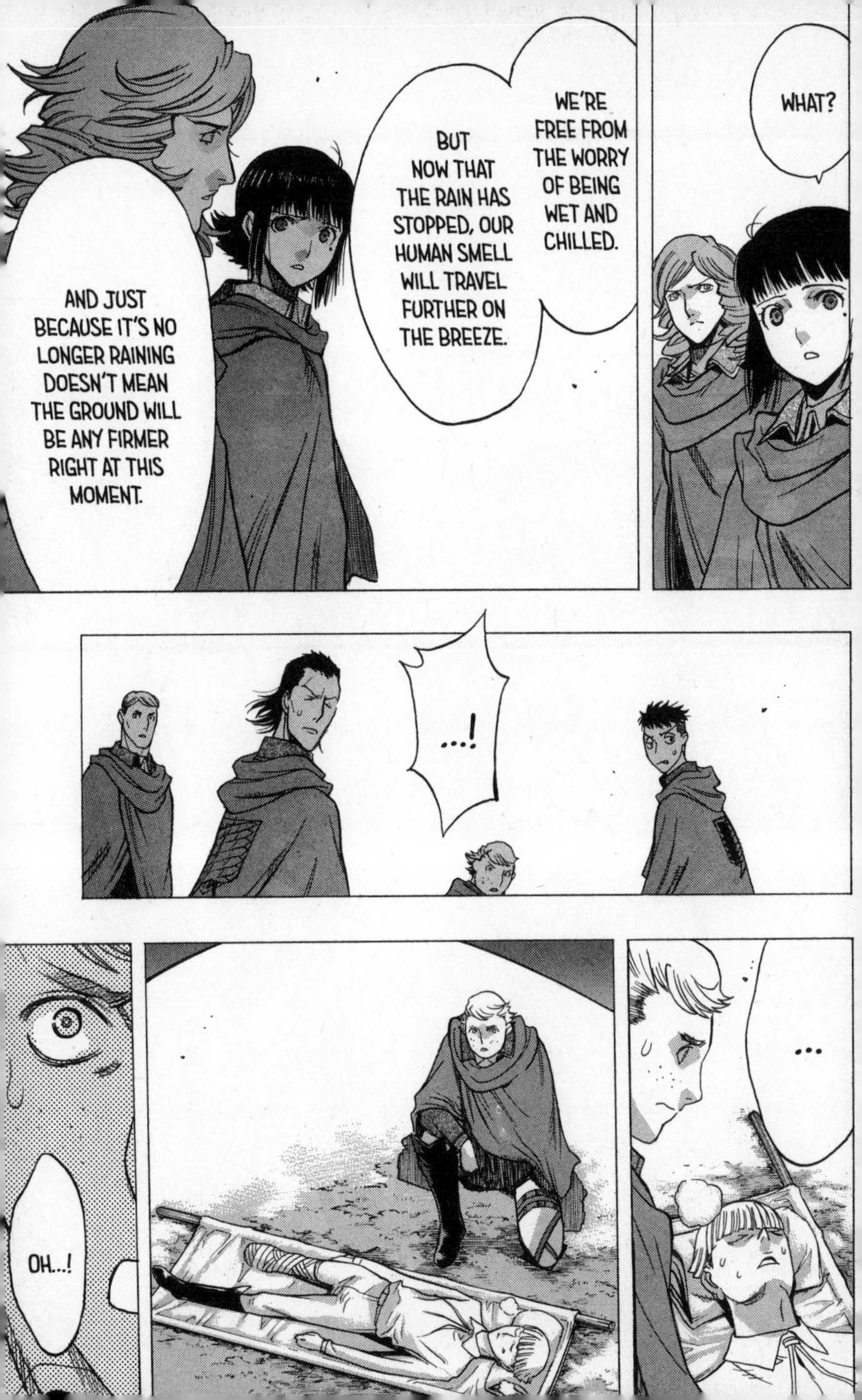
WHAT?
WE'RE FREE FROM THE WORRY OF BEING WET AND CHILLED.
BUT NOW THAT THE RAIN HAS STOPPED, OUR HUMAN SMELL WILL TRAVEL FURTHER ON THE BREEZE.
AND JUST BECAUSE IT'S NO LONGER RAINING DOESN'T MEAN THE GROUND WILL BE ANY FIRMER RIGHT AT THIS MOMENT.
...!
...
OH...!

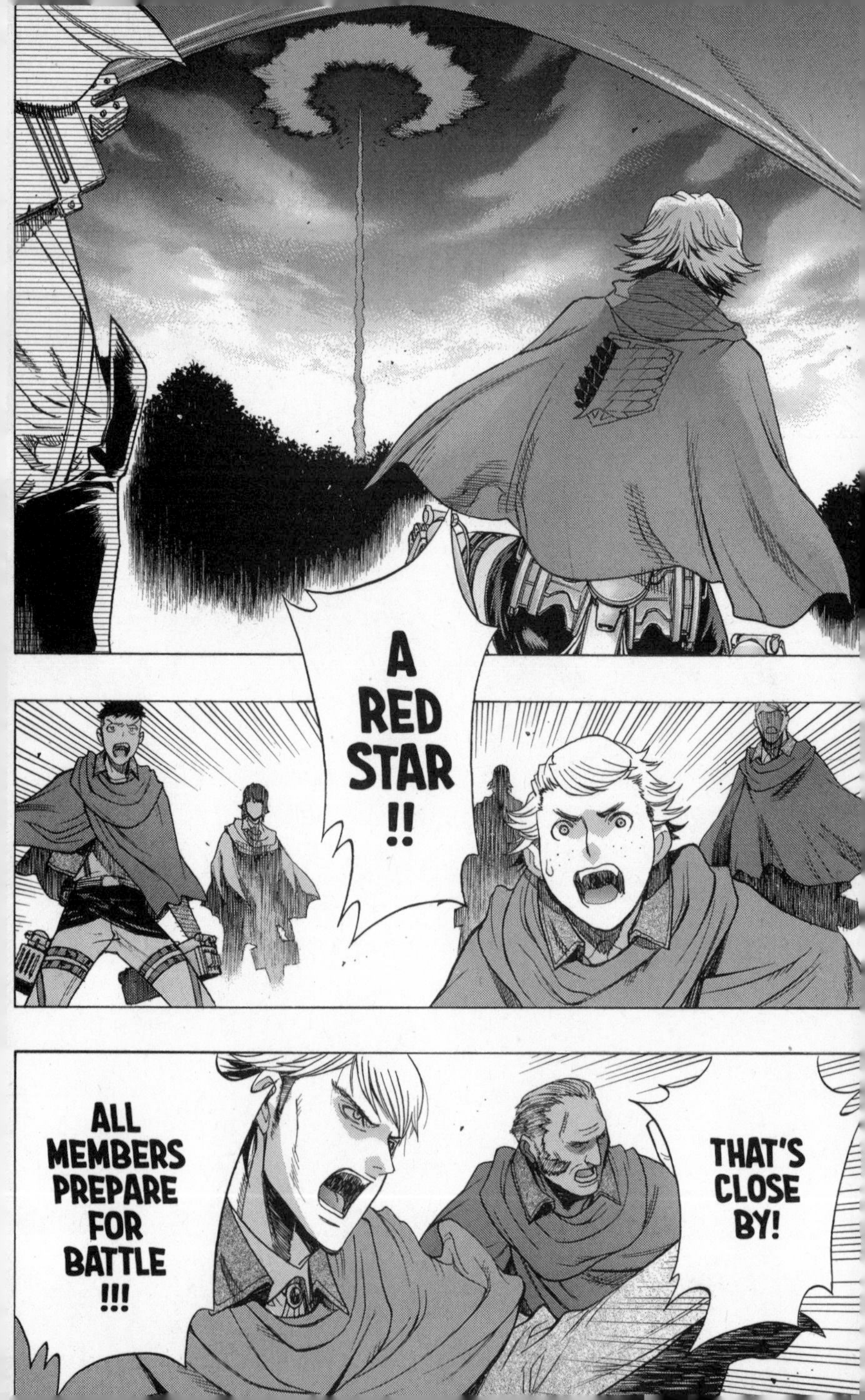
A RED STAR !!
THAT'S CLOSE BY!
ALL MEMBERS PREPARE FOR BATTLE !!!

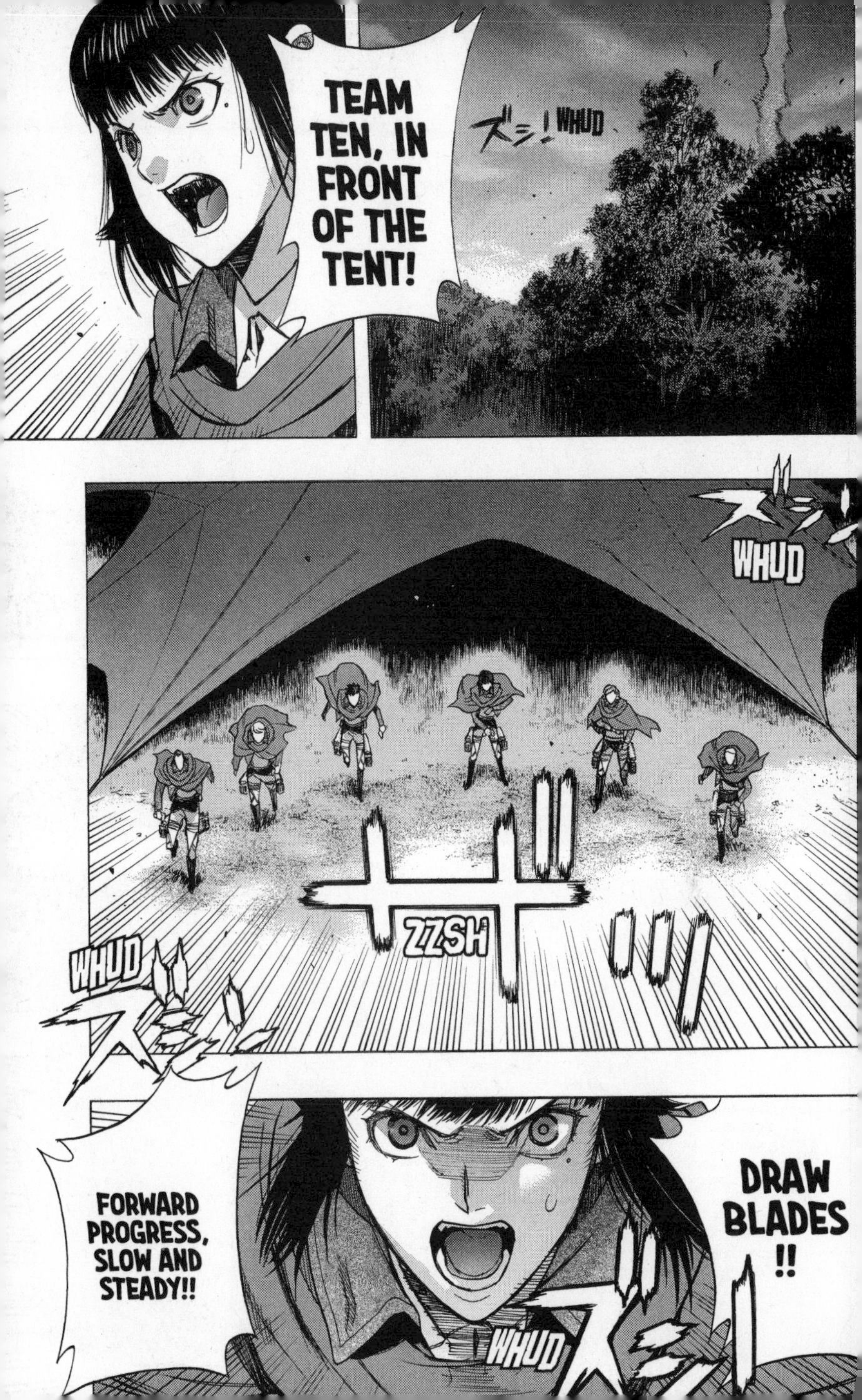
WHUD
TEAM TEN, IN FRONT OF THE TENT!
WHUD
ZZSH
WHUD
DRAW BLADES !!
FORWARD PROGRESS, SLOW AND STEADY!!
WHUD

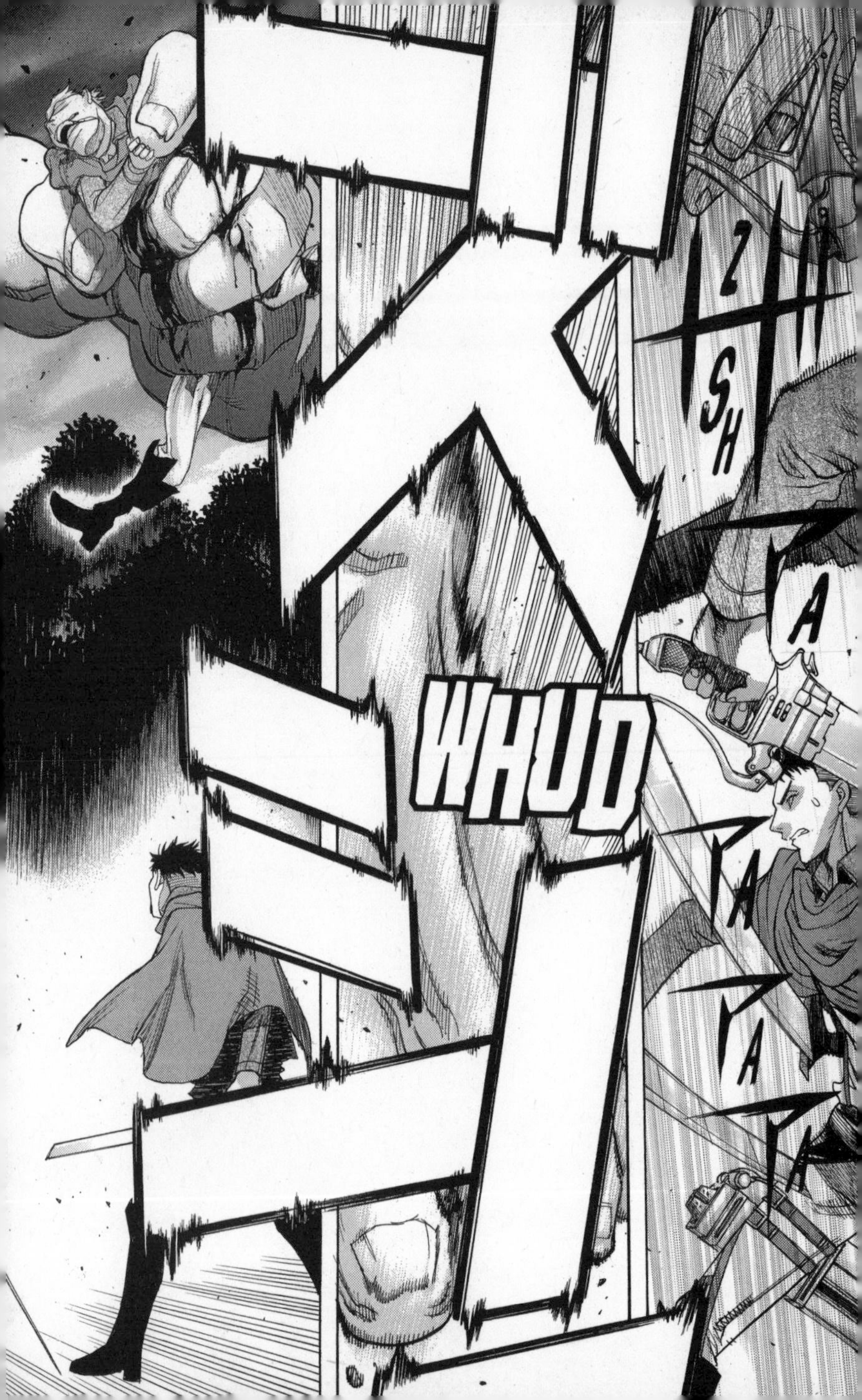
ZSH
AAAA
WHUD

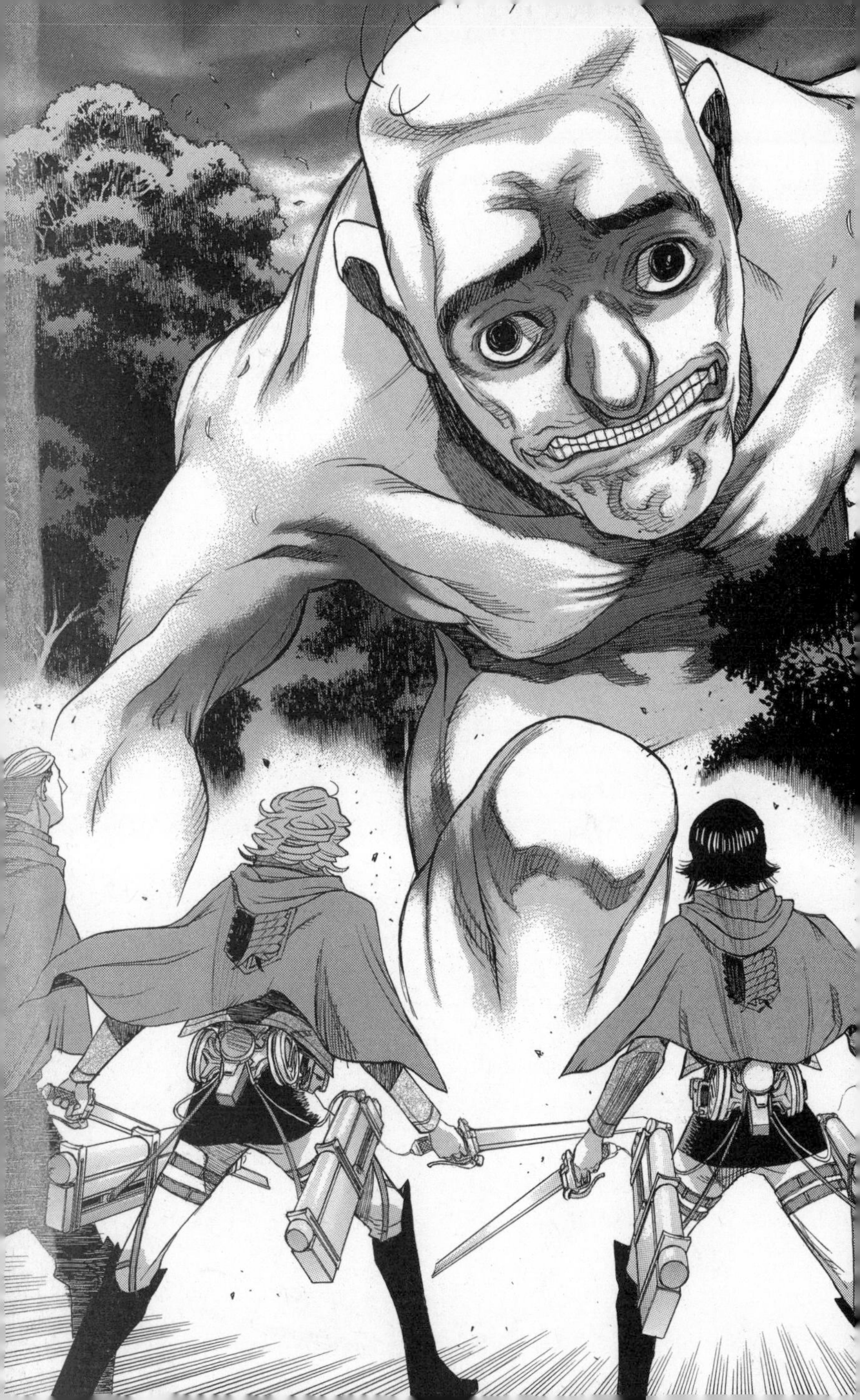

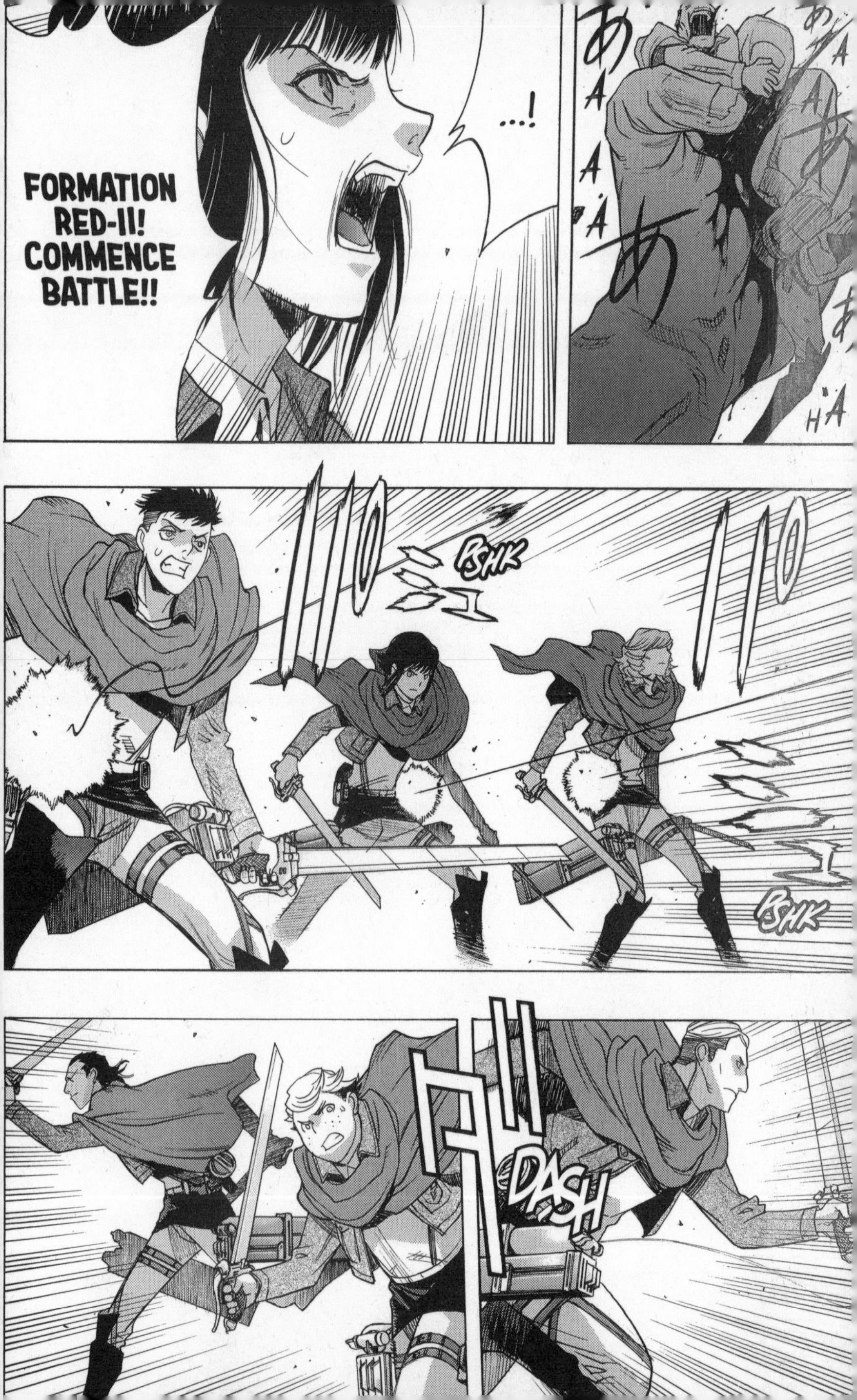
...!
FORMATION RED-II! COMMENCE BATTLE!!
PSHK
PSHK
DASH

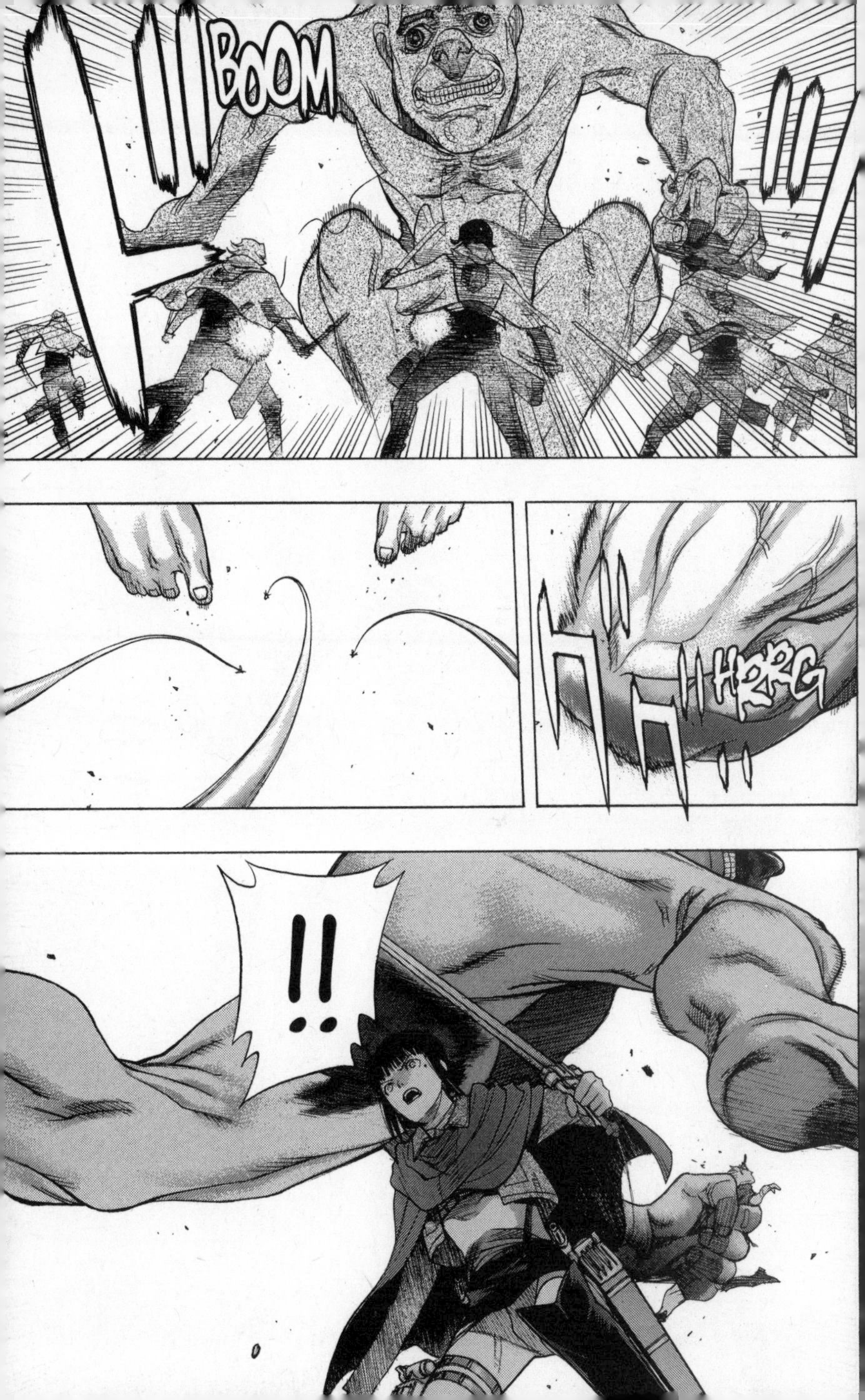
BOOM
HRRG
!!

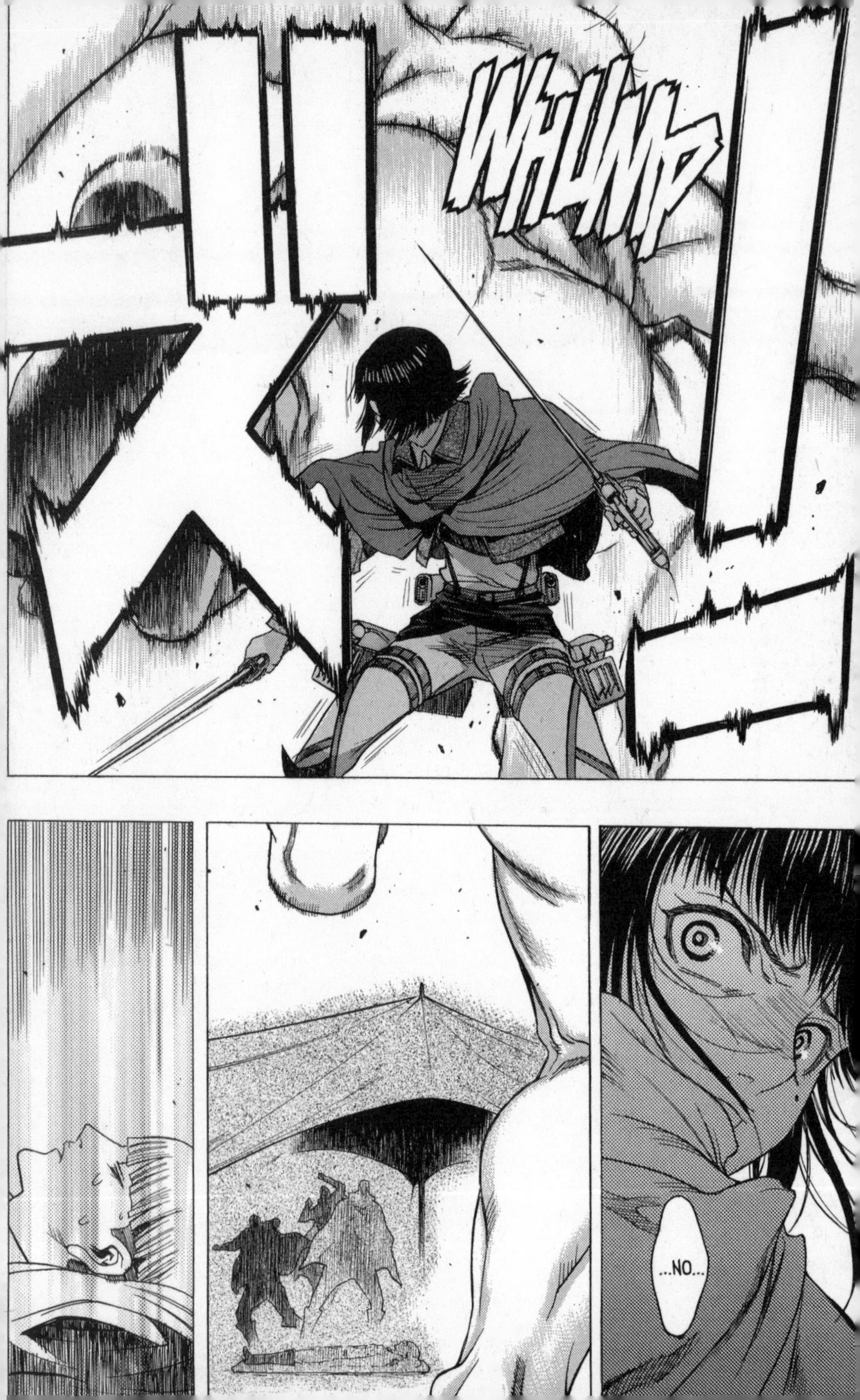
WHUMP
...NO...

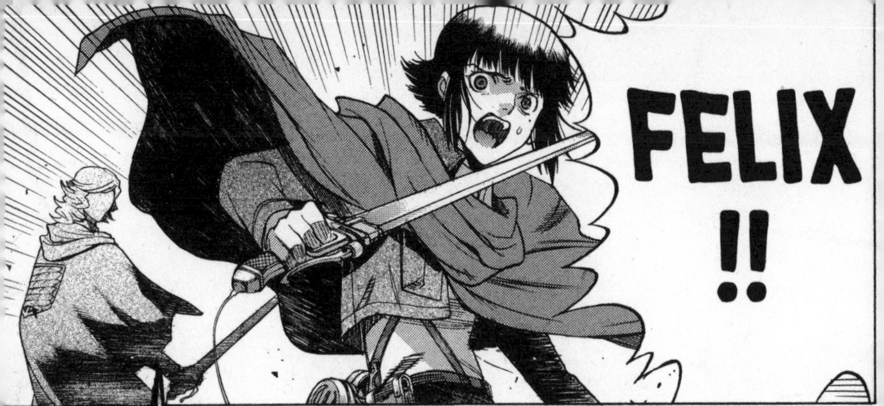
FELIX!!
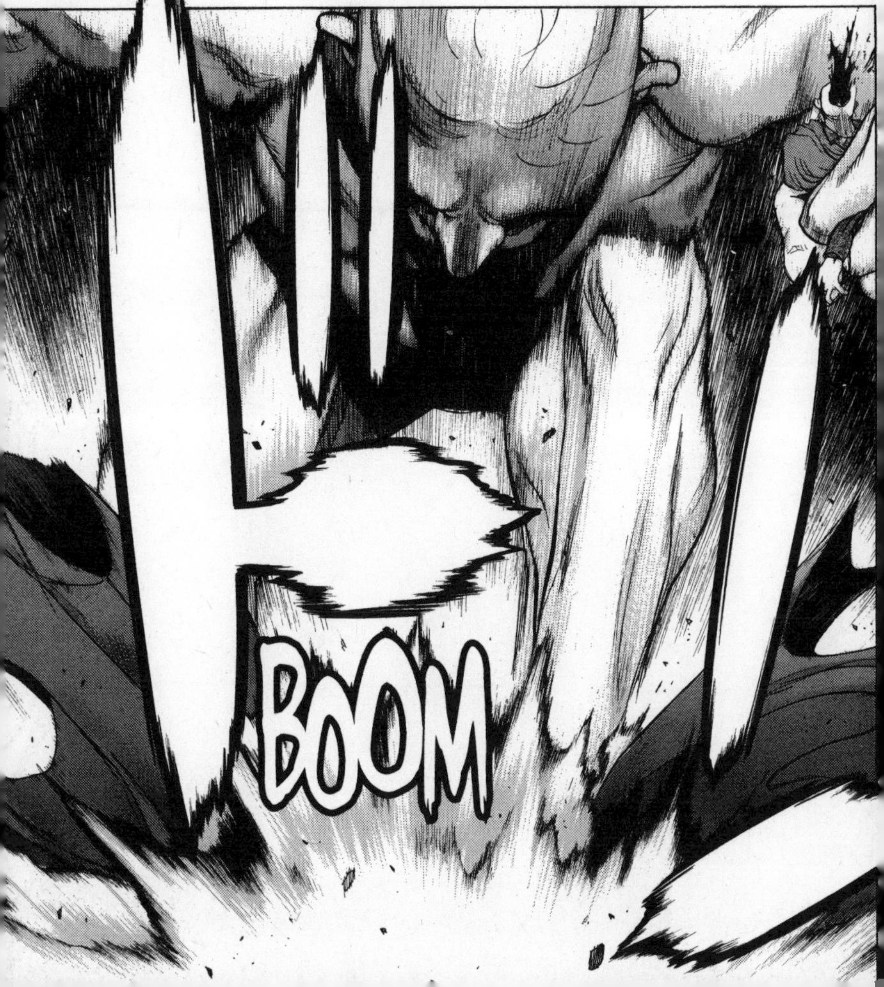
BOOM

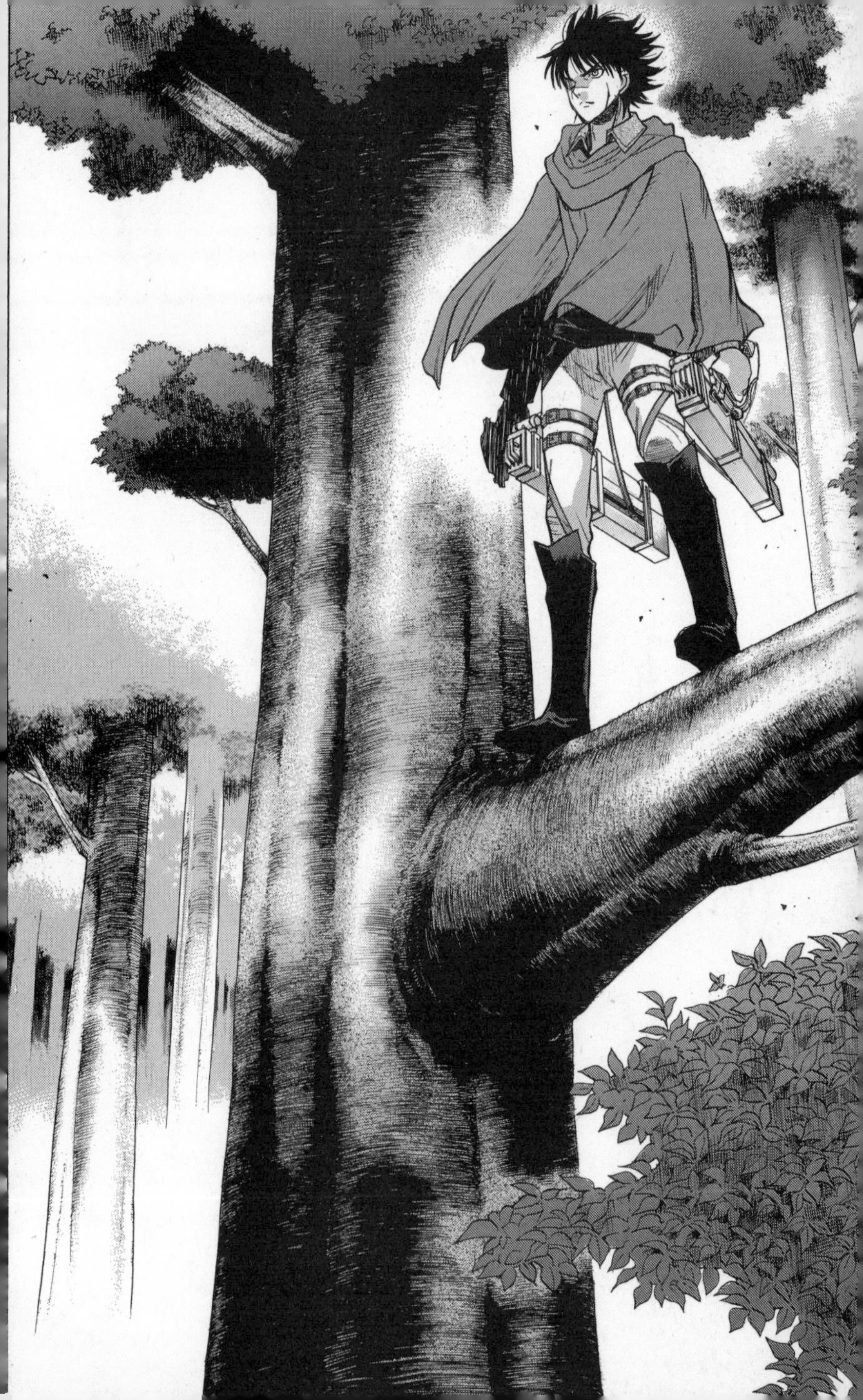

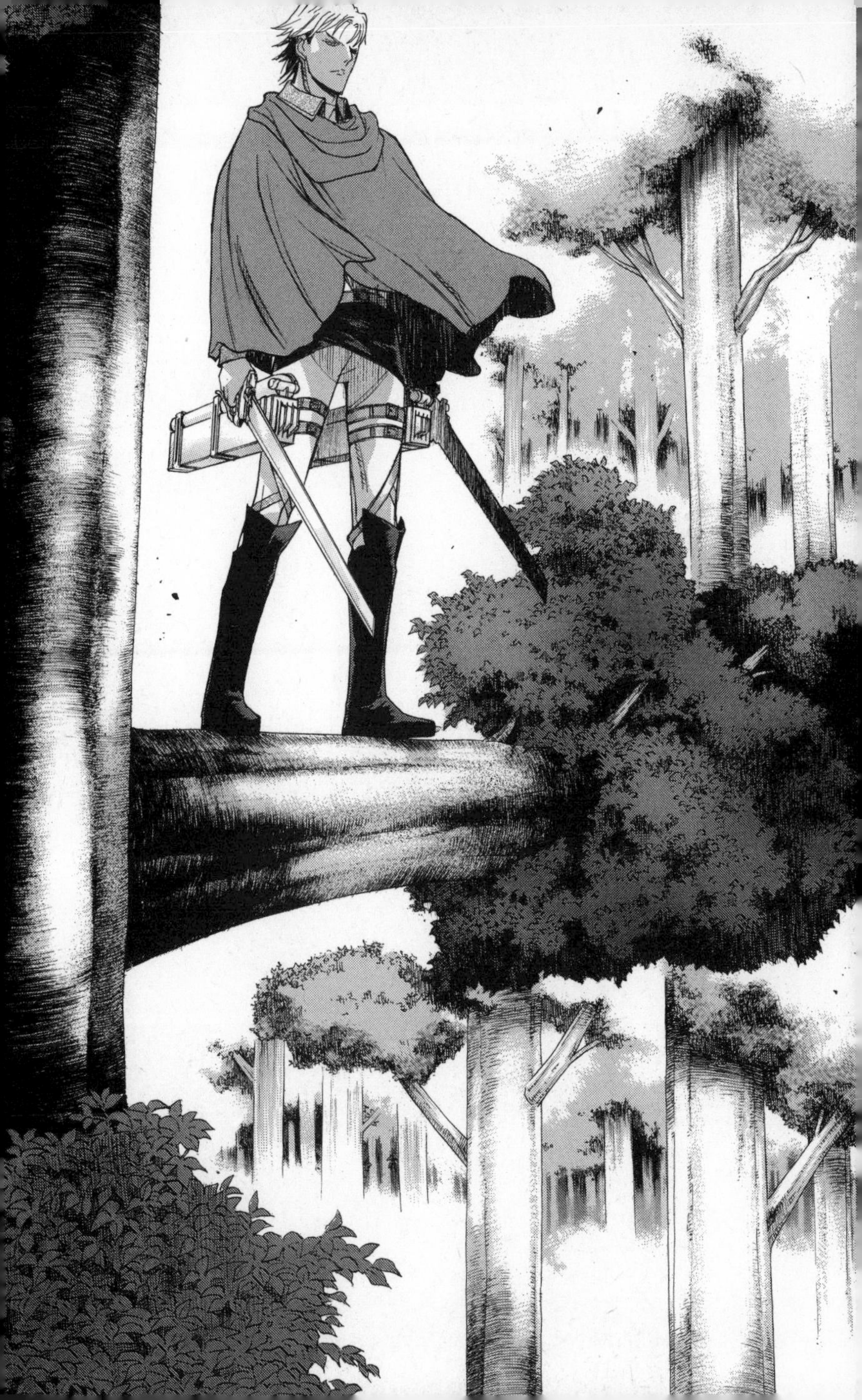

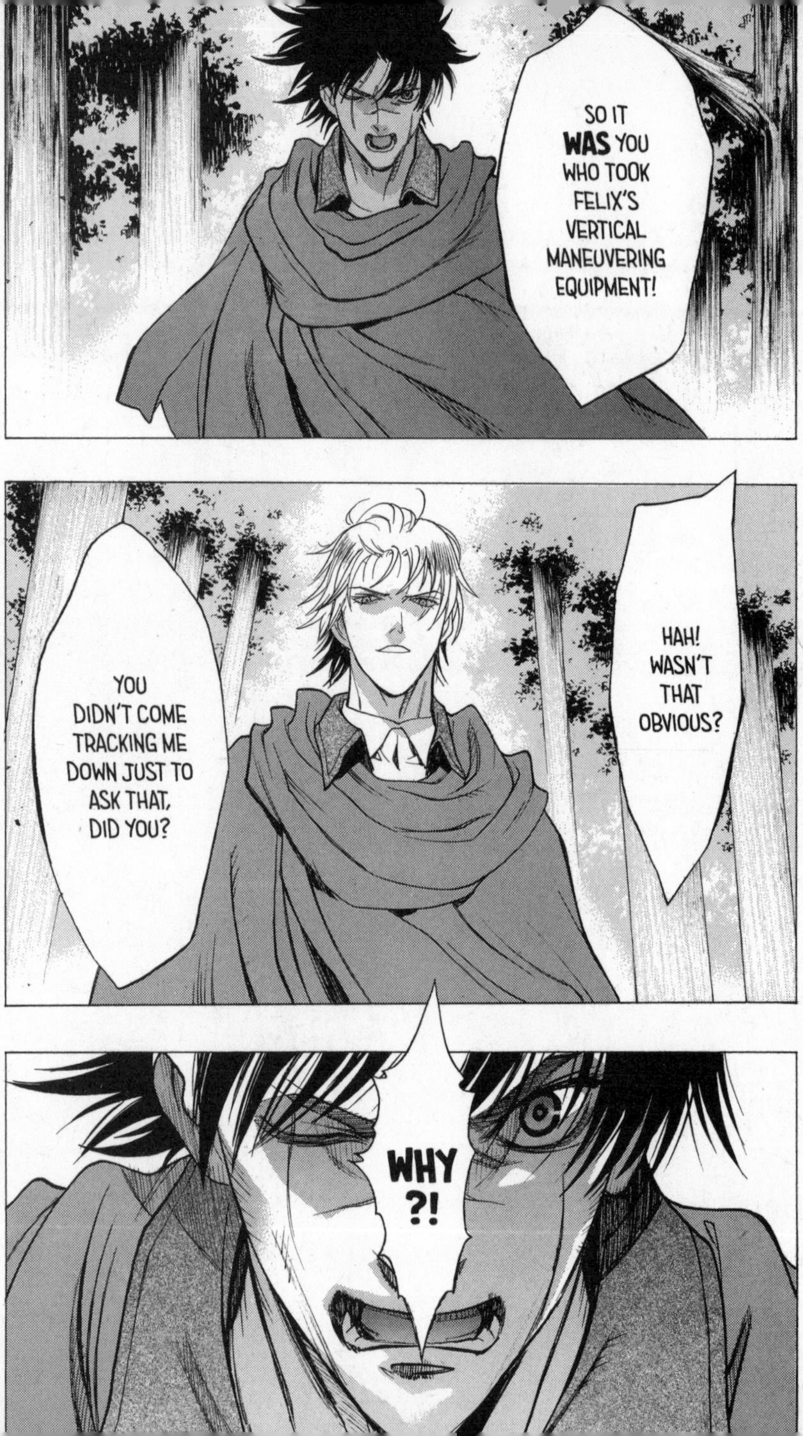
SO IT WAS YOU WHO TOOK FELIX'S VERTICAL MANEUVERING EQUIPMENT!
HAH! WASN'T THAT OBVIOUS?
YOU DIDN'T COME TRACKING ME DOWN JUST TO ASK THAT, DID YOU?
WHY?!

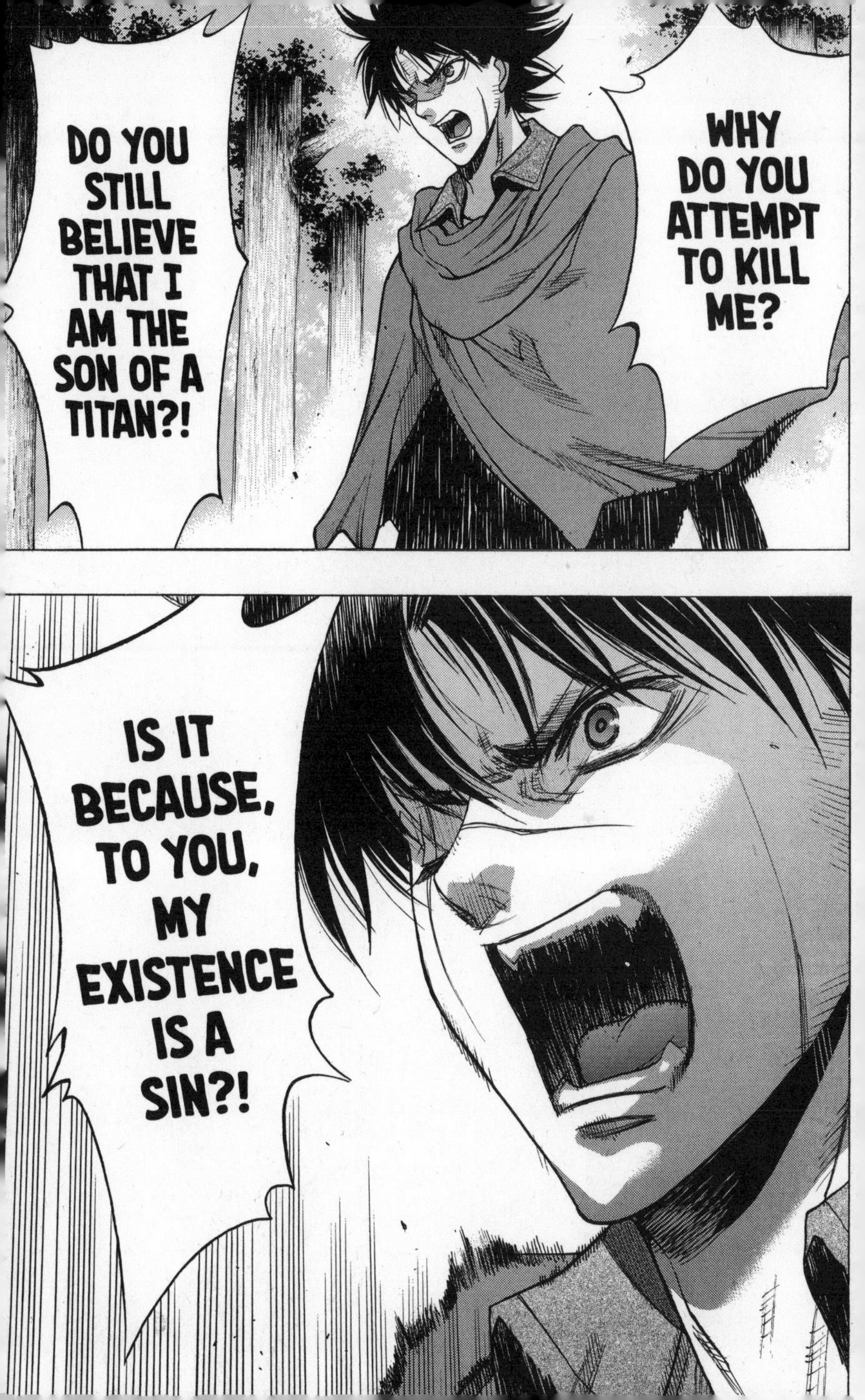
WHY DO YOU ATTEMPT TO KILL ME?
DO YOU STILL BELIEVE THAT I AM THE SON OF A TITAN?!
IS IT BECAUSE, TO YOU, MY EXISTENCE IS A SIN?!

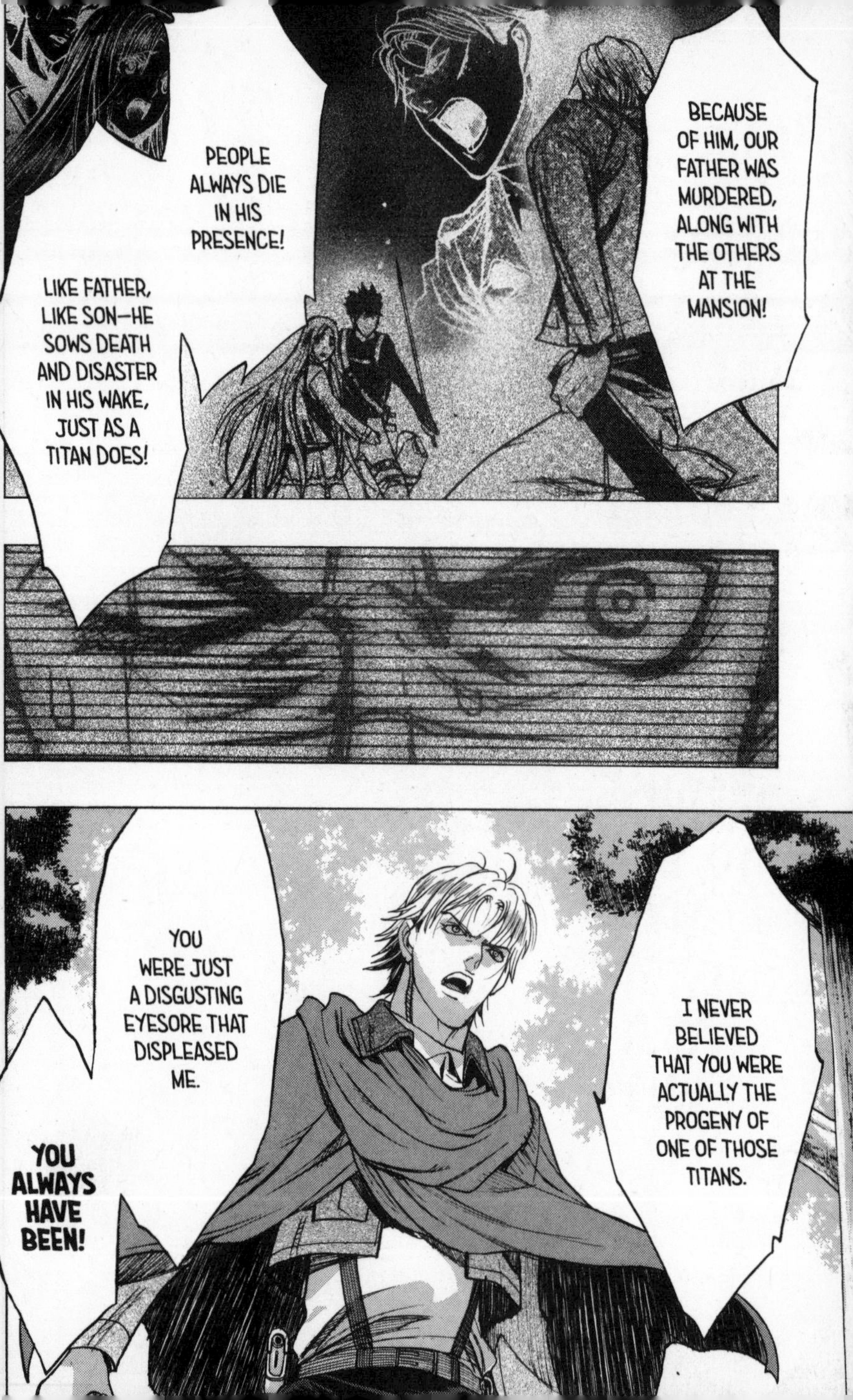
BECAUSE OF HIM, OUR FATHER WAS MURDERED, ALONG WITH THE OTHERS AT THE MANSION!
PEOPLE ALWAYS DIE IN HIS PRESENCE!
LIKE FATHER, LIKE SON—HE SOWS DEATH AND DISASTER IN HIS WAKE, JUST AS A TITAN DOES!
I NEVER BELIEVED THAT YOU WERE ACTUALLY THE PROGENY OF ONE OF THOSE TITANS.
YOU WERE JUST A DISGUSTING EYESORE THAT DISPLEASED ME.
YOU ALWAYS HAVE BEEN!

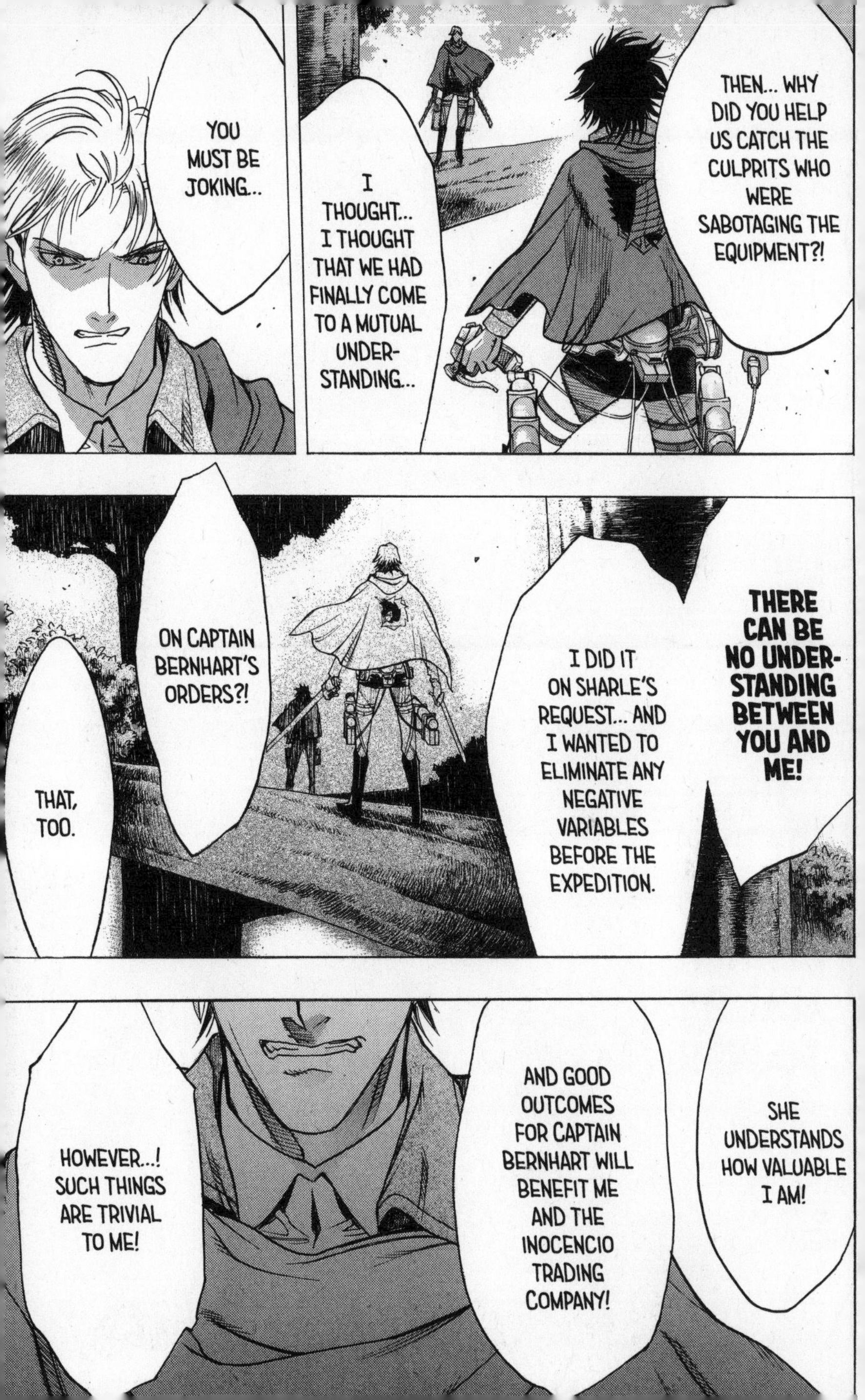
THEN... WHY DID YOU HELP US CATCH THE CULPRITS WHO WERE SABOTAGING THE EQUIPMENT?!
I THOUGHT... I THOUGHT THAT WE HAD FINALLY COME TO A MUTUAL UNDER-STANDING...
YOU MUST BE JOKING...
THERE CAN BE NO UNDER-STANDING BETWEEN YOU AND ME!
I DID IT ON SHARLE'S REQUEST... AND I WANTED TO ELIMINATE ANY NEGATIVE VARIABLES BEFORE THE EXPEDITION.
ON CAPTAIN BERNHART'S ORDERS?!
THAT, TOO.
SHE UNDERSTANDS HOW VALUABLE I AM!
AND GOOD OUTCOMES FOR CAPTAIN BERNHART WILL BENEFIT ME AND THE INOCENCIO TRADING COMPANY!
HOWEVER...! SUCH THINGS ARE TRIVIAL TO ME!

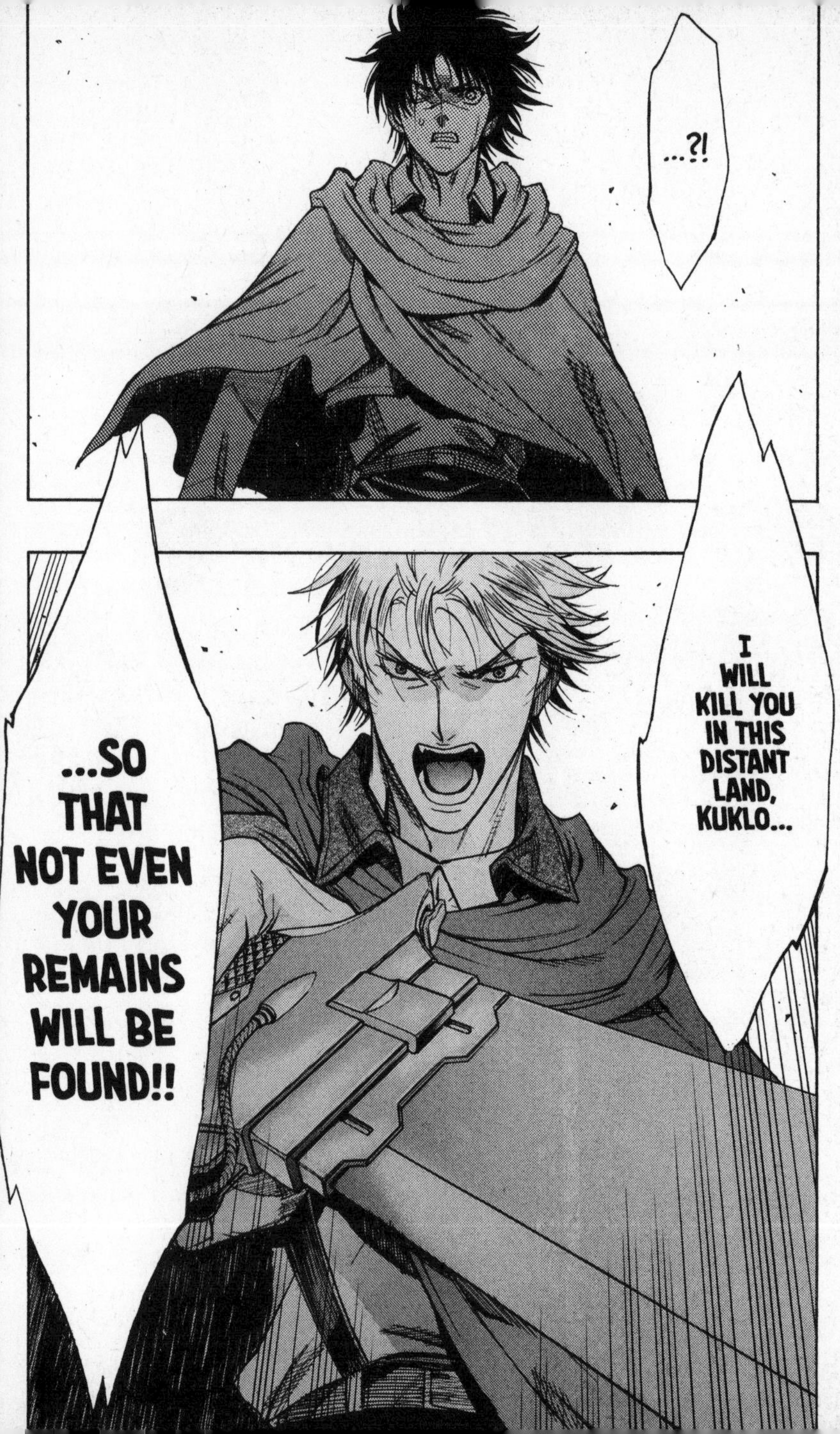
...?!
I WILL KILL YOU IN THIS DISTANT LAND, KUKLO...
...SO THAT NOT EVEN YOUR REMAINS WILL BE FOUND!!

Chapter 63: The Deadly Greenwood · End

ATTACK on TITAN
BEFORE THE FALL

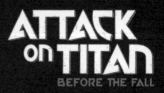

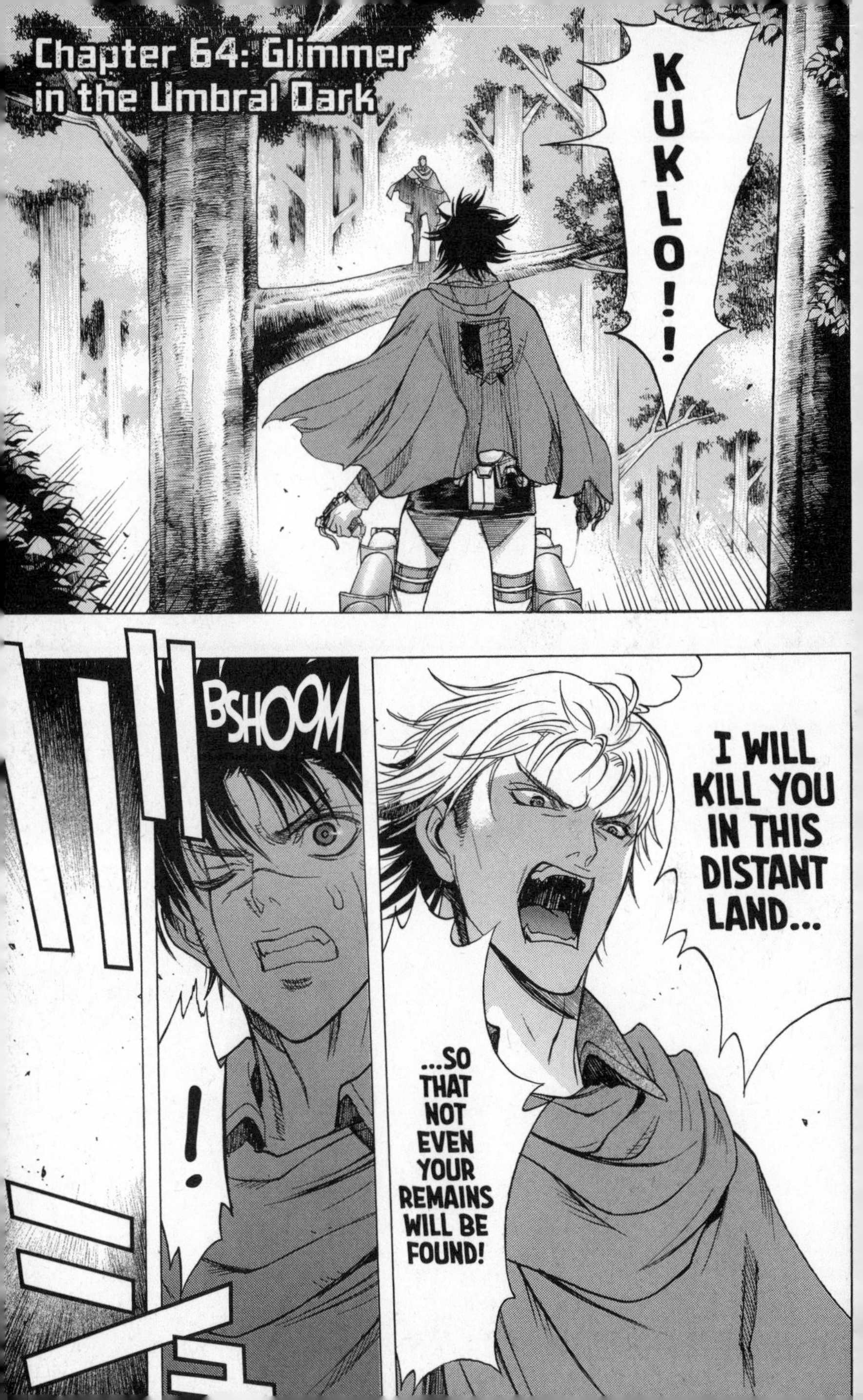
Chapter 64: Glimmer in the Umbral Dark
KUKLO!!
I WILL KILL YOU IN THIS DISTANT LAND...
...SO THAT NOT EVEN YOUR REMAINS WILL BE FOUND!
BSHOOM
!

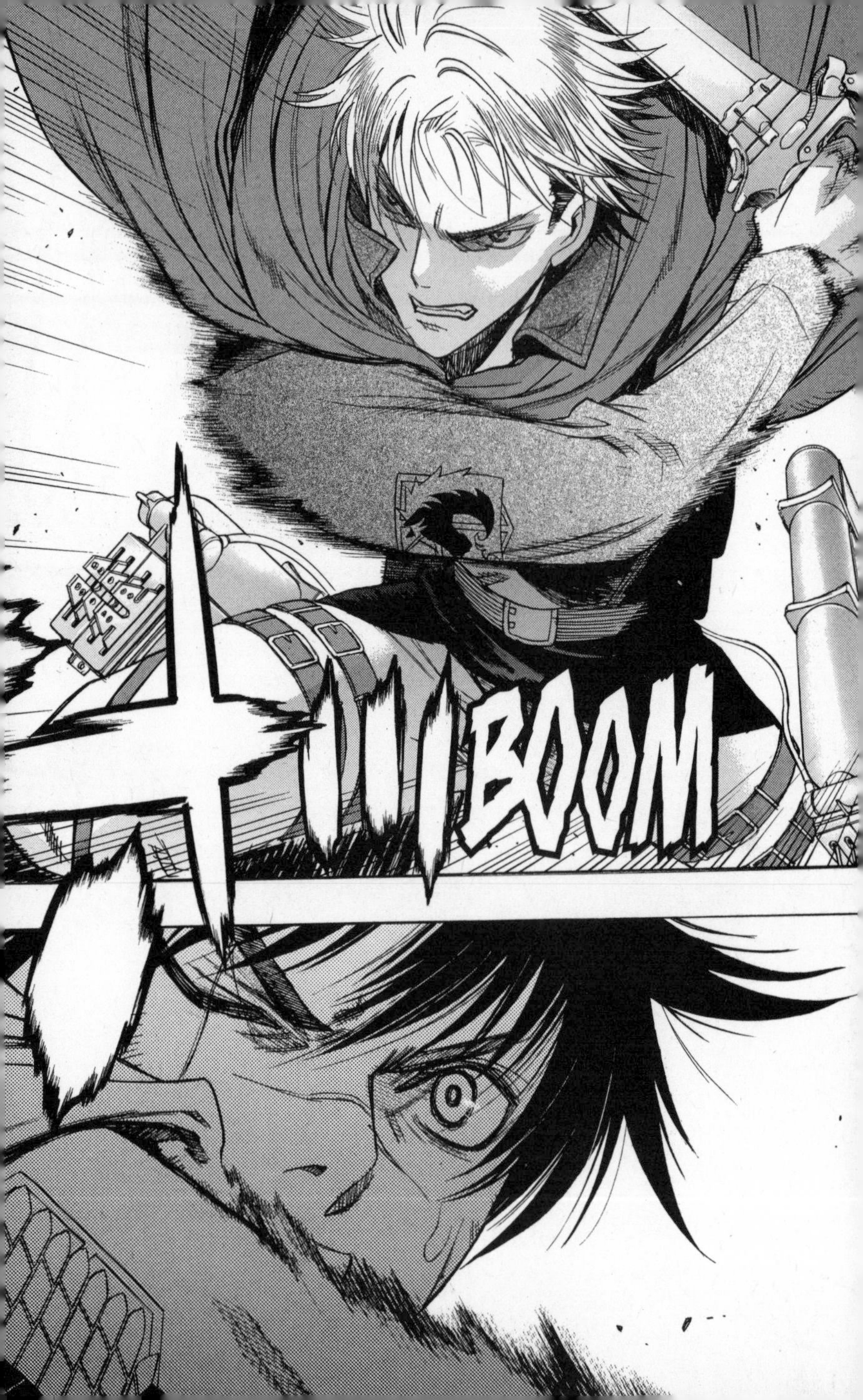
BOOM

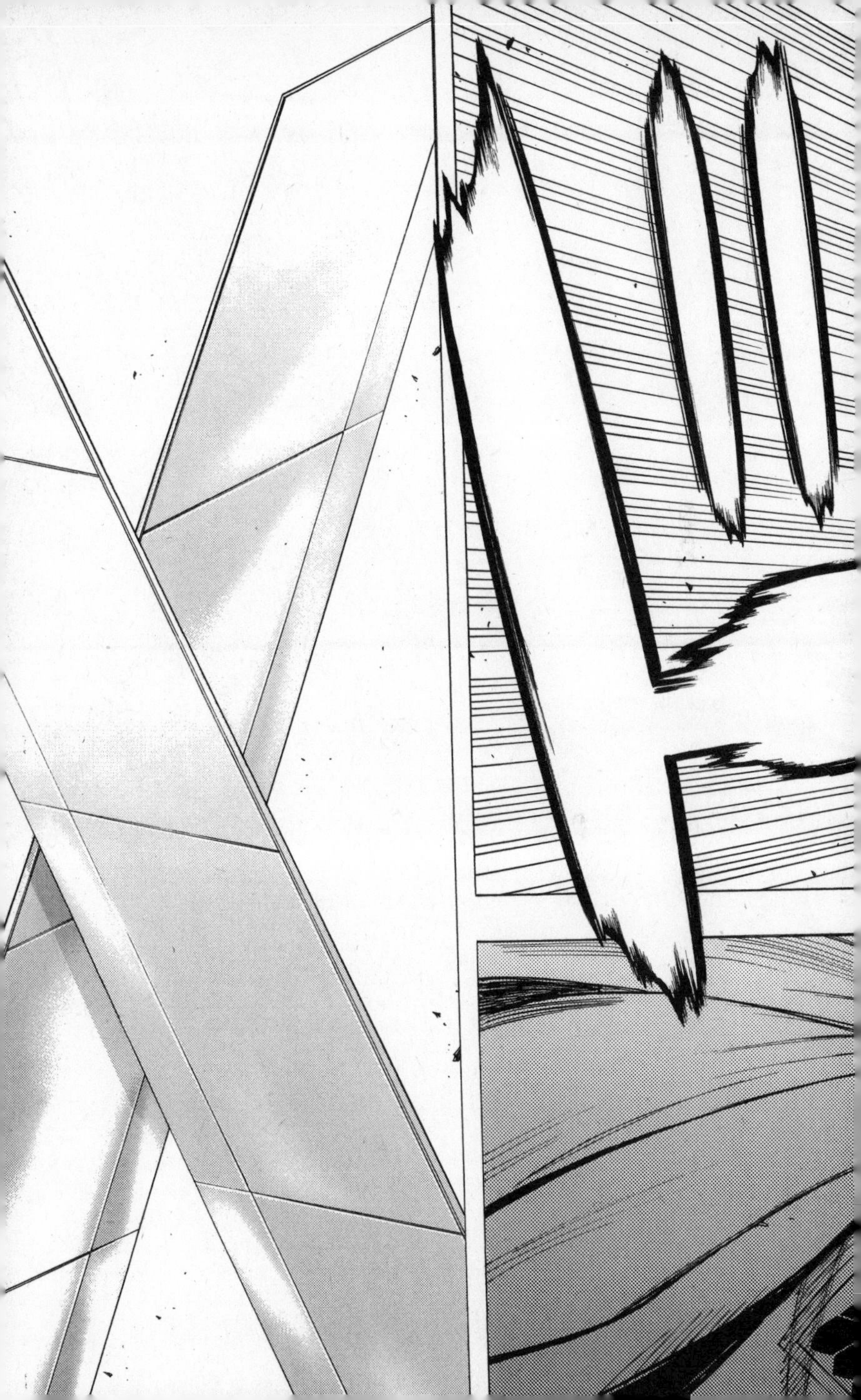

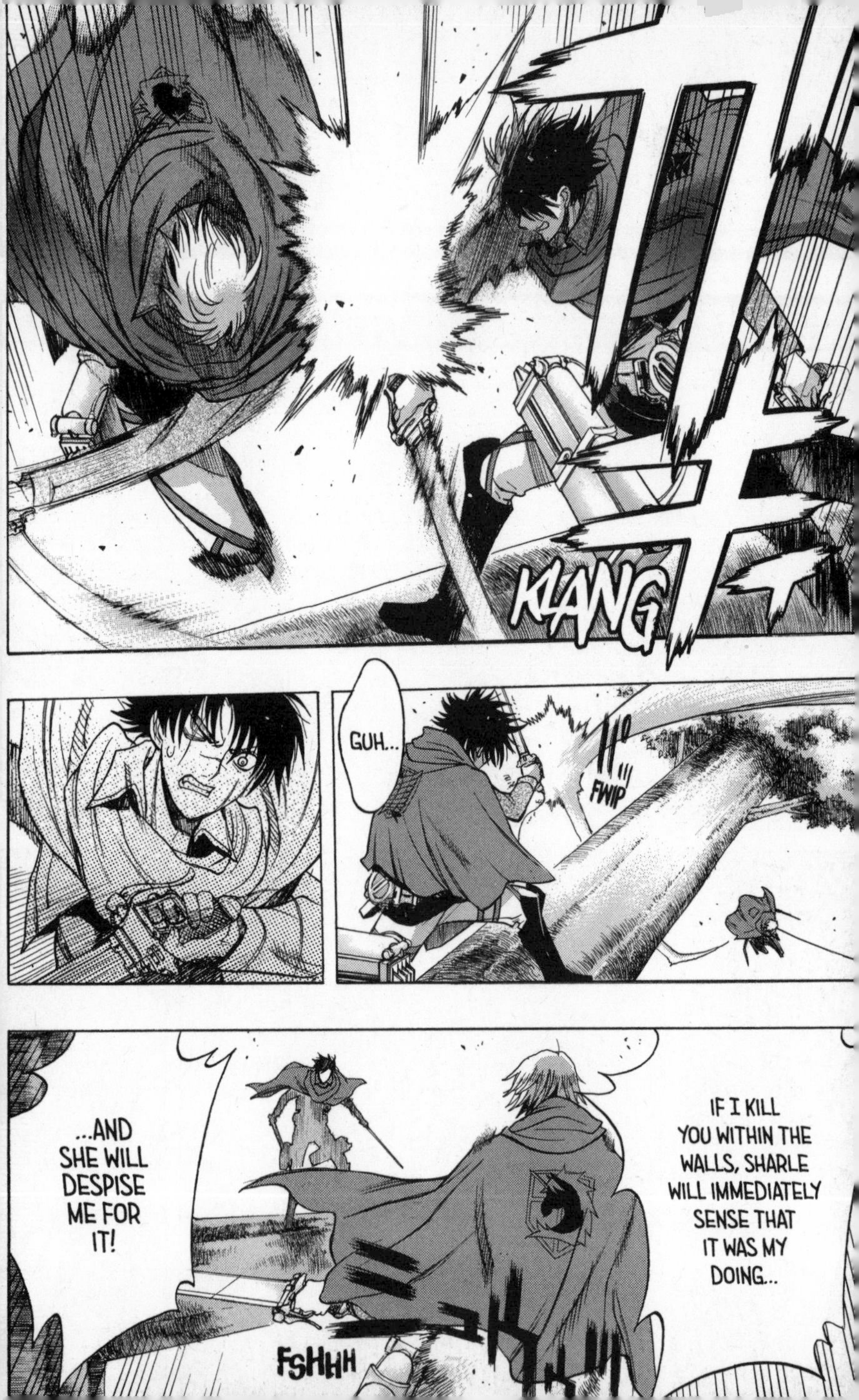
KLANG
GUH...
FWIP
IF I KILL YOU WITHIN THE WALLS, SHARLE WILL IMMEDIATELY SENSE THAT IT WAS MY DOING...
...AND SHE WILL DESPISE ME FOR IT!
FSHHH

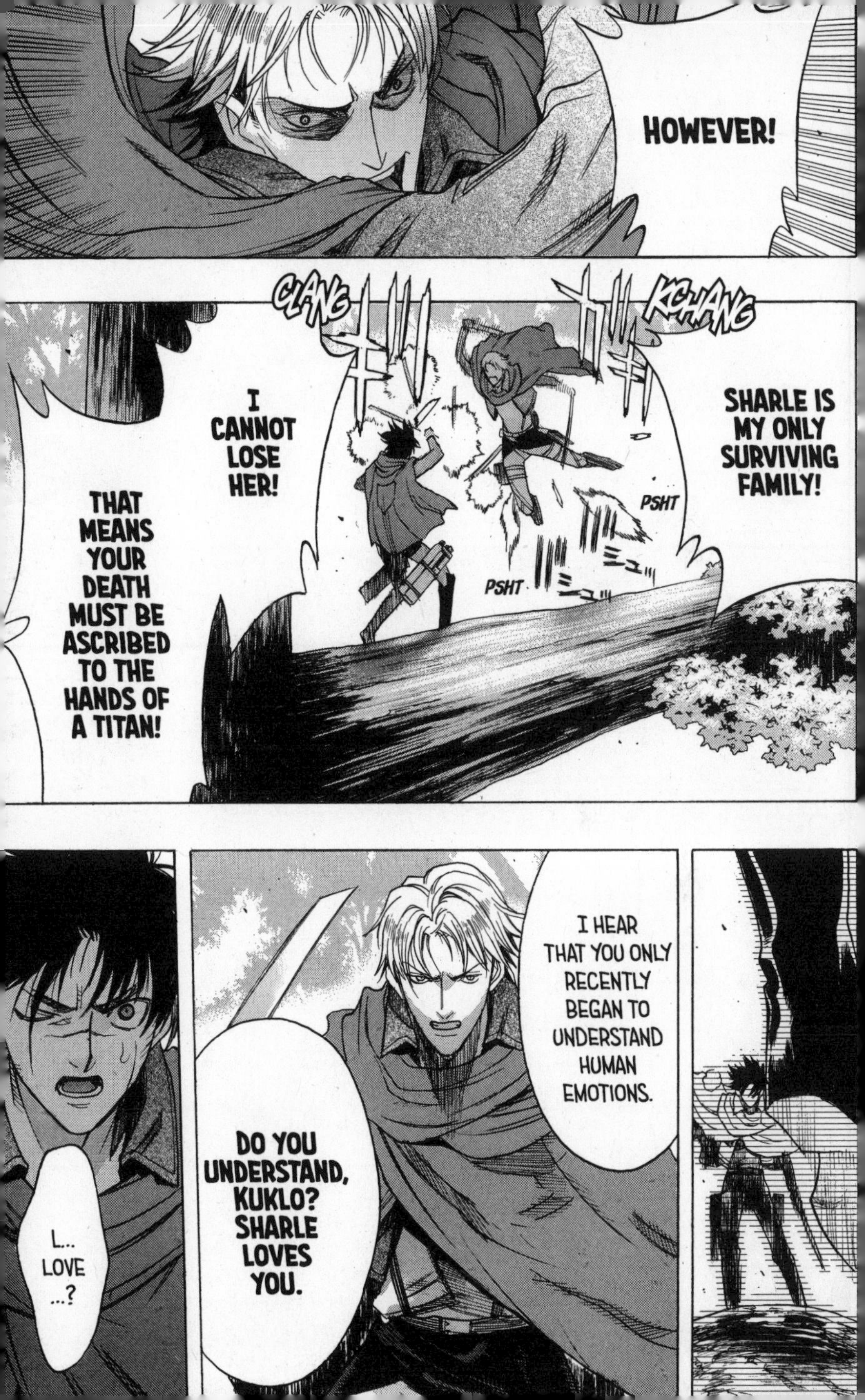
HOWEVER!
KCHANG
CLANG
SHARLE IS MY ONLY SURVIVING FAMILY!
I CANNOT LOSE HER!
PSHT
PSHT
THAT MEANS YOUR DEATH MUST BE ASCRIBED TO THE HANDS OF A TITAN!
I HEAR THAT YOU ONLY RECENTLY BEGAN TO UNDERSTAND HUMAN EMOTIONS.
DO YOU UNDERSTAND, KUKLO? SHARLE LOVES YOU.
L... LOVE ...?

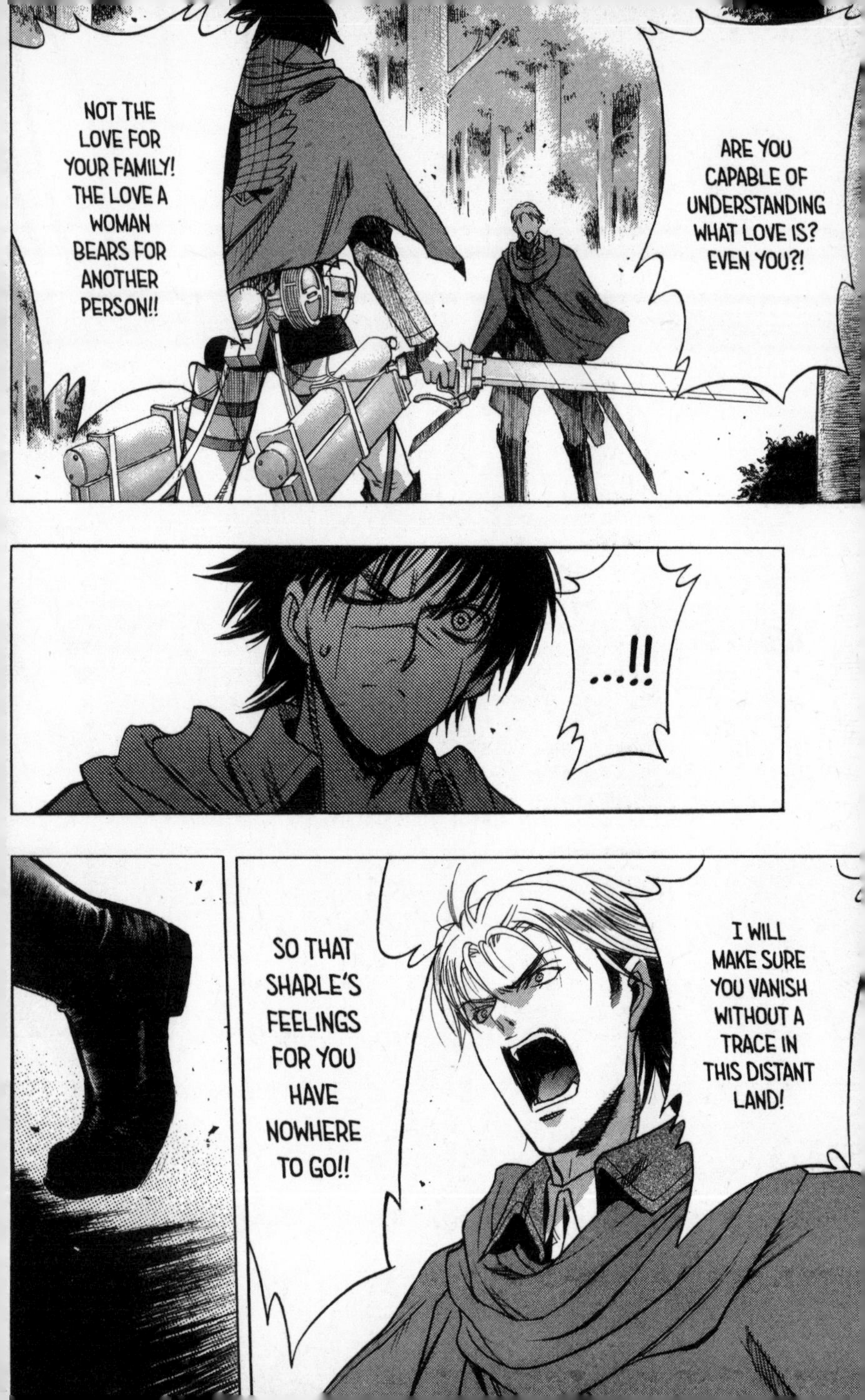
ARE YOU CAPABLE OF UNDERSTANDING WHAT LOVE IS? EVEN YOU?!
NOT THE LOVE FOR YOUR FAMILY! THE LOVE A WOMAN BEARS FOR ANOTHER PERSON!!
...!!
I WILL MAKE SURE YOU VANISH WITHOUT A TRACE IN THIS DISTANT LAND!
SO THAT SHARLE'S FEELINGS FOR YOU HAVE NOWHERE TO GO!!

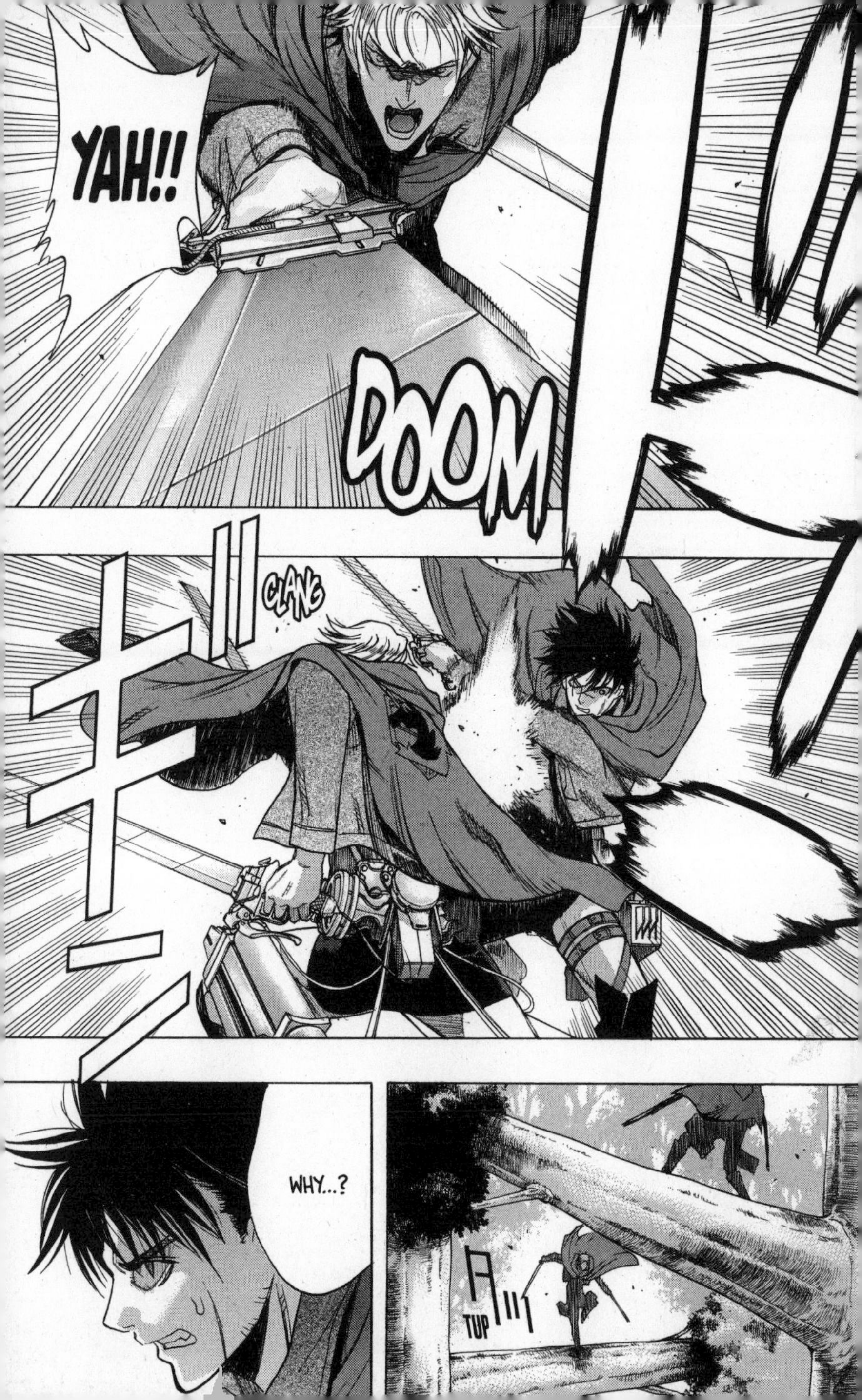
YAH!!
DOOM
CLANG
WHY...?
TUP

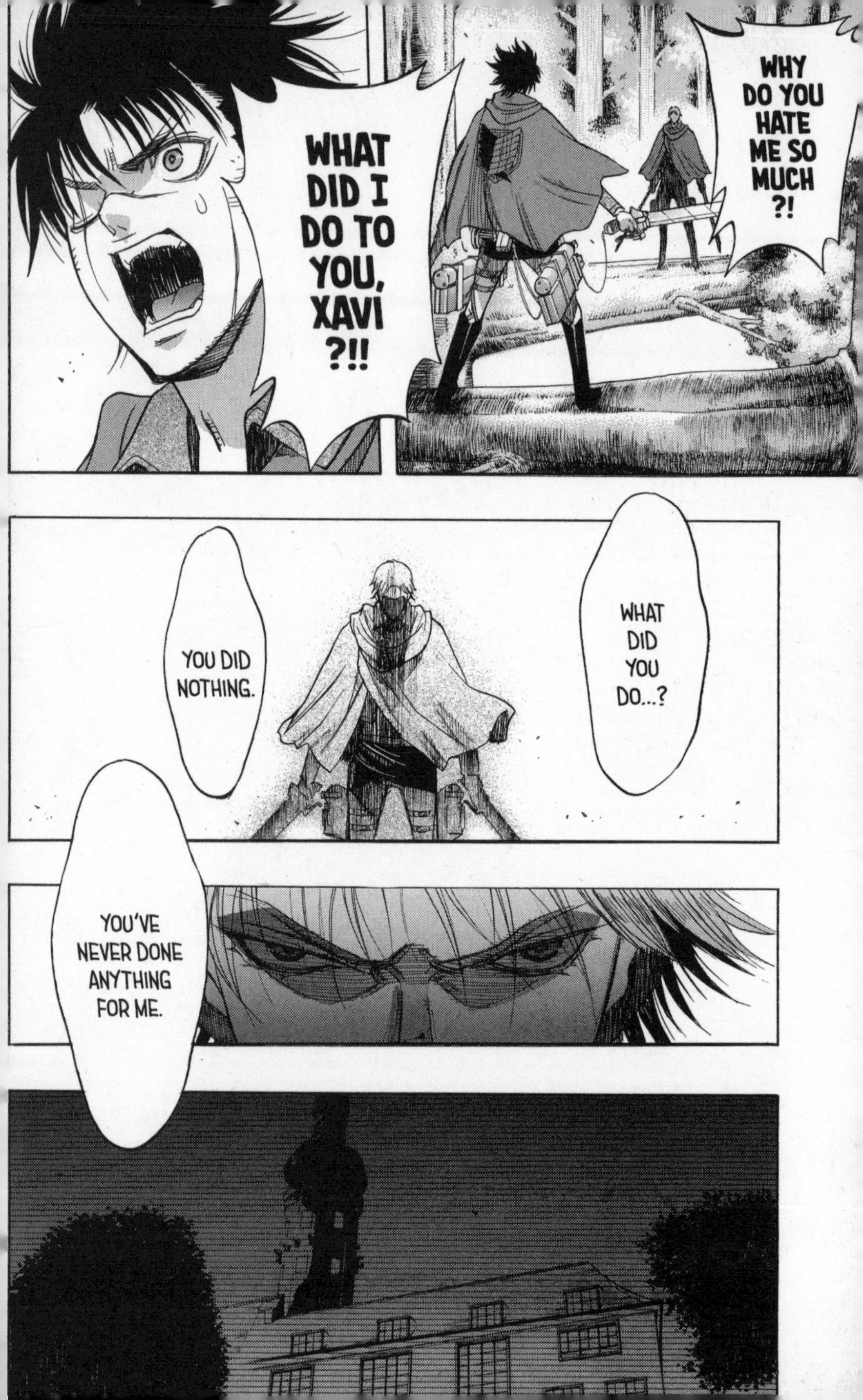
WHY DO YOU HATE ME SO MUCH?!
WHAT DID I DO TO YOU, XAVI?!!
WHAT DID YOU DO...?
YOU DID NOTHING.
YOU'VE NEVER DONE ANYTHING FOR ME.

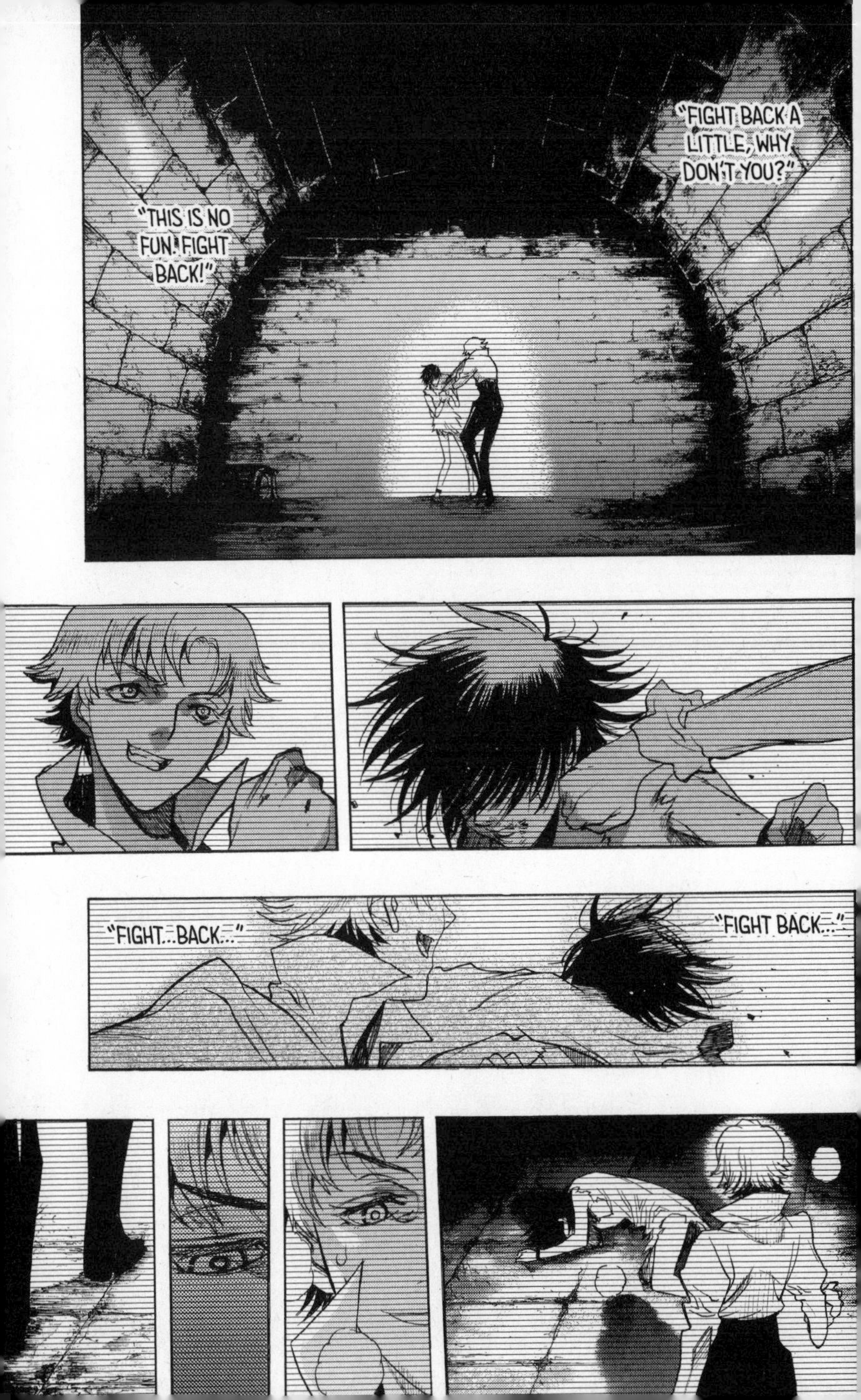
"FIGHT BACK A LITTLE, WHY DON'T YOU?"
"THIS IS NO FUN. FIGHT BACK!"
"FIGHT BACK..."
"FIGHT...BACK..."

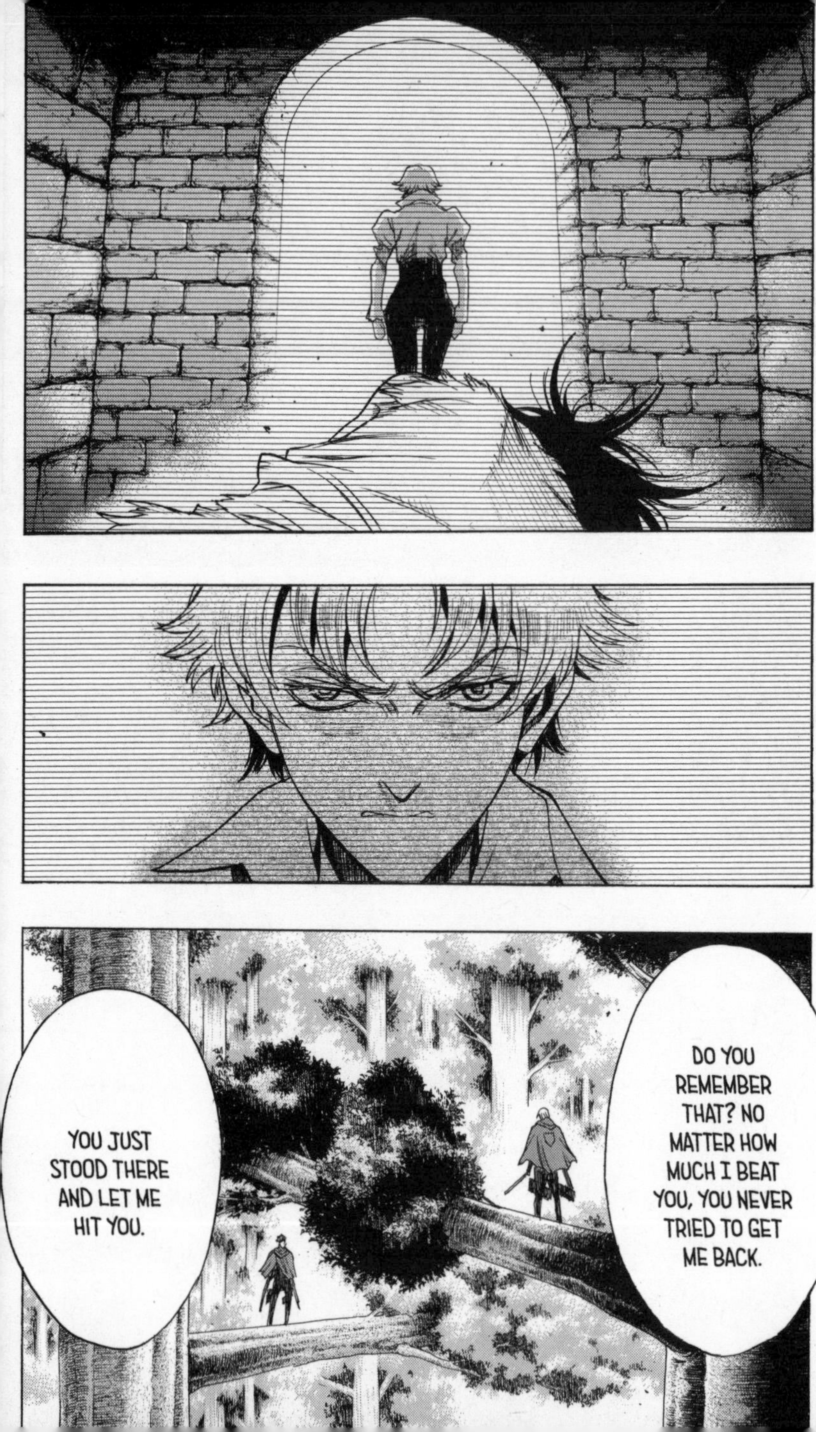
DO YOU REMEMBER THAT? NO MATTER HOW MUCH I BEAT YOU, YOU NEVER TRIED TO GET ME BACK.
YOU JUST STOOD THERE AND LET ME HIT YOU.

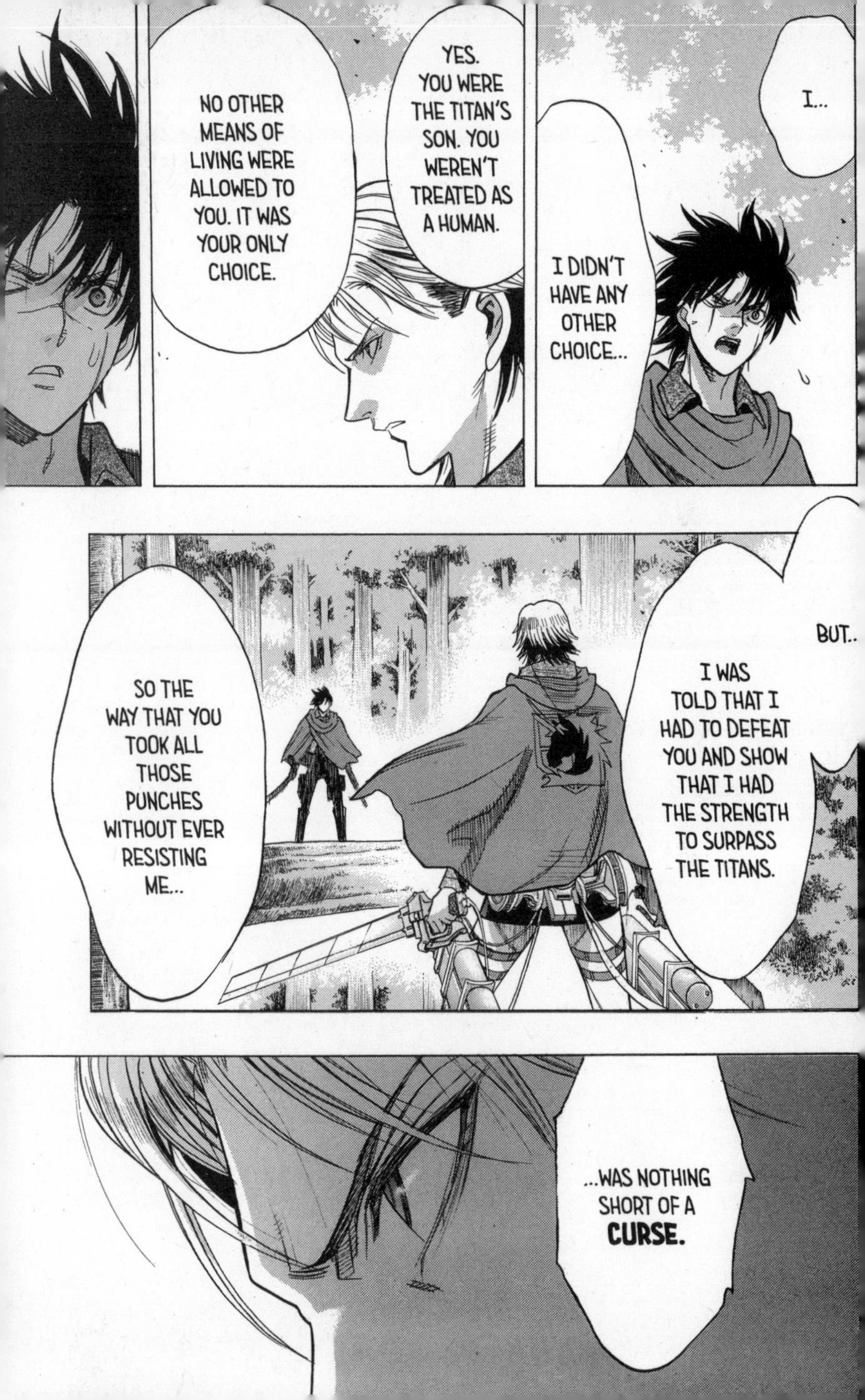
I...
I DIDN'T HAVE ANY OTHER CHOICE...
YES. YOU WERE THE TITAN'S SON. YOU WEREN'T TREATED AS A HUMAN.
NO OTHER MEANS OF LIVING WERE ALLOWED TO YOU. IT WAS YOUR ONLY CHOICE.
BUT..
I WAS TOLD THAT I HAD TO DEFEAT YOU AND SHOW THAT I HAD THE STRENGTH TO SURPASS THE TITANS.
SO THE WAY THAT YOU TOOK ALL THOSE PUNCHES WITHOUT EVER RESISTING ME...
...WAS NOTHING SHORT OF A CURSE.

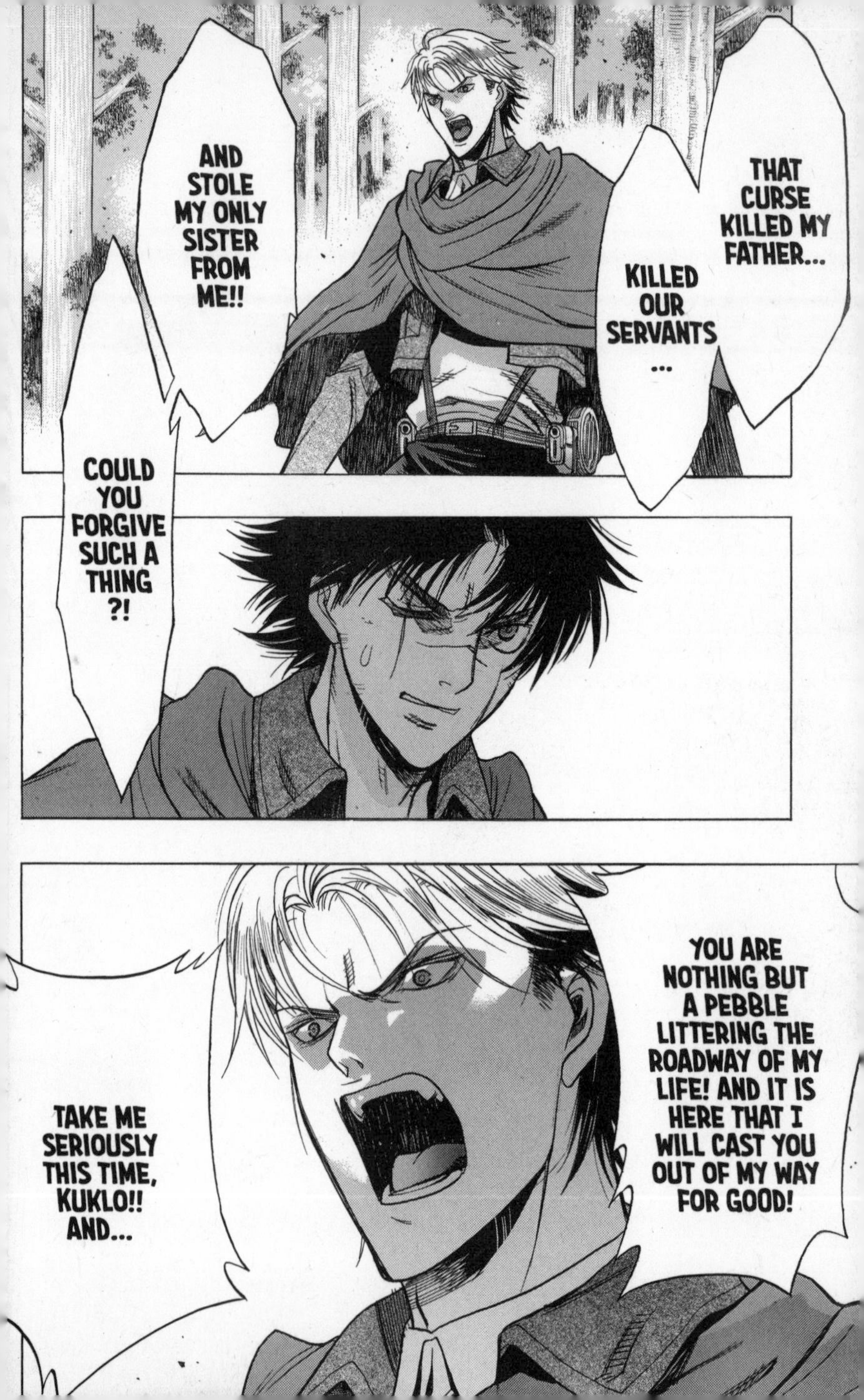
THAT CURSE KILLED MY FATHER...
KILLED OUR SERVANTS ...
AND STOLE MY ONLY SISTER FROM ME!!
COULD YOU FORGIVE SUCH A THING ?!
YOU ARE NOTHING BUT A PEBBLE LITTERING THE ROADWAY OF MY LIFE! AND IT IS HERE THAT I WILL CAST YOU OUT OF MY WAY FOR GOOD!
TAKE ME SERIOUSLY THIS TIME, KUKLO!! AND...

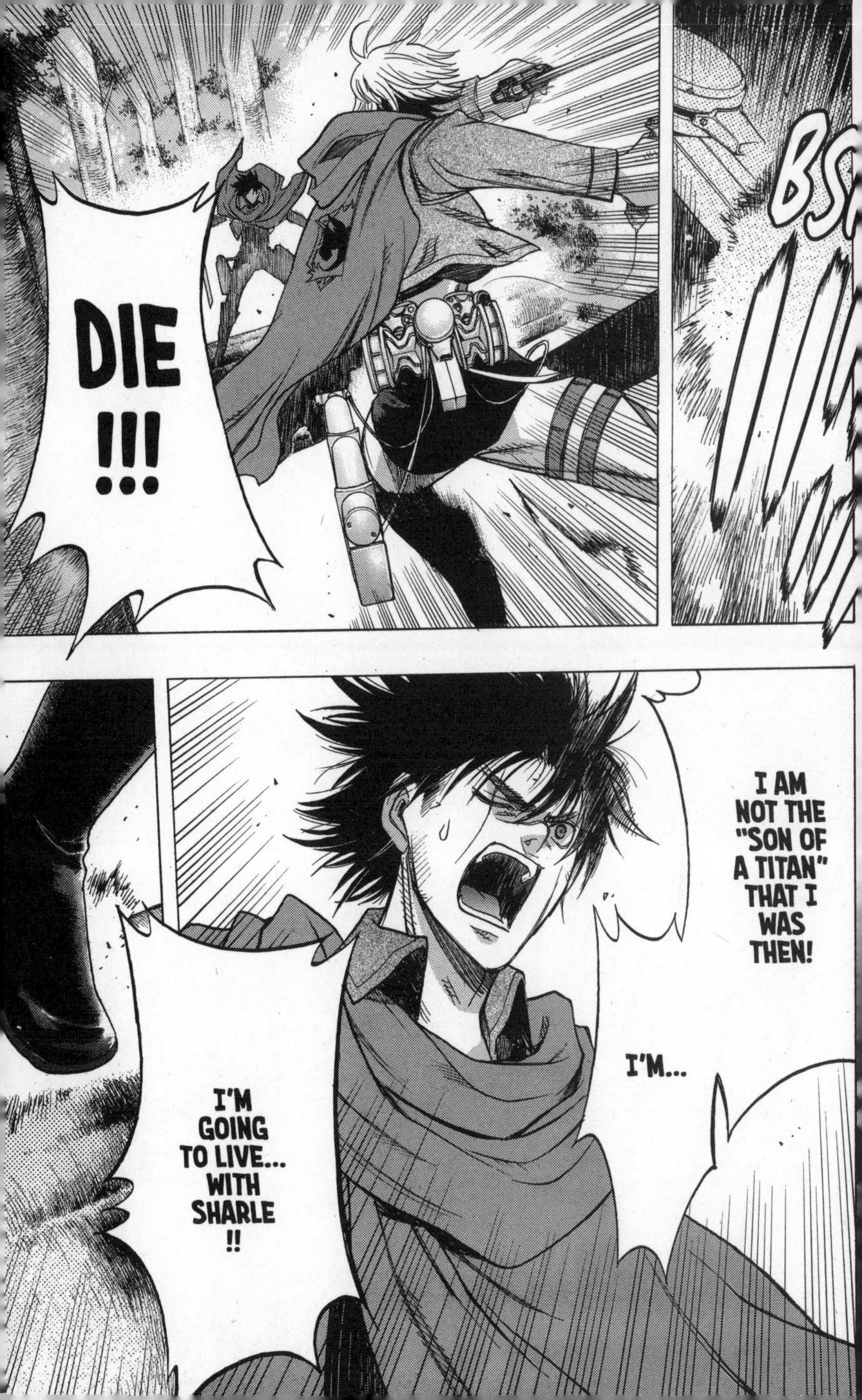
BS
DIE !!!
I AM NOT THE "SON OF A TITAN" THAT I WAS THEN!
I'M...
I'M GOING TO LIVE... WITH SHARLE !!

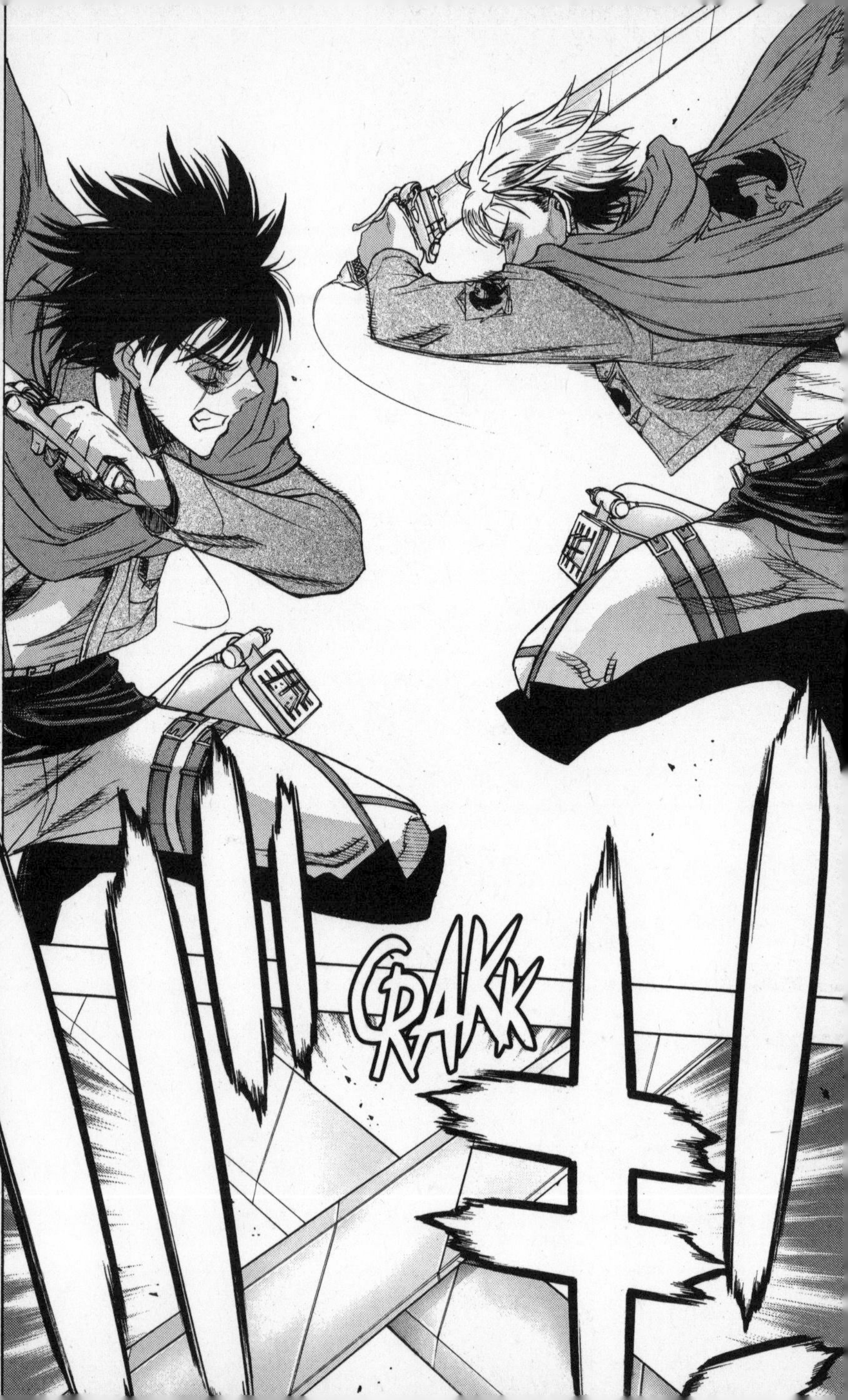
CRAKK

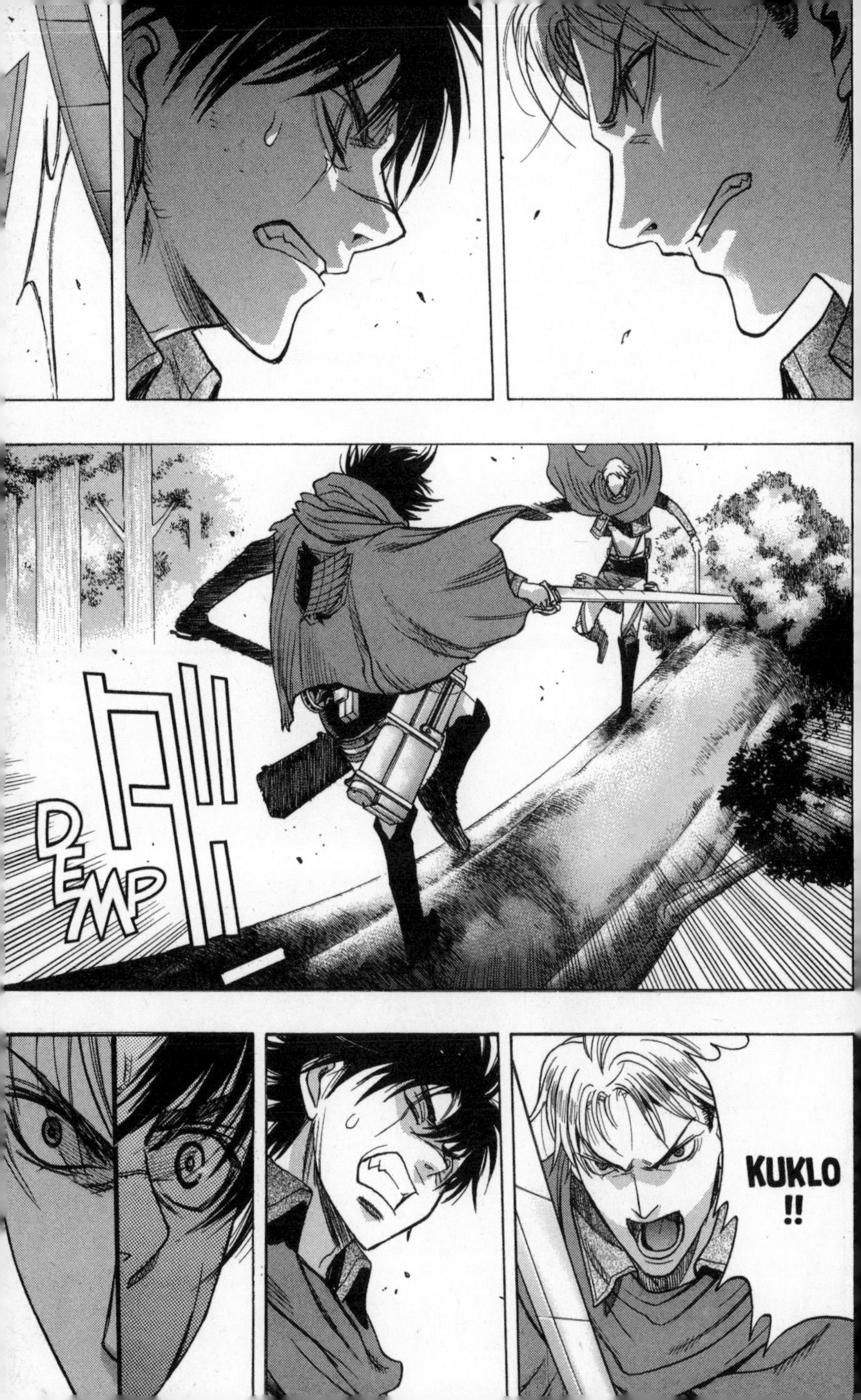
DEMP
KUKLO
!!

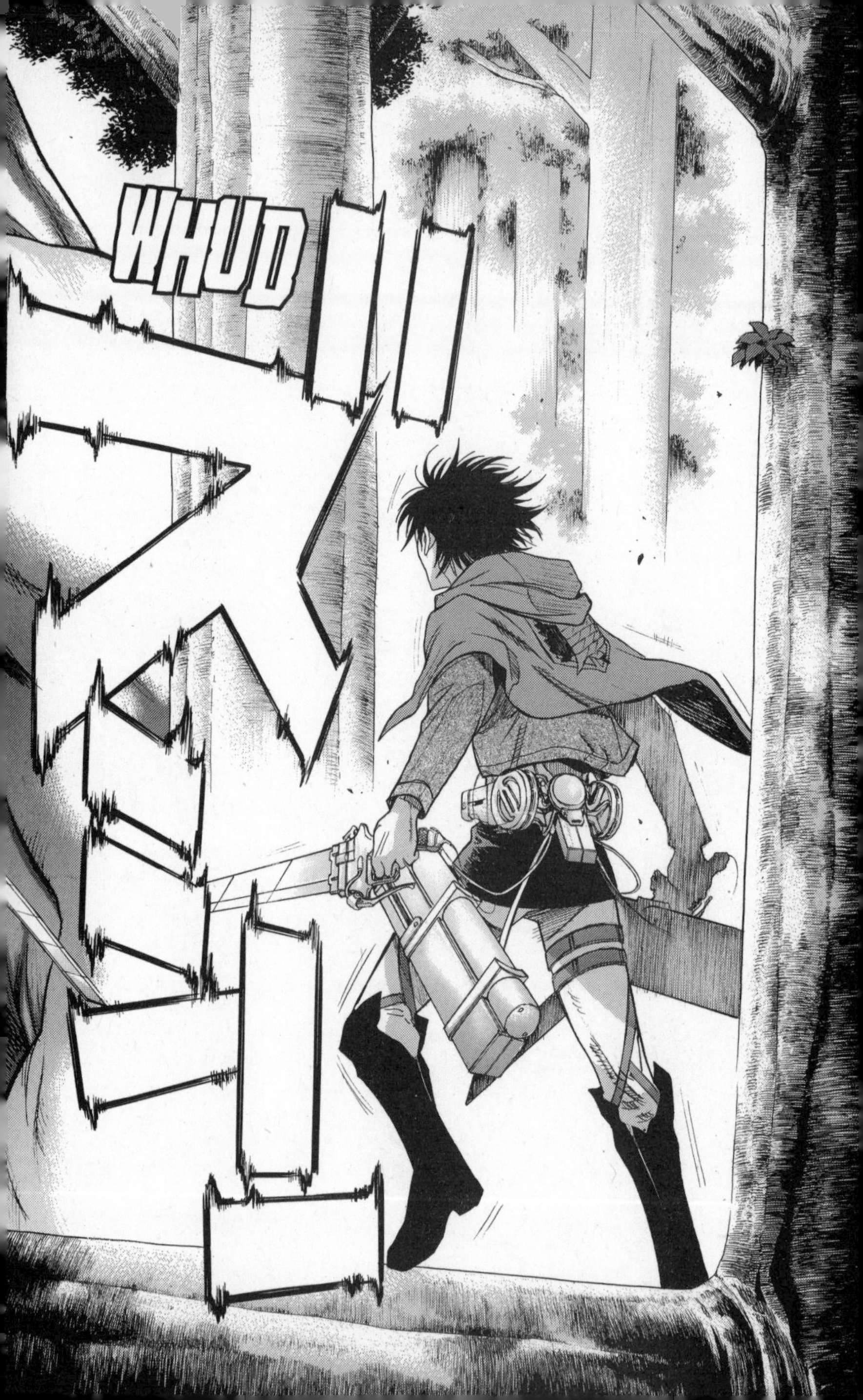
WHUD

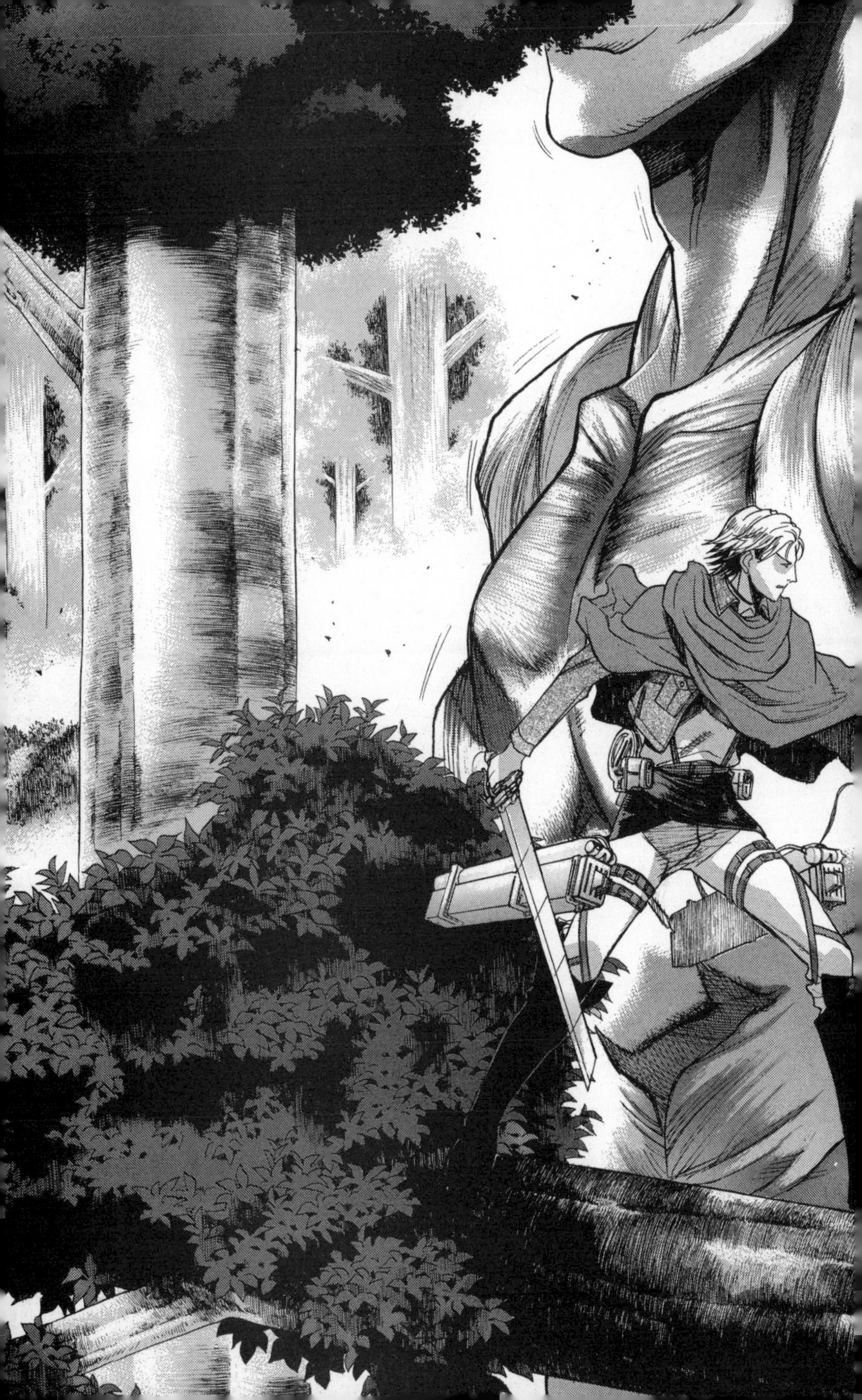

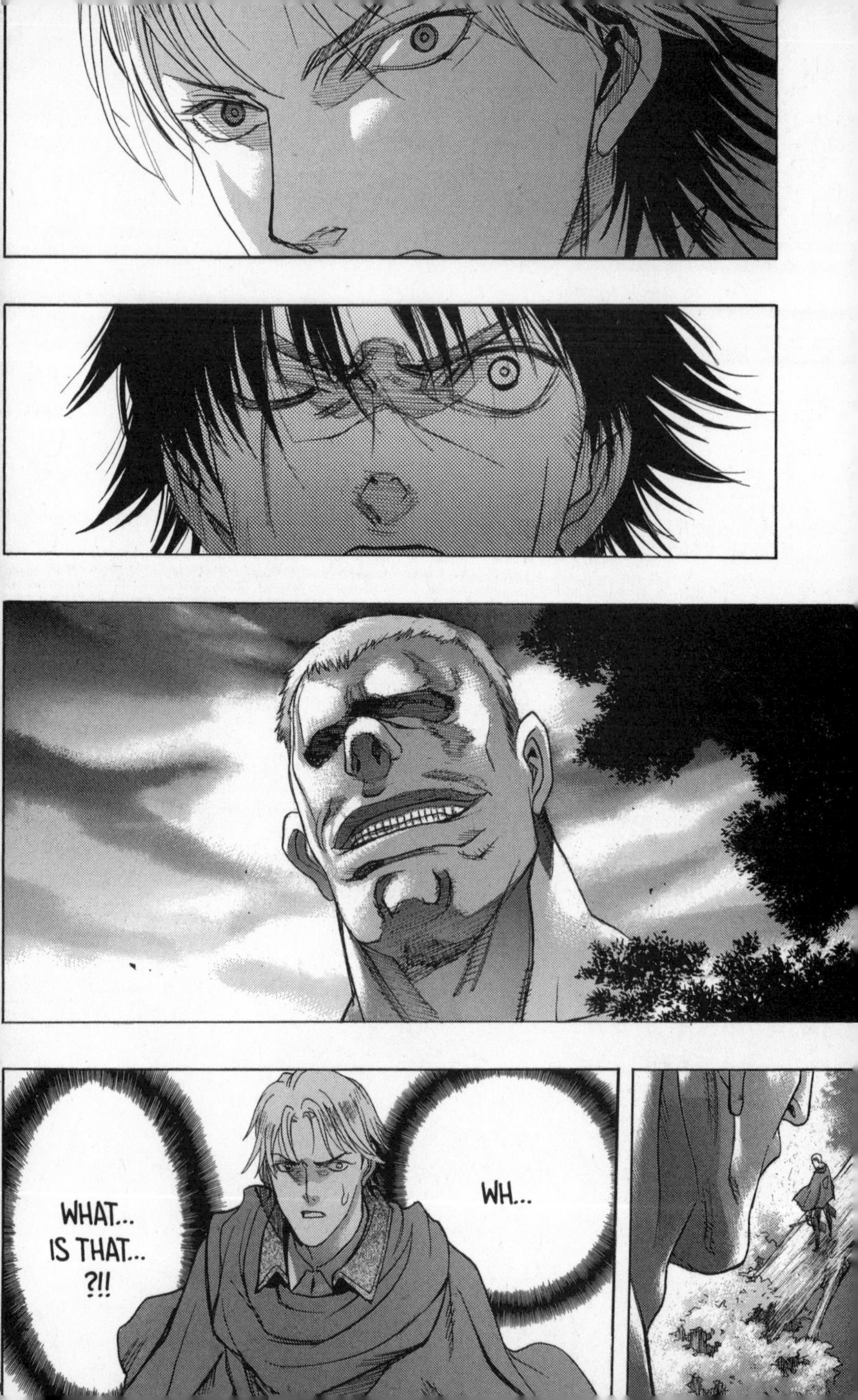
WH...
WHAT... IS THAT... ?!!

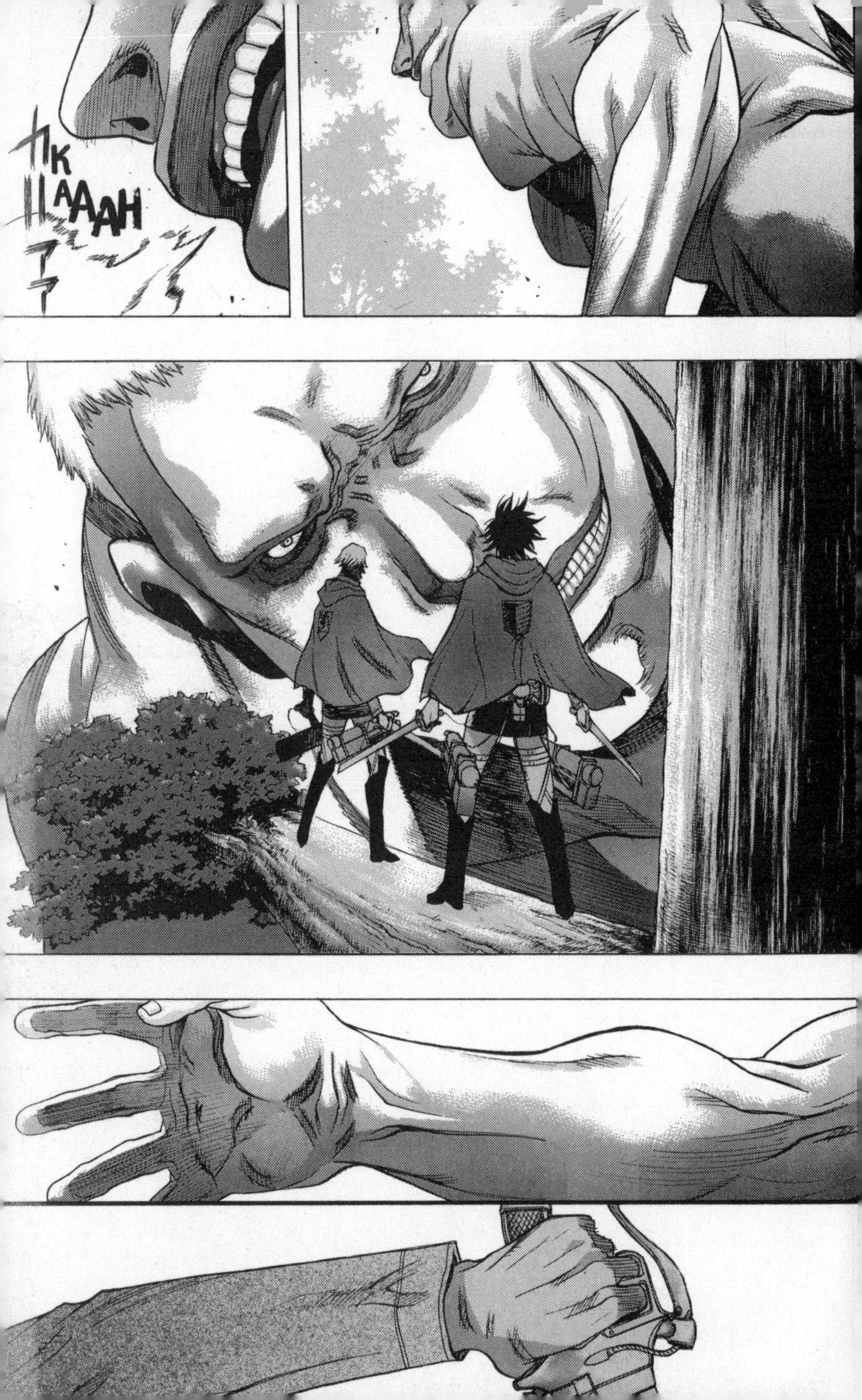

カハァァ
K
AAAH

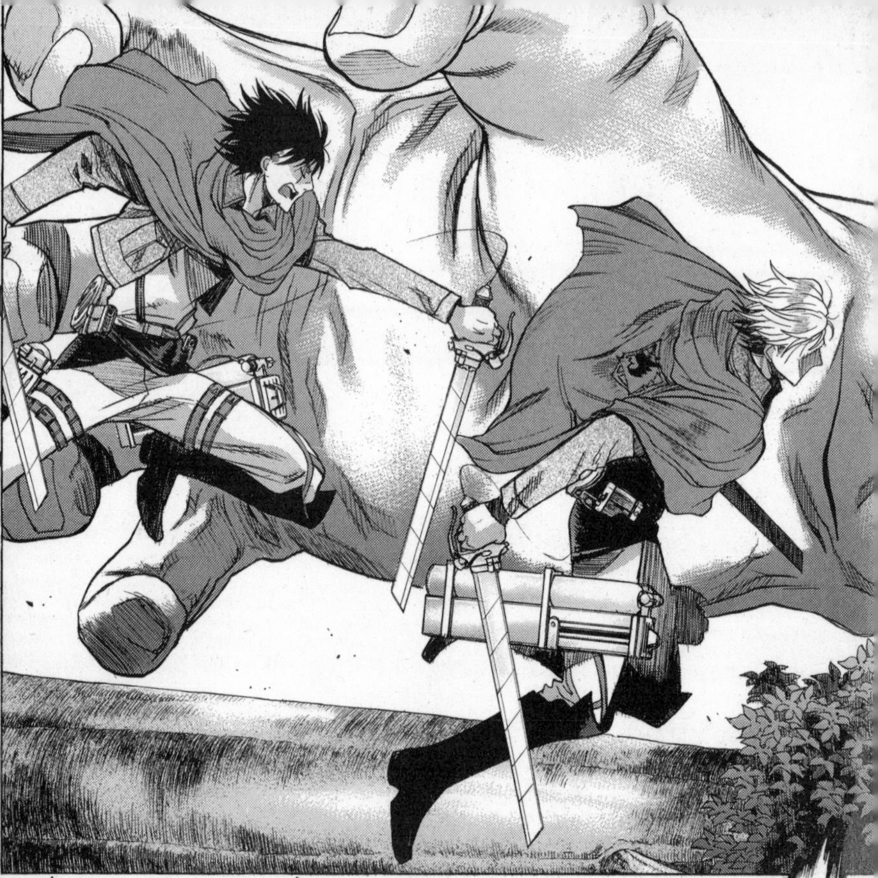
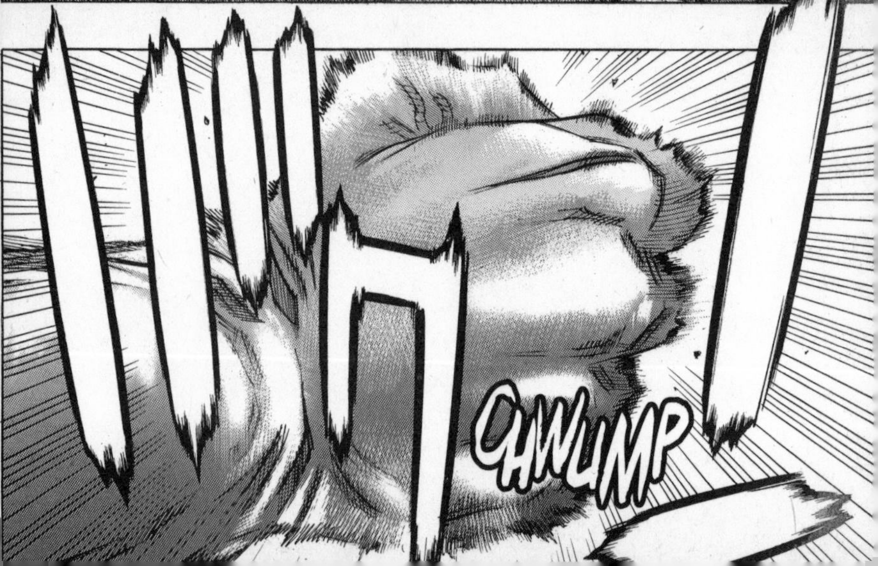
CHWUMP

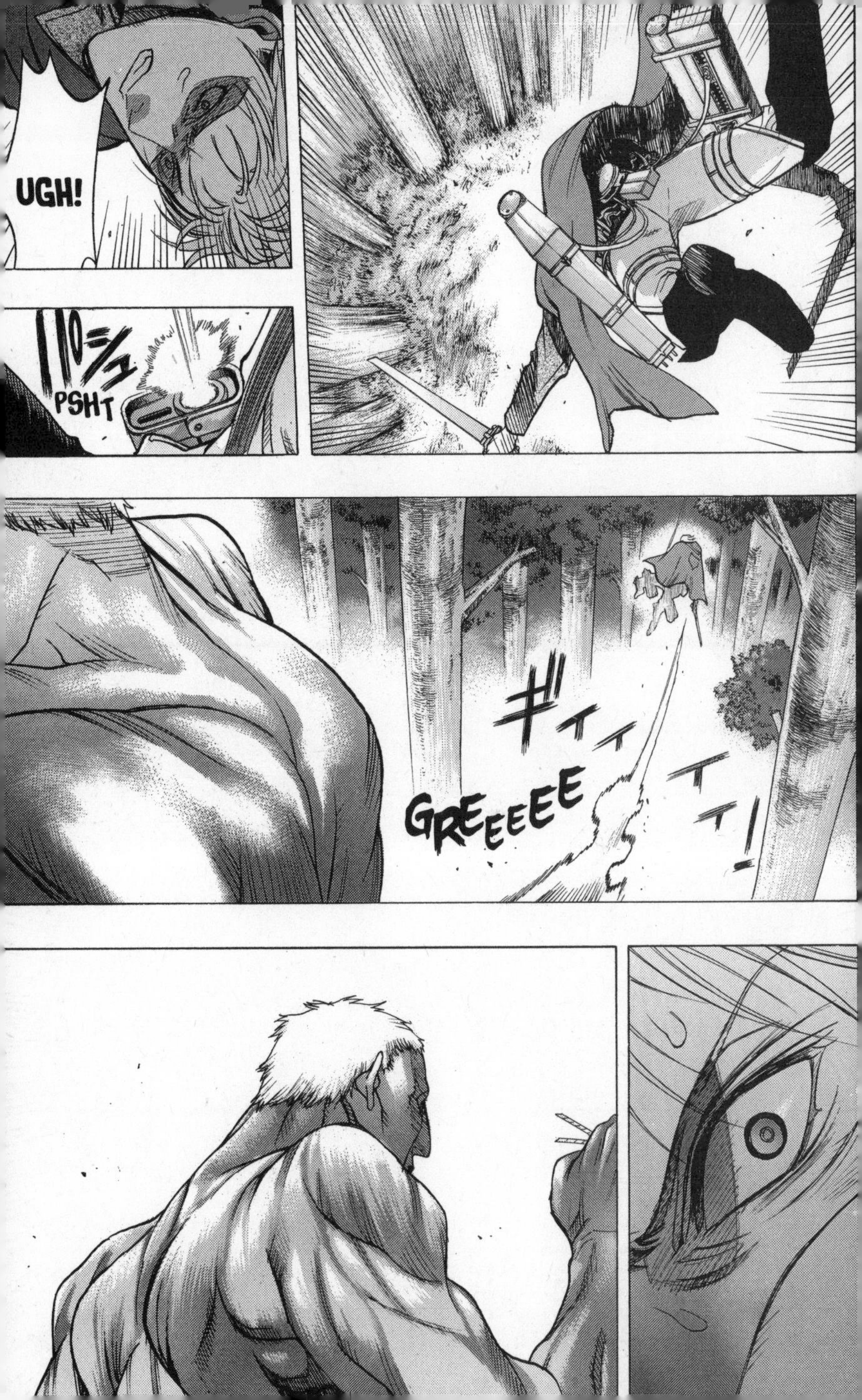
UGH!
PSHT
GREEEEE

WHOOSH

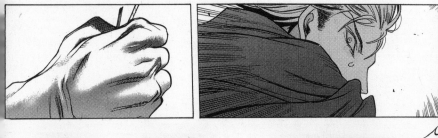

HUFF!!

HUFF!!

HUFF!!

HUFF!!

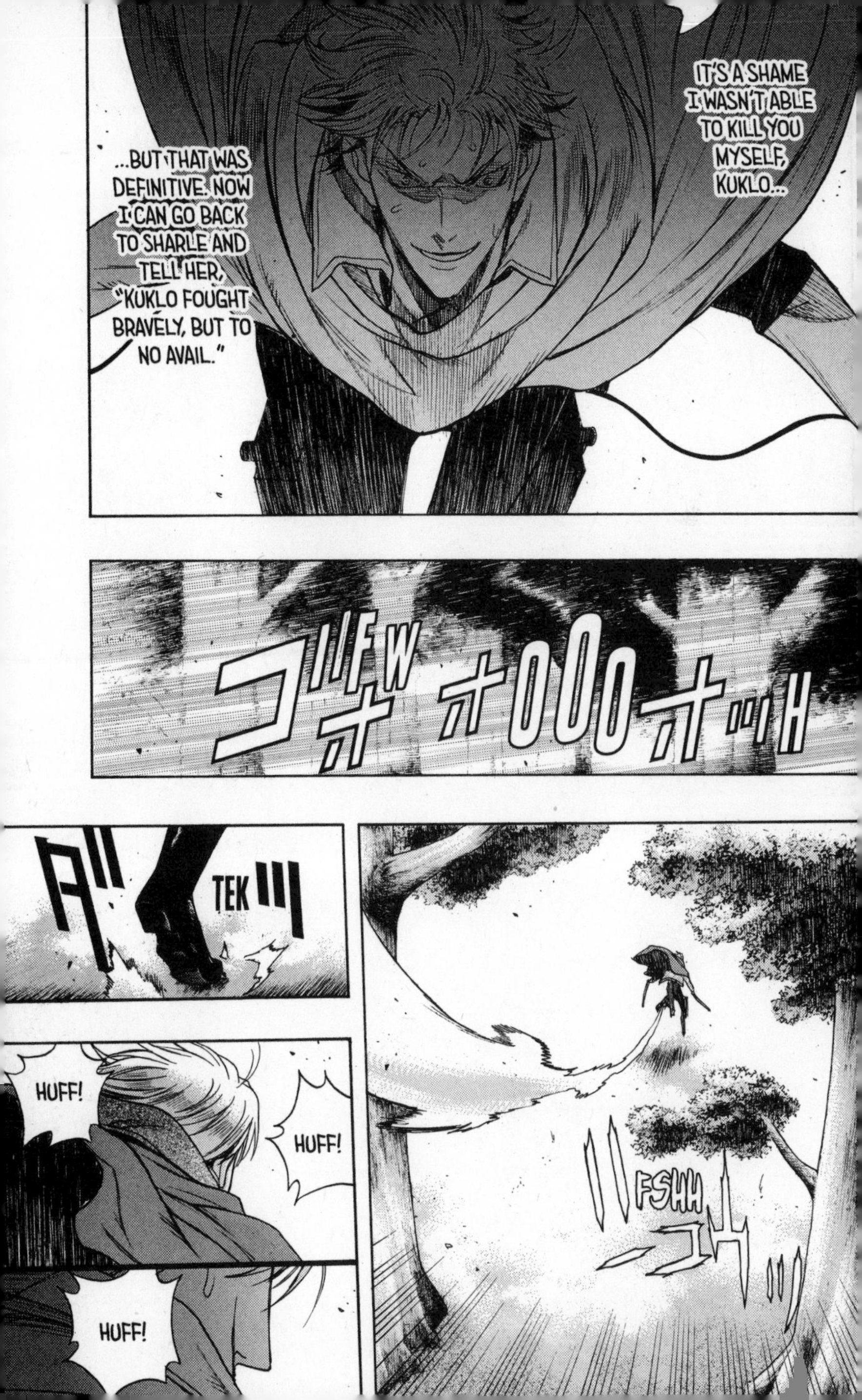
IT'S A SHAME I WASN'T ABLE TO KILL YOU MYSELF, KUKLO...
...BUT THAT WAS DEFINITIVE. NOW I CAN GO BACK TO SHARLE AND TELL HER, "KUKLO FOUGHT BRAVELY, BUT TO NO AVAIL."
FWOOOH
FSHH
TEK
HUFF!
HUFF!
HUFF!

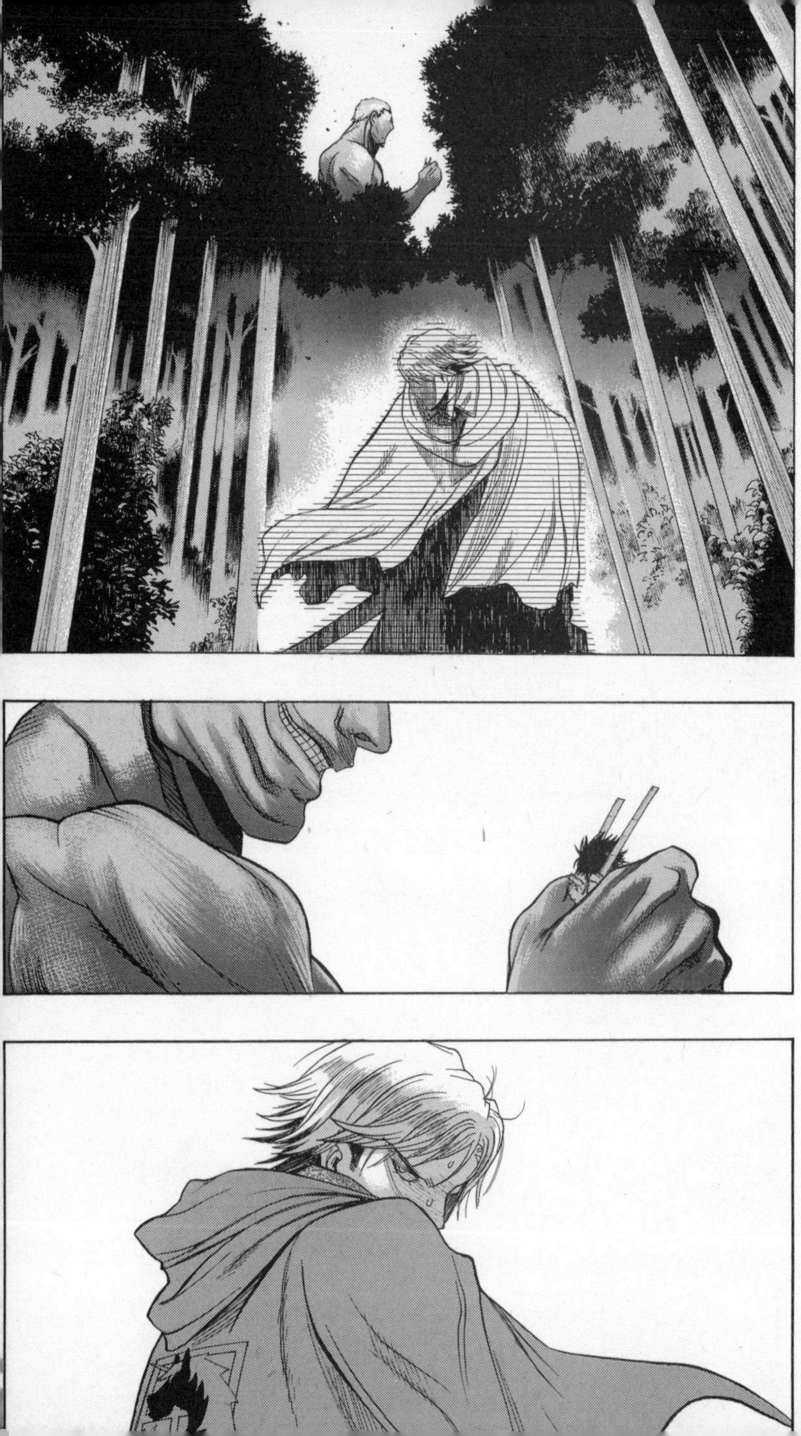

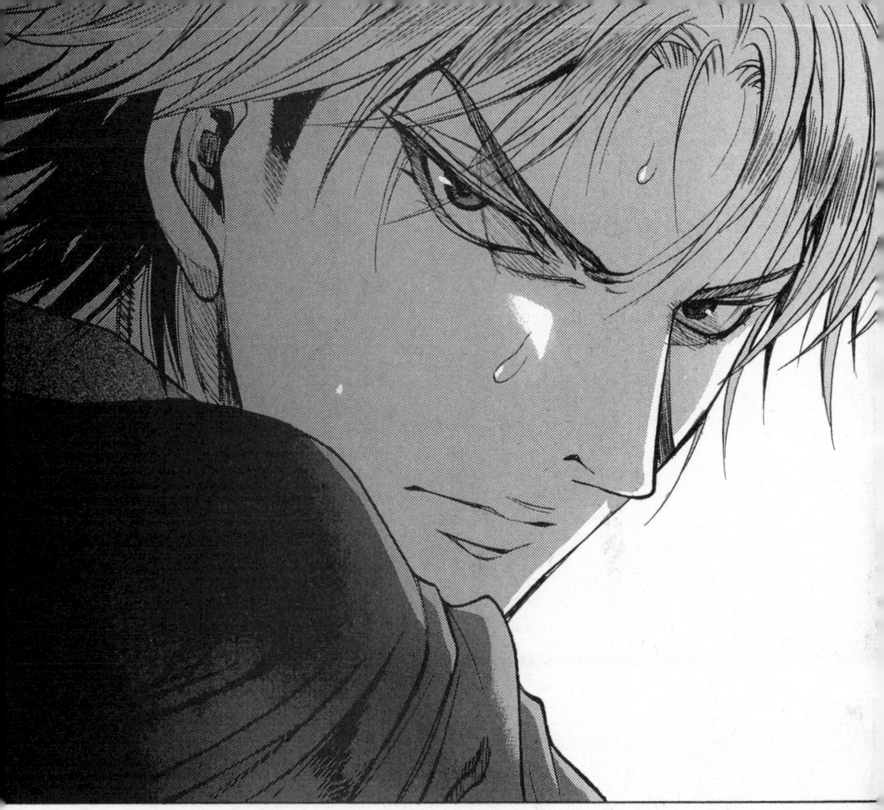

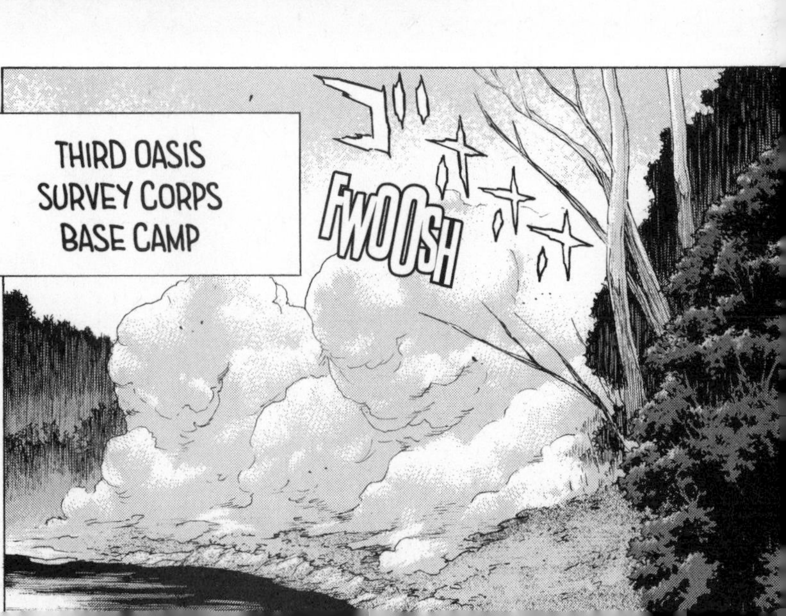
THIRD OASIS
SURVEY CORPS
BASE CAMP
FWOOSH

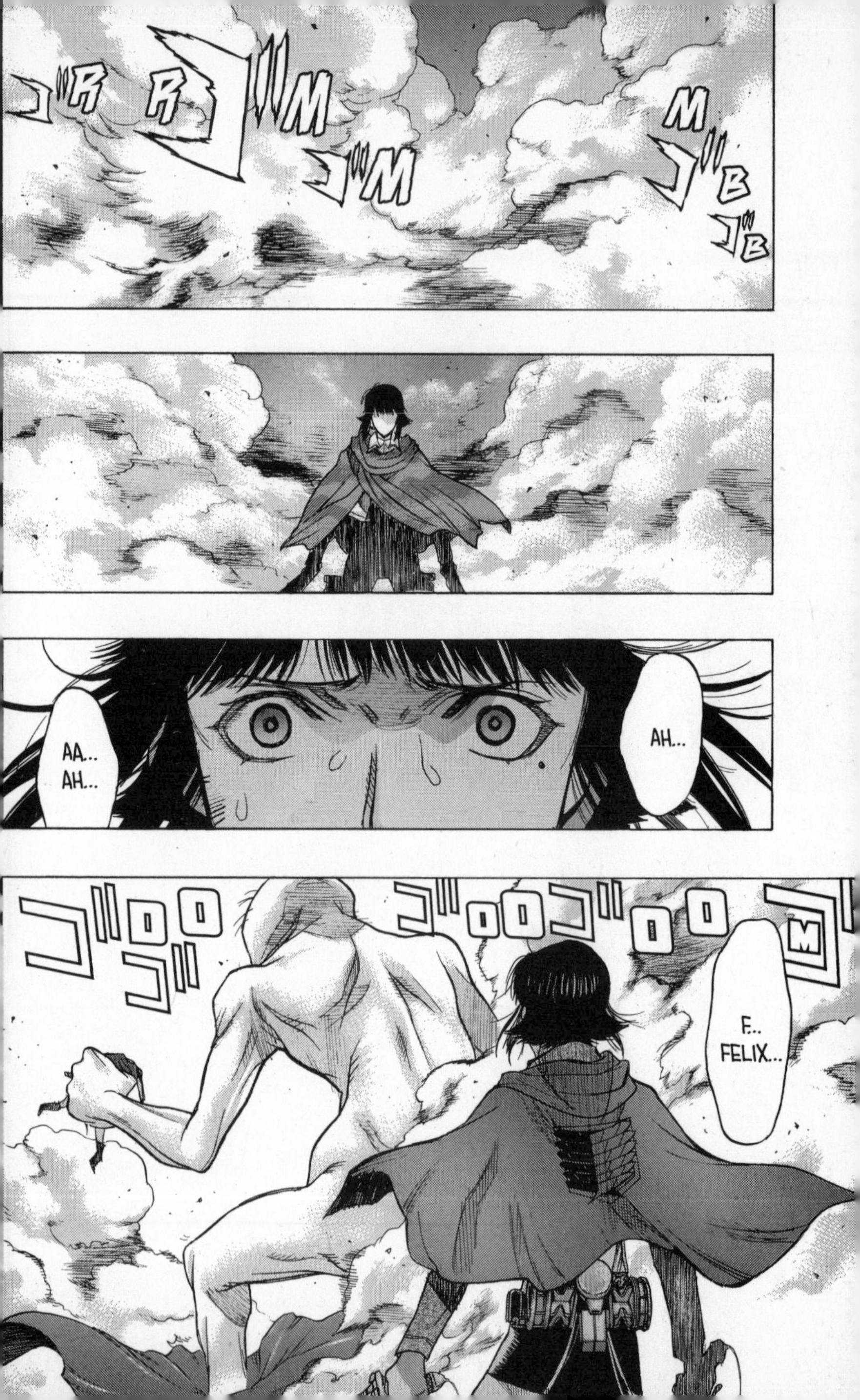
M ゴB ゴB
ゴR R ゴM ゴM
AH...
AA... AH...
ゴOOゴOO ゴM
ゴOO ゴ
F... FELIX...

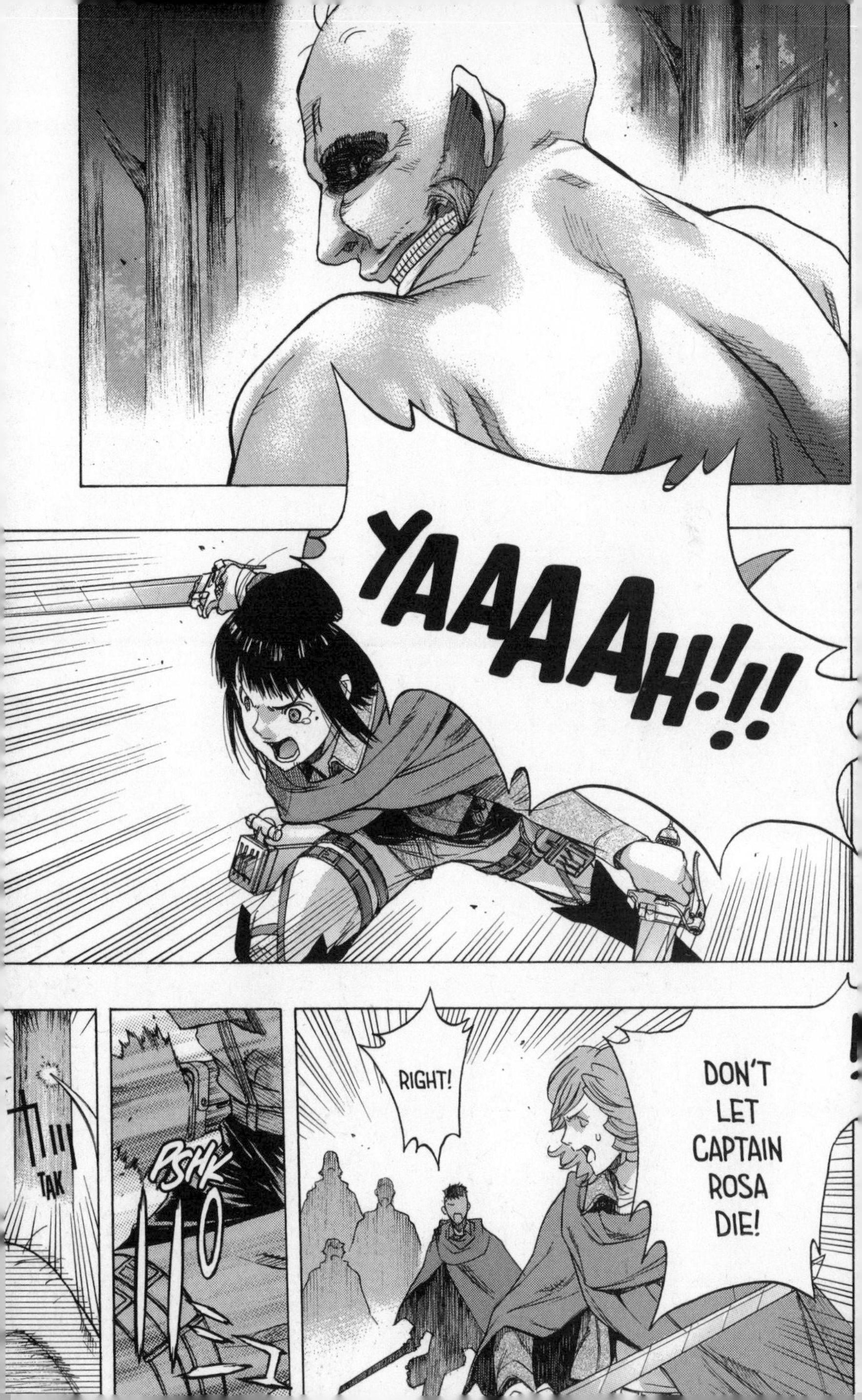
YAAAAAH!!!
DON'T LET CAPTAIN ROSA DIE!
RIGHT!
PSHK
TAK

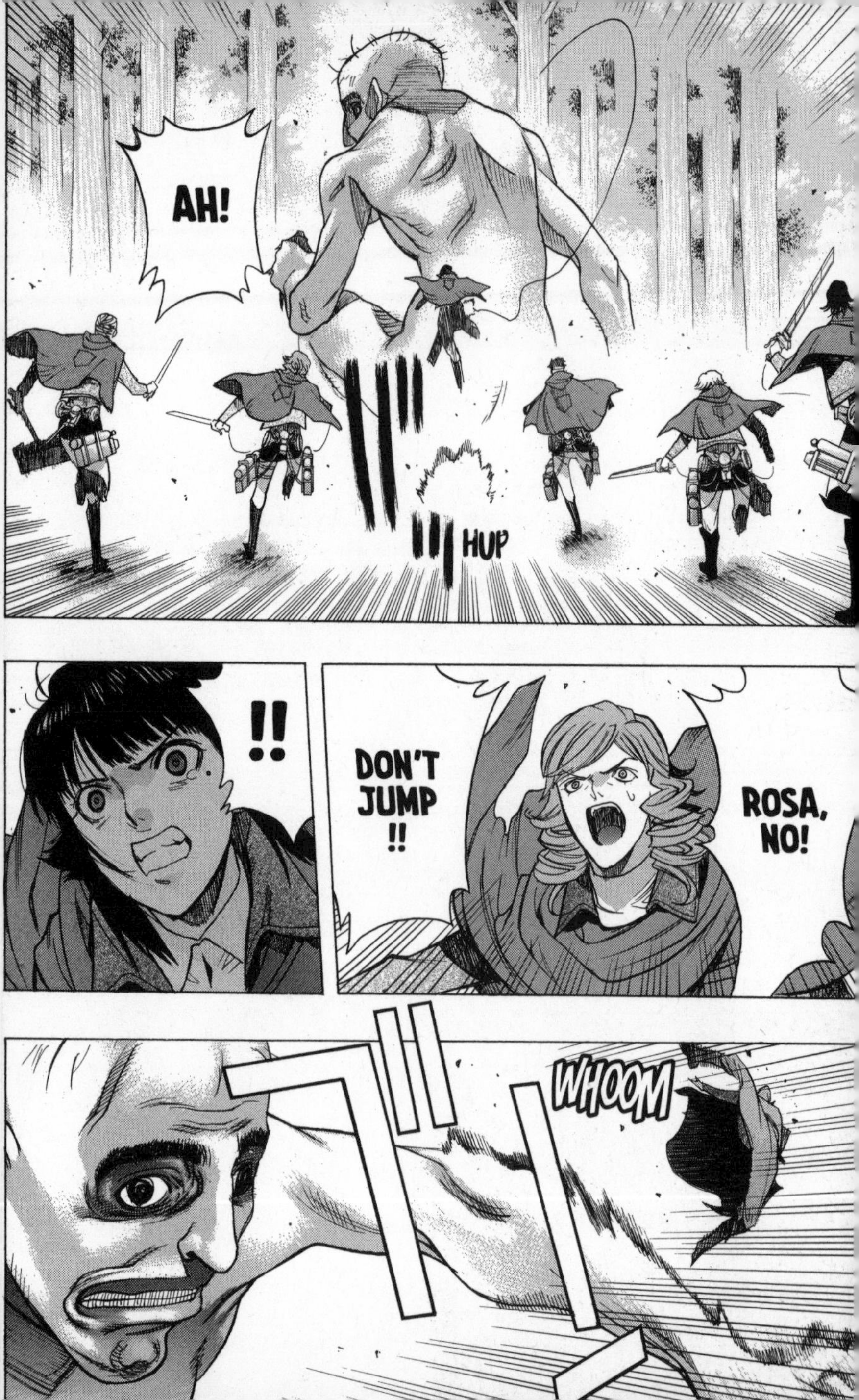
AH!
HUP
ROSA, NO!
DON'T JUMP !!
!!
WHOOM

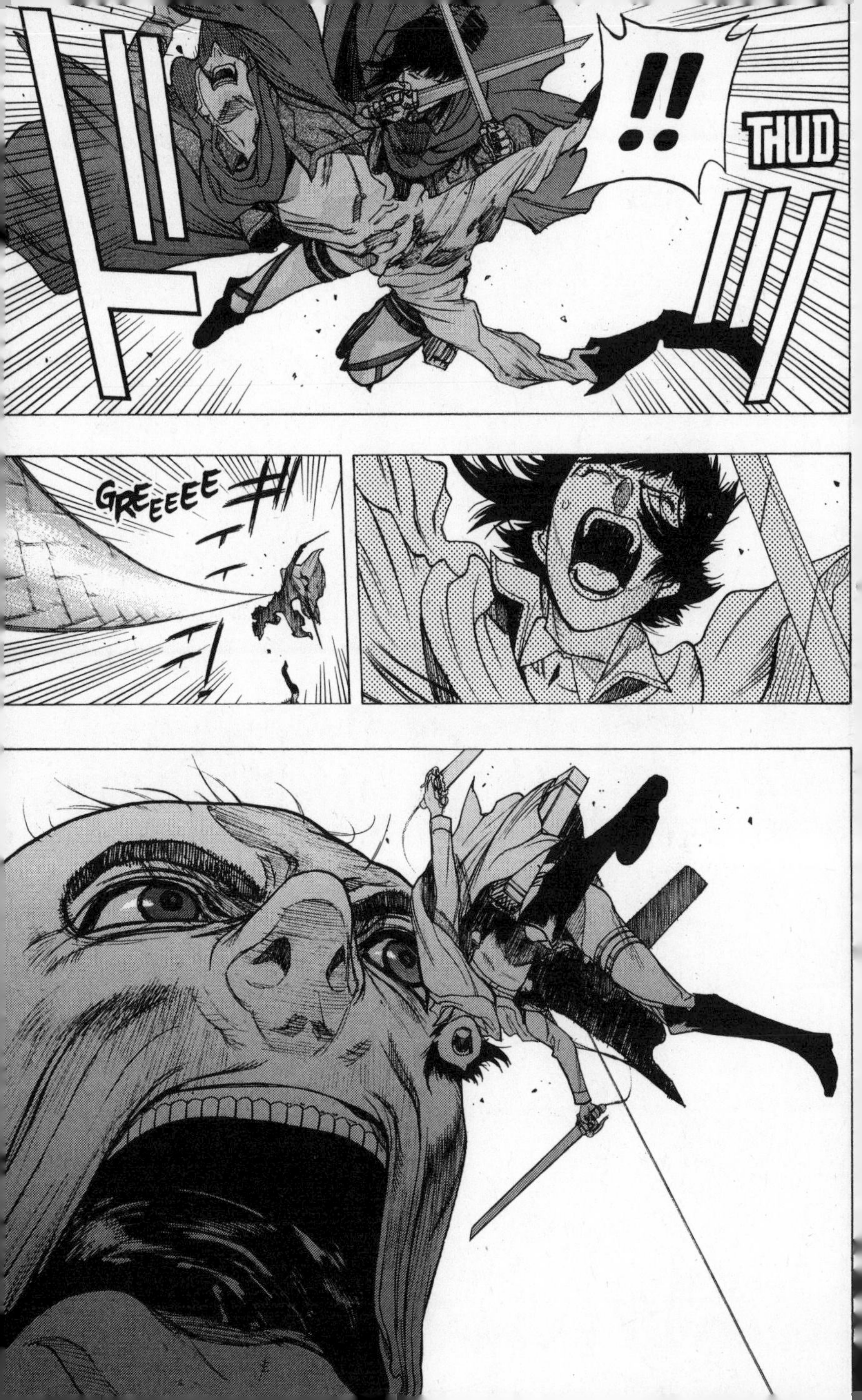
!!
THUD
GREEEEE

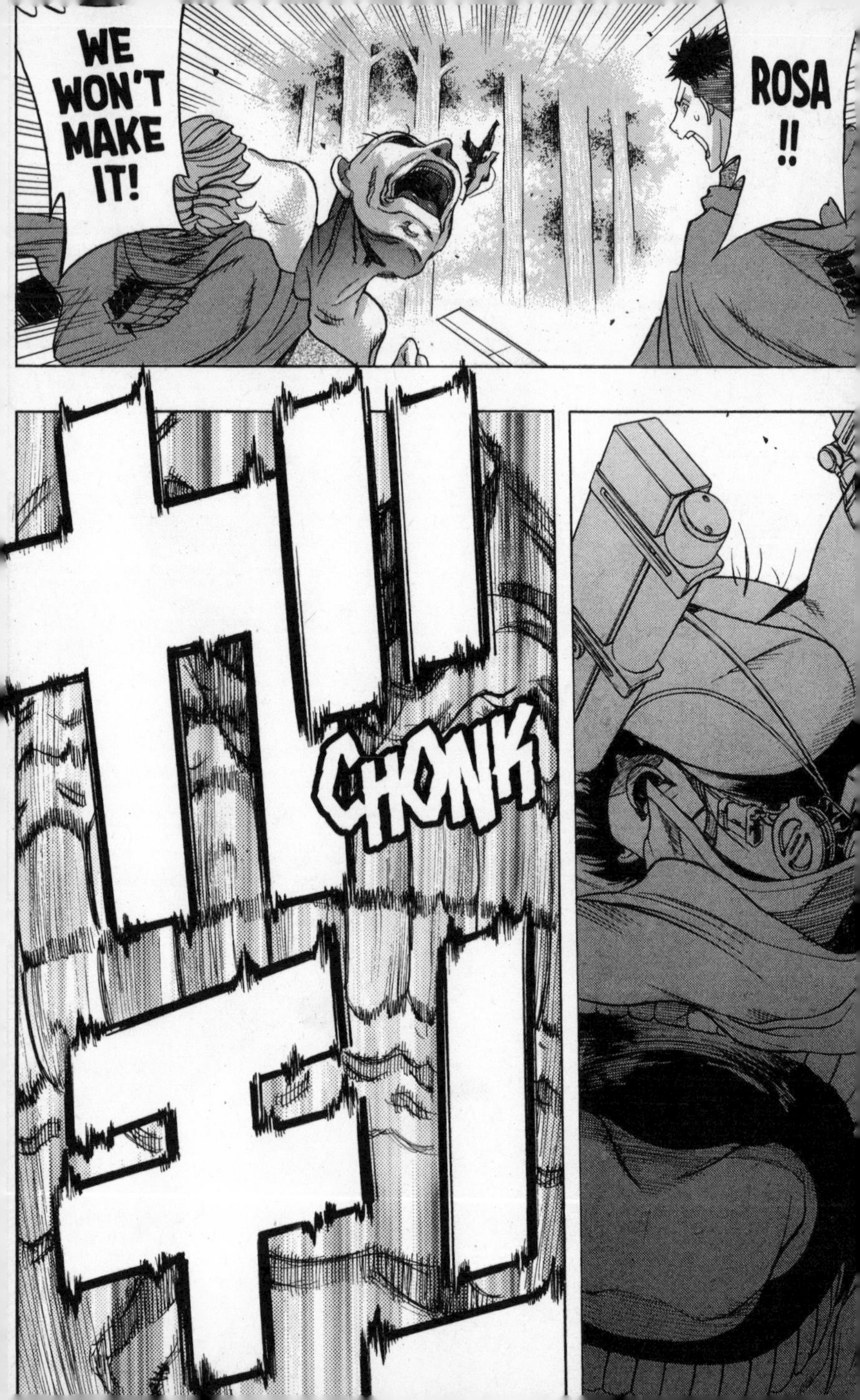
ROSA !!
WE WON'T MAKE IT!
CHONK

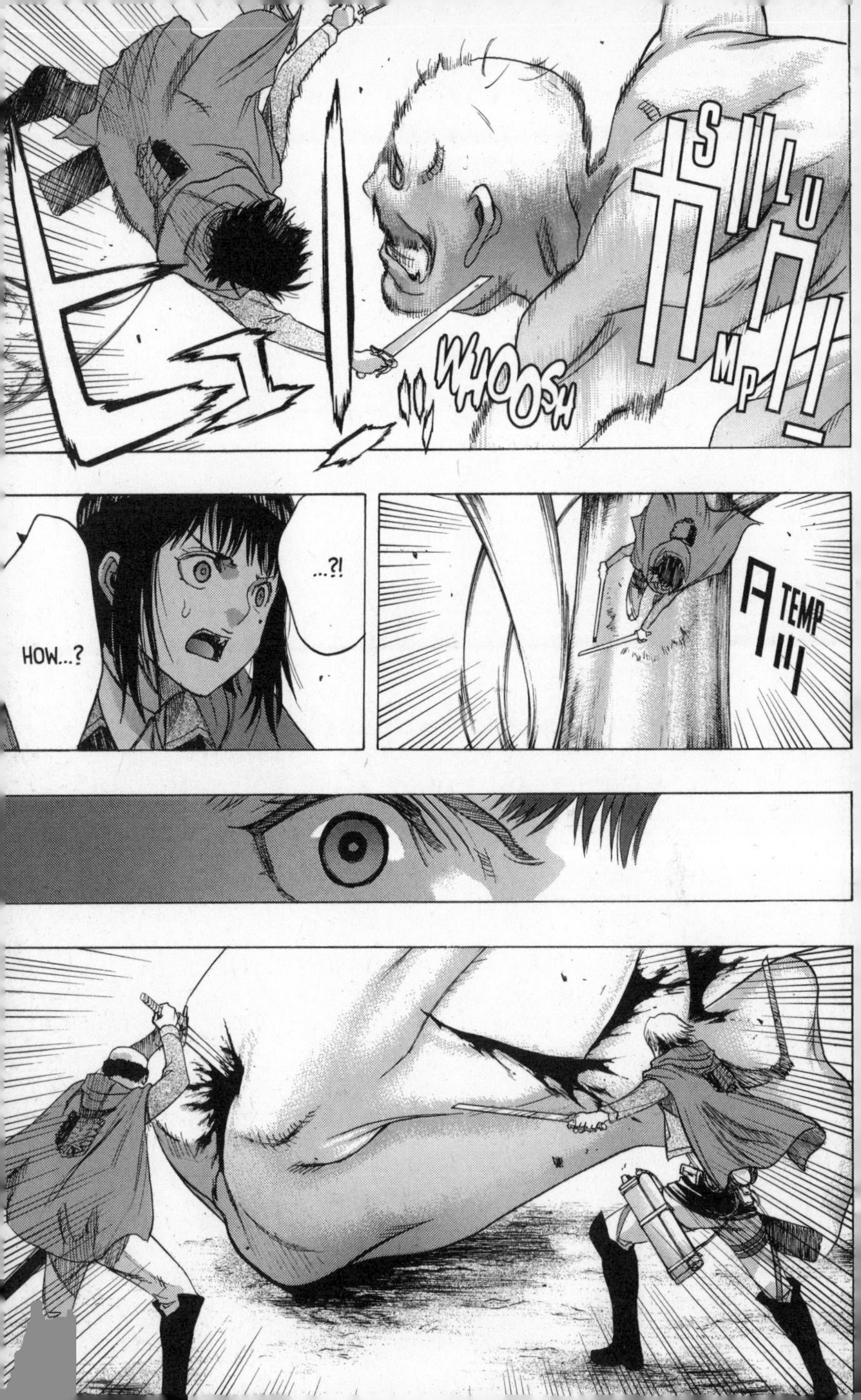
SLUMP
WHOOSH
TEMP
...?!
HOW...?

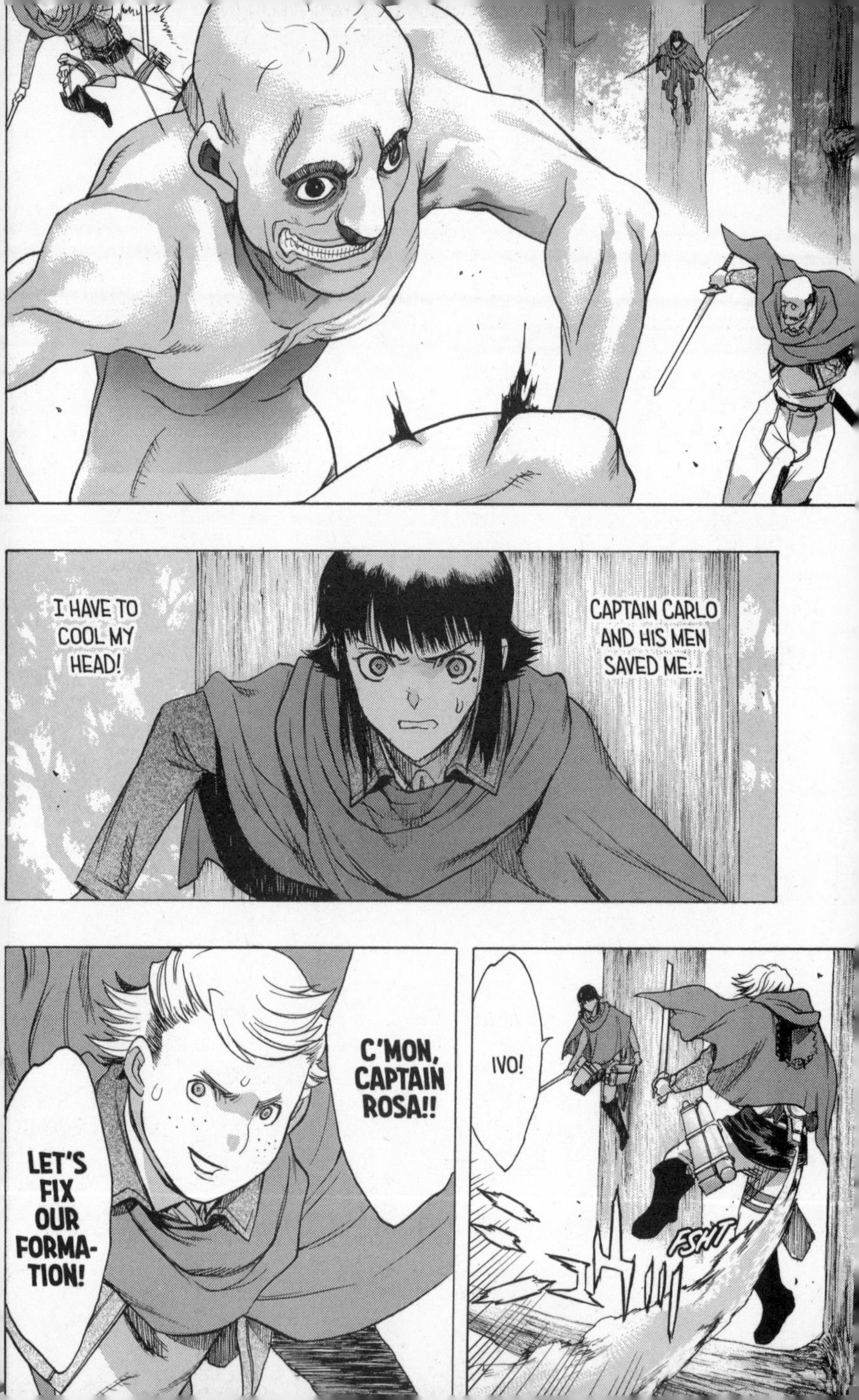
CAPTAIN CARLO AND HIS MEN SAVED ME...
I HAVE TO COOL MY HEAD!
IVO!
FSHT
C'MON, CAPTAIN ROSA!!
LET'S FIX OUR FORMATION!

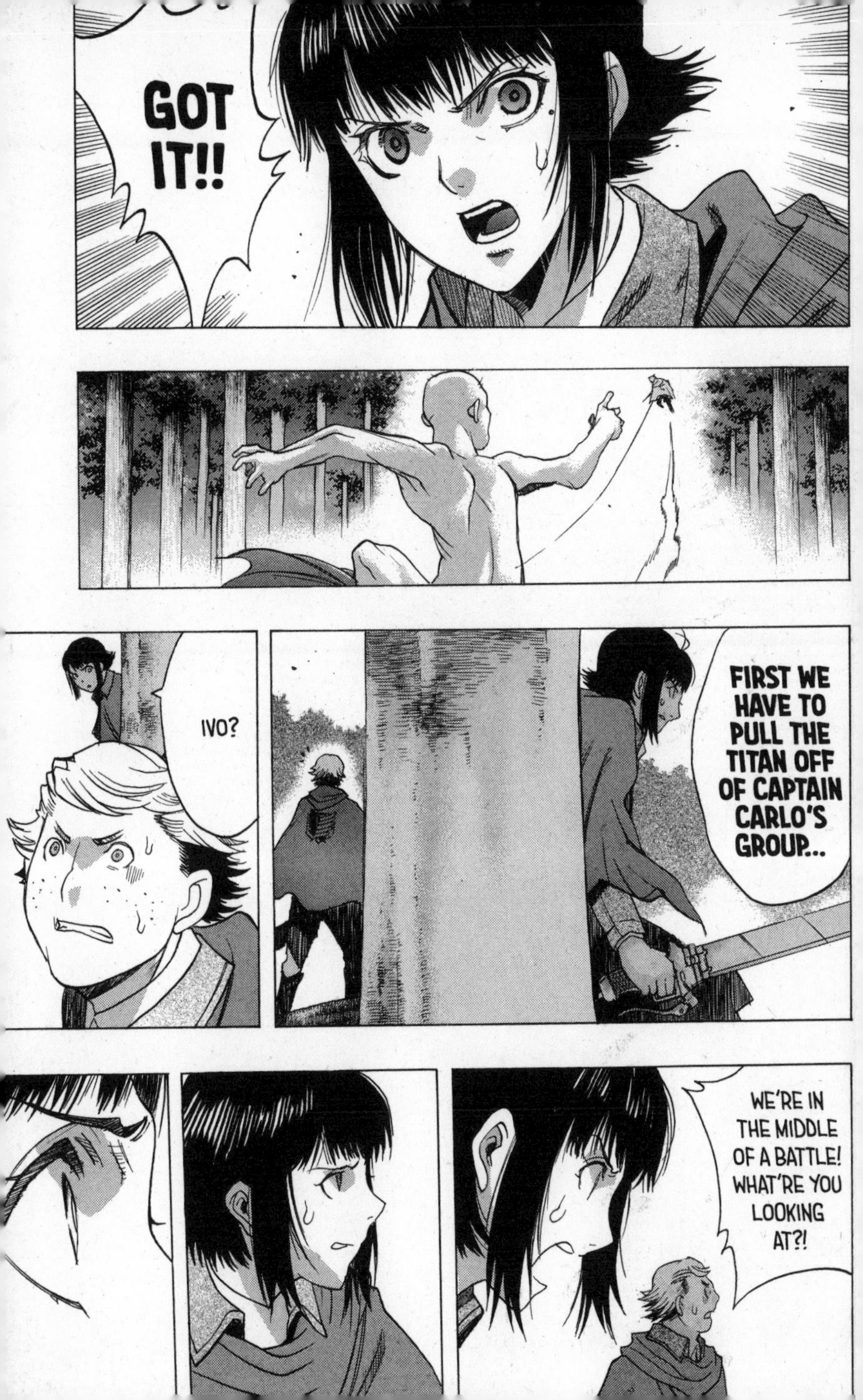
GOT IT!!
FIRST WE HAVE TO PULL THE TITAN OFF OF CAPTAIN CARLO'S GROUP...
IVO?
WE'RE IN THE MIDDLE OF A BATTLE! WHAT'RE YOU LOOKING AT?!

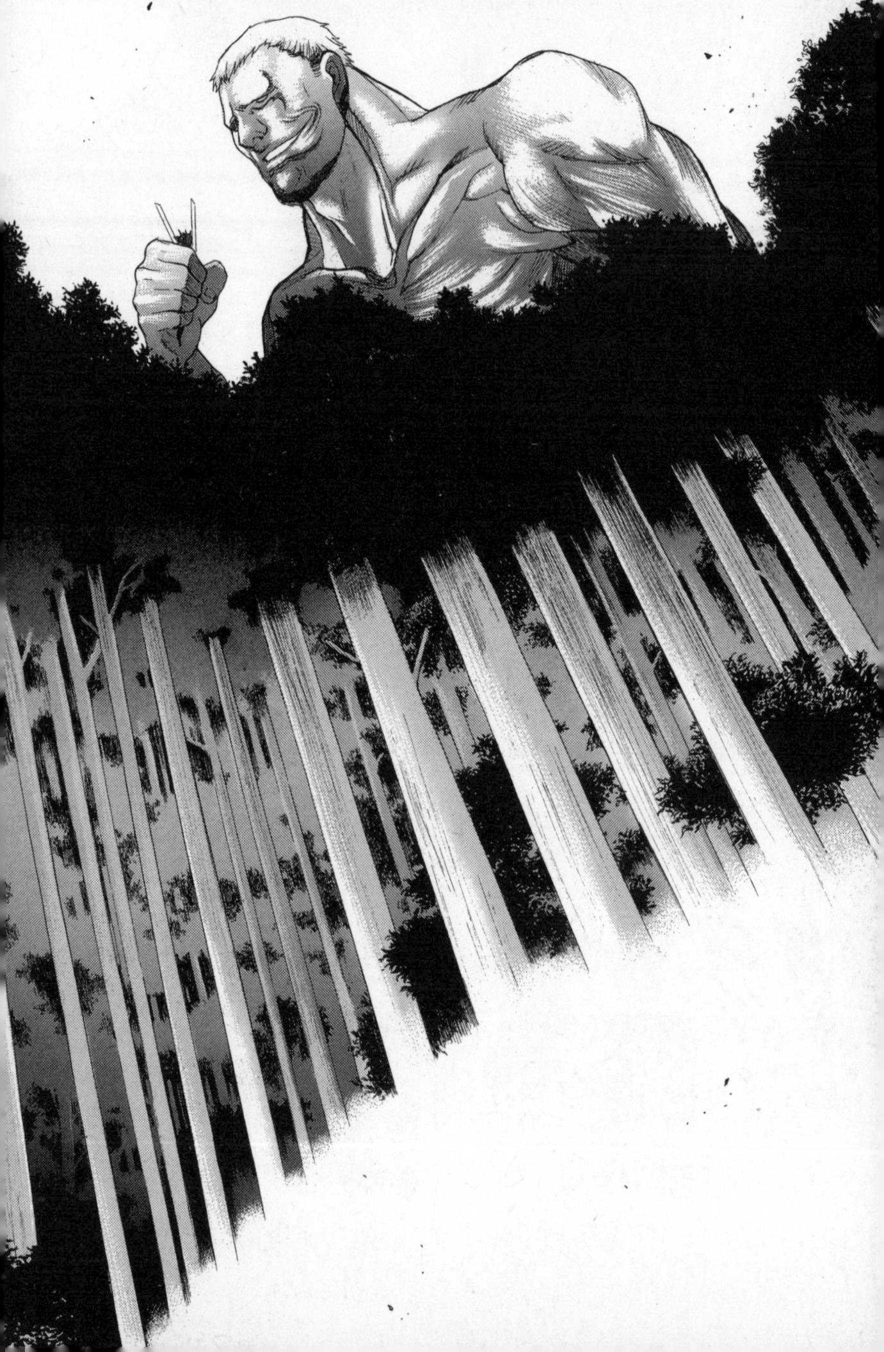

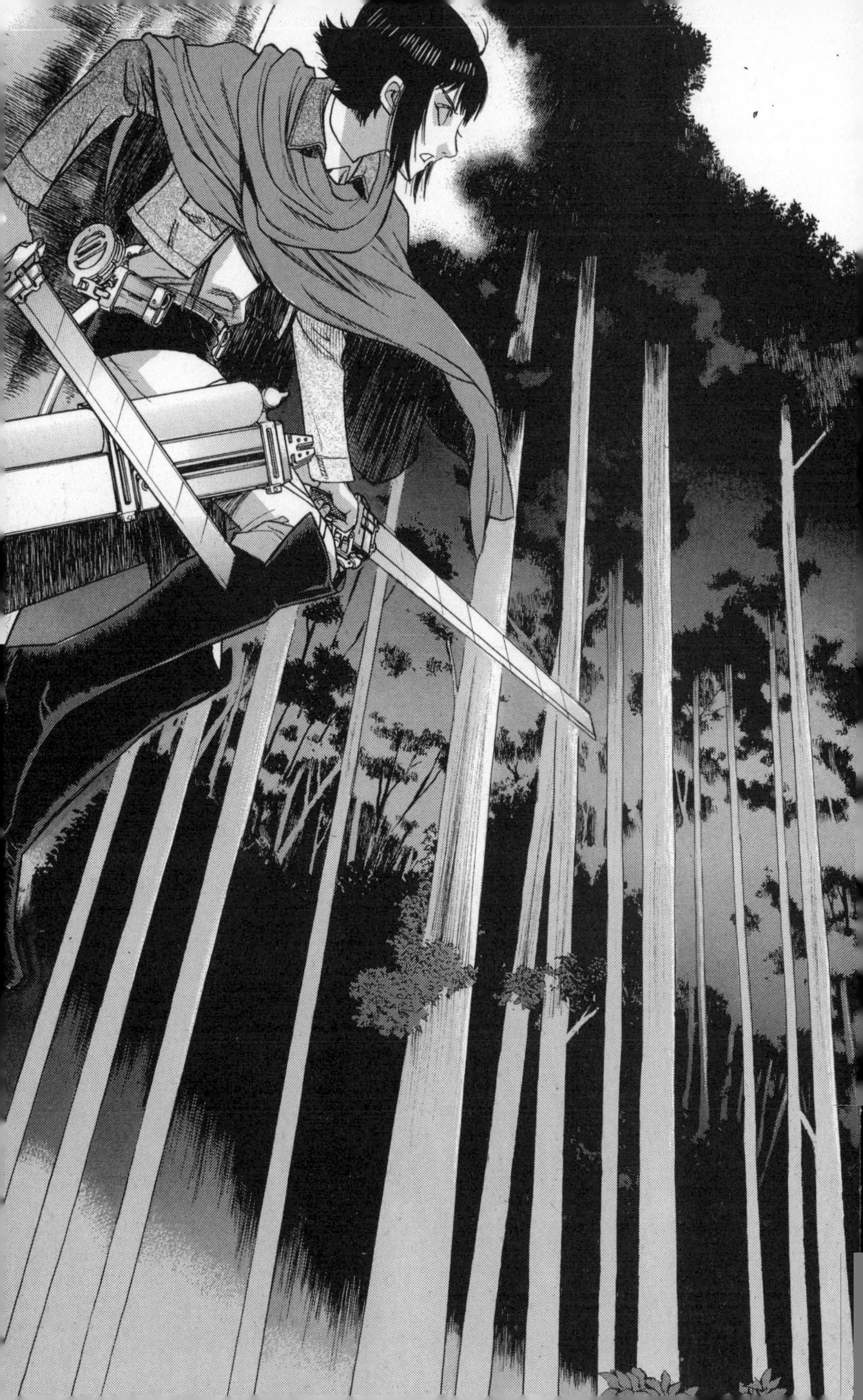

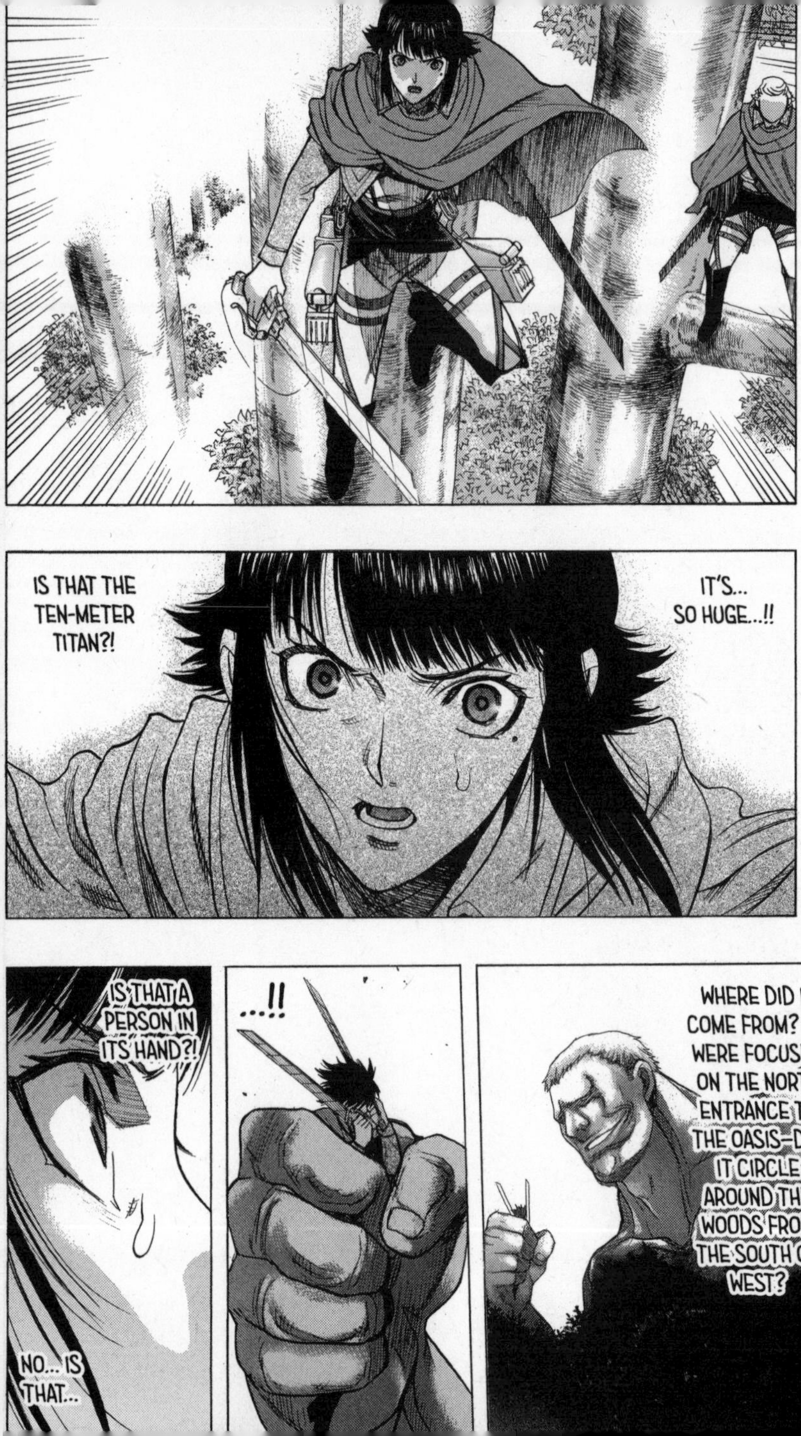
IT'S... SO HUGE...!!
IS THAT THE TEN-METER TITAN?!
WHERE DID IT COME FROM? WE WERE FOCUSED ON THE NORTH ENTRANCE TO THE OASIS—DID IT CIRCLE AROUND THE WOODS FROM THE SOUTH OR WEST?
...!!
IS THAT A PERSON IN ITS HAND?!
NO... IS THAT...

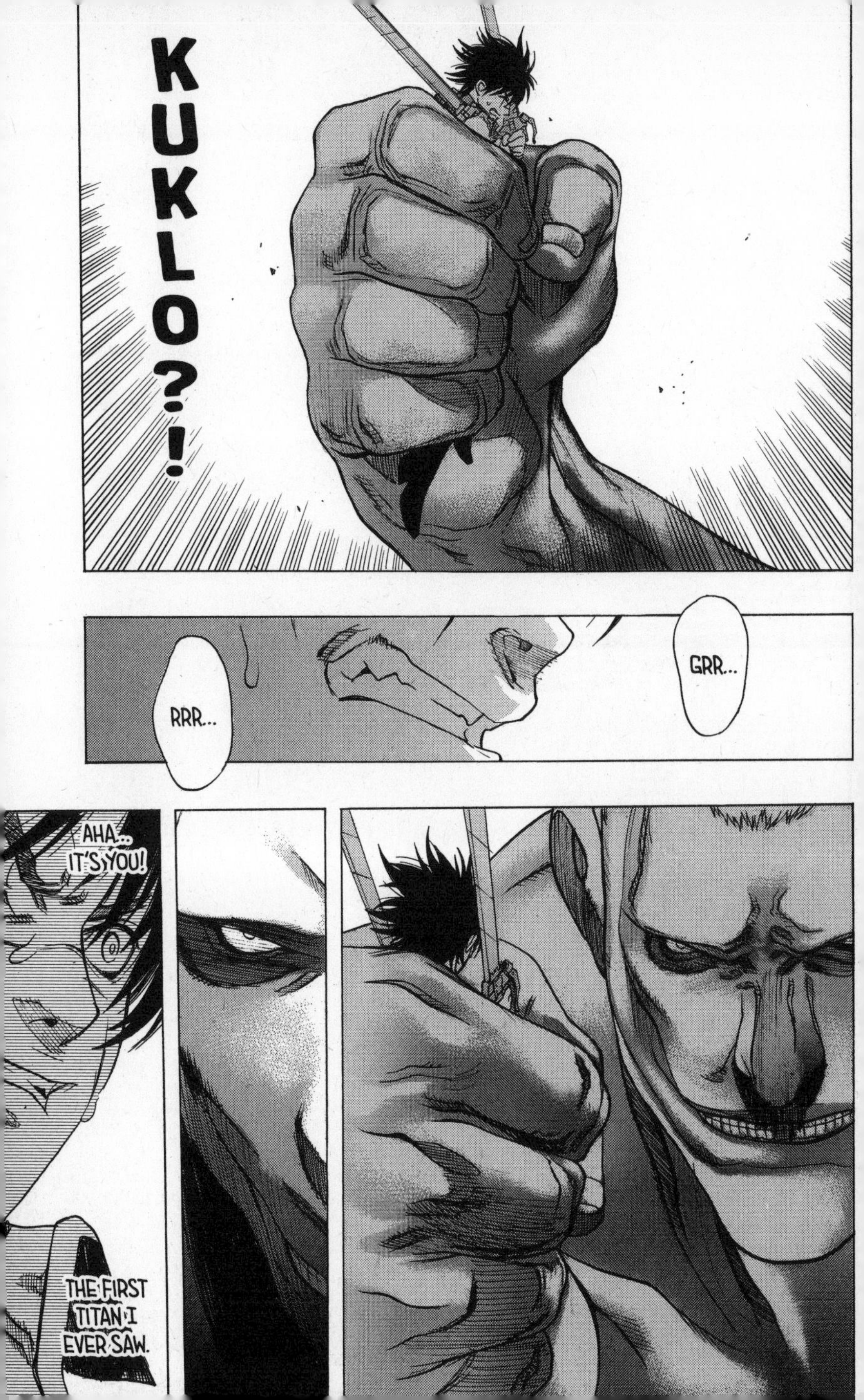
KUKLO?!
GRR...
RRR...
AHA... IT'S YOU!
THE FIRST TITAN I EVER SAW.

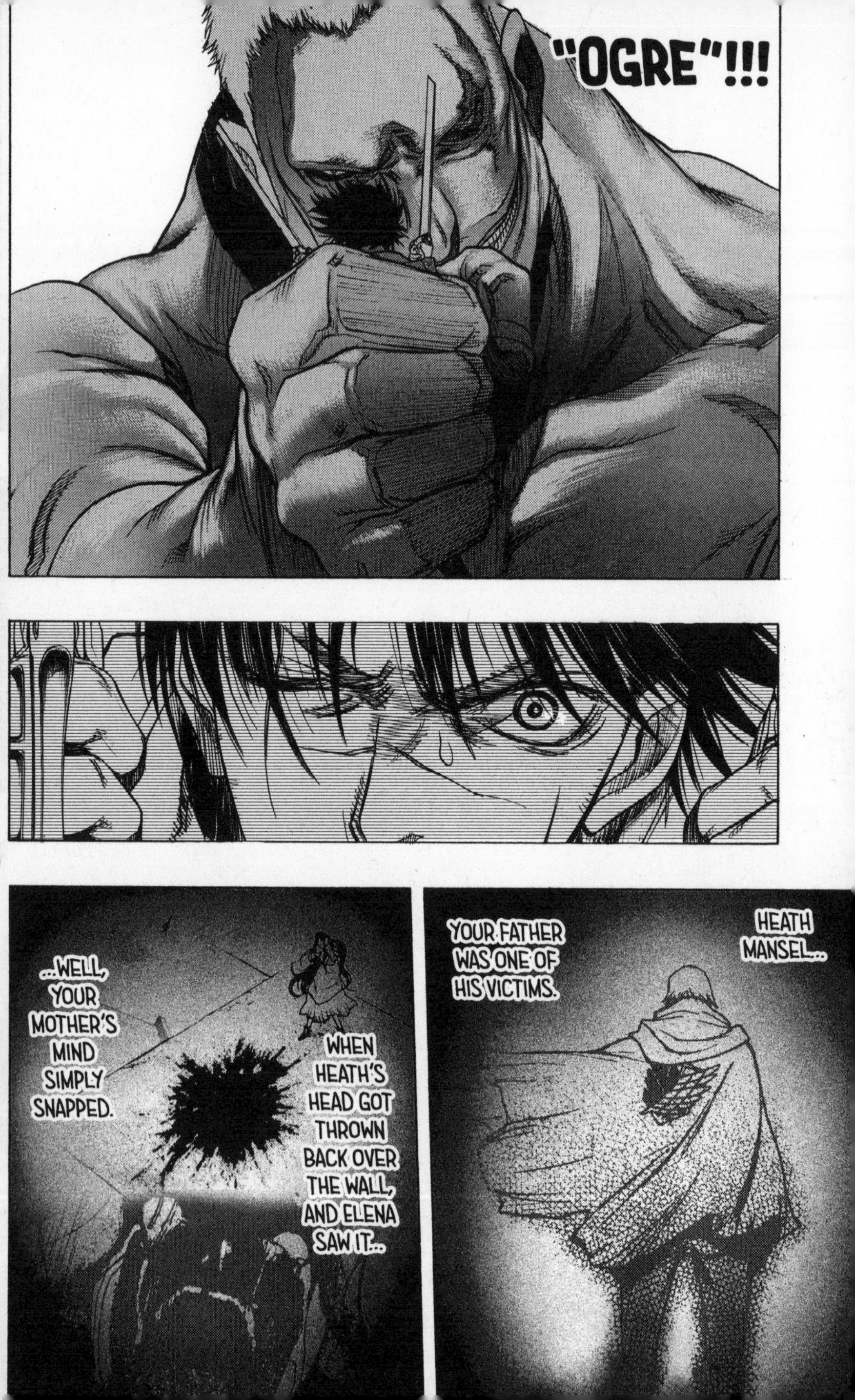
"OGRE"!!!
HEATH MANSEL...
YOUR FATHER WAS ONE OF HIS VICTIMS.
WHEN HEATH'S HEAD GOT THROWN BACK OVER THE WALL, AND ELENA SAW IT...
...WELL, YOUR MOTHER'S MIND SIMPLY SNAPPED.

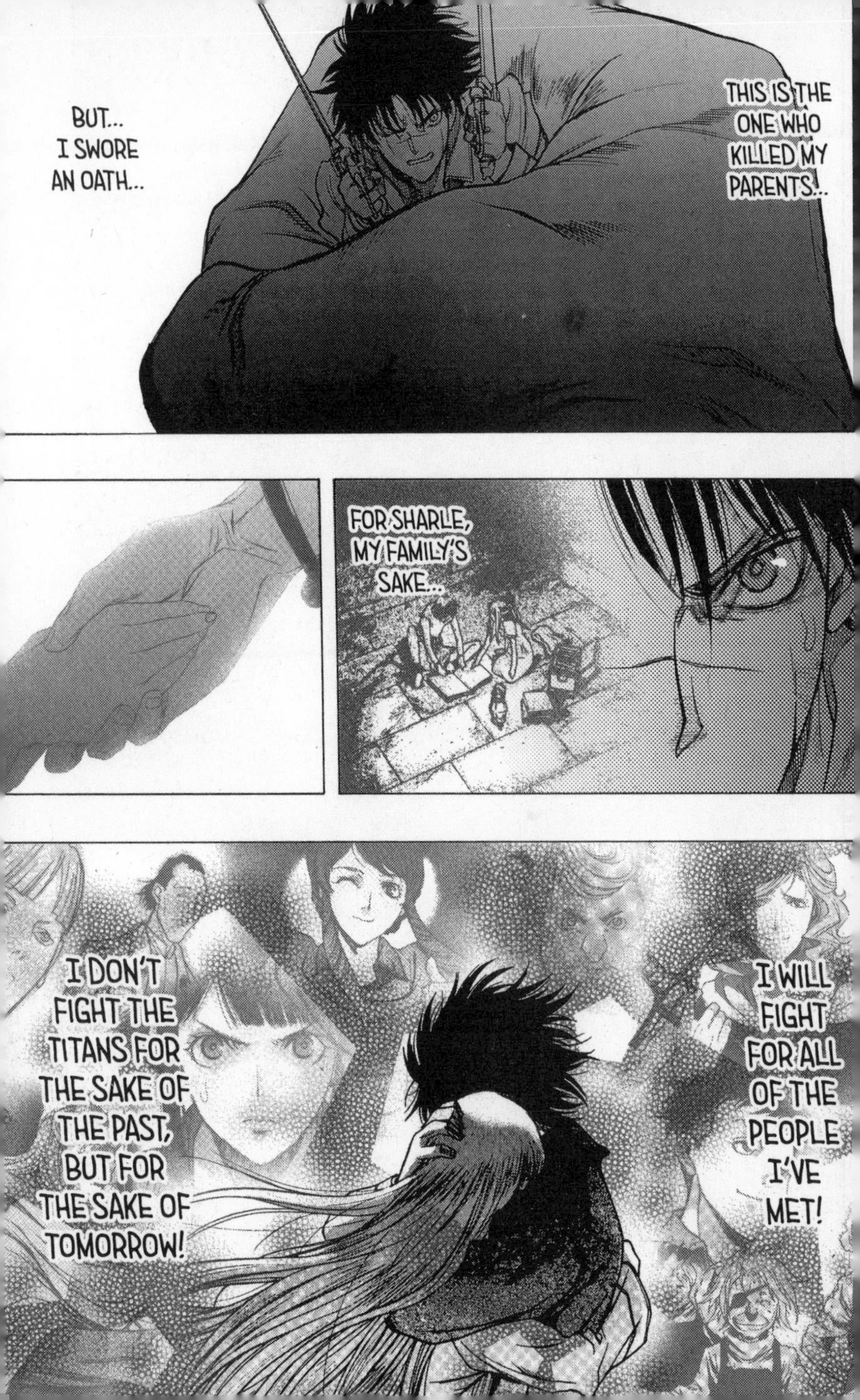
THIS IS THE ONE WHO KILLED MY PARENTS...
BUT... I SWORE AN OATH...
FOR SHARLE, MY FAMILY'S SAKE...
I WILL FIGHT FOR ALL OF THE PEOPLE I'VE MET!
I DON'T FIGHT THE TITANS FOR THE SAKE OF THE PAST, BUT FOR THE SAKE OF TOMORROW!

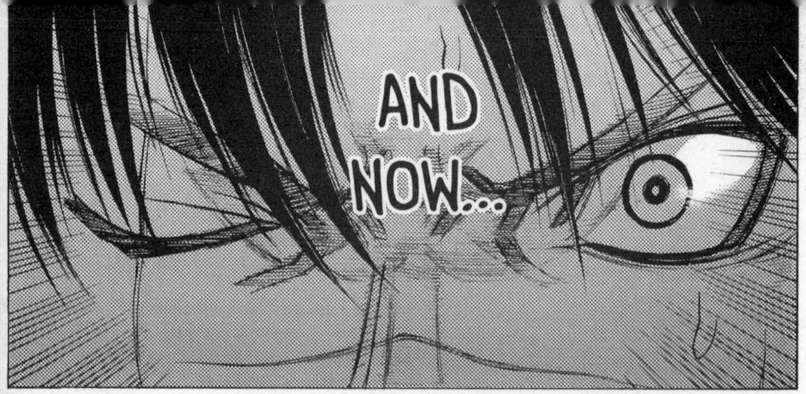
AND NOW...
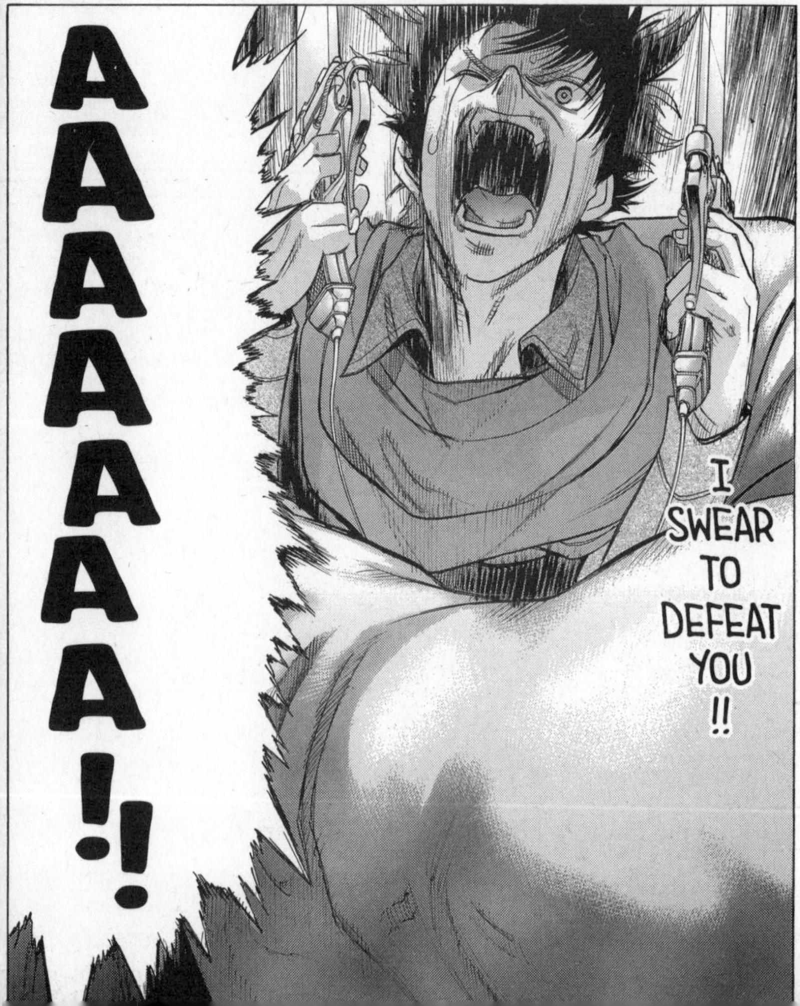
I SWEAR TO DEFEAT YOU!!
AAAAAAAA!!

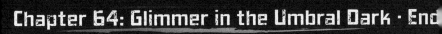

Chapter 64: Glimmer in the Umbral Dark · End

ATTACK on TITAN
BEFORE THE FALL

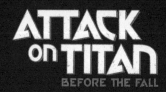

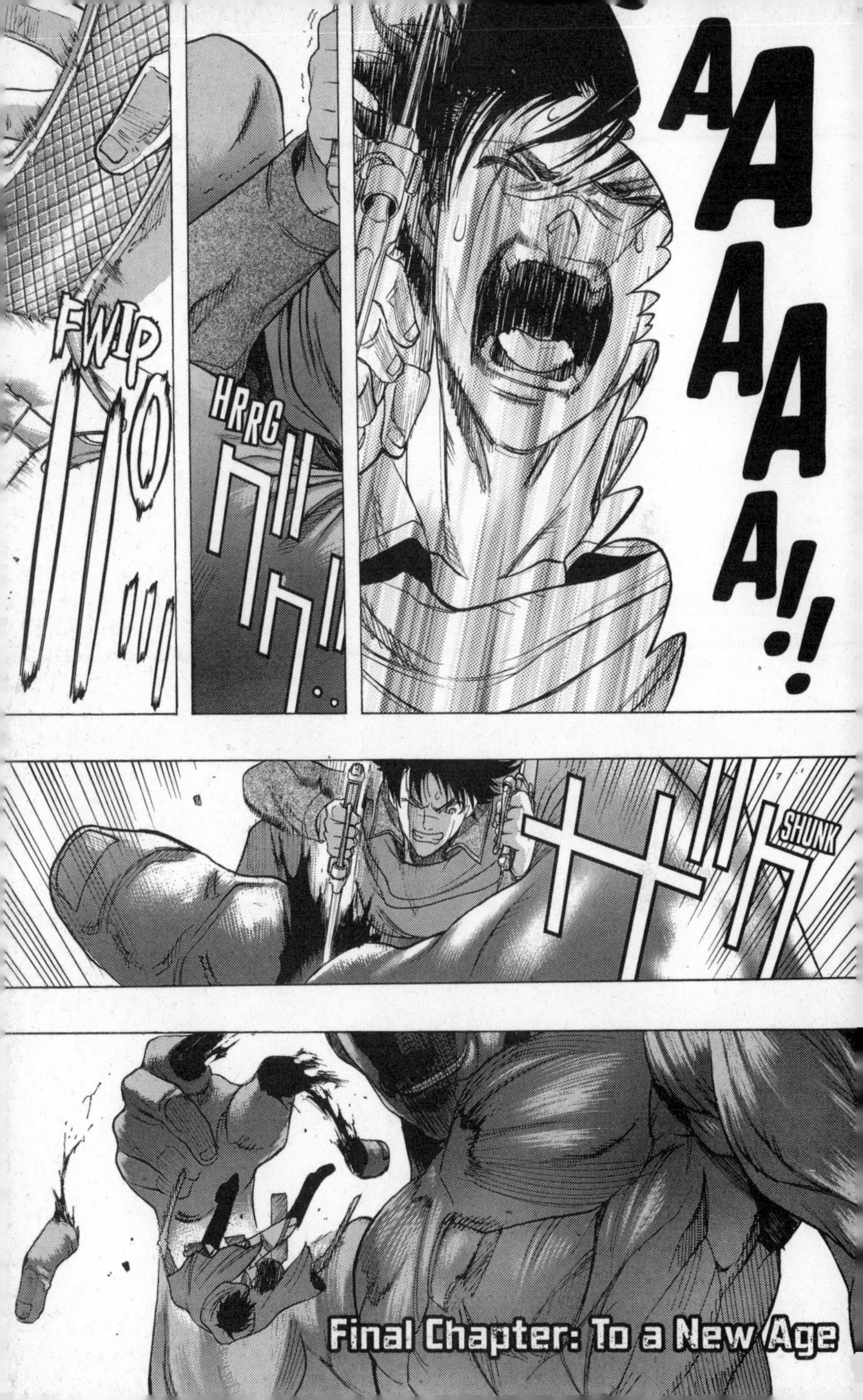
AAAAAA!!
HRRG
FWIP
SHUNK
Final Chapter: To a New Age

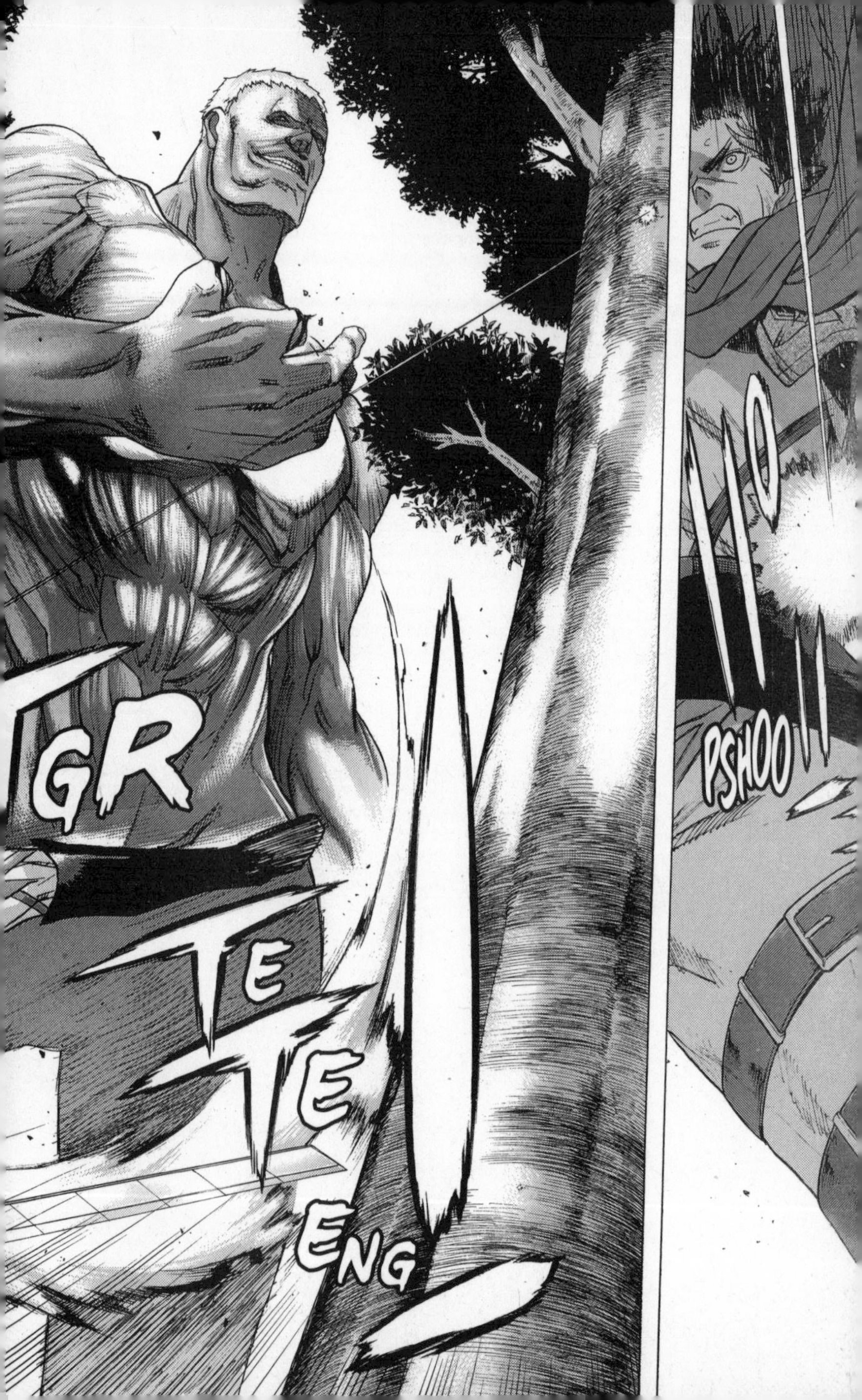
PSHOO
GR
TE
TE
ENG

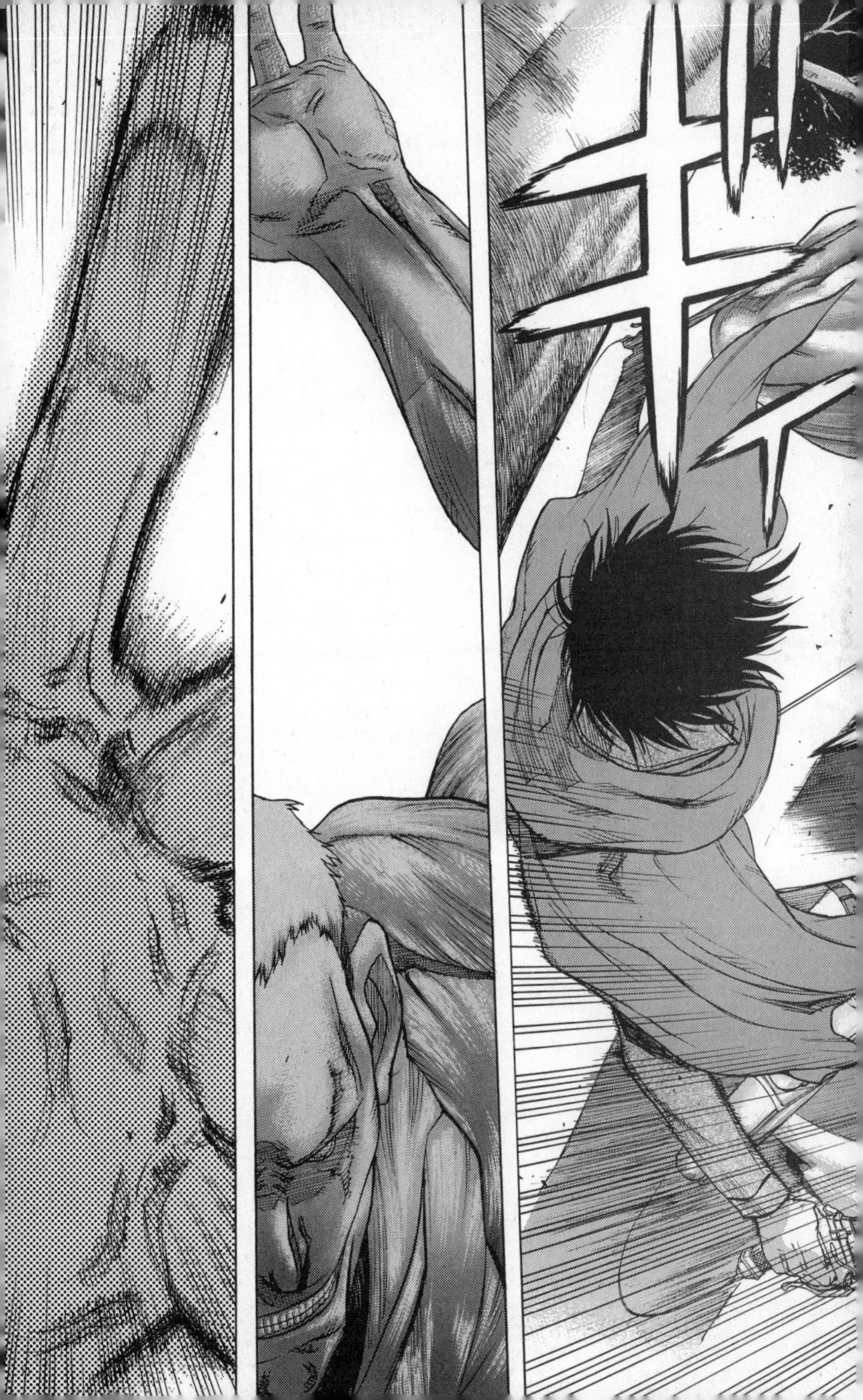

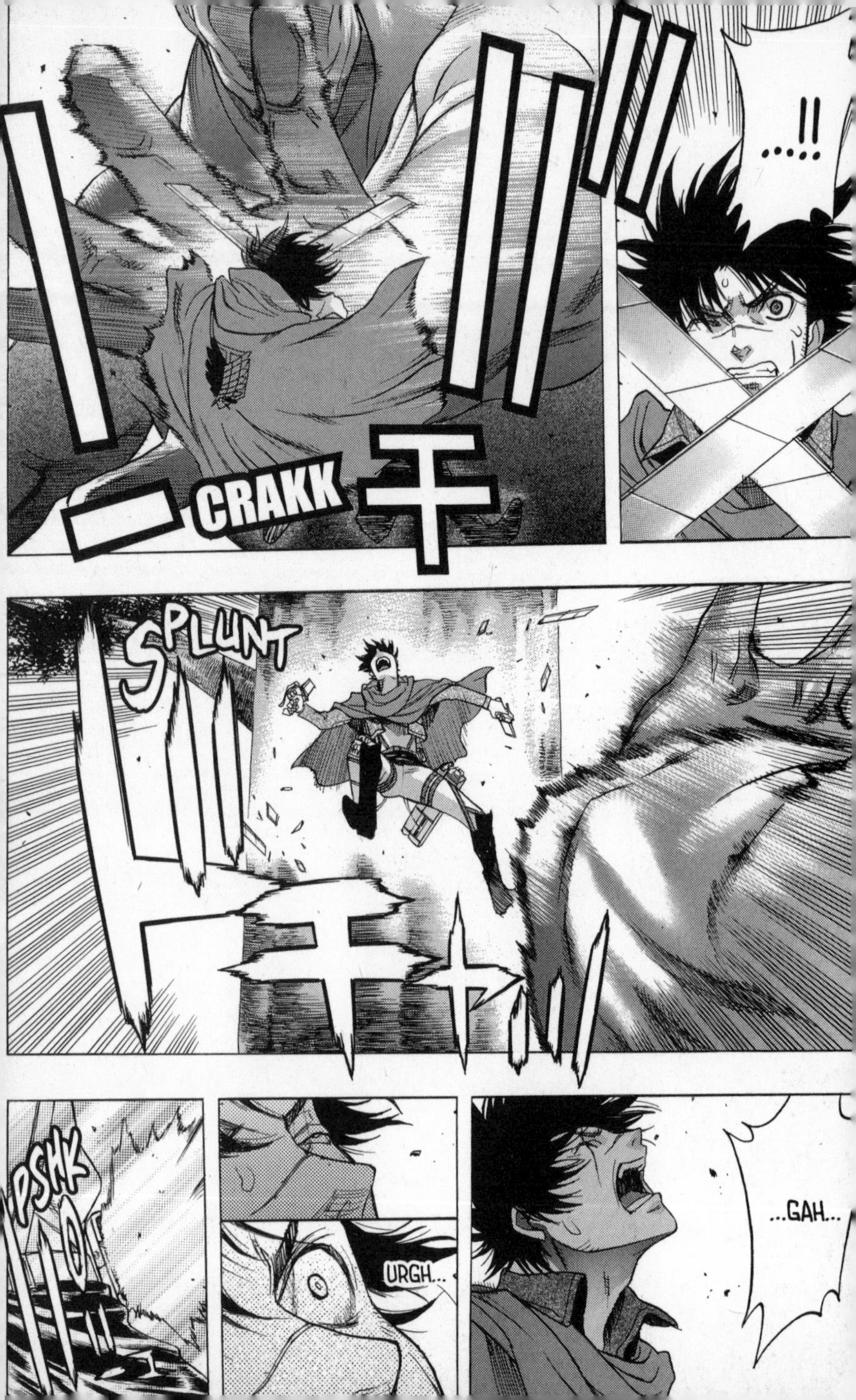
...!!
CRAKK
SPLUNT
...GAH...
URGH...
PSHK

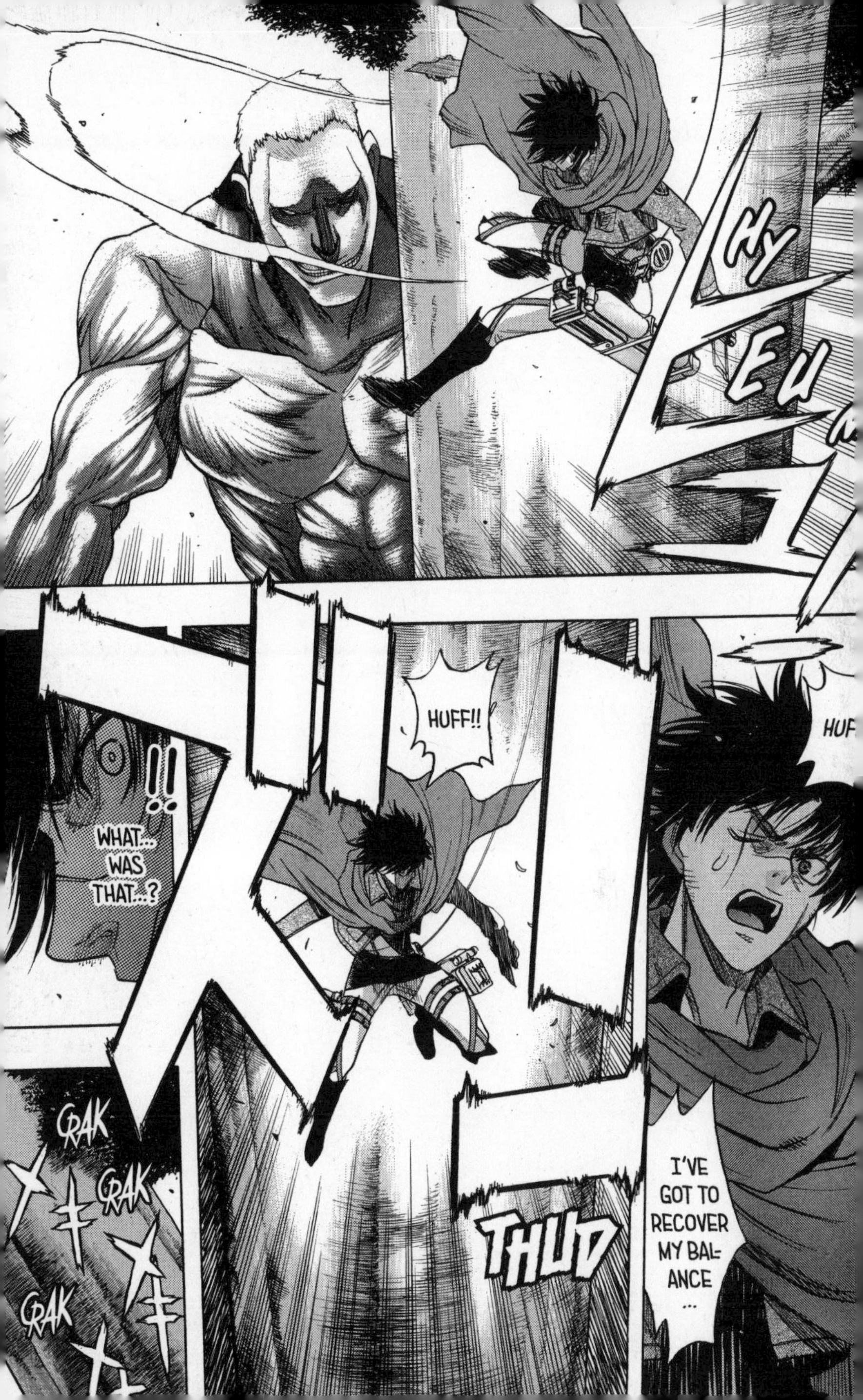
HYEUN
HUFF!!
HUF
!!
WHAT... WAS THAT...?
I'VE GOT TO RECOVER MY BAL-ANCE ...
THUD
CRAK
CRAK
CRAK

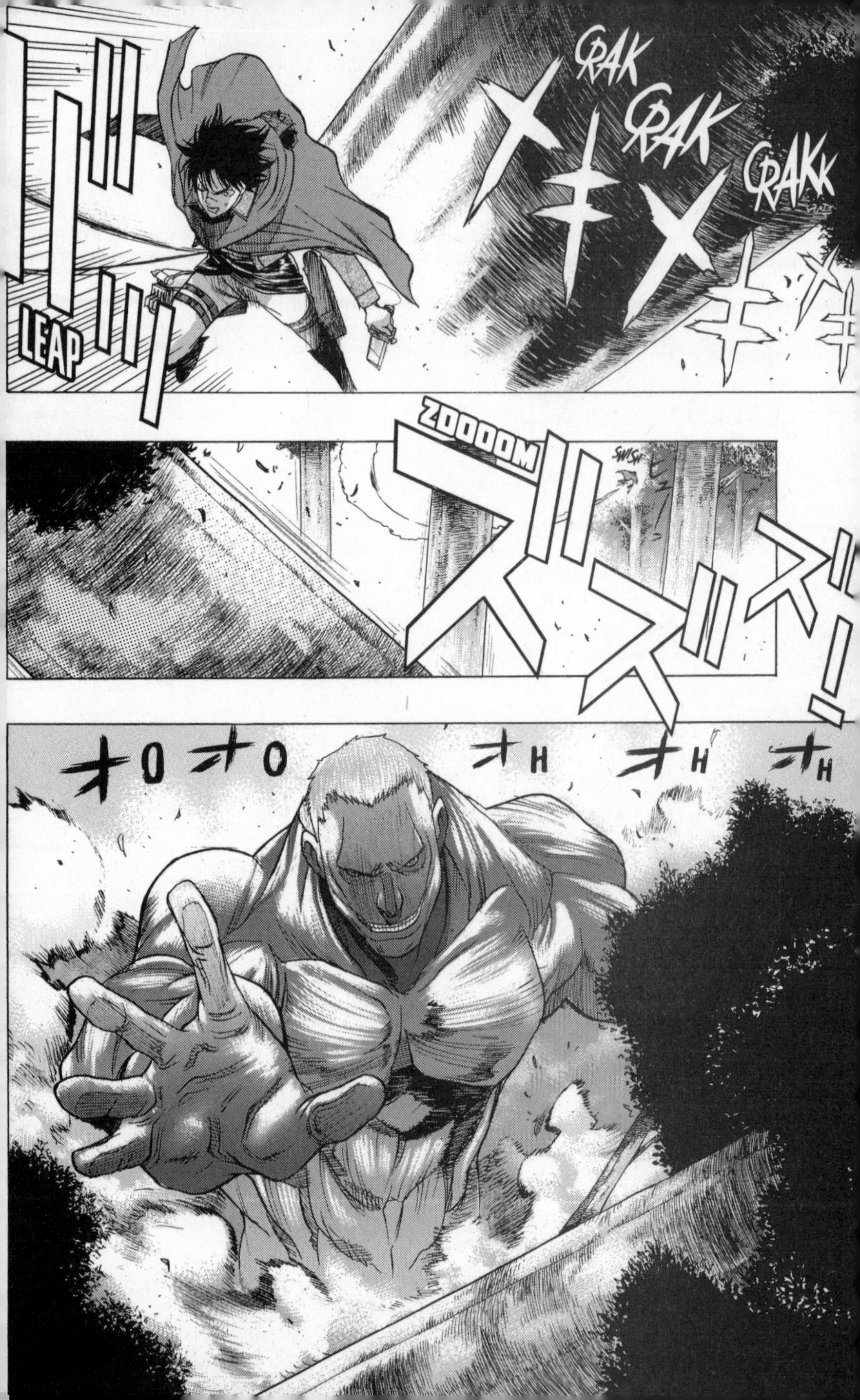
CRAK
CRAK
CRAKK
LEAP
ZOOOOM
SWISH
OH
OH
OH
O
O

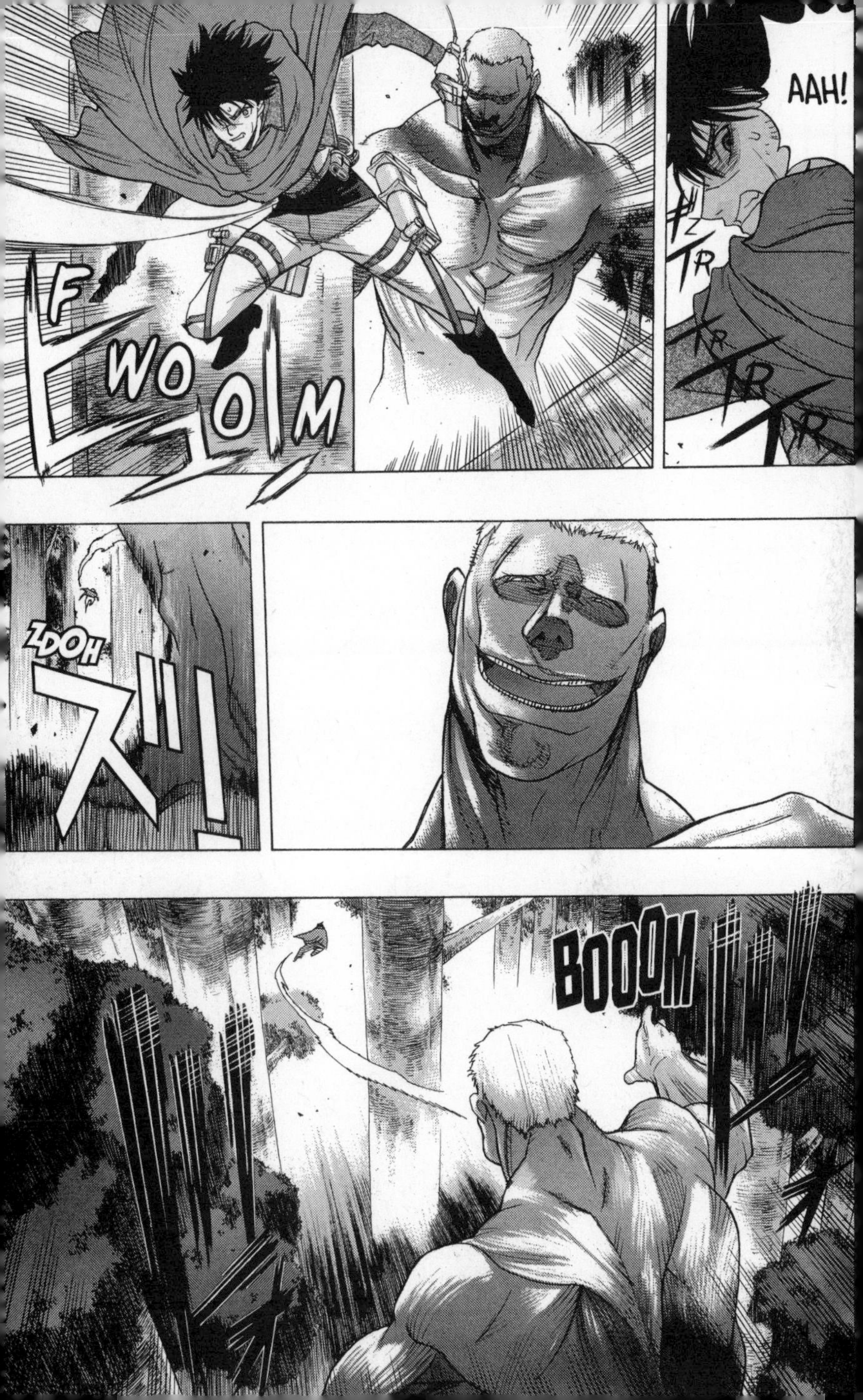
AAH!
TR TR TR TR TR
FWOOM
ZDOH
BOOOM

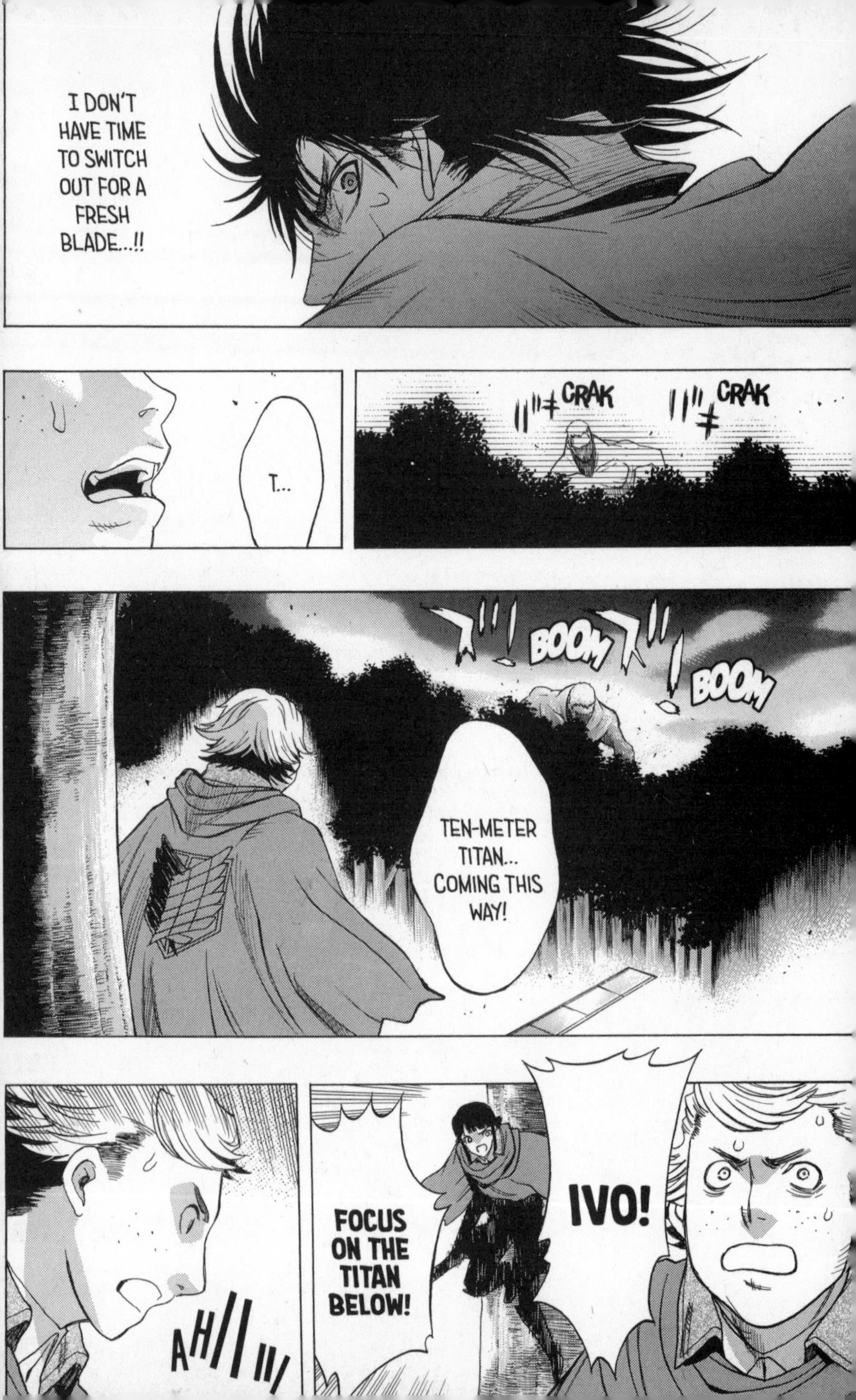
I DON'T HAVE TIME TO SWITCH OUT FOR A FRESH BLADE...!!
CRAK
CRAK
T...
BOOM
BOOM
TEN-METER TITAN... COMING THIS WAY!
IVO!
FOCUS ON THE TITAN BELOW!
AH

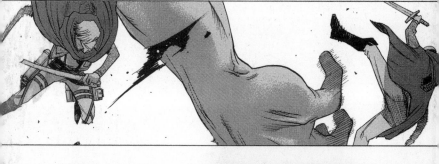

Y...

YEAH!

WE'VE GOT TO FINISH THIS ONE OFF BEFORE THE TEN-METER GETS HERE!

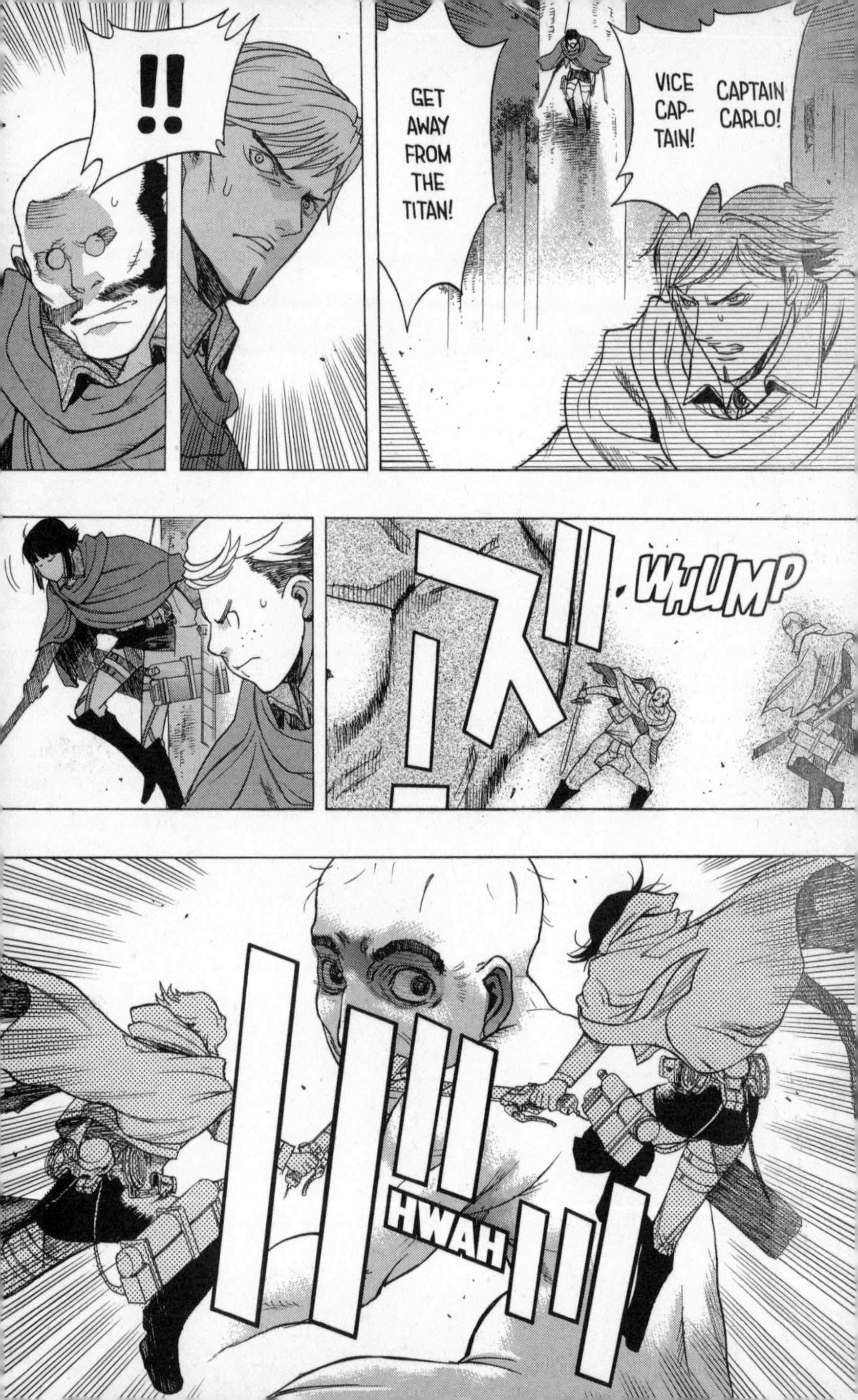
CAPTAIN CARLO!
VICE CAP-TAIN!
GET AWAY FROM THE TITAN!
!!
WHUMP
HWAH

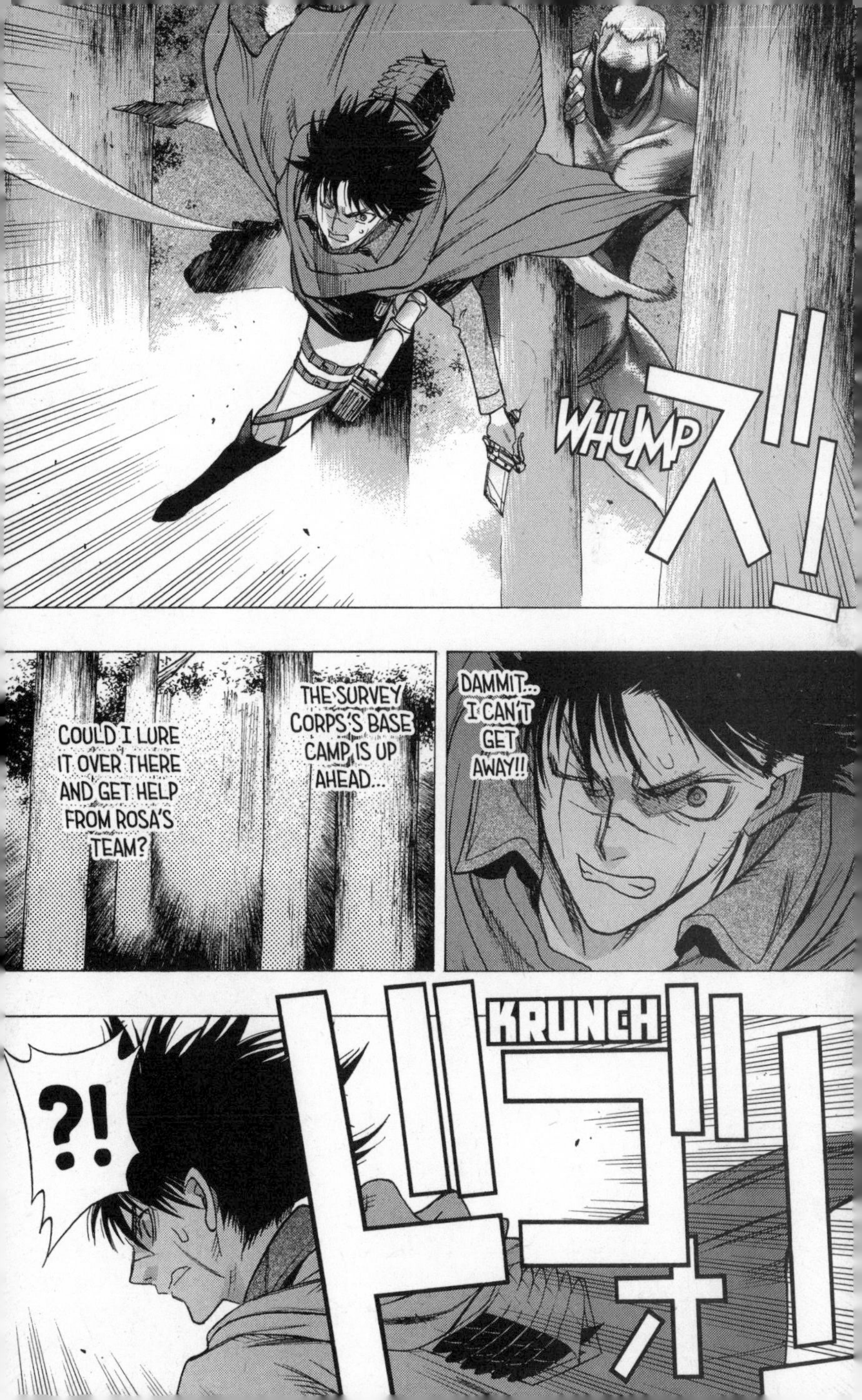
WHUMP
DAMMIT... I CAN'T GET AWAY!!
THE SURVEY CORPS'S BASE CAMP IS UP AHEAD...
COULD I LURE IT OVER THERE AND GET HELP FROM ROSA'S TEAM?
KRUNCH
?!

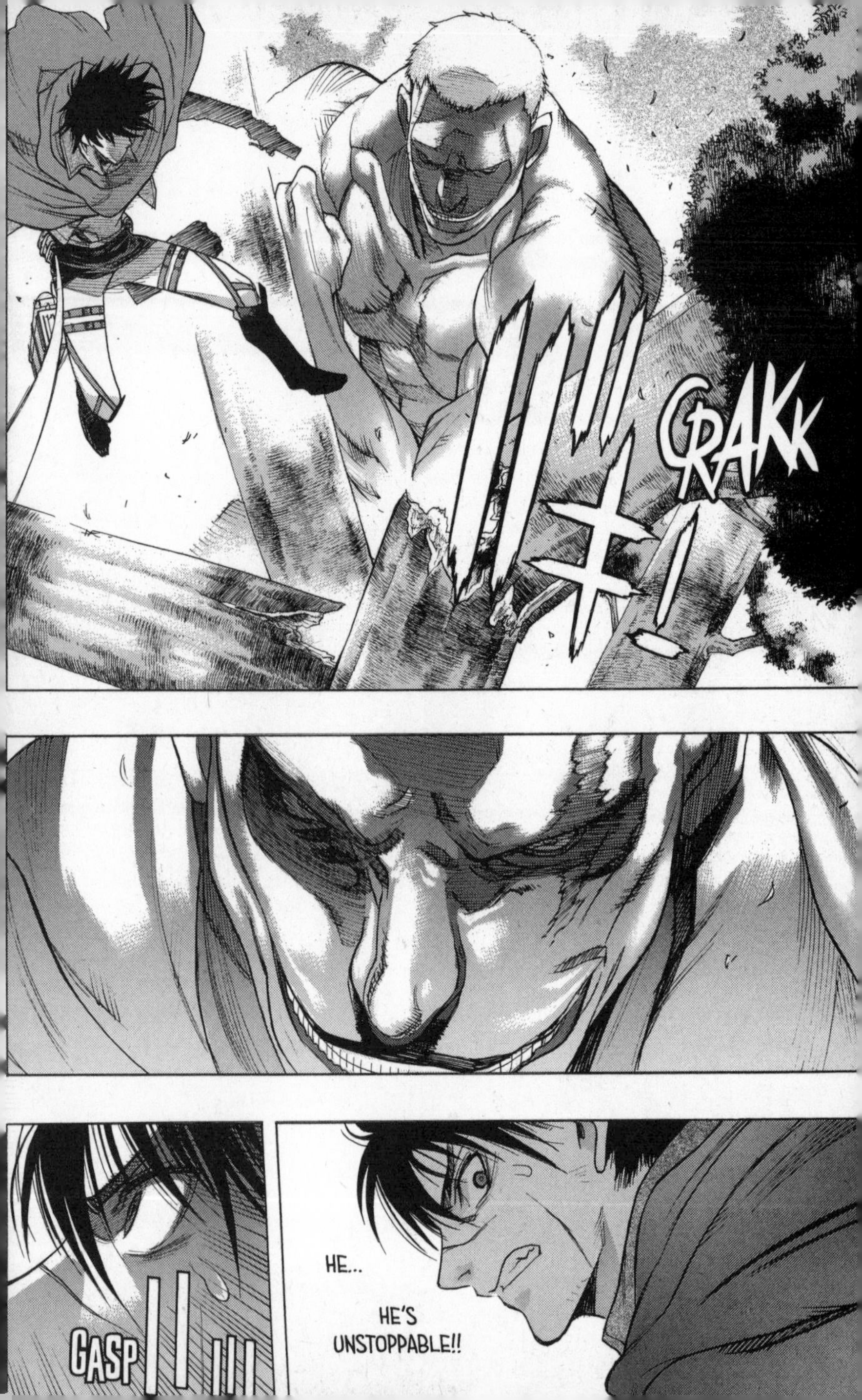
CRAKK
HE...
HE'S UNSTOPPABLE!!
GASP

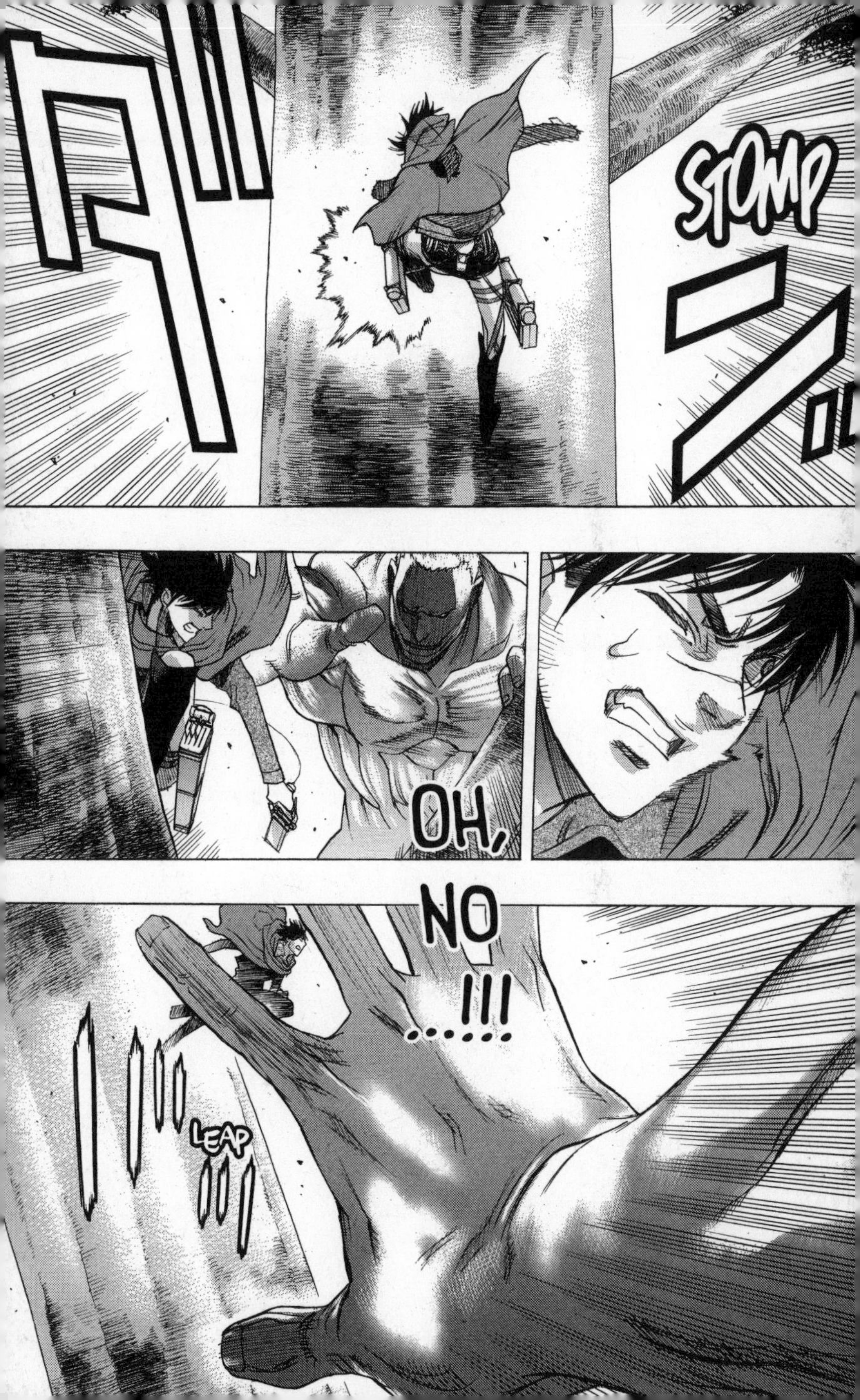
STOMP
OH, NO ...!!!
LEAP

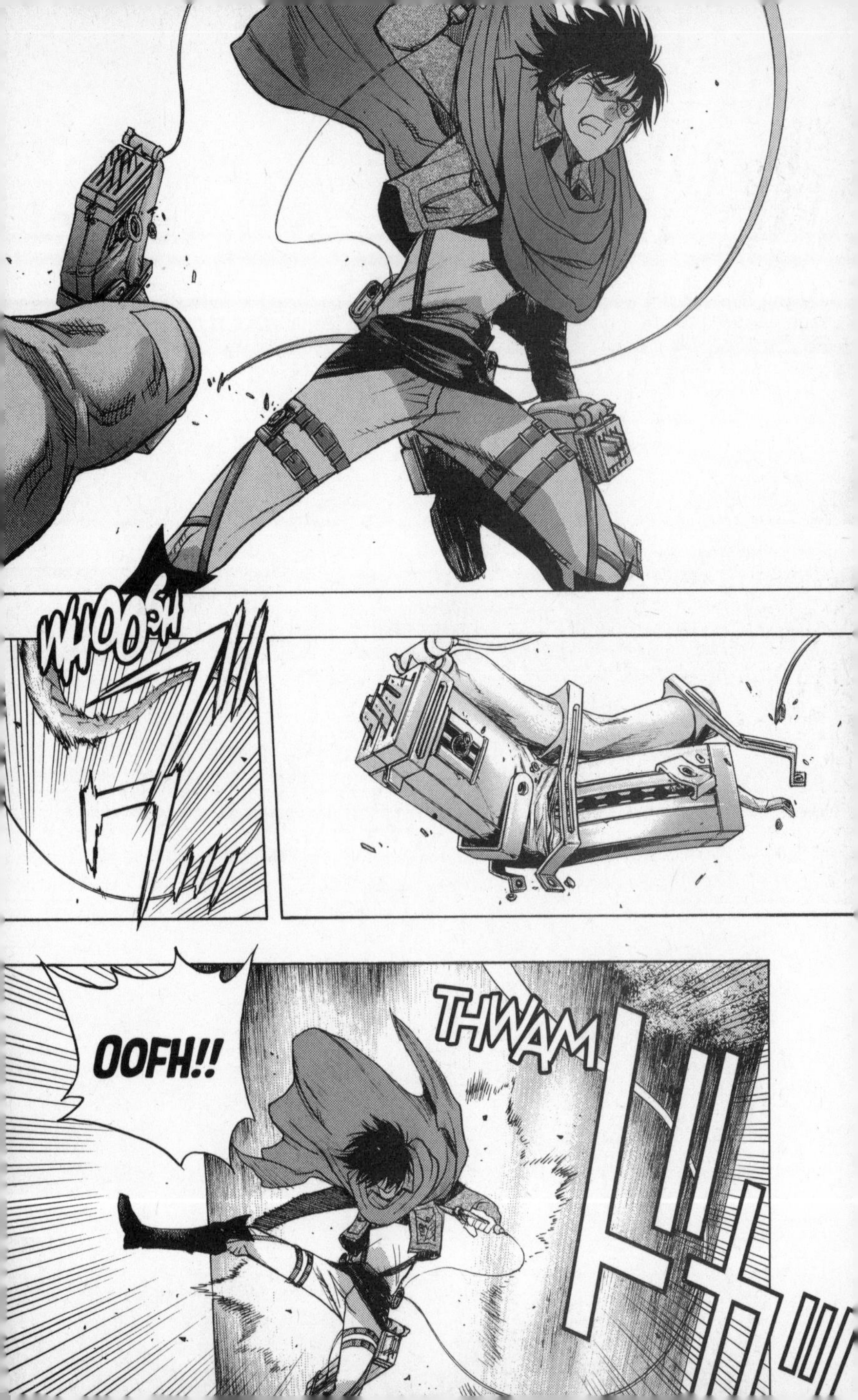
WHOOSH
THWAM
OOFH!!

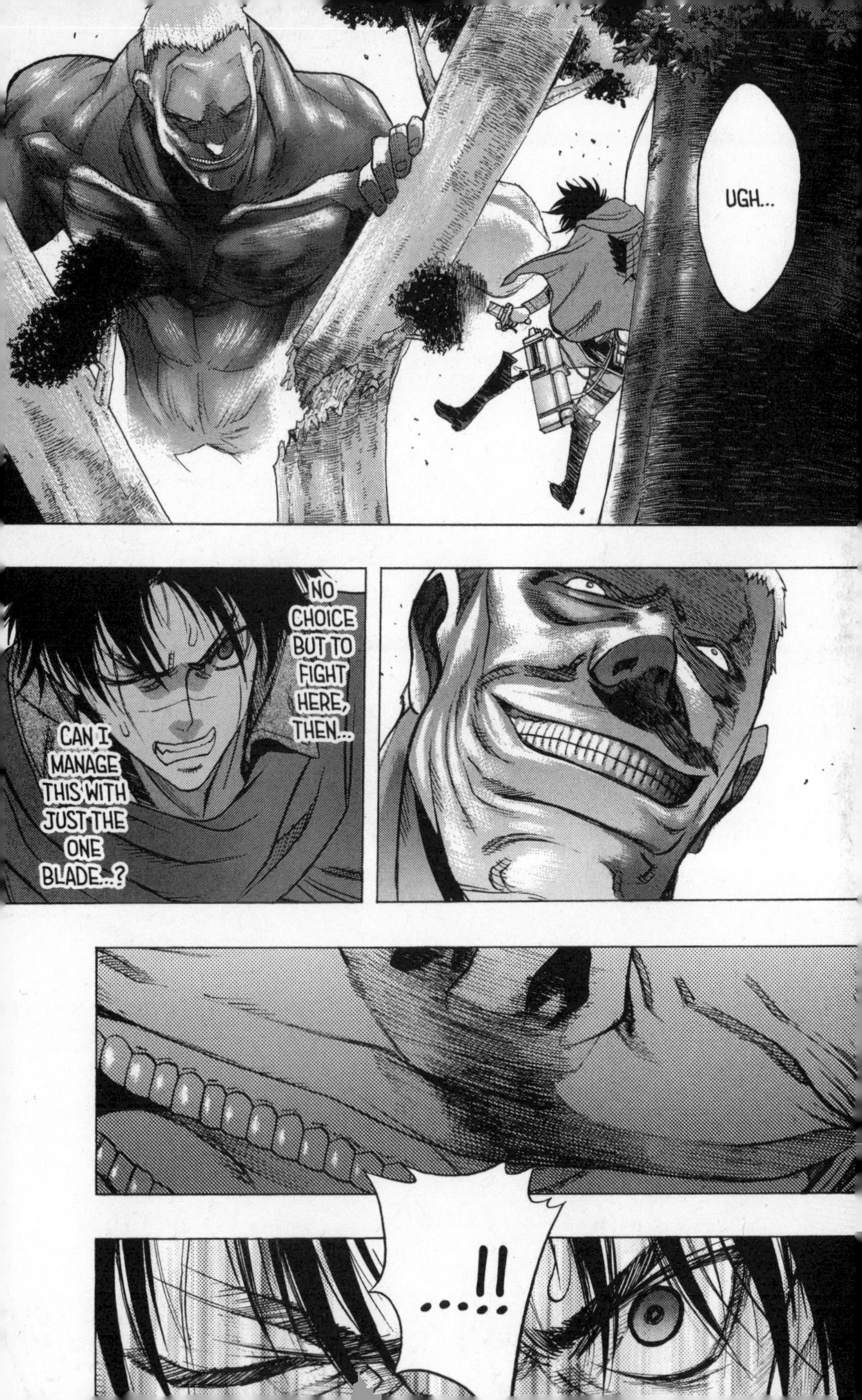
UGH...
NO CHOICE BUT TO FIGHT HERE, THEN...
CAN I MANAGE THIS WITH JUST THE ONE BLADE...?
...!!

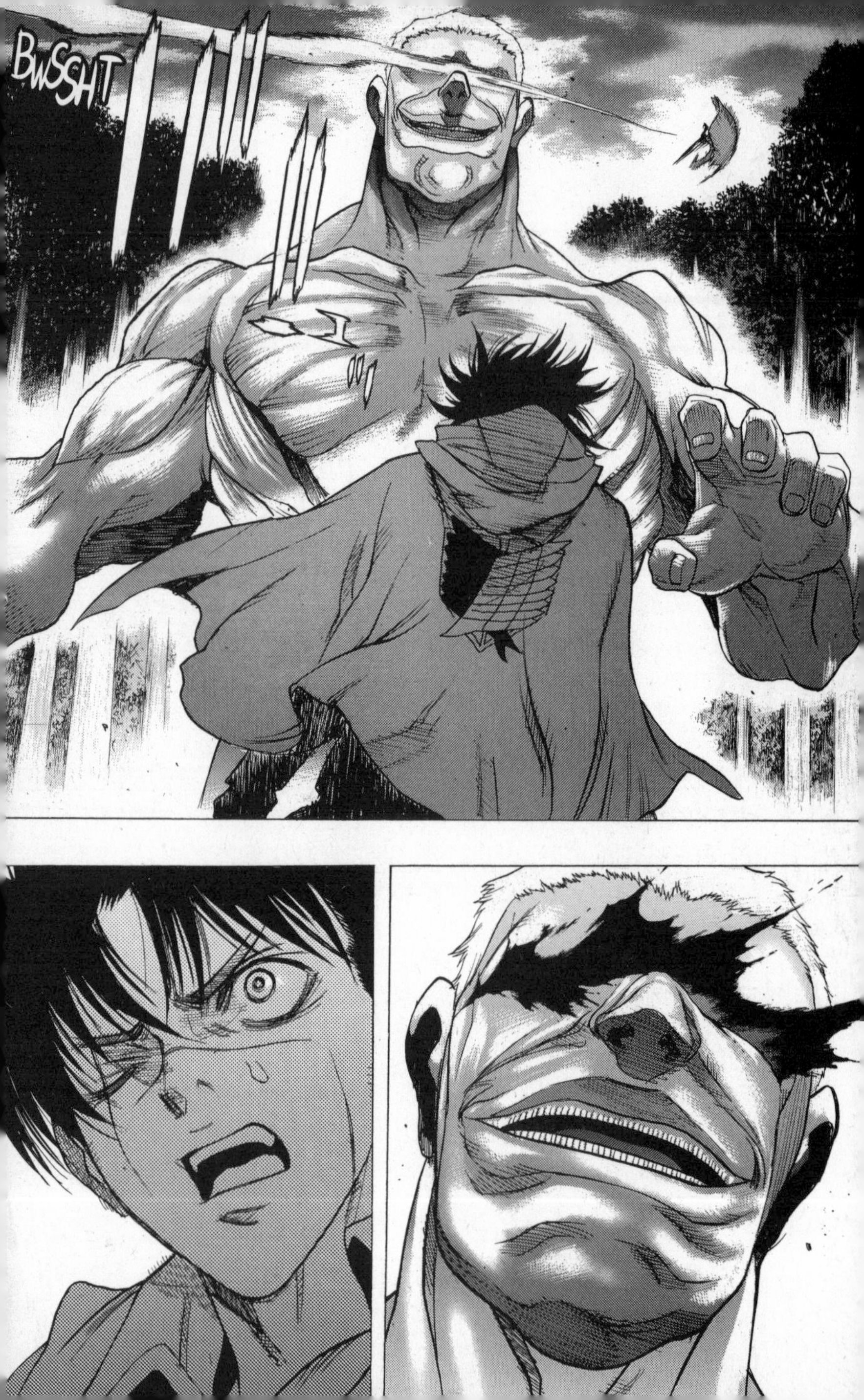
BWSSHT

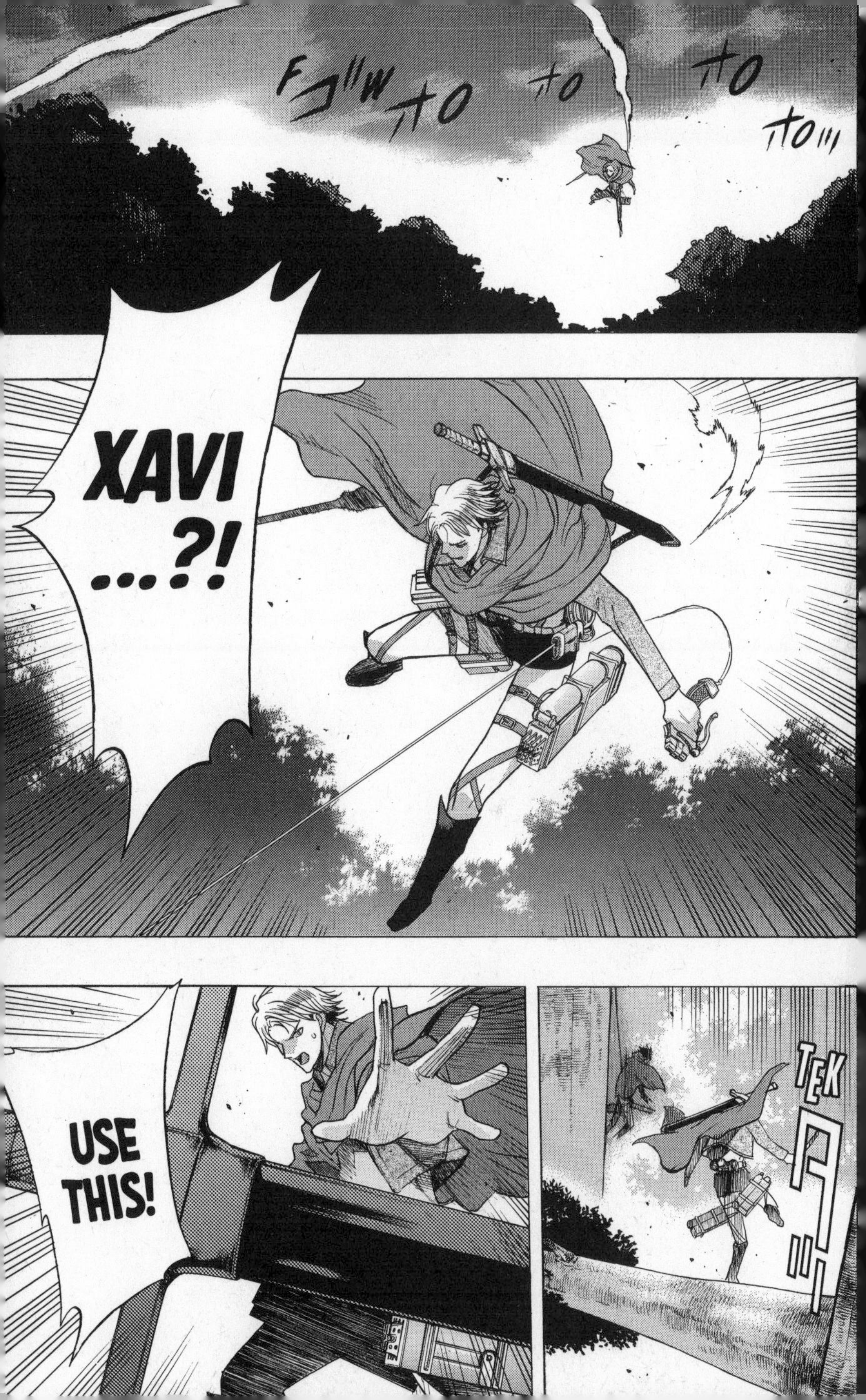
XAVI ...?!
TEK
USE THIS!

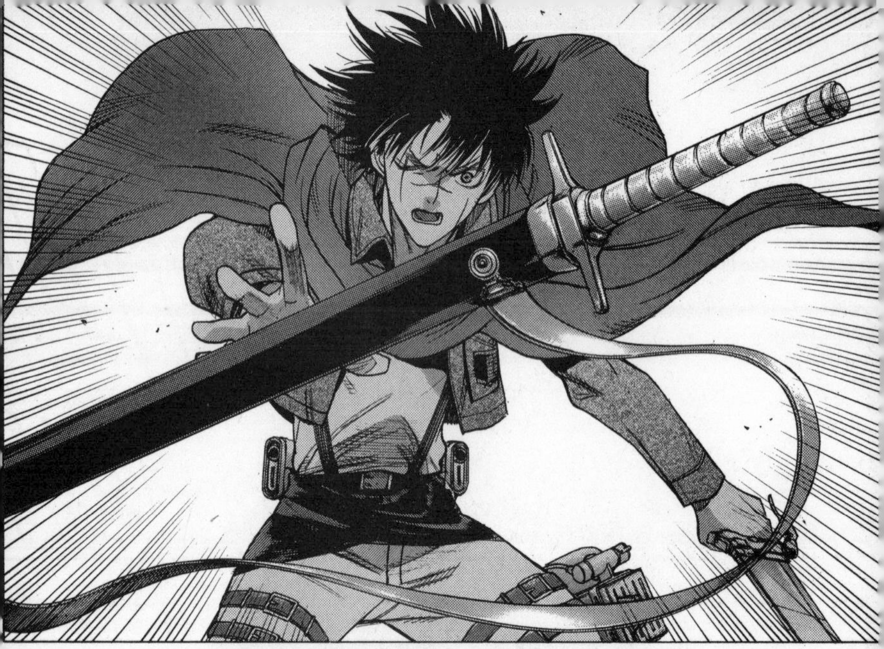
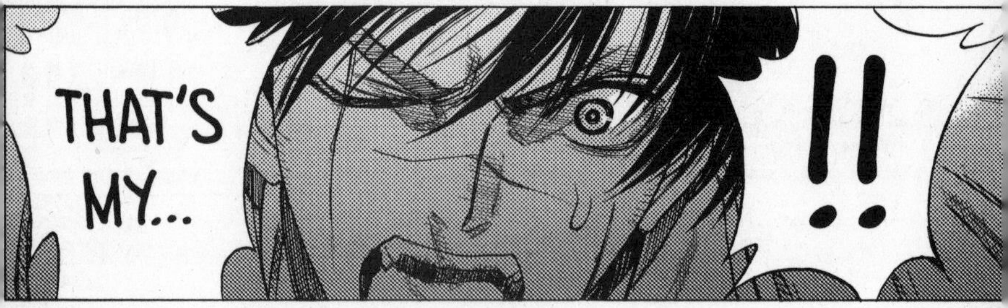
THAT'S MY...
!!
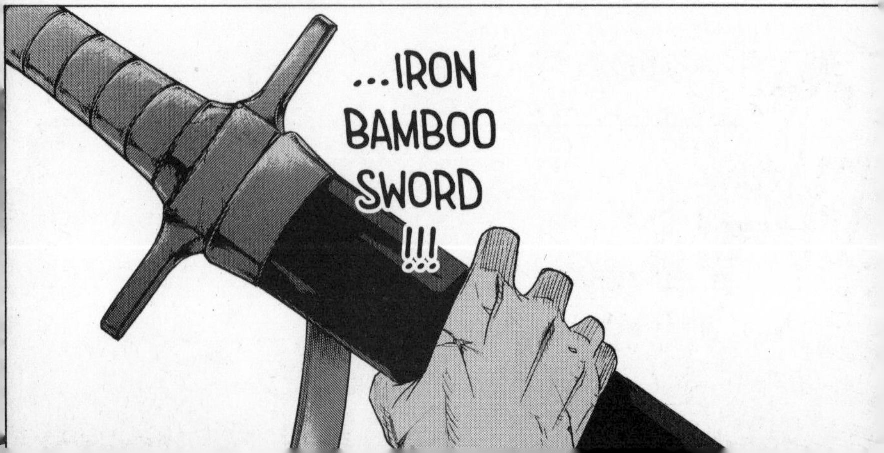
...IRON BAMBOO SWORD !!!

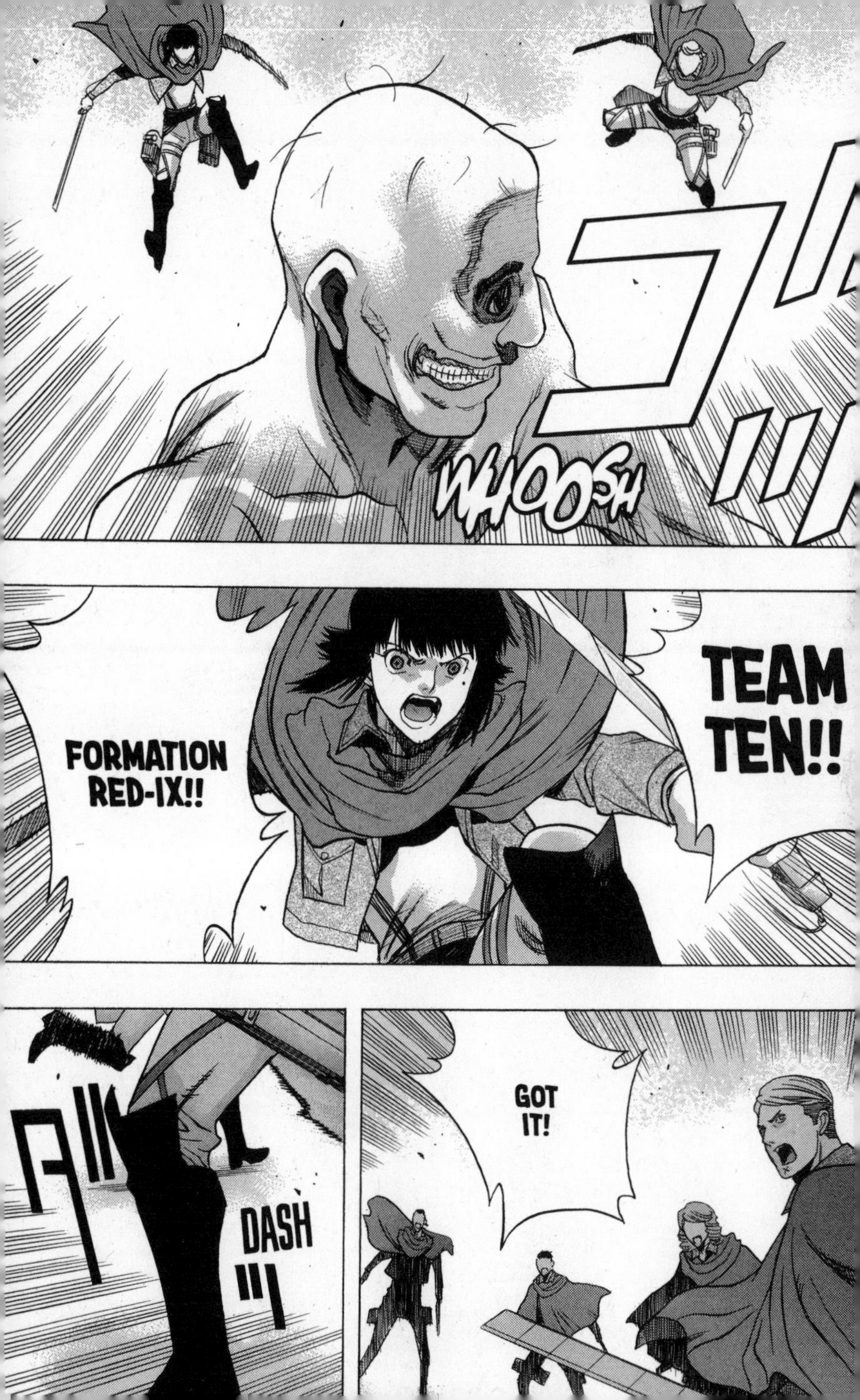
WHOOSH
TEAM TEN!!
FORMATION RED-IX!!
GOT IT!
DASH

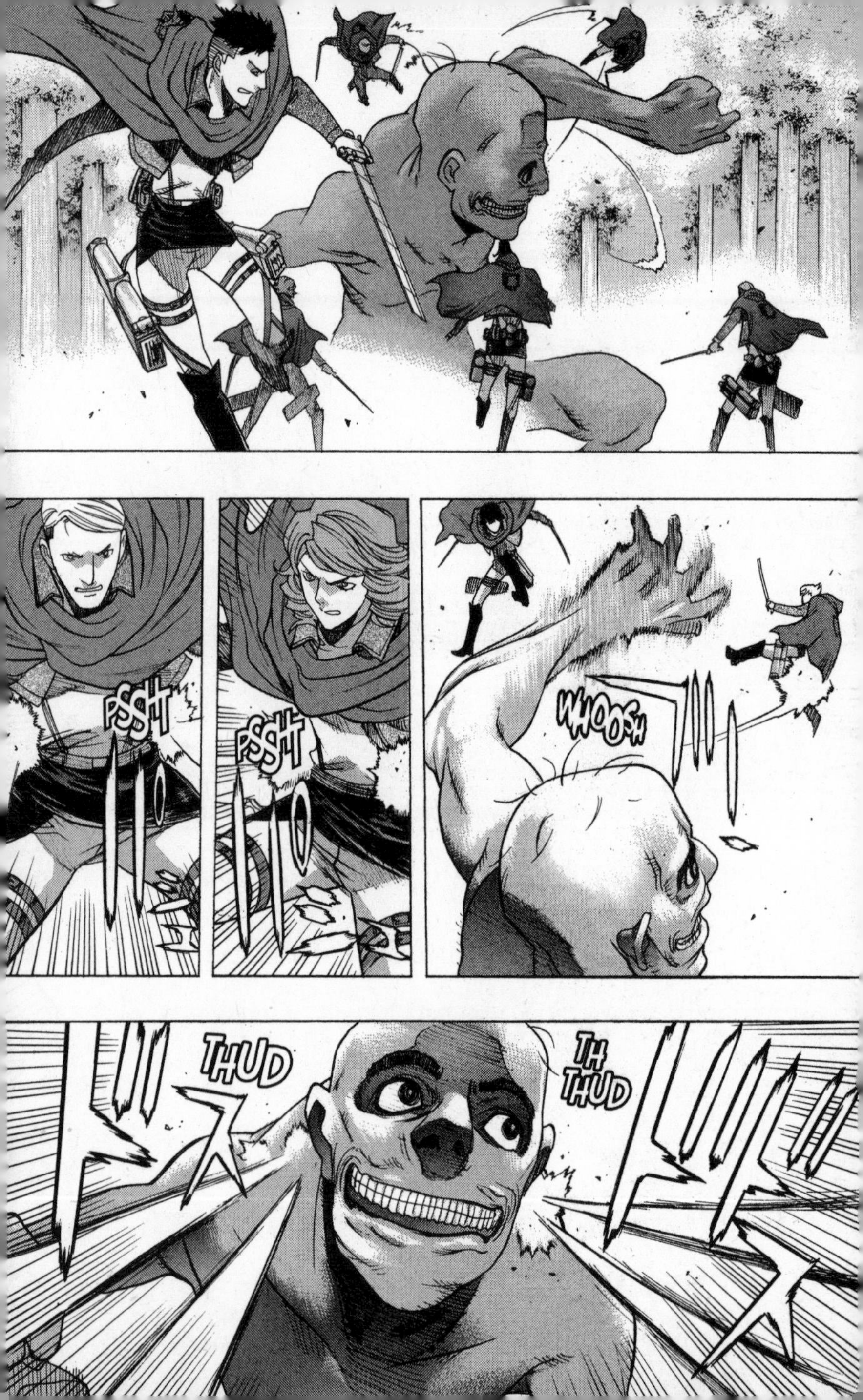
WHOOSH
PSSH
PSSH
TH THUD
THUD

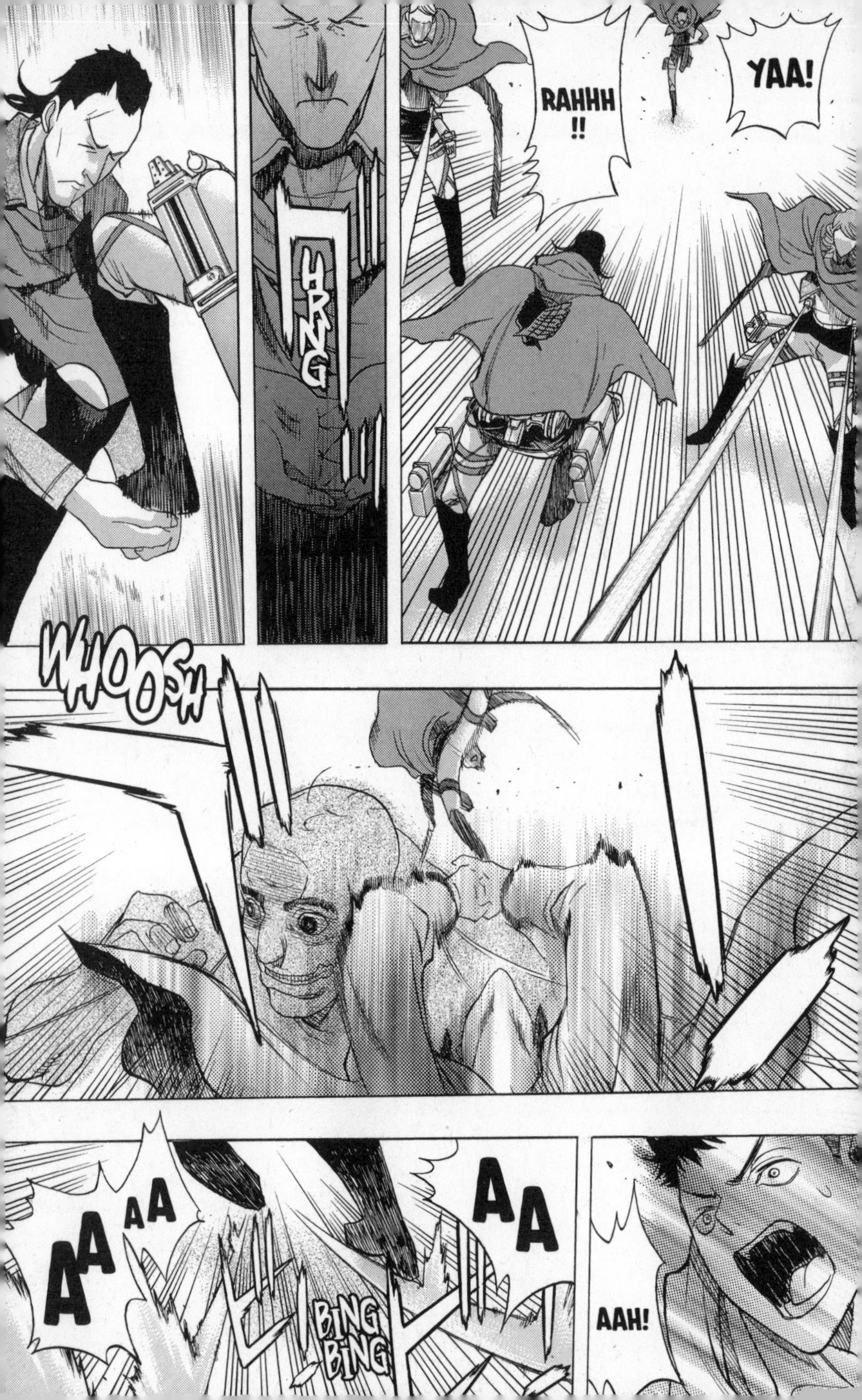
YAA!
RAHHH !!
HRNG
WHOOSH
AAH!
AA
AAA
A
BING BING

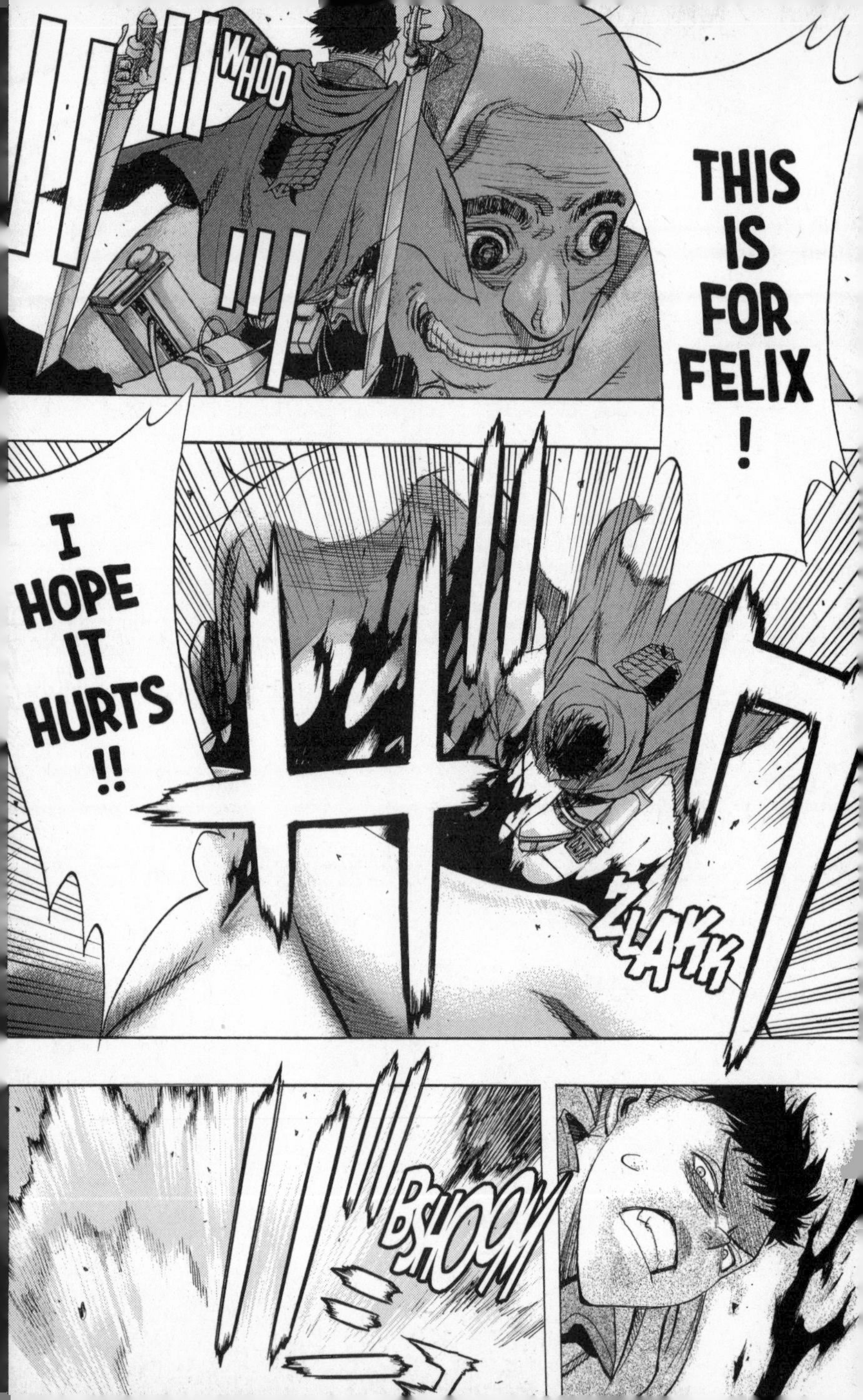
WHOO
THIS IS FOR FELIX!
I HOPE IT HURTS!!
ZLAKK
BSHOOM

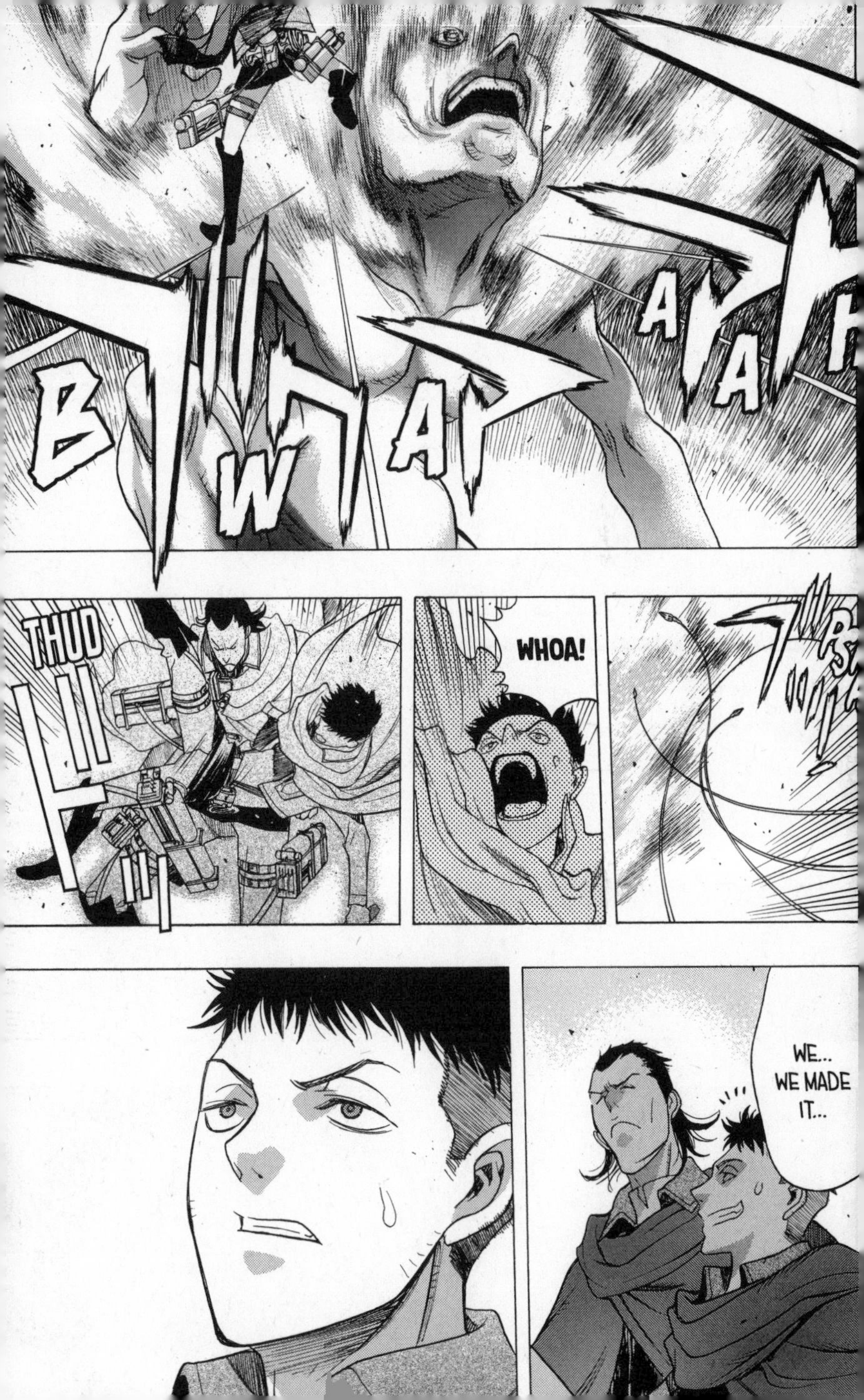
BWAAAH
WHOA!
THUD
WE... WE MADE IT...

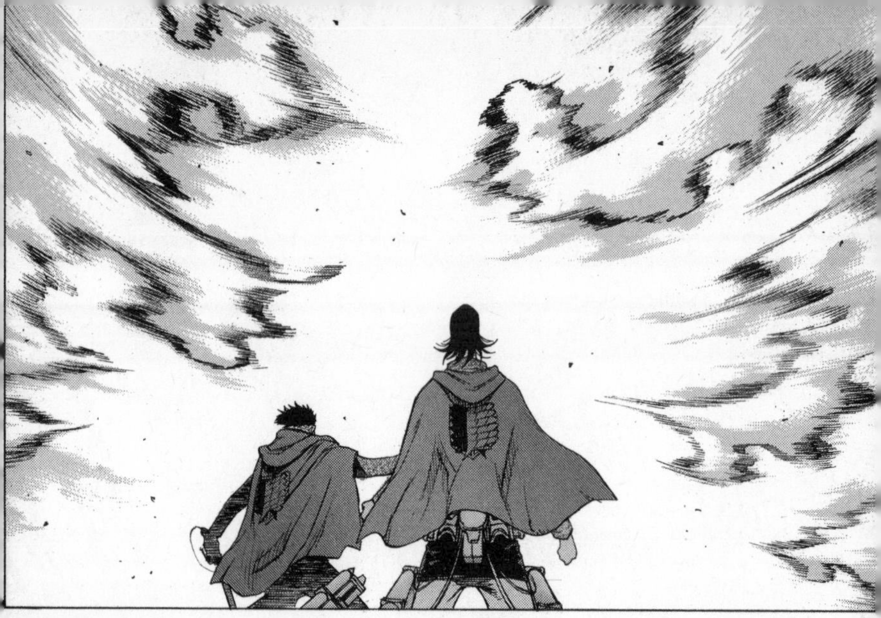
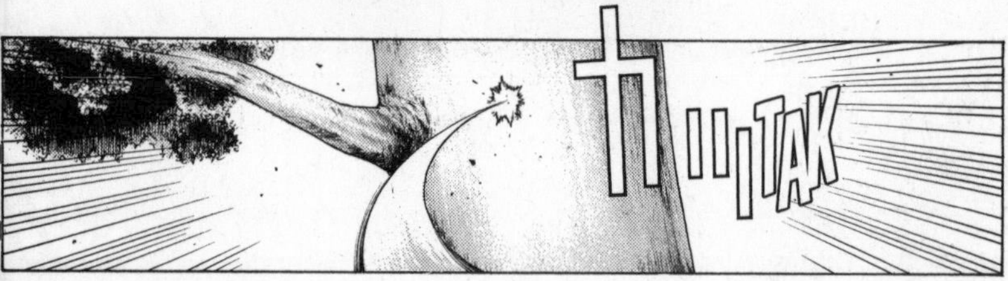
TAK
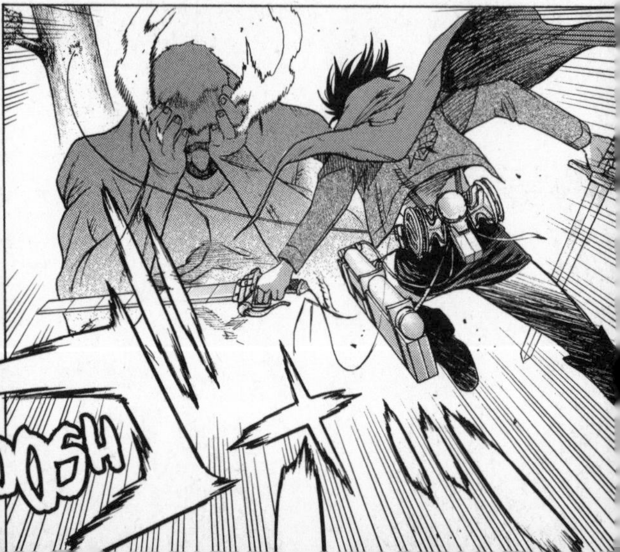
VWOOSH
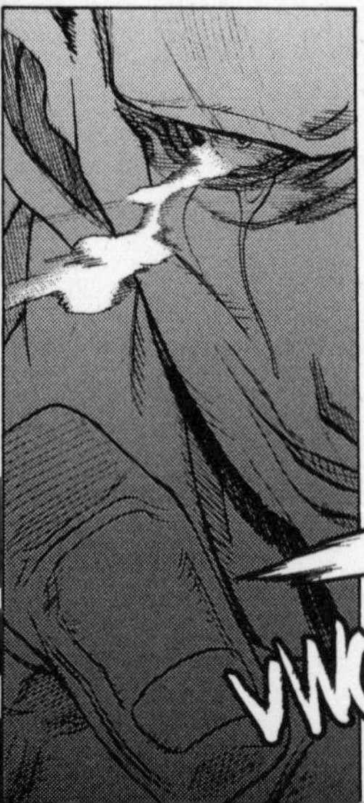

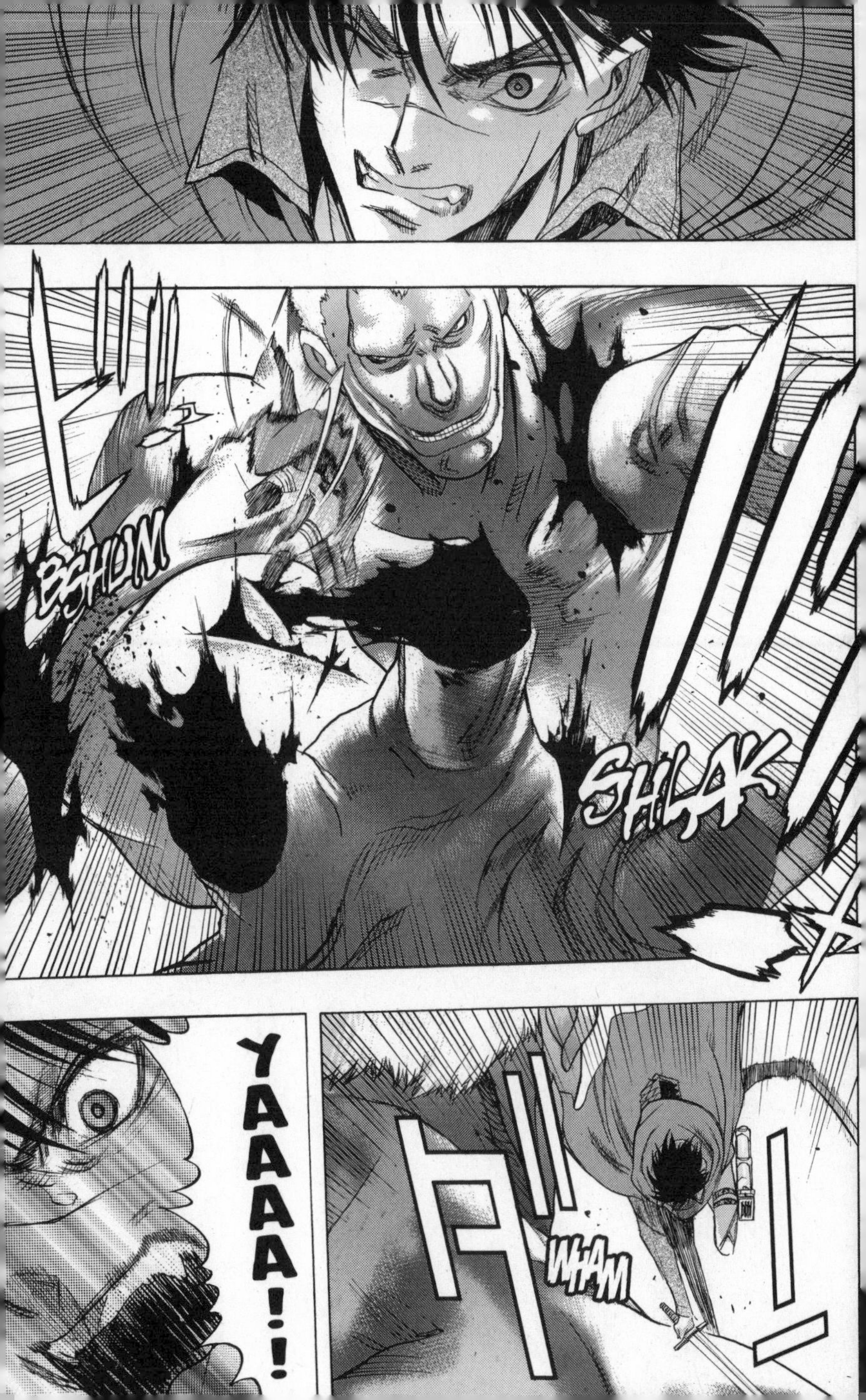
SHLAK
BSHUM
WHAM
YAAAA!!!

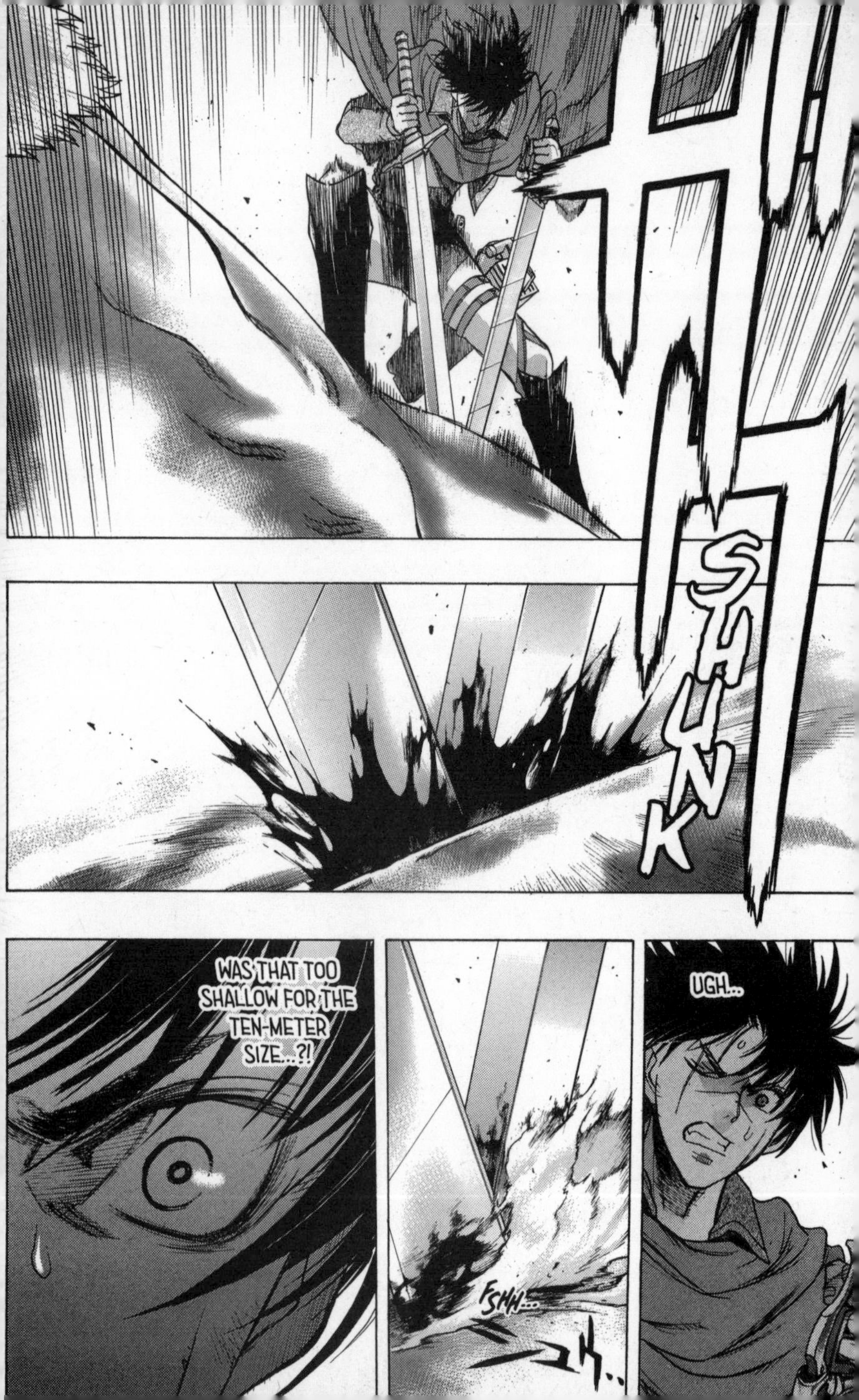
SHUNK
UGH...
FSHH...
ZK...
WAS THAT TOO SHALLOW FOR THE TEN-METER SIZE...?!

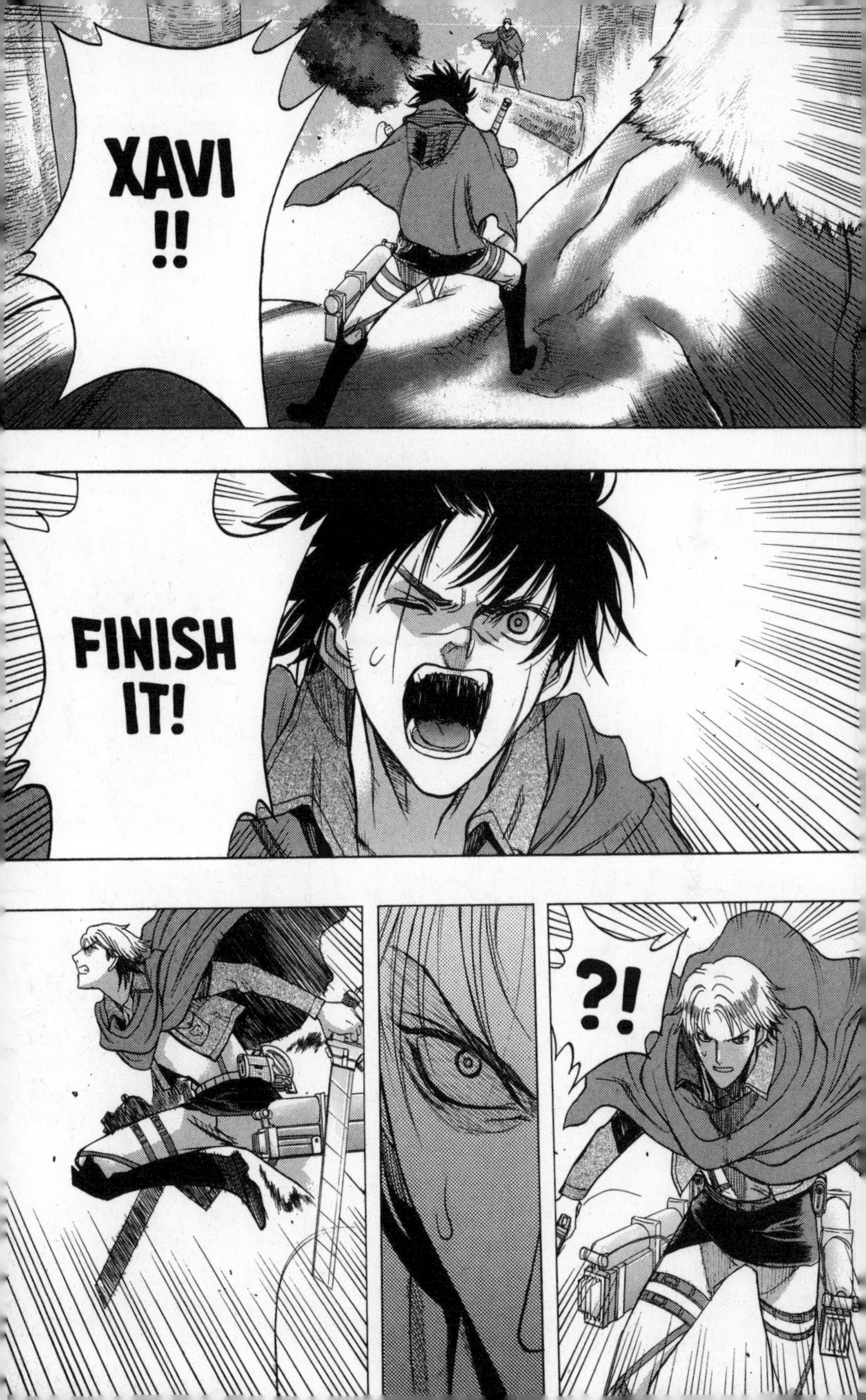
XAVI !!
FINISH IT!
?!

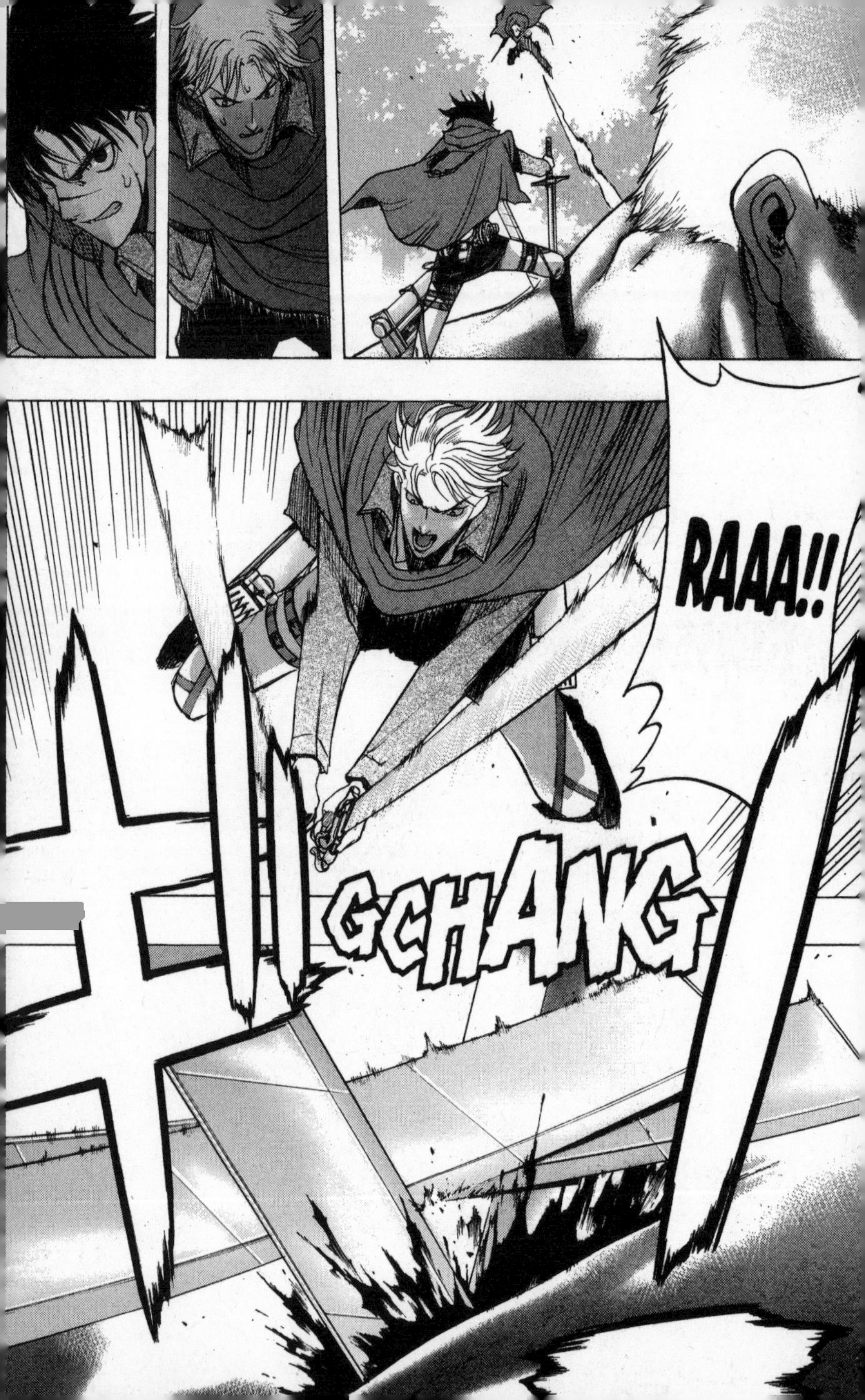
RAAA!!
GCHANG

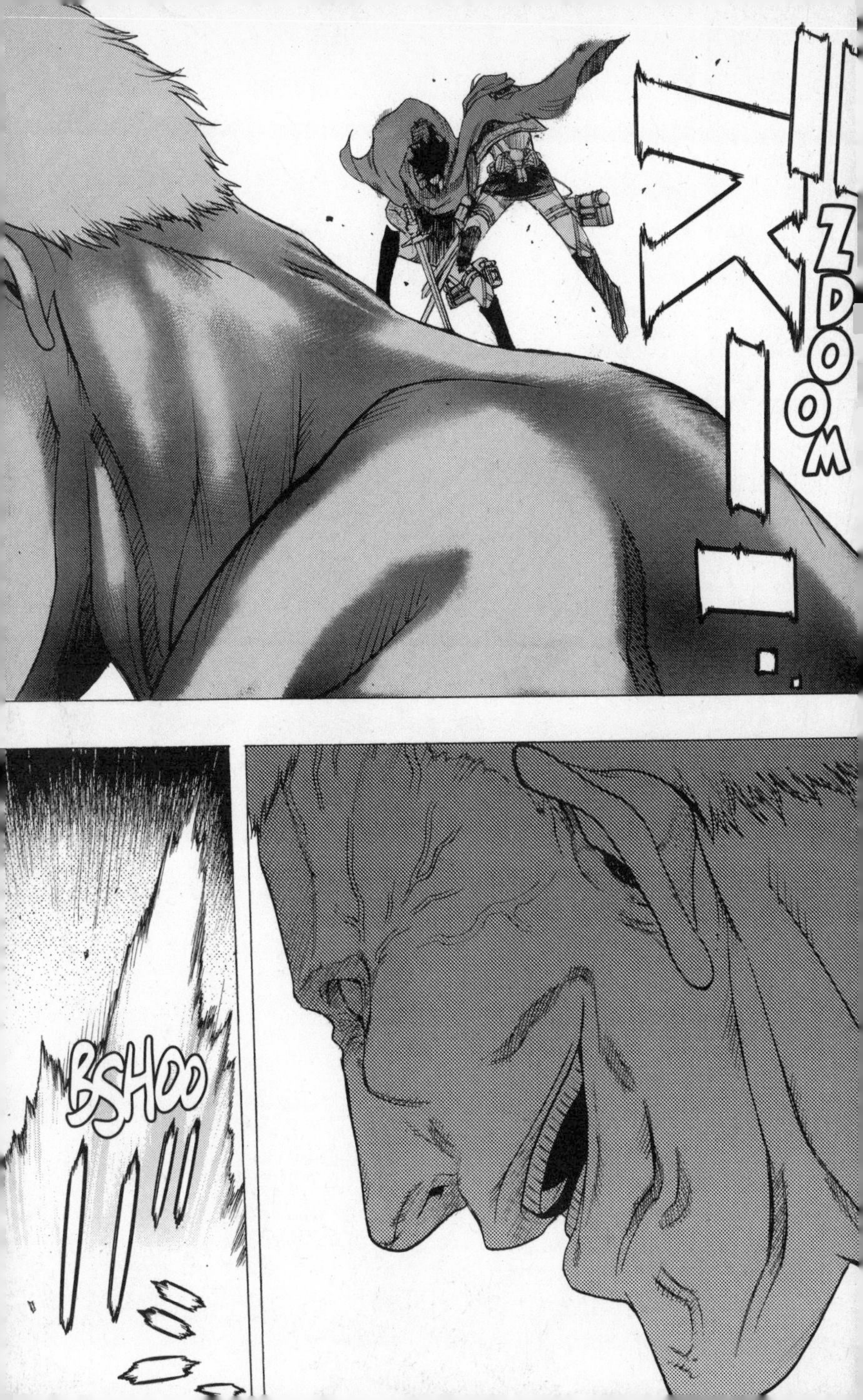
ZDOOM
BSHOO

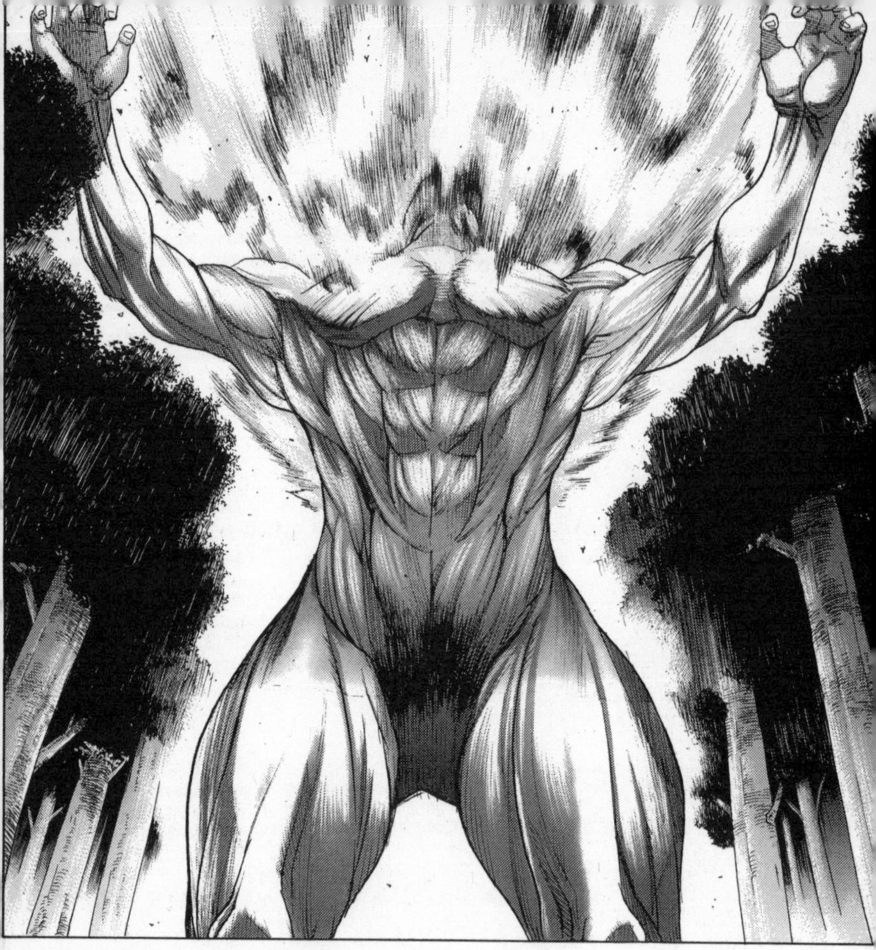

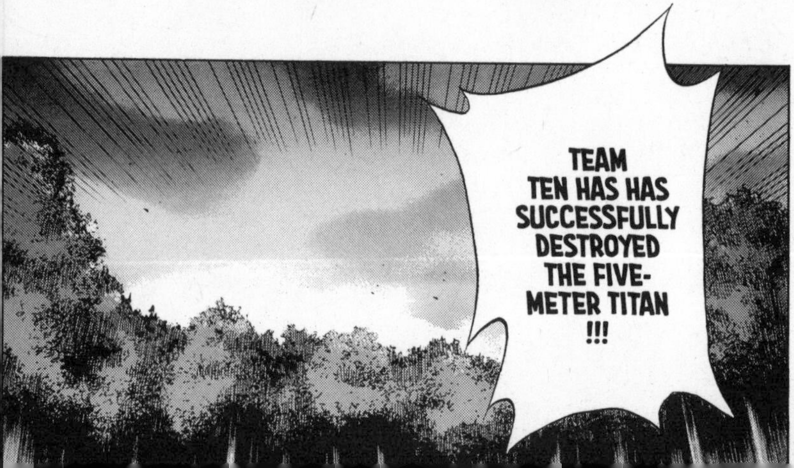
TEAM TEN HAS HAS SUCCESSFULLY DESTROYED THE FIVE-METER TITAN !!!

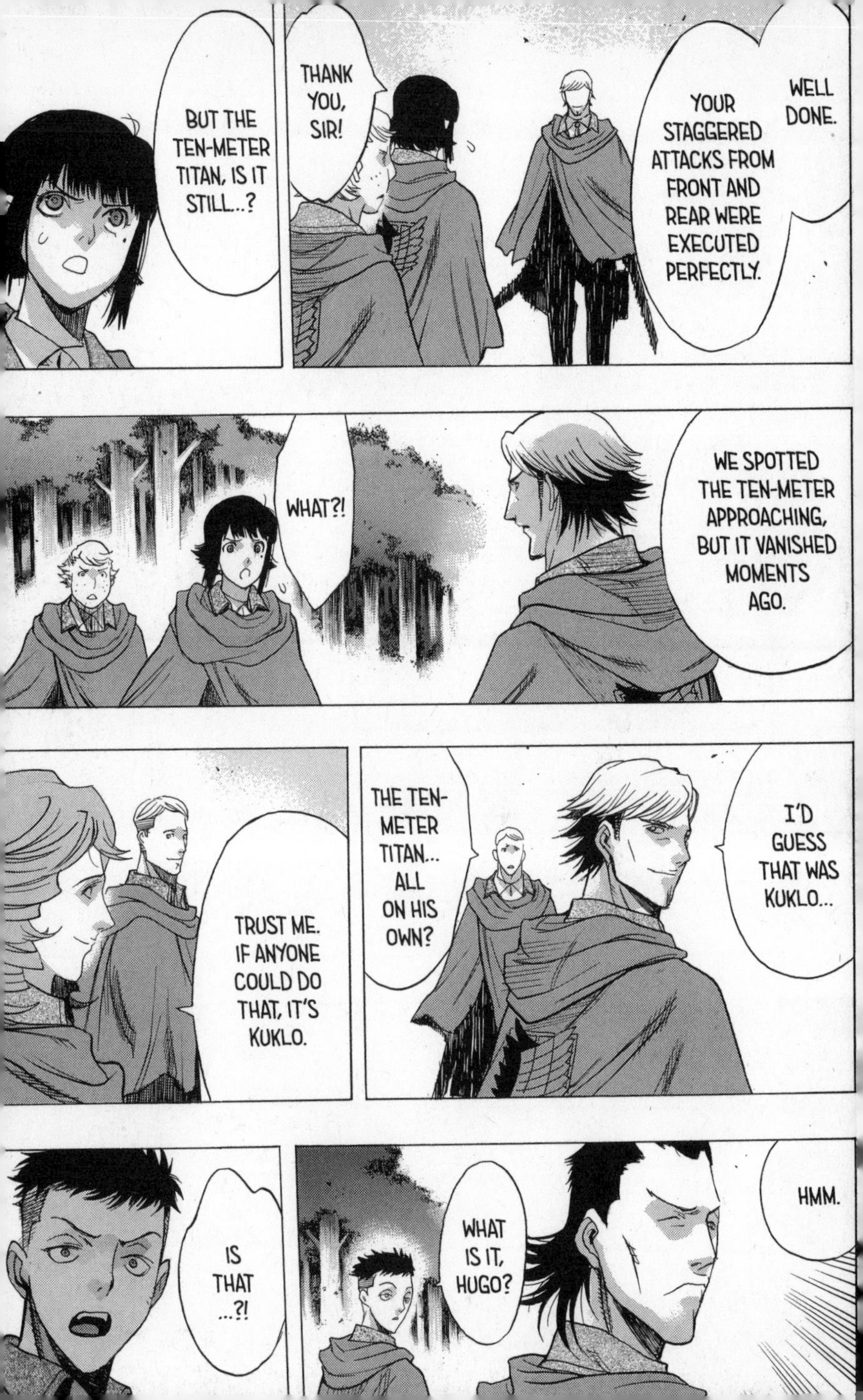
WELL DONE.
YOUR STAGGERED ATTACKS FROM FRONT AND REAR WERE EXECUTED PERFECTLY.
THANK YOU, SIR!
BUT THE TEN-METER TITAN, IS IT STILL...?
WE SPOTTED THE TEN-METER APPROACHING, BUT IT VANISHED MOMENTS AGO.
WHAT?!
I'D GUESS THAT WAS KUKLO...
THE TEN-METER TITAN... ALL ON HIS OWN?
TRUST ME. IF ANYONE COULD DO THAT, IT'S KUKLO.
HMM.
WHAT IS IT, HUGO?
IS THAT ...?!

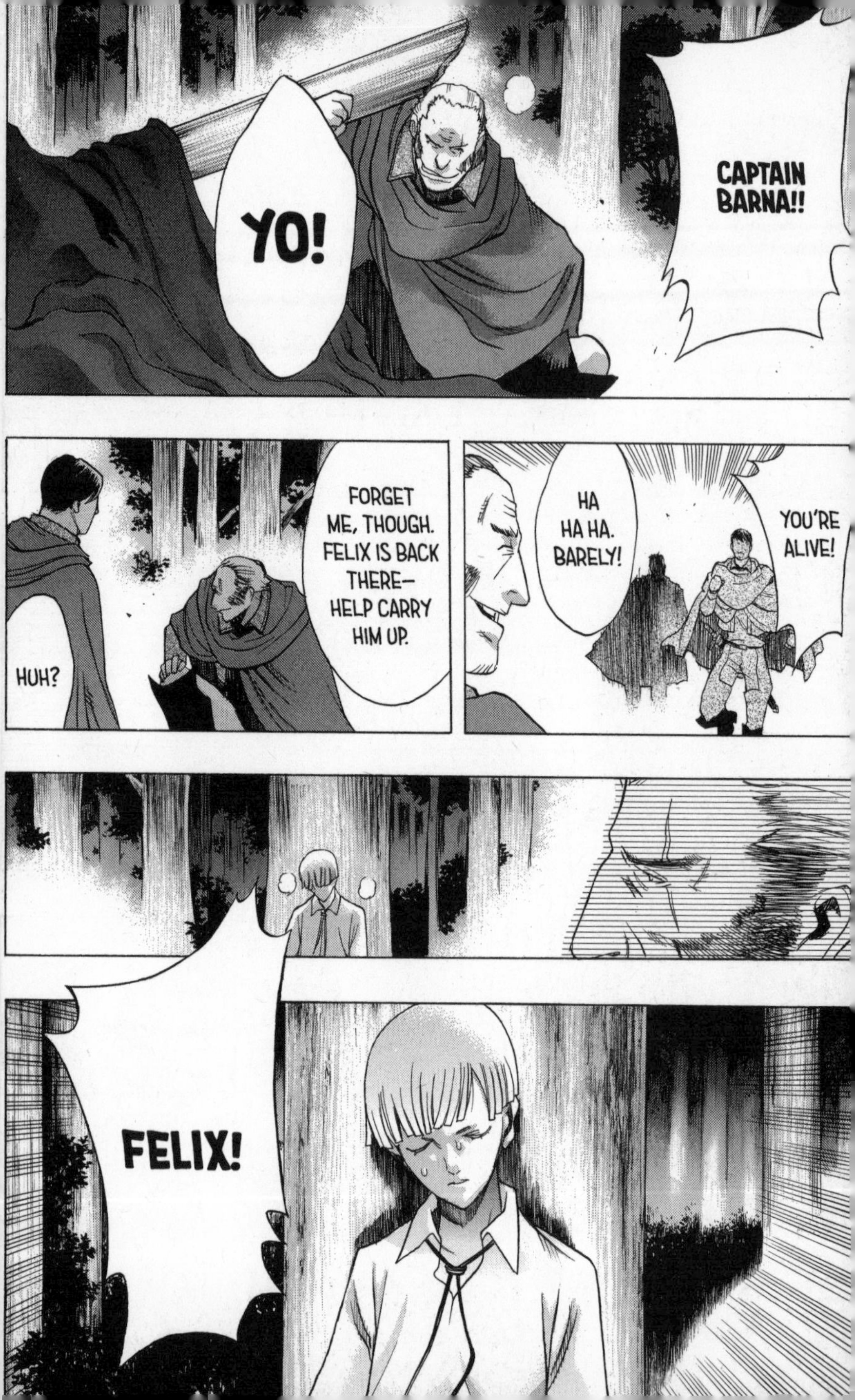
CAPTAIN BARNA!!
YO!
YOU'RE ALIVE!
HA HA HA. BARELY!
FORGET ME, THOUGH. FELIX IS BACK THERE— HELP CARRY HIM UP.
HUH?
FELIX!

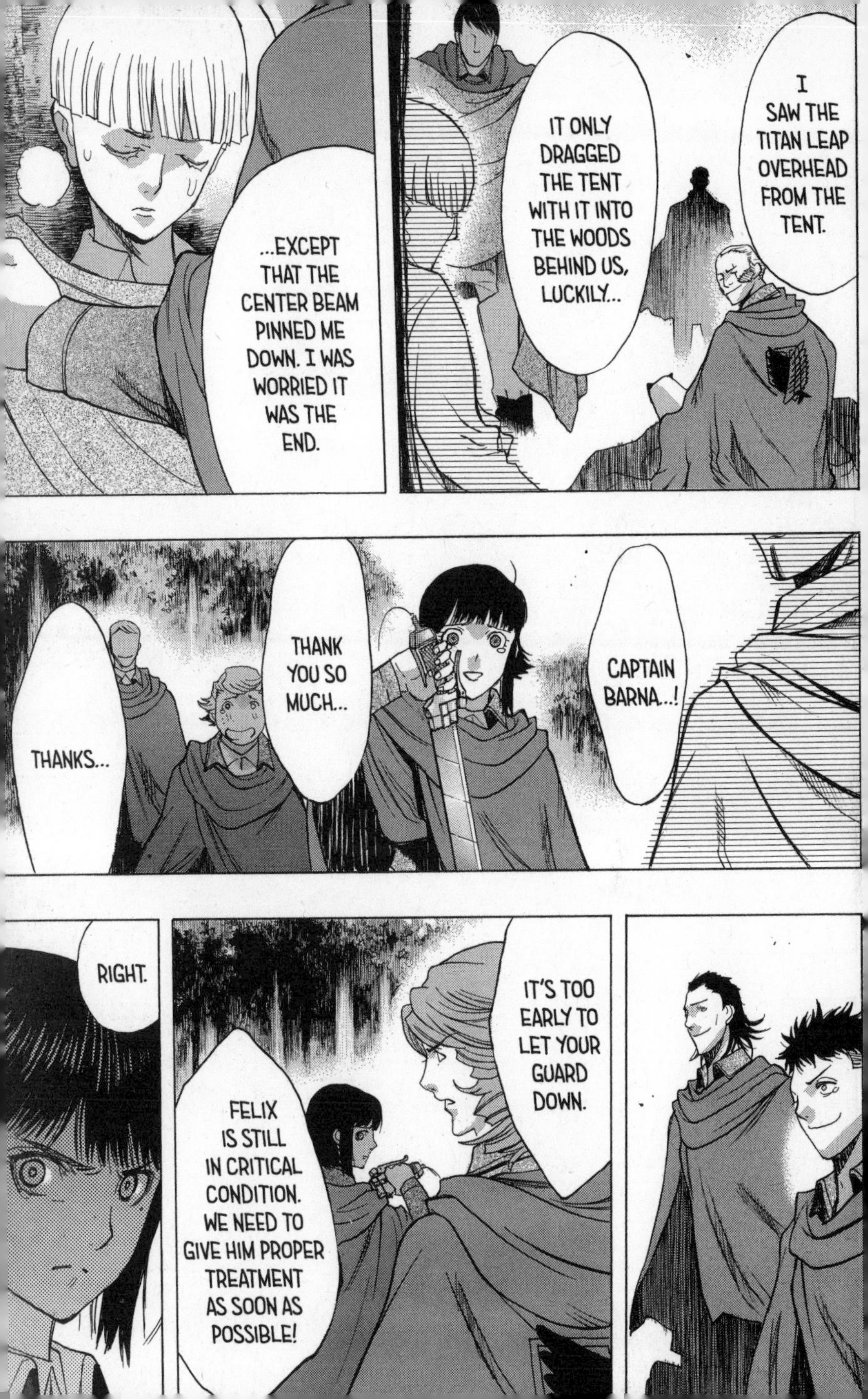
I SAW THE TITAN LEAP OVERHEAD FROM THE TENT.
IT ONLY DRAGGED THE TENT WITH IT INTO THE WOODS BEHIND US, LUCKILY...
...EXCEPT THAT THE CENTER BEAM PINNED ME DOWN. I WAS WORRIED IT WAS THE END.
CAPTAIN BARNA...!
THANK YOU SO MUCH...
THANKS...
IT'S TOO EARLY TO LET YOUR GUARD DOWN.
FELIX IS STILL IN CRITICAL CONDITION. WE NEED TO GIVE HIM PROPER TREATMENT AS SOON AS POSSIBLE!
RIGHT.

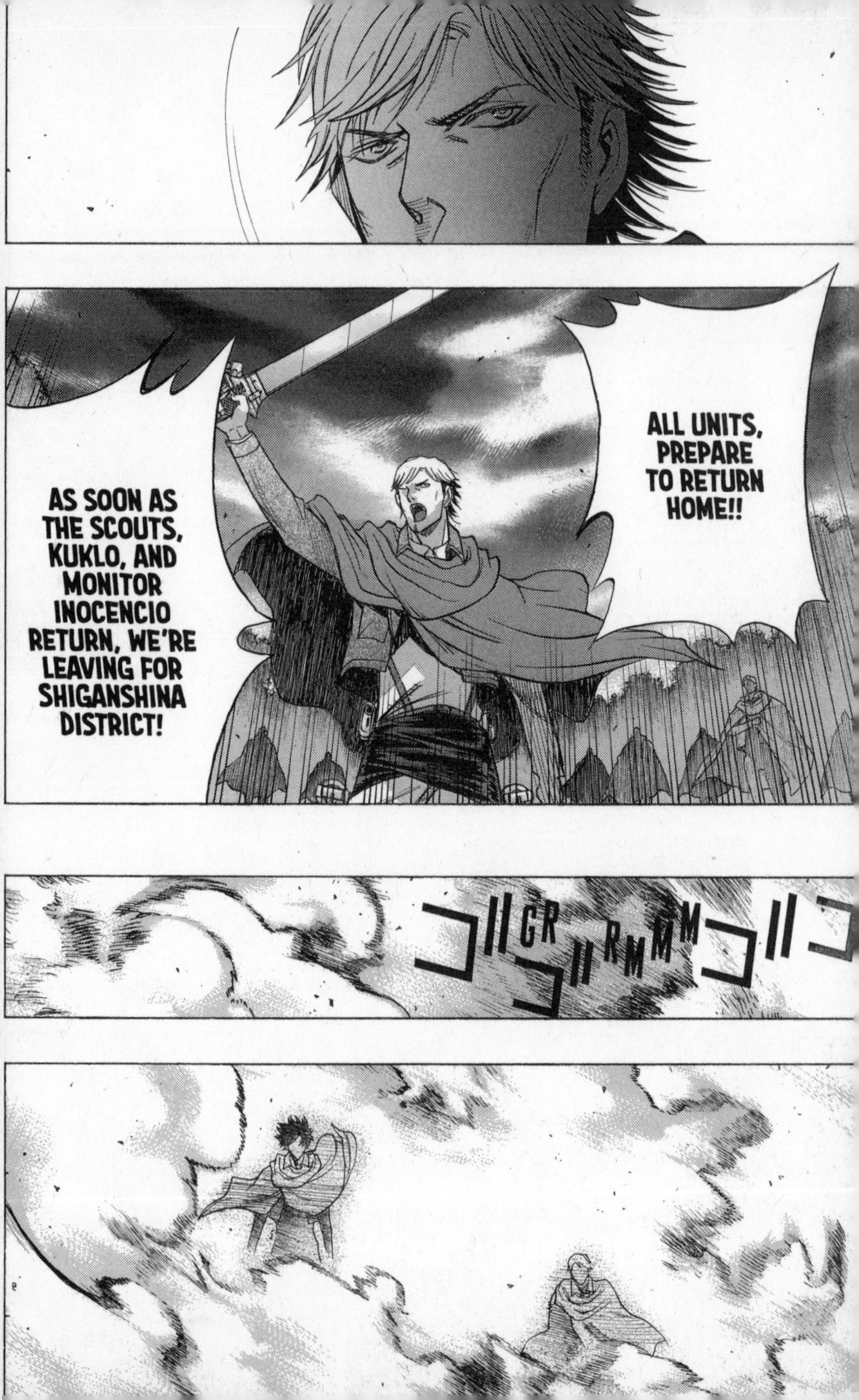
ALL UNITS, PREPARE TO RETURN HOME!!
AS SOON AS THE SCOUTS, KUKLO, AND MONITOR INOCENCIO RETURN, WE'RE LEAVING FOR SHIGANSHINA DISTRICT!
GRRMMM

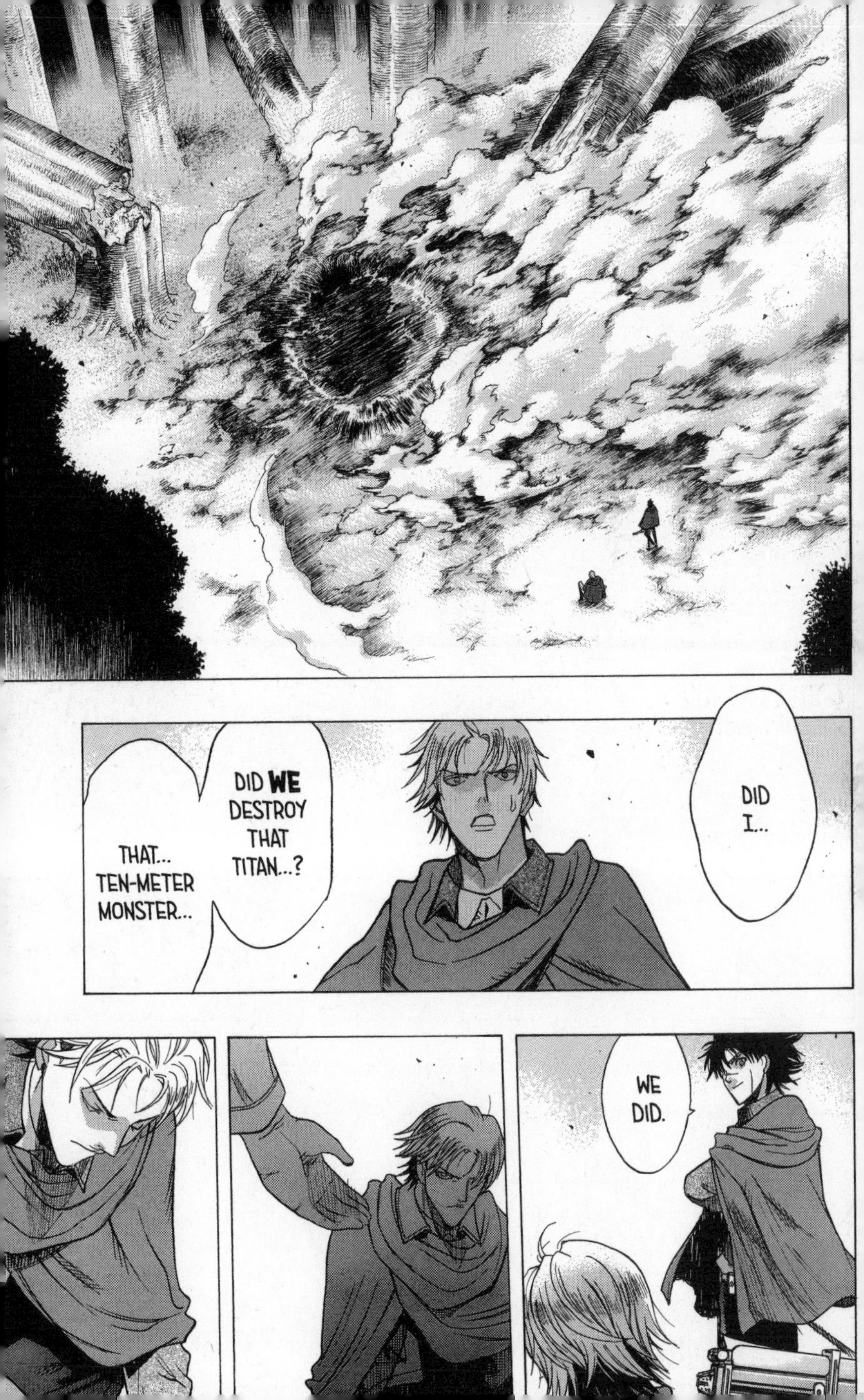
DID I...
DID WE DESTROY THAT TITAN...?
THAT... TEN-METER MONSTER...
WE DID.

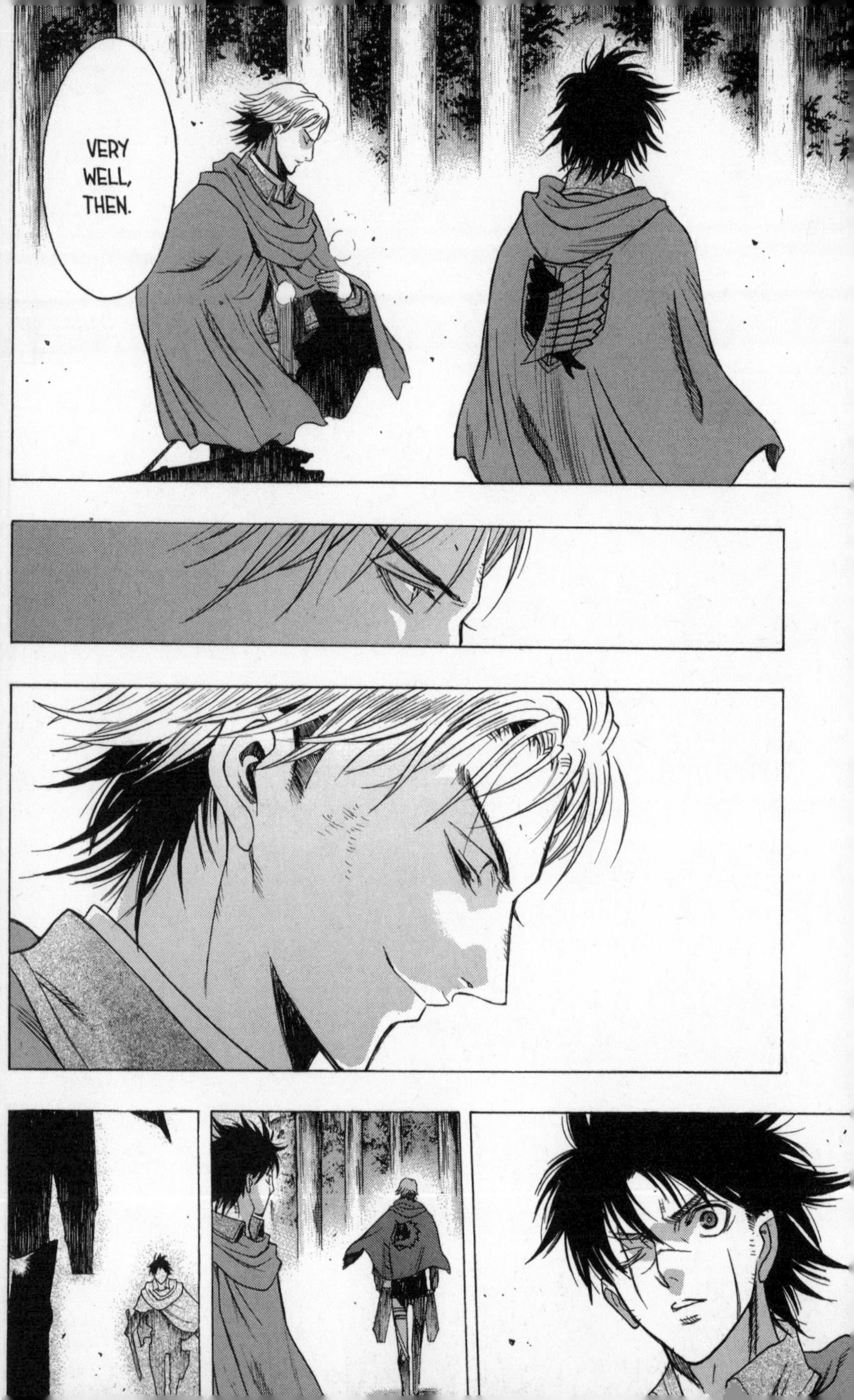
VERY WELL, THEN.

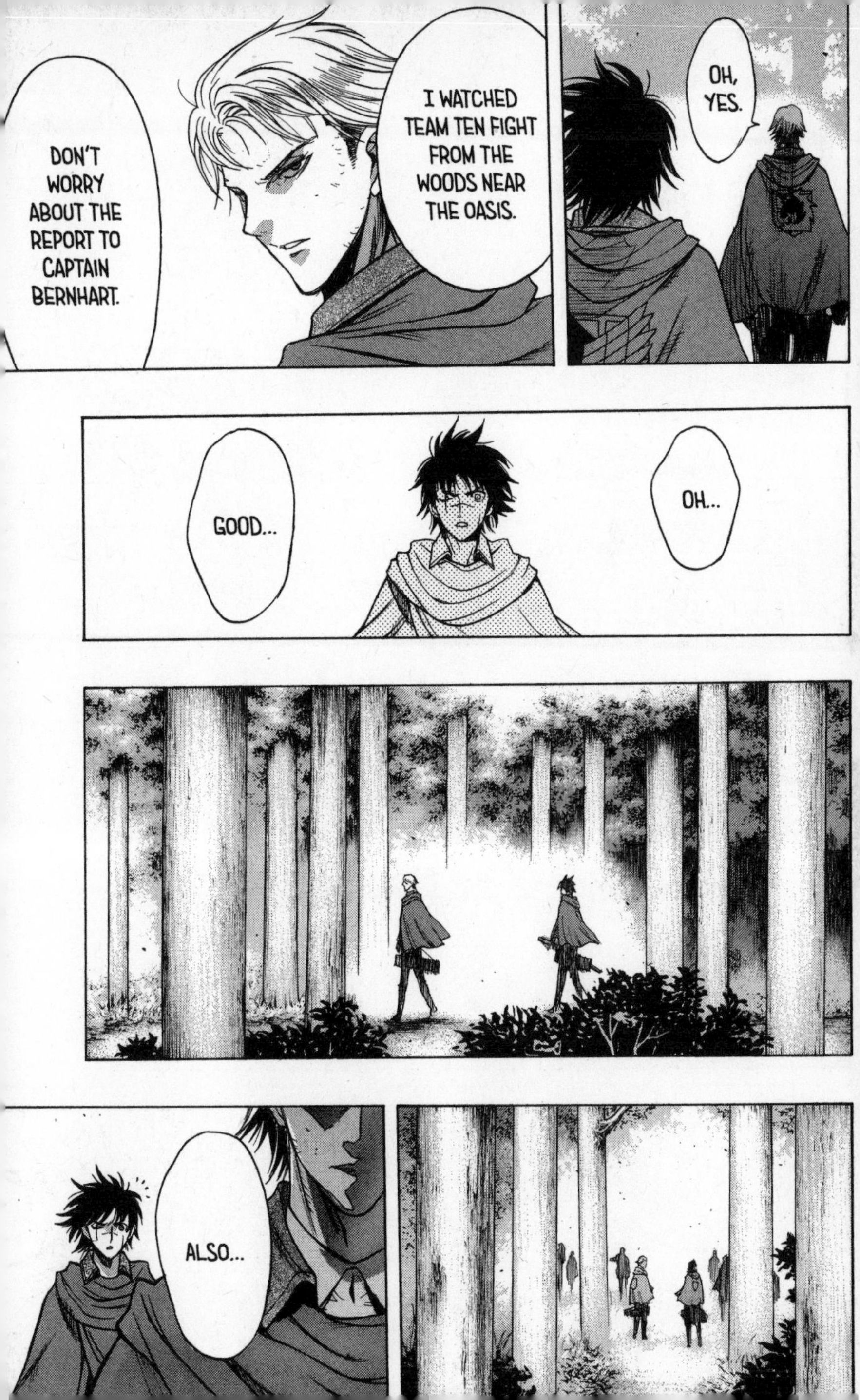
OH, YES.
I WATCHED TEAM TEN FIGHT FROM THE WOODS NEAR THE OASIS.
DON'T WORRY ABOUT THE REPORT TO CAPTAIN BERNHART.
OH...
GOOD...
ALSO...

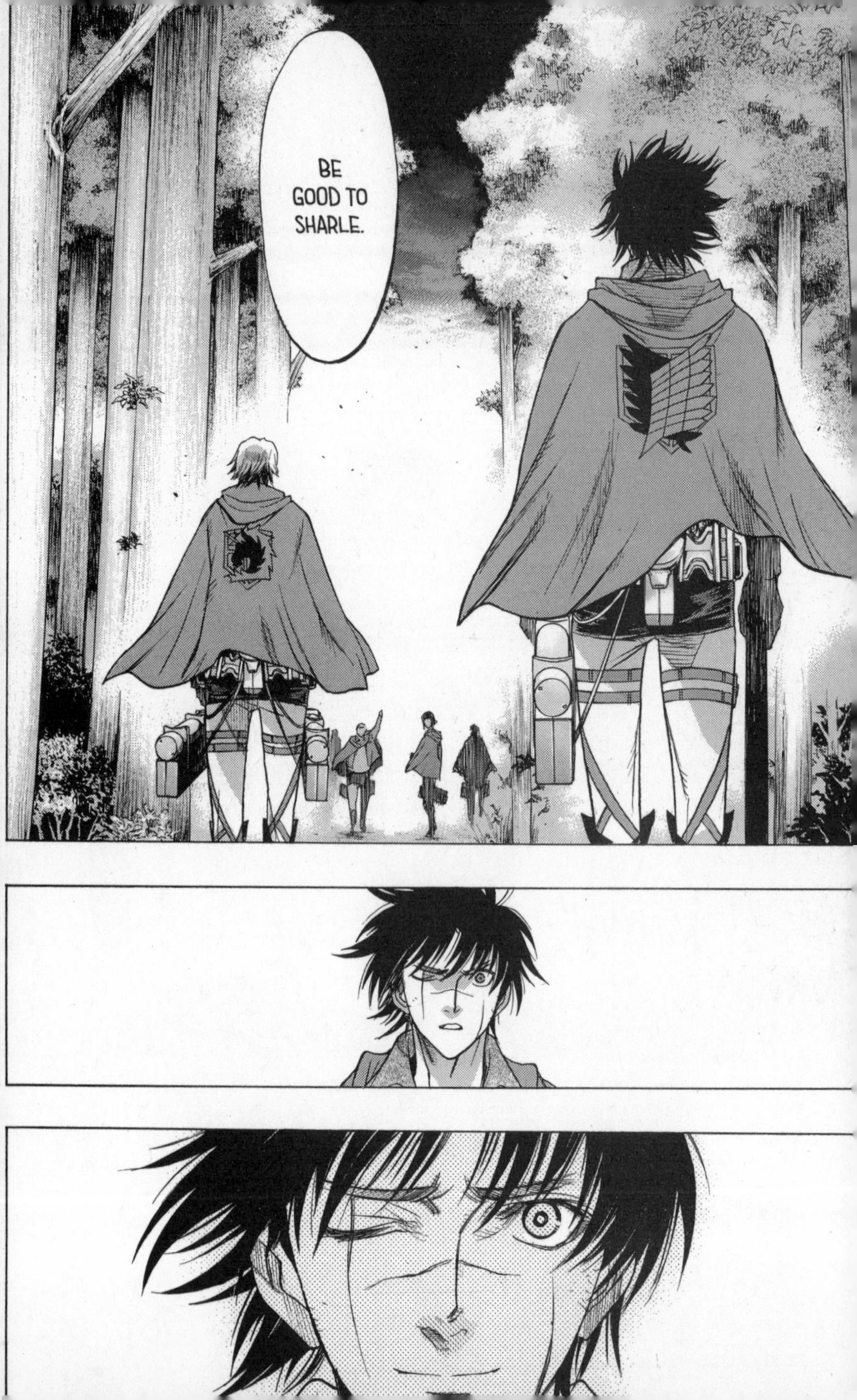
BE GOOD TO SHARLE.

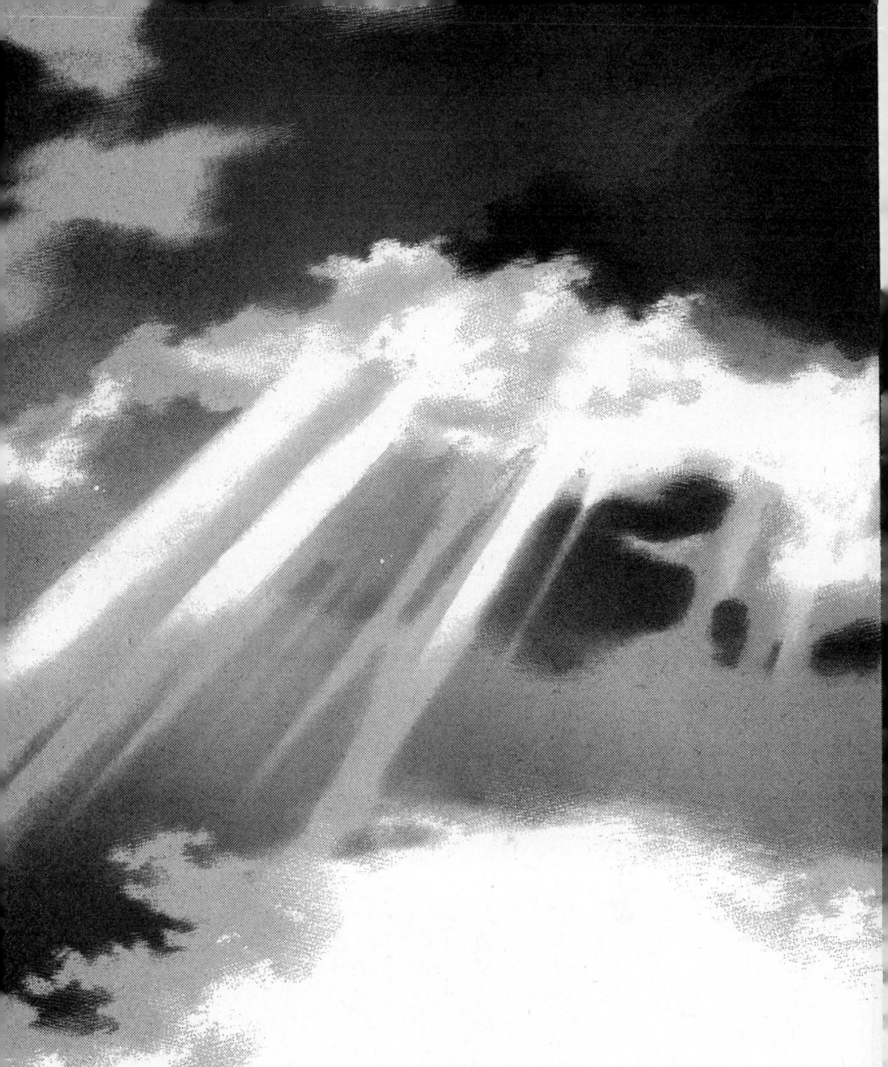

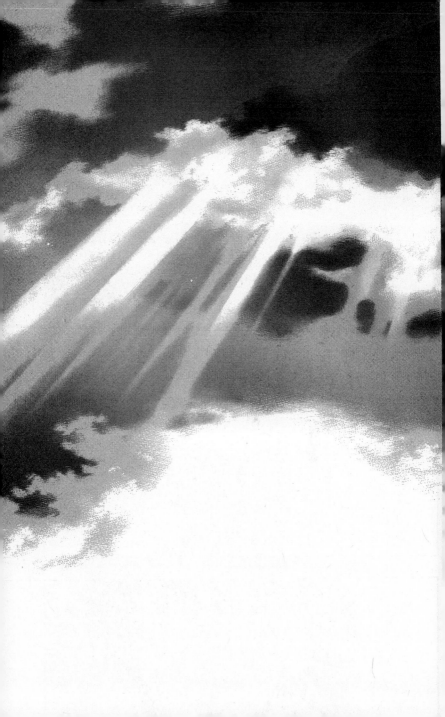

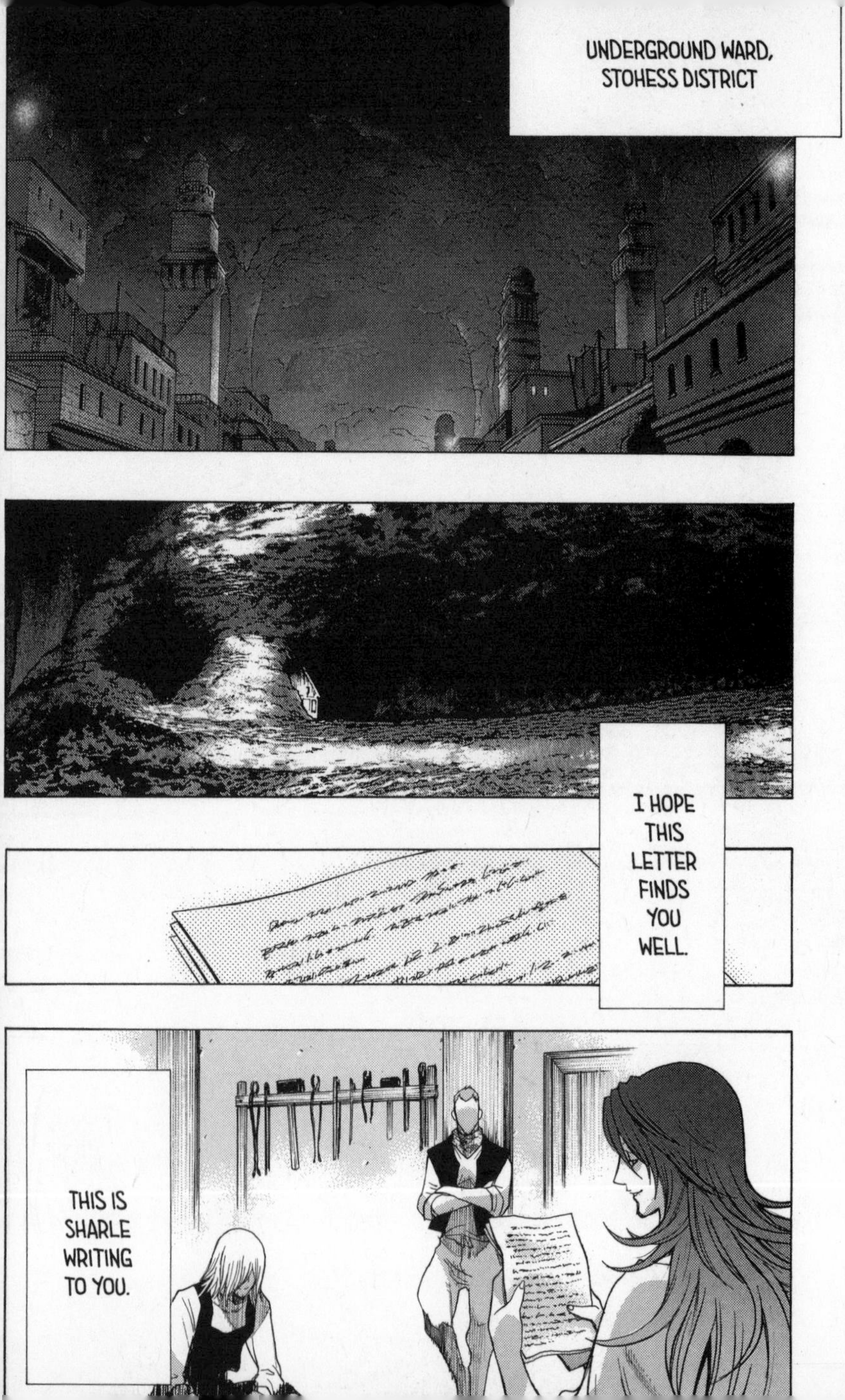
UNDERGROUND WARD, STOHESS DISTRICT
I HOPE THIS LETTER FINDS YOU WELL.
THIS IS SHARLE WRITING TO YOU.

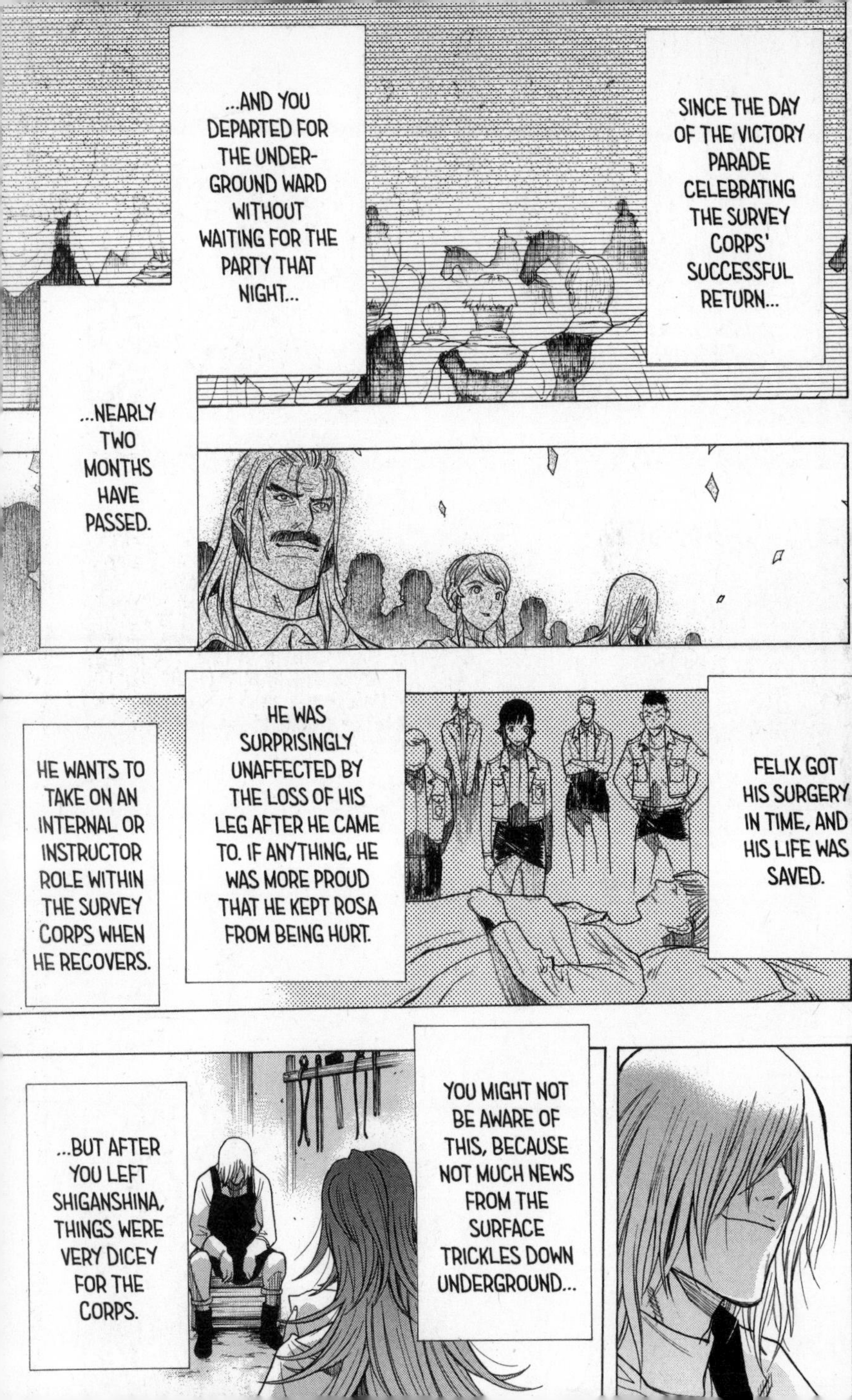
SINCE THE DAY OF THE VICTORY PARADE CELEBRATING THE SURVEY CORPS' SUCCESSFUL RETURN...
...AND YOU DEPARTED FOR THE UNDER-GROUND WARD WITHOUT WAITING FOR THE PARTY THAT NIGHT...
...NEARLY TWO MONTHS HAVE PASSED.
FELIX GOT HIS SURGERY IN TIME, AND HIS LIFE WAS SAVED.
HE WAS SURPRISINGLY UNAFFECTED BY THE LOSS OF HIS LEG AFTER HE CAME TO. IF ANYTHING, HE WAS MORE PROUD THAT HE KEPT ROSA FROM BEING HURT.
HE WANTS TO TAKE ON AN INTERNAL OR INSTRUCTOR ROLE WITHIN THE SURVEY CORPS WHEN HE RECOVERS.
YOU MIGHT NOT BE AWARE OF THIS, BECAUSE NOT MUCH NEWS FROM THE SURFACE TRICKLES DOWN UNDERGROUND...
...BUT AFTER YOU LEFT SHIGANSHINA, THINGS WERE VERY DICEY FOR THE CORPS.

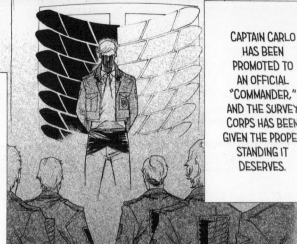

CAPTAIN CARLO HAS BEEN PROMOTED TO AN OFFICIAL "COMMANDER," AND THE SURVEY CORPS HAS BEEN GIVEN THE PROPER STANDING IT DESERVES.

BUT FOR A TIME, THE ONGOING EXISTENCE OF THE CORPS WAS IN QUESTION BECAUSE OF THE DEATH OF CAPTAIN GLORIA BERNHART OF THE MP BRIGADE.

THEN A LETTER FROM GLORIA ARRIVED AT THE INOCENCIO MANSION IN THE CAPITAL, ADDRESSED TO MY BROTHER XAVI.

IT CONTAINED VIVID DETAILS OF THE MISDEEDS AND ILLEGAL SABOTAGE PERFORMED BY HER UNCLE, VICE COMMANDER BERNHART.

IT ALSO CONTAINED INSTRUCTIONS FOR XAVI TO CARRY OUT.

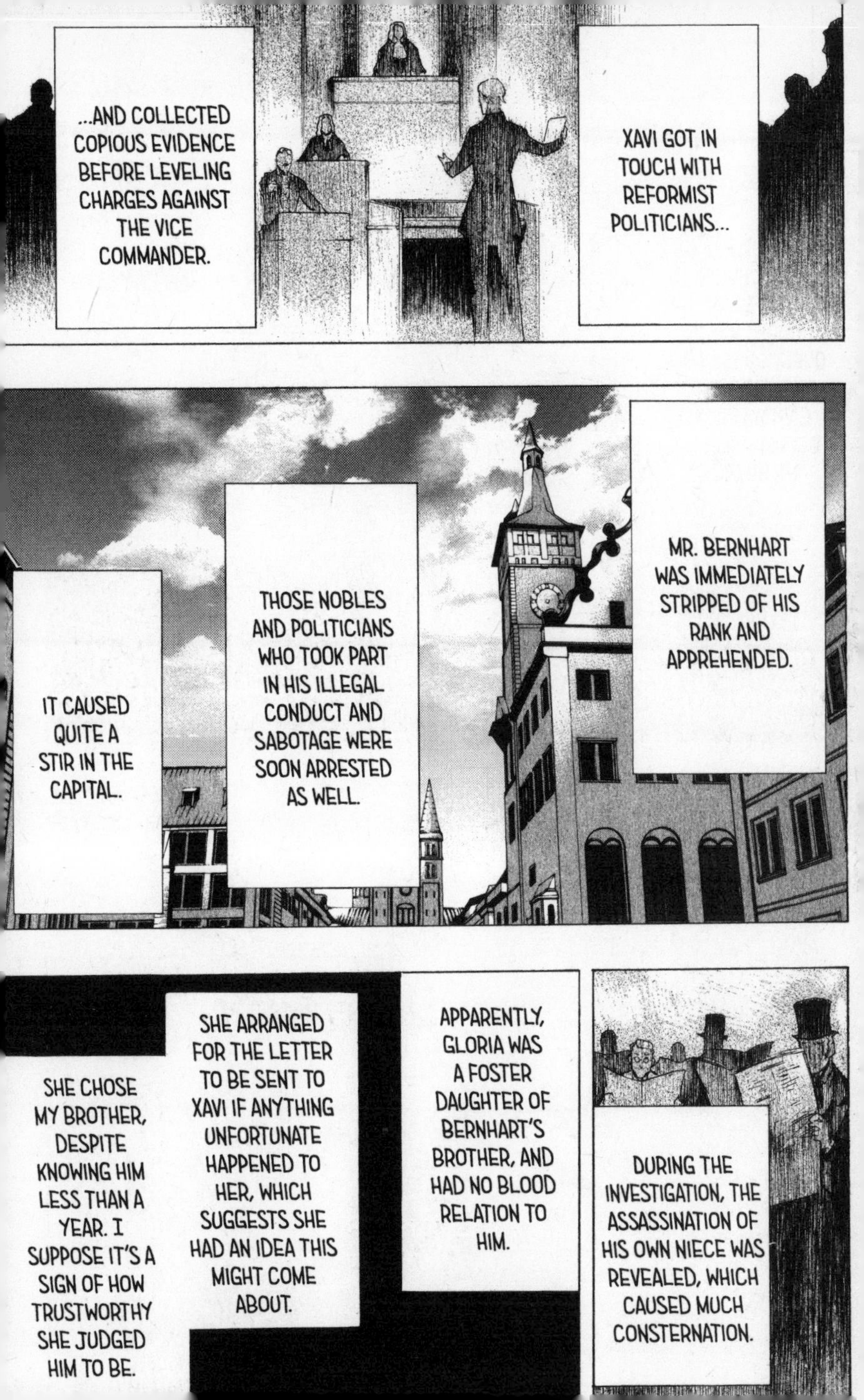
XAVI GOT IN TOUCH WITH REFORMIST POLITICIANS...
...AND COLLECTED COPIOUS EVIDENCE BEFORE LEVELING CHARGES AGAINST THE VICE COMMANDER.
MR. BERNHART WAS IMMEDIATELY STRIPPED OF HIS RANK AND APPREHENDED.
THOSE NOBLES AND POLITICIANS WHO TOOK PART IN HIS ILLEGAL CONDUCT AND SABOTAGE WERE SOON ARRESTED AS WELL.
IT CAUSED QUITE A STIR IN THE CAPITAL.
DURING THE INVESTIGATION, THE ASSASSINATION OF HIS OWN NIECE WAS REVEALED, WHICH CAUSED MUCH CONSTERNATION.
APPARENTLY, GLORIA WAS A FOSTER DAUGHTER OF BERNHART'S BROTHER, AND HAD NO BLOOD RELATION TO HIM.
SHE ARRANGED FOR THE LETTER TO BE SENT TO XAVI IF ANYTHING UNFORTUNATE HAPPENED TO HER, WHICH SUGGESTS SHE HAD AN IDEA THIS MIGHT COME ABOUT.
SHE CHOSE MY BROTHER, DESPITE KNOWING HIM LESS THAN A YEAR. I SUPPOSE IT'S A SIGN OF HOW TRUSTWORTHY SHE JUDGED HIM TO BE.

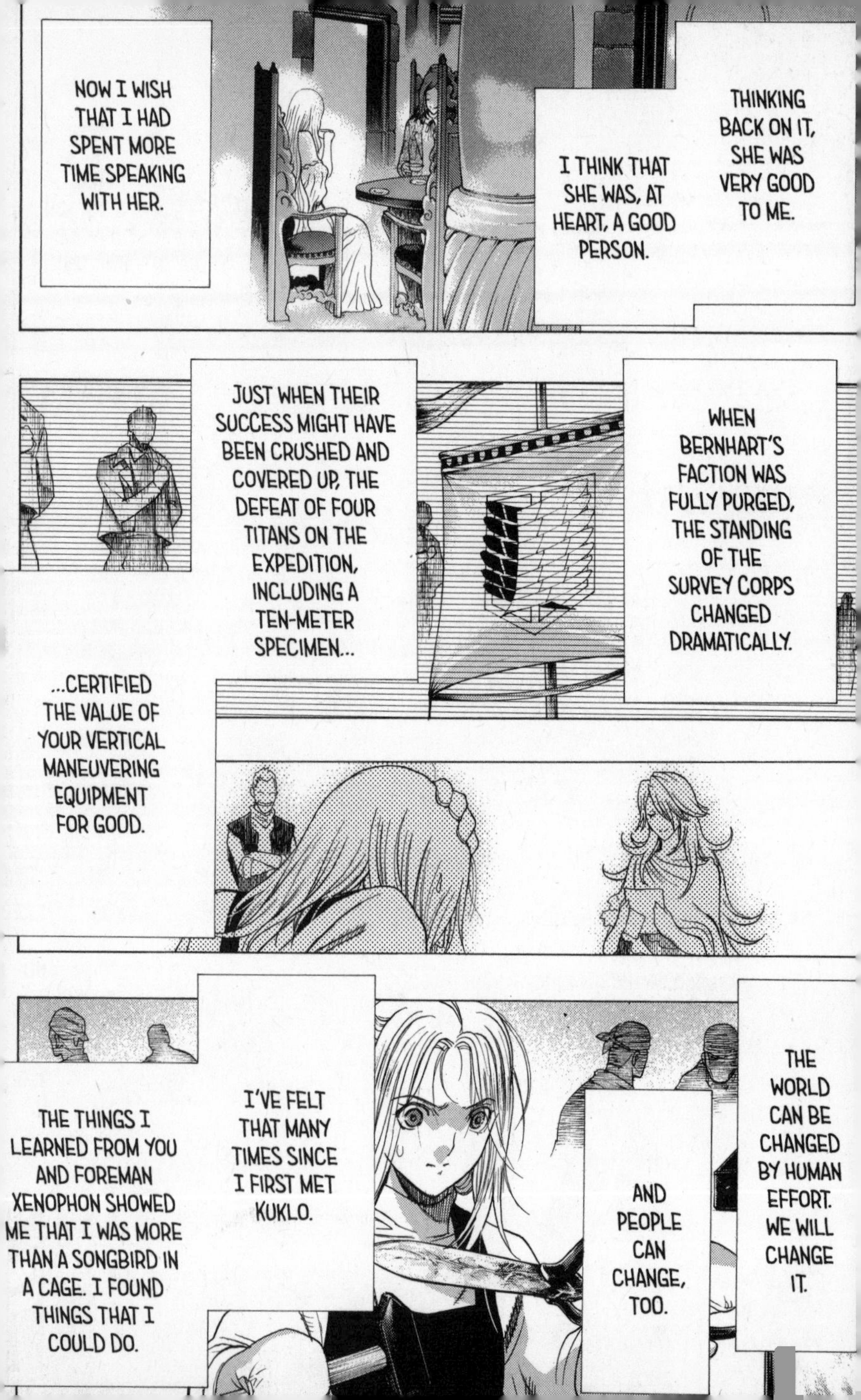
THINKING BACK ON IT, SHE WAS VERY GOOD TO ME.
I THINK THAT SHE WAS, AT HEART, A GOOD PERSON.
NOW I WISH THAT I HAD SPENT MORE TIME SPEAKING WITH HER.
WHEN BERNHART'S FACTION WAS FULLY PURGED, THE STANDING OF THE SURVEY CORPS CHANGED DRAMATICALLY.
JUST WHEN THEIR SUCCESS MIGHT HAVE BEEN CRUSHED AND COVERED UP, THE DEFEAT OF FOUR TITANS ON THE EXPEDITION, INCLUDING A TEN-METER SPECIMEN...
...CERTIFIED THE VALUE OF YOUR VERTICAL MANEUVERING EQUIPMENT FOR GOOD.
THE WORLD CAN BE CHANGED BY HUMAN EFFORT. WE WILL CHANGE IT.
AND PEOPLE CAN CHANGE, TOO.
I'VE FELT THAT MANY TIMES SINCE I FIRST MET KUKLO.
THE THINGS I LEARNED FROM YOU AND FOREMAN XENOPHON SHOWED ME THAT I WAS MORE THAN A SONGBIRD IN A CAGE. I FOUND THINGS THAT I COULD DO.

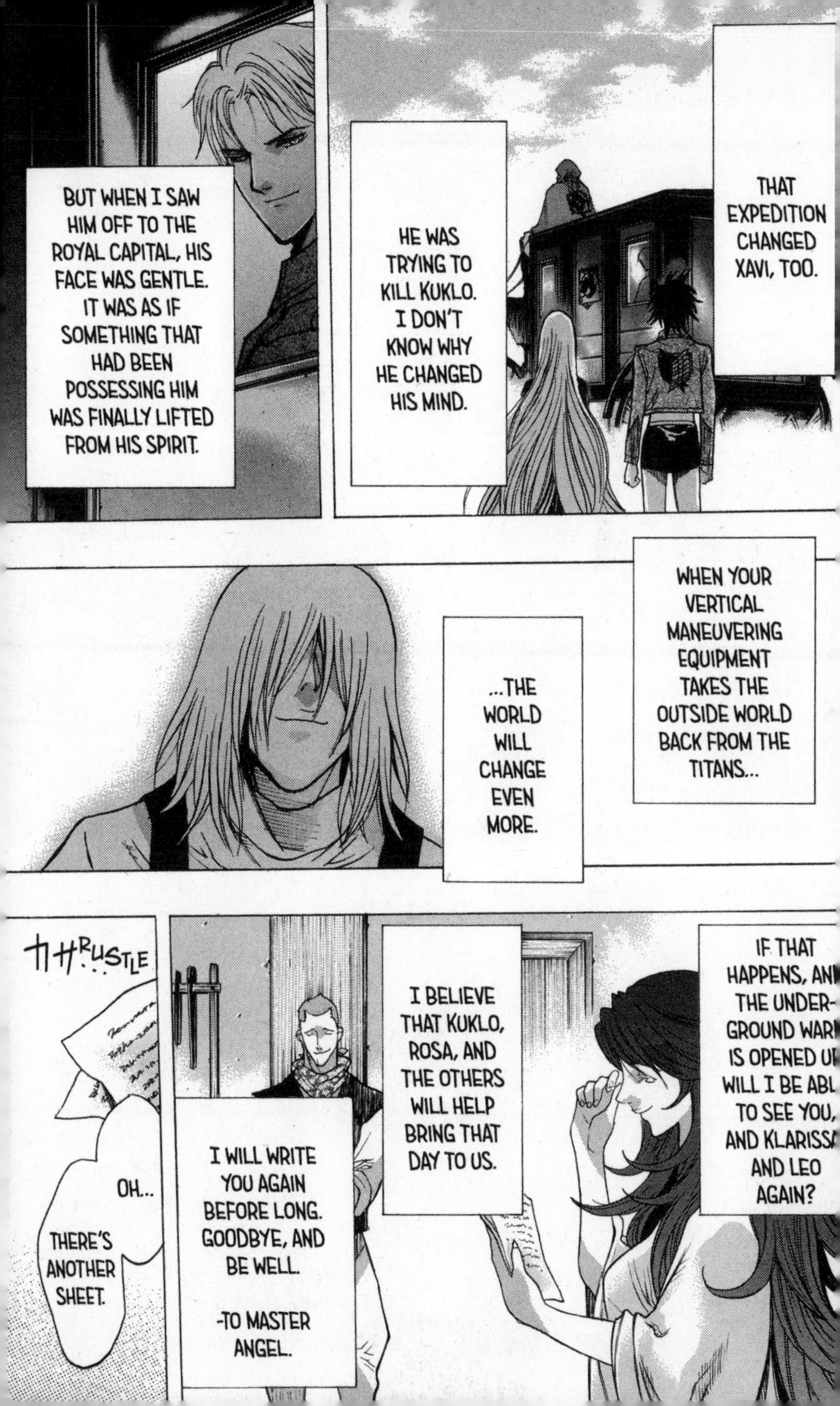
THAT EXPEDITION CHANGED XAVI, TOO.
HE WAS TRYING TO KILL KUKLO. I DON'T KNOW WHY HE CHANGED HIS MIND.
BUT WHEN I SAW HIM OFF TO THE ROYAL CAPITAL, HIS FACE WAS GENTLE. IT WAS AS IF SOMETHING THAT HAD BEEN POSSESSING HIM WAS FINALLY LIFTED FROM HIS SPIRIT.
WHEN YOUR VERTICAL MANEUVERING EQUIPMENT TAKES THE OUTSIDE WORLD BACK FROM THE TITANS...
...THE WORLD WILL CHANGE EVEN MORE.
IF THAT HAPPENS, AN THE UNDER- GROUND WAR IS OPENED U WILL I BE ABL TO SEE YOU, AND KLARISS AND LEO AGAIN?
I BELIEVE THAT KUKLO, ROSA, AND THE OTHERS WILL HELP BRING THAT DAY TO US.
RUSTLE...
I WILL WRITE YOU AGAIN BEFORE LONG. GOODBYE, AND BE WELL.
-TO MASTER ANGEL.
OH...
THERE'S ANOTHER SHEET.

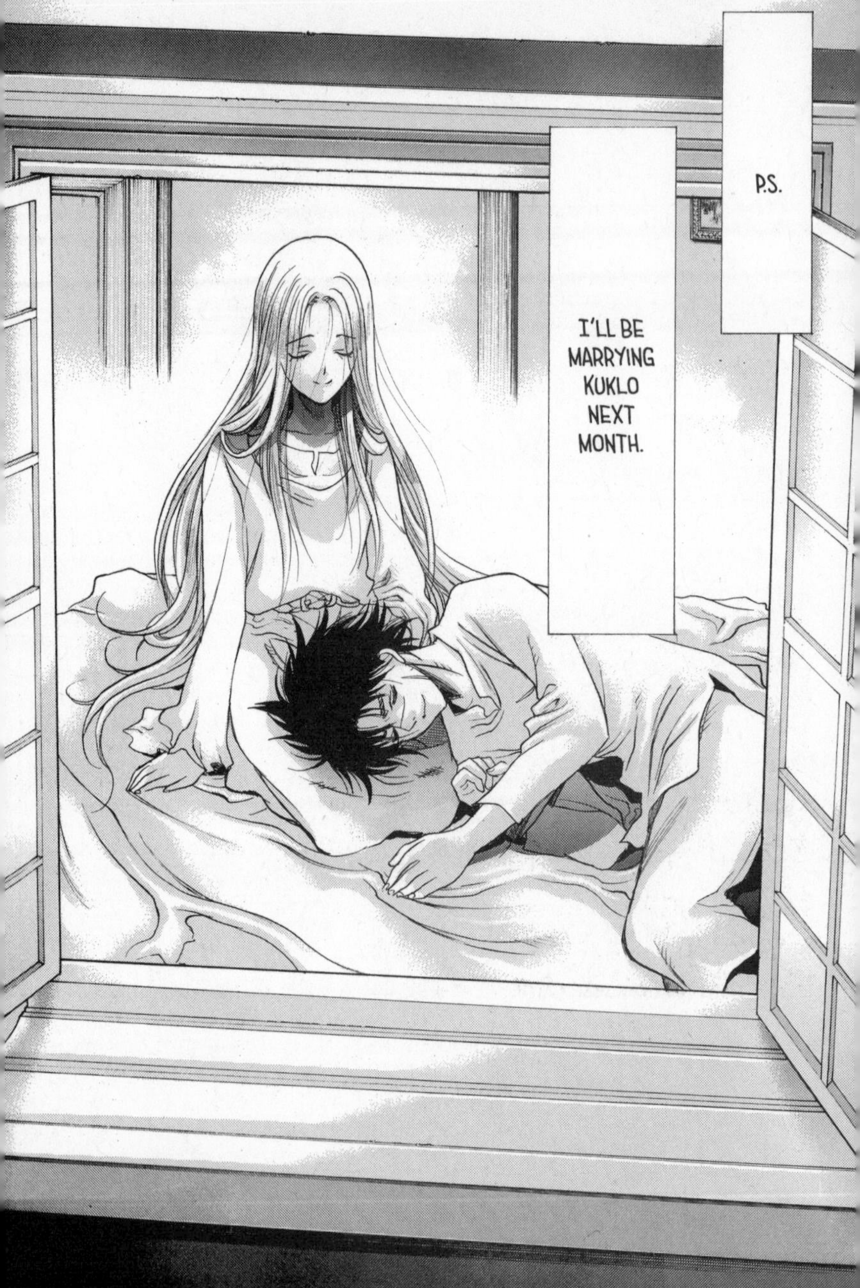
P.S.
I'LL BE MARRYING KUKLO NEXT MONTH.

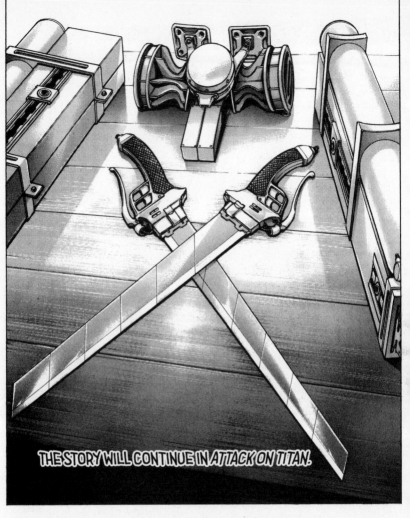

THE STORY WILL CONTINUE IN *ATTACK ON TITAN*.

The Tale of the Vertical Maneuvering Equipment's Creation

ATTACK ON TITAN
BEFORE THE FALL

The End

A Kodansha Comics Trade Paperback Original
Attack on Titan: Before the Fall volume 17 copyright © 2019 Hajime Isayama/
Ryo Suzukaze/Satoshi Shiki
English translation copyright © 2019 Hajime Isayama/Ryo Suzukaze/Satoshi Shiki

Published in the United States by Kodansha Comics, an imprint of
Kodansha USA Publishing, LLC, New York.

Publication rights for this English edition arranged through
Kodansha Ltd, Tokyo.

First published in Japan in 2019 by Kodansha Ltd., Tokyo
as *Shingeki no kyojin Before the fall*, volume 17.

ISBN 978-1-63236-875-1

Character designs by Thores Shibamoto
Original cover design by Takashi Shimoyama and Kayo Hasegawa (Red Rooster)

Printed in the United States of America.

www.kodanshacomics.com

9 8 7 6 5 4 3 2 1
Translation: Stephen Paul
Lettering: Steve Wands
Editing: Haruko Hashimoto
Kodansha Comics edition cover design by Phil Balsman